CONFLICTS OF COLONIALISM

Based around the life of Mademba Sèye, an African born in the colonial town of Saint Louis du Sénégal in 1852, who transformed himself with the help of his French patrons from a telegraph clerk into an African king, this book examines Mademba's life and career to reveal how colonialism in French West Africa was articulated differently at different times and how Mademba survived these changes by periodically reinventing himself. Investigating Mademba's alleged abuses of power and crimes that pitted French colonial indirect rule policy with its foundations in patronage and loyalty against its stated commitment to the rule of law and the civilizing mission, *Conflicts of Colonialism* sheds light on conflicts between different forms of colonialism and the deep ambiguities of the rule of law in colonial societies, which, despite serious challenges to Mademba's rule, allowed him to remain king until his death in 1918.

RICHARD L. ROBERTS is the Frances and Charles Field Professor in History and Professor of African History at Stanford University. A long-time member of the editorial board of Cambridge University Press's African Studies series, he has authored numerous books himself, such as *Litigants and Households: African Disputes and Colonial Courts in the French Soudan* (Heinemann, 2005) and *Two Worlds of Cotton: Colonialism and the Regional Economy of the French Soudan, 1800–1946* (Standford University Press, 1996).

African Studies Series

The African Studies series, founded in 1968, is a prestigious series of monographs, general surveys, and textbooks on Africa covering history, political science, anthropology, economics, and ecological and environmental issues. The series seeks to publish work by senior scholars as well as the best new research.

CONFLICTS OF COLONIALISM

The Rule of Law, French Soudan, and Faama Mademba Sèye

RICHARD L. ROBERTS

Stanford University

CAMBRIDGE
UNIVERSITY PRESS

CAMBRIDGE
UNIVERSITY PRESS

University Printing House, Cambridge CB2 8BS, United Kingdom

One Liberty Plaza, 20th Floor, New York, NY 10006, USA

477 Williamstown Road, Port Melbourne, VIC 3207, Australia

314–321, 3rd Floor, Plot 3, Splendor Forum, Jasola District Centre, New Delhi – 110025, India

103 Penang Road, #05–06/07, Visioncrest Commercial, Singapore 238467

Cambridge University Press is part of the University of Cambridge.

It furthers the University's mission by disseminating knowledge in the pursuit of
education, learning, and research at the highest international levels of excellence.

www.cambridge.org
Information on this title: www.cambridge.org/9781009098045
DOI: 10.1017/9781009106849

First published 2022

A catalogue record for this publication is available from the British Library.

Library of Congress Cataloging-in-Publication Data
Names: Roberts, Richard L., 1949 - author.
Title: Conflicts of colonialism : the rule of law, French Soudan, and Faama Mademba
Sèye / Richard L. Roberts.
Description: Cambridge, United Kingdom ; New York, NY : Cambridge University Press, 2022.
| Series: African studies series ; 158 | Includes bibliographical references and index.
Identifiers: LCCN 2021047774 (print) | LCCN 2021047775 (ebook) | ISBN 9781009098045
(hardback) | ISBN 9781009107686 (paperback) | ISBN 9781009106849 (epub)
Subjects: LCSH: Sèye, Mademba, 1852-1918. | Bambara (African people)–Kings and
rulers–Biography. | Sansanding (Ségou, Mali)–Kings and rulers–Biography. | France–Colonies–
Africa–Administration–History. | Mali–Politics and government–1898-1959. | Africa,
French-speaking West–History–1884-1960. | BISAC: HISTORY / Africa / General
Classification: LCC DT551.72.S49 R63 2022 (print) | LCC DT551.72.S49 (ebook) | DDC 969.3092
[B]–dc23/eng/20211027
LC record available at https://lccn.loc.gov/2021047774
LC ebook record available at https://lccn.loc.gov/2021047775

ISBN 978-1-009-09804-5 Hardback

CONTENTS

FIGURES

MAPS

TABLES

PREFACE

I first bumped into Mademba, king of Sinsani, in the Archives Nationales du Mali up on Kouluba Hill overlooking Bamako more than four decades ago. At that time, the national archives were located in a small stone house located on the outer edge of the President's "palace," which was formerly the home of the governor of the French Soudan. When I say that I bumped into Mademba back in the mid-1970s, this was not a physical encounter, since Mademba had been dead for nearly sixty years. Instead, I bumped into Mademba through the rich colonial government papers collected and maintained by a group of extraordinarily dedicated archival staff working on a shoestring budget in a physical setting that was challenging to the preservation of documents. At the time, I did not quite know what to do with my encounter with Mademba.

In the mid-1970s, my original research focused on the economy and political economy of precolonial and early colonial history of the Middle Niger with Sinsani at the center. Sinsani – also referred to as Sansanding in the sources – was a major commercial town situated along the Niger River not far from Segu, which became the capital of the Segu Bambara kingdom. As a commercial town within the orbit of the Segu Bambara kingdom, Sinsani had never had kings and never aspired to expansive political authority. Sinsani had chiefs but delegated wider political overrule to Segu. Thus, finding references to Mademba as *faama* (Bambara: king, ruler) of Sinsani or as the French often referred to it as the *État de Sansanding et Dépendances* struck me as an anomaly. Historians interested in social change are constantly on the lookout for both patterns and ruptures. Anomalies become wake-up calls to pay more attention to patterns in order to detect changes and then to assess whether or not these changes were significant. Mademba entered the historical record through the colonial period, which coincided with the French conquest of the Middle Niger Valley in the late nineteenth century. Who was Mademba and how did he become king over a commercial town that had never had kings before? This was an intriguing question, but it was not one that I was interested in pursuing at the time.

Mademba, it turned out, was an African born in the French colonial town of Saint Louis du Sénégal in 1852, who joined the French colonial civil service as a clerk in the nascent Senegalese Post and Telegraph Department in 1869.

Mademba's career was quite ordinary during the 1870s and would likely have remained ordinary if he had not been posted to the Upper Senegal region in 1879, just as the French military was preparing for its aggressive phase of conquest of the Soudanese interior. Serendipity happens. Mademba was charged with helping to lay the telegraph system that was so essential to military communications. Mademba was both competent and eager to help the French proceed with conquest. French military leaders understood their military prowess but also their vulnerabilities because they did not fully understand local political and cultural landscapes. The French thus relied on Africans, especially Africans whom they could trust and who had proven their loyalties. The French were quick to reward Africans loyal to them and to their cause. Mademba's fortunes in the French colonial system rose along with conquest.

Serendipity also happens in the archives. I kept finding evidence of Mademba as I pursued archival and oral history research in Bamako, Segu, Sinsani, and Dakar, where the excellent Archives Nationales du Sénégal has the records of the government-general of French West Africa, which oversaw the operation of France's widespread West African empire, and in France's national collection of colonial and overseas archives. At some point in my many return research visits to West Africa, I came across a huge file entitled "Affaire Mademba," located in the Dakar archives. The "Affaire Mademba" dossier contains correspondence and evidence relating to the 1899–1900 investigation into Mademba's alleged crimes, misdemeanors, and abuses of power. The "Affaire Mademba" actually contains evidence of three nested investigations into these alleged crimes and the debates about how to proceed with overwhelming but contradictory evidence of Mademba's wrongdoing. I was still unready to pursue deeper research into Mademba, in part because I had other books to write and because I was hesitant to focus on one individual's life. I am much more interested in how ordinary people effect change and how change affects them.

My interest in Mademba persisted, but with waxing and waning intensity. Mademba made a cameo appearance in my first book that explored the broad changes in the political economy of the Middle Niger Valley because Sinsani remained a central locus of the story. In 1991, I published my preliminary interpretation of the legal case against Mademba in the book I coedited with Kristin Mann on law in colonial Africa. Several years before, Kristin and I discovered our shared interest in legal sources that each of us was using to help make sense of economic and social change. My preliminary interpretation, "The Case Against Faama Mademba Sy and the Ambiguities of Legal Jurisdiction in Early Colonial French Soudan," was neither right nor wrong, it was just preliminary. Nevertheless, it did suggest further avenues to pursue. However, I still was not ready. Instead, Mademba made another cameo appearance in my second book that explored the long history of cotton and

colonial development in French West Africa. In that book, Mademba's appearance surrounded his role as an early adopter of American varieties of cotton so
much in demand in French textile mills. After finishing the cotton book,
I thought that I could finally begin to make sense of the case against
Mademba, but first I had to understand what I meant in the 1991 essay in
which I raised the issue of the "ambiguities of legal jurisdiction." I thus
embarked on a decade-long effort to make sense of colonial court records
for the French Soudan. That third monograph used over 2,000 entry-level civil
disputes to help me make sense of how the colonial legal system operated and
what court records could actually tell me as a social historian. I did not forget
Mademba, who appears on a single page in that book. Writing that book also
made me realize that evidence I had for Mademba's legal case was actually not
formally brought before a court, as I had assumed in 1991.

While I have been collecting evidence on Mademba for over four decades
and drafted bits and pieces of his story, I still faced challenges many of my own
making. As a historian of social change, I use evidence of individual lives to
illustrate larger trends. I remained uncomfortable dedicating a whole book to
the life of one individual. As I note in the Introduction, biography has a long
and storied place in the history profession, but most biographies involve a level
of intimacy and empathy with the subject that I just did not have. Then,
suddenly, my disposition changed in 2016.

I would never have anticipated that Donald J. Trump's political campaign
and election as president would have inspired me in any way. Much to my
chagrin, Trump effectively became my muse for this book on Mademba.
Trump did so precisely because he and Mademba seemed to share so many
similar attributes: both were driven by narcissism and insecurities; both were
outsiders aided by powerful minority parties; both were consumed with the
legitimacy of their authority; both were deeply misogynistic and abused
women; both demanded loyalty and were quick to punish what they saw as
disloyalty; both demanded adoration and public submission precisely because
they had weak legitimacy; both saw conspiracies all around them; and both
were subject to unwelcome scrutinies by administrative powers. Actually, the
list of similarities runs deeper: both Mademba and Trump faced refugee crises,
although Trump's involved immigrants while Mademba faced emigration;
both faced numerous accusations of rape and sexual assault; both faced
accusations of witness tampering and obstruction of justice; and both challenged the rule of law. In addition, both periodically sought to remake
themselves. This book is not about these comparisons, but my addiction to
the nightly news provided me with insights into Mademba's behavior that
I might not otherwise have noticed, let alone tried to understand.

I am not the first person to write about Mademba. Mademba's son and
decorated war hero, Abd-el-Kader Mademba, wrote a hagiographical account
of his father's life during the era of nostalgia for both the Great War and the

French Empire in the late 1920s. In 1994, Barbara Lefebvre produced an excellent, but unpublished, Sorbonne (Université Paris I) Master's thesis on Mademba, based on several months of archival research in Mali and France. Abd-el-Kader's book about his father remains, however, the standard account, despite its obvious self-interest. Several of Mademba's children died fighting for France during the Great War and others went on to become high-ranking professional soldiers, leading educators, and prominent businessmen. Among Mademba's grandchildren and great-grandchildren are a former Senegalese ambassador and other prominent dignitaries. Mademba's investment in his children's education and in their commitment to public service is one of his enduring legacies. Precisely because of this legacy, I am certain that this book's critical analysis of Mademba will spark debate. This is as it should be. Just as there are many sides to Mademba, there are also many more sources to tap into in the archives and in oral histories in order to provide fuller and perhaps different interpretations of Mademba. Just as this book on Mademba has clearly been influenced by the contemporary issues dominating the world in which I live, others will certainly find other aspects of Mademba's long and prominent life to write about.

ACKNOWLEDGMENTS

There are at least two truisms in all historical research and writing: the first is that all of our work is collaborative; and the second is that precisely because we can never know everything, all of our work is provisional. Robert Merton famously noted in his 1936 discussion of the unintended consequences of public policies that all policies will be flawed because policy makers cannot know everything and thus cannot anticipate all possible consequences. But Merton did not appreciate that the very questions we pose are shaped by structured ways of knowing that limit the questions we ask. Thus, all knowledge is provisional, and all knowledge is shaped by political biases.

To further complicate the production of knowledge is the fact that all of our research builds on the work of those who have laid the foundations for the research we conduct. We depend on the memories of our informants, whose work is not only to remember but to recount and reorder their memories and traditions in ways that are meaningful to them. We depend equally on the women and men who wrote things down, those who collected them, and those who organized them into forms that are retrievable. Not everything is remembered or written down or even kept. Everyone forgets and all of us discard paper and notes that we no longer need without usually thinking about others who might want to work with those discarded or forgotten things. Thus, the universe of potential things to study is immense but never stable: this universe constantly expands and contracts. So, what we know and how we know it are central to the tasks of thinking, learning, and producing history.

Archival research is a core part of our discipline. What we read in the archives is part of the constructed and curated collection of past records that fit the visions both of those who wrote reports, memos, orders, letters, and all sorts of written forms and those who have organized and helped to make legible the collections of evidence from the past. Both sets of visions deeply shape what we find, what we read, what order we read them in, and what sense we make of the evidence we find. Silences form a huge hole in any body of archival sources we use. Oral sources do not merely fill these holes; instead, our oral informants curate their own versions of the past. They are in many ways our historian colleagues. But silences abound in the oral records as well. Each body of evidence about the past is deeply shaped by structures of power in no small part because knowledge is power and controlling knowledge contributes to power. That said, this project on Mademba has benefitted from the willingness of my elderly informants to share their interpretations of the past with me and from the tireless work of archivists and staff in the Archives Nationales du Mali, Archives Nationales du Sénégal, the Archives Nationales de France d'Outre-Mer, the Archives Nationales République de France at Franc-Bourgeois, and the Service Historique de la Défense at Vincennes. In addition to appreciating the work of archivists who organize raw material into legible categories, I also appreciate the work of the archives' staff who bring us the cartons of raw material, but who also reshelf and preserve the archives. In Mali, I want to acknowledge the former director, Ali Onguiba, and especially Timothée Saye, who has provided sustained assistance on my many projects over the years. In Senegal, I especially want to thank both the former director, Saliou M'Baye, and the current director, Mme. Fatoumata Cissé Diarra, for their commitments to the production of knowledge and to their hard work in making the archives in Dakar one of the premier collections in Africa. In Dakar, I am especially grateful to Cheikhou Oumar Tall, with whom I have collaborated now for several years on projects relating to African colonial employees, of whom Mademba was one.

I owe a special debt to Babacar Fall, whose encouragement of this project goes back to when we were both fellows at Stanford Humanities Center. Mademba is an outgrowth of our efforts to promote and sustain collaboration between the Faculté des Sciences et Technologies de l'Éducation et de la Formation (FASTEF), the Université Cheikh Anta Diop de Dakar (UCAD), the Archives Nationales du Sénégal, and Stanford University. Our initial and ongoing collaboration focused on the huge but rarely used archival collection of African colonial employees of the French colonial state and especially of the government-general of l'Afrique Occidentale Française (AOF). All along the way, Babacar provided inspiration and encouragement to all of us involved in the project and to me especially. Indeed, Babacar early in this project suggested that the shift in Mademba's patronym from Sèye to Sy was a sign of a much larger change in how Mademba presented himself. Babacar has also devoted his tireless energy to building the Institut d'Études Avancées de Saint Louis du Sénégal and serving as its inaugural director. I want to acknowledge the work of Phil Schwartzberg, who produced the maps included in this book from the bits and pieces of colonial era maps. Charles Becker played an essential role in the preparation and publication of the French version of this book. All of the translations from French to English in this book and all of the errors contained in them are my own.

All work of scholarship is collaborative. All of us build on what other scholars have written and what others have collected. Over the nearly four decades in which I have ever so tentatively collected evidence on Mademba, so many people have provided feedback and suggestions. Some have been nudges to think more about certain aspects and others have been more robust criticism. But I am deeply appreciative of all who have taken the time to read bits and pieces of this book in its various stages over this long period and especially to those who have engaged in the heroic effort to read through the entire work. Many of my current and former students have had to trudge their way through pieces of this book. Every nudge or deep criticism along the way has helped make this a better book. But it is not a perfect book, precisely because there is still so much that we do not know. I remain in awe of anyone who reads what I write.

Martin Klein and David Robinson saw in a rather inchoate PhD dissertation a sparkle that was to become this book. Mademba had a cameo appearance in that dissertation. Bouboucar Barry encouraged my thinking on this and many of my other history projects. Support for my research on Mademba has come from many sources, including the National Endowment for the Humanities, the Guggenheim Foundation, the Stanford Humanities Center, the Stanford Center for African Studies, and the office of the dean of Humanities and Sciences at Stanford, all of which provided funding and time to both collect and begin the process of writing. Stanford University, the Stanford History Department, and Stanford's Center for African Studies have supported and sustained my research by providing an intellectual community of fellow scholars and a stream of wonderfully talented graduate students. At Stanford, I want to shout out my appreciation especially to my fellow Africanists Jim Campbell, Joel Cabrita, Gabrielle Hecht, Steven Press, and Sean Hanretta (now at Northwestern), as well as Jim Ferguson, Grant Parker, Joel Samoff, Larry Diamond, Laura Hubbard, and David Abernethy, among so many others. Even further afield, I appreciate the criticism, insights, and ongoing friendship of Kristin Mann, Andreas Eckert, Alessandro Stanziani, Allen Isaacman, Fred Cooper, Bruce Hall, Greg Mann, Bill Worger, Tom Spear, Marie Rodet, Trevor Getz, Kelly Duke Bryant, Owen White, and Tom Bassett. Several of my former students have provided some of the most piercing criticism, but also the most helpful insights and sustained collaboration. Benjamin Lawrance, Emily Burrill, Emily Osborn, Liz Thornberry, Rachel Jean-Baptiste, Thom McClendon, and Jim Mokiber have been fellow travelers in the broader field of African legal history. Rebecca Wall and Wallace Teska have not only engaged with Mademba but have also used some of their precious time in the archives in Mali and Senegal while conducting their own research to keep a look out for additional evidence on Mademba that I missed; and, no doubt, there is much more that we all have missed.

A core component of scholarship lies in the hidden side of the publication process that takes on relatively inchoate arguments and narratives and helps transform them into meaningful and readable scholarship. I want to thank not only the anonymous reviewers for this book, who pushed me in very different ways to make this a better book, but also Atifa Jiwa and Maria Marsh with whom I have worked for many years on the African Studies Series of Cambridge University Press and who are instrumental in this process of producing scholarship.

Having worked on this project for four decades, it is as if Mademba has become a long-term house guest who was fun to have around for a short visit but whose seemingly unending residence has become challenging. Mademba has shared my household for longer than I could ever have imagined and I could never have managed to encourage him out of the door except for the love and support I have received from Amy, Sam, Sophie, and their families. To them, I owe the greatest thanks.

ABBREVIATIONS

ACC	Association Cotonnière Coloniale
ANM	Archives Nationales du Mali
ANOM	Archives Nationales de France d'Outre-Mer
ANS-AOF	Archives Nationales du Sénégal section l'Afrique Occidentale Française
bull.	bulletin
cmdt. sup.	commandant supérieur
doss. pers.	dossier personnel
gouv.	gouverneur
gouv.-gen.	gouverneur-général
gouv. Sén., p.i.	gouverneur Sénégal, per interim
gouvt.-gen.	gouvernement-général
inspecteur-gen.	inspecteur-general
JAH	*Journal of African History*
JOAOF	*Journal officiel de l'Afrique Occidentale française*
JOHSN	*Journal officiel du Haut-Sénégal-Niger*
lt.-col.	lieutenant-colonel
lt.-gouv.	lieutentant-gouverneur
Min. Col.	minister of colonies
Min. Marine	minister of marine (Navy)
nd	no date
np	no place
p.i.	par interim
pol.	politique
PT	postes et télégraphe
rap.	rapport/s
Sén.	Sénégal
Sén. et Dépend.	Sénégal et Dépendances
SHD	Service Historique de la Défense (Vincennes)

~

Introduction

In 1900, less than a decade after the French had conquered the vast interior of French West Africa, Faama Mademba Sèye, the king of the states of Sansanding and dependencies along the banks of the Niger River, found himself under house arrest in the colonial capital of Kayes. Mademba had been ordered to Kayes as the colonial administration conducted further investigations into the allegations that he had systematically abused his power, engaged in ritual murder, raped countless women, and extorted significant wealth from his subjects. While under house arrest, Mademba wrote to the governor-general of French West Africa demanding that he be given the opportunity to clear his name in front of a French court. Mademba's request went as far as the minister of colonies in Paris, who bluntly denied Mademba's request. "[I]n no case should Mademba be permitted to bring this [case] before French courts."[1] The governor-general argued further that "the Mademba affair . . . is at once more delicate and more serious than it would appear" in the official investigations into Mademba's alleged abuses.[2] Why was the minister of colonies so afraid of letting Mademba try to clear his name in a French court? What made this case so "delicate" and so "serious"? How could Mademba, an African born in the French colonial town of Saint Louis du Sénégal, attempt to bring such a case before French courts, whose jurisdiction was limited to those who had French or European citizenship? And what did this case against Mademba reveal about the intersection of colonialism and the rule of law?

This book is a history of the early phase of colonialism: from conquest and the scrapping together of a colonial administration under military supervision to the development of a civilian administration. It examines how the moving parts that constituted colonialism adhered and repelled each other periodically. This study of colonialism also reveals that plans developed in the

---

[1] Min. Col. confidential letter to Gouv.-Gen., Mar. 24, 1900, Paris, ANS-AOF 15 G 176.
[2] Gouv.-gen. Chaudié, Suite Donnée à la Vérification par l'Administration ou par la Division compétente, Kayes, Feb. 1, 1900, in Danel, Service du Fama de Sansanding, Segu, Jan. 14, 1900, ANS-AOF 15 G 176.

metropole, in the colonial headquarters in Africa, or even in the forward barracks of the military command were rarely implemented as designed. Few colonial administrators understood the complexities on the ground, which differed from region to region and group to group. Nonetheless, colonialism was not merely an exercise in improvisation. Out of the constant give and take between changing metropolitan policy agenda and local conditions, broad patterns of rule were eventually established. This study focuses on the period when colonialism was still a work in progress, even as muscular efforts were undertaken to create order and regularity.

One of the defining features of colonialism was that it required the active or passive collaboration of subjected peoples. Force alone was never enough. Colonial subjects and colonial powers entered into bargains of collaboration that changed over time as colonial states evolved. This book examines an individual, Mademba Sèye, as he traversed the early phases of colonial rule, during which he transformed himself with the help of his French patrons from a telegraph clerk into an African *faama* (Bambara: king, ruler). Just as colonialism was a series of moving parts that articulated differently at different times, Mademba survived these changes by transforming and adapting himself to changed circumstances. Despite changes to colonialism and despite serious challenges to Mademba's rule, Mademba remained *faama* until his death in 1918.

Tracing Mademba's experiences within the emerging and maturing colonial state illuminates the conflicts of different forms of colonialism and the deep ambiguities of the rule of law in colonial societies. Mademba's life was shaped by his embeddedness in these processes. As a student in the French colonial school for sons of chiefs and hostages and as an entry-level clerk in the nascent Post and Telegraph Department, Mademba spent almost all of his childhood and adulthood affiliated with the colonial state. As Mademba moved up the administrative ladder, he became even more enmeshed with the colonial state. This has implications for the nature of the sources I have. As research on biography makes clear, most of the evidence we have on subaltern lives is generated from "institutions of domination and regulation," forcing the researcher to be explicit about his or her methods, about how those institutions produced those records, and about the wider silences in the historical record.[3] This is also the case with Mademba; most of the documentary

---

[3] See, among others, Sue Peabody, "Microhistory, Biography, and Fiction: The Politics of Narrating the Lives of People under Slavery," *Transatlantica: Revue d'études américaines, American Studies Journal* 2 (2012), 1–19; Trevor R. Getz and Liz Clarke, *Abina and the Import Men: A Graphic History* (New York: Oxford University Press, second edition, 2016); Thomas V. Cohen, "The Macrohistory of Microhistory," *Journal of Medieval and Early Modern Studies* 47 (1) 2017, 55–73.

evidence that I have about him and written by him was produced through official correspondence, which shaped the nature of the evidence itself. I also have a handful of personal letters Mademba wrote to Louis Archinard, his long-time patron, which sometimes provide glimpses into the intimate worlds otherwise neglected in official correspondence. And I have oral histories collected in Sinsani and surroundings from elderly informants who at best were children when Mademba ruled his kingdom and whose interpretations of Mademba were shaped by their families' experiences and subsequent history. There is a lot I still do not know about Mademba's life.

Given the evidence I have, I share Alice Kessler-Harris's unease about how an individual life could speak to larger historical processes.[4] In many ways, this project cleaves closest to the challenge laid out by Charles Tilly regarding the task of European social history: "reconstructing ordinary people's experiences of large structural changes." Tilly had in mind the rise of nation-states and rise of industrial capitalism.[5] While neither the modern nation-state nor industrial capitalism emerged in late nineteenth-century French West Africa, the changes unleashed by colonial conquest were no less transformational. In addition, Tilly, who called for a collective biography of working people who lived these big transformations, would unlikely recognize this study in the terms he framed. However, this book is about how one individual lived these big transformations and how he used these transformations to transform himself. Circumstances provided the raw material for how Mademba transformed himself, but he was the actor who often recognized the changes underway and seized the opportunities available to him. My approach to Mademba and his life is much like the one proposed by Kessler-Harris:

> Rather than offering history as a background, or introducing it in order to locate an individual in time, I want to ask how the individual life helps us make sense of a piece of historical process. I want to see through the life ... I think an individual life might help us to see not only into particular events but into the larger cultural and social and even political processes of a moment in time.[6]

This study of Mademba's life astride the transformations of colonialism provides texture to the processes of change unleashed by French conquest. In so doing, it illuminates three significant bodies of scholarship: the changing nature of colonialism; intermediaries and bargains of collaboration; and the rule of law.

---

[4] Alice Kessler-Harris, "AHR Roundtable: Why Biography?" *American Historical Review* 114 (3) 2009, 625.

[5] Charles Tilly, "Retrieving European Lives," in *Reliving the Past: The Worlds of Social History*, ed. Olivier Zunz (Chapel Hill: University of North Carolina Press, 1985), 15–16.

[6] Kessler-Harris, "AHR Roundtable," 626.

Changing Nature of Colonialism

In a memorial lecture celebrating the life and work of Frederick Lugard given in 1963, former French colonial governor and scholar Hubert Deschamps reflected on the practices of French and British native policies and on their consequences for newly independent African states. Deschamps argued that while both British and French native policies failed to achieve their stated goals, they both nonetheless succeeded "belatedly and inadequately" in generating modern political institutions that promoted independence. In making his case, Deschamps argued in a retrospective justification of colonialism that despite periodic efforts to promote "assimilation" as native policy, the French relied on native authorities to manage colonial rule, as did the British. By assimilation, Deschamps meant the effort to normalize French metropolitan political forms in colonial Africa, which had been abandoned in the nineteenth century with colonial conquest only to be applied again in the 1930s, abandoned again during Vichy, and applied again in the period after 1945. In this mock conversation with the deceased Lugard, Deschamps argued that "In black Africa, everywhere where we found kings, except in extreme cases where we had fierce opposition or a lack of traditional institutions, we have inducted them, we made them our superior agents, just like the British and for the same reasons: convenience for the conquest, facilitating the administration [of conquered lands], and for economic stability."[7]

Michael Crowder took issue with Deschamps's comparison of French and British reliance on African chiefs and rulers. Admitting that both used African chiefs in their native administration, Crowder argued "What *is* important is the very different way in which these authorities were used" and how the use of chiefs fit into a coherent colonial policy.[8] In his defense of British colonial policy of indirect rule, Crowder missed the significant challenge Deschamps raised: that despite their invocation of grand theories of colonial rule, both French and British colonialism were inherently pragmatic and improvisational. D. K. Fieldhouse better captured Deschamps's insight.

> Colonialism was not a rational or planned condition. It was rather the product of a unique set of circumstances before and during the later nineteenth century that resulted unpredictably in the formal partition of much of the world between the great powers. Few of these, it was argued, had a coherent preconceived idea of what they would do with these territories they claimed or of the problems these would create. Colonial rule was thus a complex improvisation and an ideology of empire was evolved to justify what it was found necessary to do.[9]

---

[7] Hubert Deschamps, "Et Maintenant, Lord Lugard," *Africa* 33 (4) 1963, 297–298.

[8] Michael Crowder, "Indirect Rule: French and British Style," *Africa* 34 (3) 1964, 197, emphasis in the original.

[9] David Kenneth Fieldhouse, *Colonialism 1870–1945: An Introduction* (London: Weidenfeld and Nicolson, 1981), 41–42.

A. G. Hopkins distinguished between the two classic forms of colonial rule: direct, which had a strong military component; and indirect, which relied on local collaborators. Hopkins wrote that "direct rule was more likely to be oppressive, usually created a focus for resistance, and even terrorism. It was also costly. Indirect rule was less visible and far cheaper, but it obliged the colonial authorities to meddle in local society and to juggle endlessly with landlords, warriors, bureaucrats, merchants and peasants."[10] Philip Curtin went even further. He argued that "[t]heorists of administration constructed elaborate frameworks on paper in which they argued the advantages of 'direct' or 'indirect' rule." In practice, however, "[t]he first stages of colonial rule, to about 1920, were marked by a great variety of administrative expediencies."[11] Expediency, improvisation, and meddling had their own unintended consequences requiring periodic intervention and colonial reform.

With its elaborate bureaucracy and clearly identifiable hierarchy, the Sokoto Caliphate served as the ideal model for Lugard's indirect rule policy that he first laid out in his 1906 *Political Memoranda* and then set to the level of imperial ideology in his *The Dual Mandate in Tropical Africa*, published in 1922.[12] Already by the time he published his *Dual Mandate*, it was clear that indirect rule along the caliphate model could not apply seamlessly throughout British colonial Africa. Where indigenous chiefs with robust institutions did not exist – or were not legible to colonial officials – British policy was to "invent" them. Such invention could take many forms, including the warrant chiefs of southeastern Nigeria and what Moses Ochonu has labeled as subcolonialism – in which Africans drawn from regions with denser institutions of rule and higher levels of "civilization" were employed in regions with weaker institutions of rule. "The reality of colonial rule," Ochonu writes, "is that colonial regimes sometimes broke the habit of ruling through indigenous elites in the interests of governing ease ... In fact, flexible and improvised colonial practices were more common than one might discern from the colonial archive. For the African colonial state, the range of flexibility in colonial practices was nearly infinite."[13] To the British, as with other European colonial officials, the most significant attribute of colonial rule was

---

[10] Antony Gerald Hopkins, "Lessons of 'Civilizing Missions' Are Mostly Unlearned," *New York Times*, March 23, 2003, sec. 4, 5.

[11] Philip Curtin, "The Impact of Europe," in *African History: From Earliest Times to Independence*, eds. Philip Curtin, Steven Feierman, Leonard Thompson, and Jan Vansina (New York and London: Longman, second edition, 1995), 425.

[12] Frederick John Dealtry Lugard, *Political Memoranda, Revision of Instructions to Political Officers on Subjects Chiefly, Political and Administrative 1913–1918* (original London: F. Cass, 1906; republished 1970); Baron Frederick John Dealtry Lugard, *The Dual Mandate in Tropical Africa* (Edinburgh and London: W. Blackwood and Sons, 1922).

[13] Moses E. Ochonu, *Colonialism by Proxy: Hausa Imperial Agents and Middle Belt Consciousness in Nigeria* (Bloomington: Indiana University Press, 2014), 6. See also

whatever worked. "Functionality," according to Ochonu, "sometimes trumped colonial doctrine no matter how elaborate or canonical such doctrine had become."[14]

As Thomas Spear reminds us, there were limits to what could be invented in terms of African political institutions under colonial rule. Africans retained a robust sense of history and historical precedent that provided legitimacy to political institutions. Those institutions invented by colonial officials in collaboration with Africans that did not resonate with ongoing political discourse might well fail to be seen as legitimate and result in disputes and rebellions.[15] Sara Berry remarked that such "hegemony on a shoestring" often gave rise not to stability but to a proliferation of disputes over customs and authority. By making so-called traditional systems of authority the cornerstones of their strategies for colonial rule, the colonial administrators built colonial rule on conflict and change rather than on age-old stability.[16] Conflict and change necessitated further intervention in African societies, thus employing increasingly elaborate improvisation and experimentation of colonial rule.

All of these historians who have debated the flexibility of colonialism seem to have missed the importance of the legal underpinnings of empire, namely the protectorate. As I discuss more fully in Chapter 3, the protectorate emerged in the late eighteenth and early nineteenth centuries as the prominent instrument of international law that furthered imperial expansion. At its most basic, the protectorate was an arrangement "whereby one state, while retaining to some extent its separate identity as a state, is subject to a kind of guardianship by another state."[17] The protectorate usually came into being through military conquest or a treaty ceding a certain degree of sovereignty to the superior power. Alfred Kamanda, a Sierra Leonean scholar and one of the few students of the protectorate treaty, argues that "by reason of its very vagueness and nebulousness, [the protectorate] could be a cloak for many different, and even diametrically opposed, administrations in practice."[18] According to Steven Press, a protected polity established a "quasi-sovereign position," or

Adiele Eberechukwu Afigbo, *The Warrant Chiefs: Indirect Rule in Southeastern Nigeria, 1891–1929* (London: Longman, 1972).

[14] Ochonu, *Colonialism by Proxy*, 214.

[15] Thomas Spear, "Neo-traditionalism and the Limits of Invention in British Colonial Africa," *JAH* 44 (1) 2003, 3–27. See also Terence Ranger, "The Invention of Tradition in Africa," in *The Invention of Tradition*, eds. Eric Hobsbawm and Terence O. Ranger (Cambridge: Cambridge University Press, 1983), 211–262.

[16] Sara Berry, *No Condition Is Permanent: The Social Dynamics of Agrarian Change in Sub-Saharan Africa* (Madison: University of Wisconsin Press, 1993), 29.

[17] Robert Jennings and Arthur Watts (eds.), *Oppenheim's International Law* (Harlow: Longman, ninth edition, 1992), vol. 1, 278.

[18] Alfred M. Kamanda, *A Study of the Legal Status of Protectorates in Public International Law* (Ambilly: The Graduate Institute, Geneva, 1961), 97–98.

as Mary Lewis argues in the case of Tunisia, a "co-sovereign" in relationship to the colonizing power that permitted a variety of subterfuges regarding who or what the colonizing power was and permitted significant changes over time.[19] At its base, however, the protectorate had its origins in the circumstances that obliged the second party to submit to the protection of the first, most often through force or the threat of force.[20] In his classic 1929 study of French colonial policy, Stephen Roberts compared French policy of association, which was in vogue at the time of his writing, to the protectorate. Roberts understood these different forms of colonial rule through the lens of British indirect rule. "Association stresses a compulsory advance suitable to native mentality and to the existing situation, but still imposed by Europeans; whereas a 'protectorate' implies development by the natives, with Europeans supervising to a lesser degree, and not interfering unless given practices are considered anti-social."[21] In the protectorate, Roberts argues, the "native authorities have been maintained ... The natives govern themselves under French supervision, and this has done much to minimize the disruptive features of the changes in their moods of existence, especially because with the utilization of native officials went a large degree of toleration for native customs, even those directly opposed to European concepts."[22] Such a policy of colonial rule fits neatly the agenda of colonial military leaders, whose objectives were to conquer territories often preemptively and to protect conquered territories once acquired. During the active phase of conquest, few colonial military leaders wanted to invest time and resources in administering conquered territories at the expense of chasing further glory on the battlefield.[23] The protectorate, whether established with relatively minor chiefs or strong kingdoms, provided the means to acquire territory, quickly establish some semblance of rule drawing on real or imagined native authorities, and keep pursuing military victories. Stephen Roberts understood this when he noted that the "conquest of the Omars and the Ahmadous and the Samorys made the

---

[19] Steven Press, *Rogue Empires: Contracts and Conmen in Europe's Scramble for Africa* (Cambridge, MA: Harvard University Press, 2017), 33, 159–160, 238–251; Mary Dewhurst Lewis, *Divided Rule: Sovereignty and Empire in French Tunisia, 1881–1938* (Berkeley: University of California Press, 2014), 11–12, 96–97. Lewis describes the protectorate as a "wonderfully flexible legal instrument," 42. See also Lauren Benton, *A Search for Sovereignty: Law and Geography in European Empires, 1400–1900* (New York: Cambridge University Press, 2010), chapter 5.

[20] Frantz Despagnet, "Les protectorats" in *Les colonies françaises: Petite encyclopédie coloniale publiée sous la direction de M. Maxime Petit* (Paris: Larousse, 1902), vol. I, 53–54.

[21] Stephen H. Roberts, *History of French Colonial Policy (1870–1925)* (London: P. S. King and Son, 1929), vol. 1, 121.

[22] Ibid., I, 316.

[23] Alexander Sydney Kanya-Forstner, *The Conquest of the Western Sudan: A Study in French Military Imperialism* (Cambridge: Cambridge University Press, 1969).

occupation of West Africa far and away the most difficult task of France. But there was a curious compensation that, to some extent, this pre-existing organization could be utilized for instance, when it came to reviving the economic life of the occupied areas" and, of course, to establish forms of native administration.[24]

Improvisation clearly remained central to colonial rule, but it was improvisation within the context of changing ideas about colonialism. That was what Deschamps was trying to explain in his fictive debate with Lugard. Changing ideas about colonialism matter for our story of Mademba because he was caught up in the swirling tides of changing policies. Upon his appointment to direct a crew that was establishing the telegraph system in the Upper River region in 1879, Mademba joined the aggressive phase of colonial conquest of the Soudan. Building and maintaining the telegraph proved Mademba's worth to the military leadership and he was increasingly drawn into the inner circle of advisors and counselors to the supreme military leader as the French planned and executed their military advance. Concerned more with the security of their troops and the advance of their mission to conquer, the French military leaders probably thought little about what the administration of conquered territories would be like. They were likely drawn to the protectorate, which had been applied in Egypt under Napoléon and in Algeria.[25] It had also been used in Senegal under Governor Louis Faidherbe's expansion. As the French moved into the Soudan, they established protectorates with chiefs and rulers who sided with them and in polities that they conquered militarily. Colonel Louis Archinard, who oversaw the largest territorial conquests in the Soudan, raised the standard for the protectorate when in the course of the campaign against the Umarian state at Segu, he justified conquest by claiming to want to return the kingdom to its rightful Bambara rulers, who had themselves been conquered by the Umarians.

In Archinard's hands, as I examine more fully in Chapters 3 and 4, French efforts to apply a variant of indirect rule through the reinstatement of legitimate African rulers in Segu failed miserably. Archinard's model of indirect rule worked somewhat better in Bandiagara, where he placed Aguibu, one of al hajj Umar's sons who has broken with Umar's eldest son and successor and sided with the French.[26] Archinard's policy of indirect rule attained its most improvisational form at Sinsani, where in 1891 Archinard made Mademba king in a region that had never had kings before and over which Mademba had no obvious claim on indigenous legitimacy. Between French conquest in 1890 and

---

[24] Roberts, *History of French Colonial Policy*, vol. 1, 304–306.

[25] See Jean-Loup Amselle, *Vers une multiculturalisme française: L'empire de la coutume* (Paris: Aubier, 1996).

[26] Yves Saint-Martin, "Un fils d'El Hadj Omar: Aguibou, roi du Dinguiray et du Macina (1843?–1907)," *Cahiers d'études africaines* 8 (29) 1968: 144–178.

1893, widespread rebellions convulsed the wider region around Segu and Sinsani that necessitated significant French military intervention. Archinard then suppressed his effort at indirect rule at Segu, but maintained Mademba and Aguibu in power.

Even if colonial conquest was popular among the public, French metropolitan parliamentarians resented the military leadership's independence, their disregard for ministerial orders, and the constant budget overruns.[27] After Archinard was recalled in 1893, the Minister of the Navy, who was charged with oversight over overseas colonies, appointed a civilian, Alfred Grodet, as governor of the Soudan. Grodet, who had served as governor in Martinique and French Guyana, saw his role in part to tame the French military and to establish civilian rule. As I shall discuss, Grodet sought to tame the military by promoting the rule of law. Two aspects of Grodet's efforts stand out: he ordered military officers to suppress the slave trade, which had been prohibited in French territories since 1848, and to suppress corporal punishment, which the French military considered necessary to control their African subjects. Grodet's policies to shape colonial rule in the Soudan through French metropolitan ideas of civilization and civilian rule of law bumped up against the French military's sense of its mission, its prerogatives, and its own rule of law. Most French military officers in the Soudan disregarded Grodet's orders and Grodet was recalled before his term had fully ended.[28]

Grodet's concern with regularity and the rule of law foreshadowed the reforms underway in metropolitan France. In 1894, the Ministry of Colonies was formed out of the Ministry of the Navy with broad mandates to reform the much enlarged French empire. The year 1894 also marked the onset of the Dreyfus Affair, which tightly enveloped the French military leadership and led to sustained political instability in France and the colonies. As part of its reform of empire, the new Ministry of Colonies created the French West Africa Federation (Afrique Occidentale française) in 1895 under the authority of a governor-general based in Dakar. Jean-Baptist Chaudié, a former administrator of the Ministry of the Navy and a senior officer in that ministry's General Inspection Service, served as the first governor-general with a mandate to oversee the budget of the colonies of this far-flung federation, to establish order and uniformity among the disparate colonies, and to hold lieutenant-governors accountable.[29] With Grodet's recall in 1895, the minister of colonies appointed Colonel Louis Edgar de Trentinian as

[27] Kanya-Forstner, *The Conquest of the Western Sudan*, chapter 8.
[28] Richard Roberts, *Warriors, Merchants and Slaves: The State and the Economy in the Middle Niger Valley, 1700–1914* (Stanford, CA: Stanford University Press, 1987), 153.
[29] Colin Newbury, "The Formation of the French West Africa Federation," *JAH* 1 (1) 1960, 111–128; Alice L. Conklin, *A Mission to Civilize: The Republican Idea of Empire in France and West Africa, 1895–1930* (Stanford, CA: Stanford University Press, 1997), 23–37.

lieutenant-governor of the French Soudan. Trentinian was an officer in the
infantry of the Marines, and thus part of the military ensconced in administrative and leadership positions in the colony, whose formative colonial
military experience was mostly in Indochina. Trentinian was thus simultaneously an outsider to the core of French military leaders in the Soudan whose
careers were shaped by conquest but also deeply part of the ethos of the
Marines.[30] As such, Trentinian treaded a delicate path through the mandates
emanating from Dakar and Paris to regularize colonial practice, to promote
economic development, to control budgetary expenses, and yet to assist his
military colleagues eager to complete the conquest of the region. It was under
Trentinian that Mademba received his first administrative sanction for his
alleged abuse of power, which I explore more fully in Chapter 5. Under
Trentinian's leadership, the military completed its conquest of the region by
1898. But also under Trentinian's leadership, the Voulet–Chanoine mission,
which was charged with demarcating the vague boundaries between French
and British territories, spun drastically out of control and resulted in a major
scandal that further shook the French military and colonial establishment. As
I explore in Chapter 6, in order to impose additional constraints on the
leadership of the French Soudan and to punish the military for its persistent
budgetary indiscipline, in 1899, the Ministry of Colonies reorganized the
colony and allocated some of its parts to neighboring colonies. In the face of
this decision, Trentinian resigned in protest.

Trentinian's resignation coincided both with the aftereffects of the Voulet–
Chanoine scandal and with the emerging scandal surrounding the investigations into Mademba's alleged crimes and abuses of authority. The three
nested investigations into these allegations form a central point of inflection in
the history of French colonialism in the Soudan. These investigations pitted
the colonialism of Archinard's indirect rule against the colonialism of
regularity and the rule of law. These investigations also illuminated the
practices of relying on African intermediaries whose position and authority
were founded on loyalty to the French against the stated goals of the mission
to civilize. I unpack these investigations in Chapter 7.

Amédée William Merlaud-Ponty, know more widely as William Ponty, who
assumed the position of lieutenant-governor following Trentinian's resignation, oversaw the investigations into Mademba. Ponty, whose real title was
delegate of the governor-general in the French Soudan, was a civilian with
significant military and administrative experience in the Soudan. Ponty served
as Archinard's private secretary and in the course of this role had firsthand

---

[30] G. Wesley Johnson, "William Ponty and Republican Paternalism in French West Africa
(1866–1915)," in *African Proconsuls: European Governors in Africa,* eds. Lewis Henry
Gann and Peter Duignan (New York: Free Press, 1978), 130–131; Kanya-Forstner, *The
Conquest of the Western Sudan,* chapter 9.

experience of challenges facing the French in building a colonial empire. He also served together with Mademba in at least one military excursion.[31] Upon assuming the role of lieutenant-governor, Ponty was obliged to deal with the results of the Mademba investigations, which raised significant challenges to his stated goals of promoting the rule of law.[32] Faced with the prospects of yet another potential scandal regarding France's African empire, Ponty, Governor-general Chaudié, and the minister of colonies closed ranks around Mademba, made oblique noises about constraining his unlimited authority, sent Mademba back to his kingdom, and ordered a relatively low-level employee of the Native Affairs Department to serve as "resident," presumably to oversee Mademba's administration and to keep his inclinations in check.

Chastised but not exonerated, Mademba returned to his kingdom in the fall of 1900 eager to refurbish his image among the French administrators who had yet again saved him from himself. With conquest now complete, the French redoubled their efforts to promote economic development. Mademba, who had understood the colonial rhetoric of the civilizing mission, of progress, and the need to develop economically, immersed himself in promoting cotton production for export, and in the process remade himself into a colonial modernizer. Cotton became the means through which Mademba rehabilitated himself during a strategic visit to France in September and October 1906, as I examine in Chapter 8. At the Colonial Exposition in Marseilles and at the Parisian banquet of the Association of Colonial Cotton, Mademba was feted as the innovator and promoter of export-oriented cotton that would free France's industry from its dependence on cotton exported from the United States. Mademba used interviews with French journalists to plant the seeds of a revised narrative of his long and steadfast loyalty to France, his commitment to France's civilizing mission in Africa, and his progressive administration of his kingdom along the banks of the Niger River. Even as Mademba was promoting Soudanese cotton to French industrialists, his own cotton kingdom was collapsing in the face of the end of slavery and the rebellion of his army of prisoners of war, who along with slaves, were now demanding their freedom. Without these armies of forced labor, Mademba's ability to produce cotton waned. Mademba nonetheless managed to surf the changing economic and political conditions in the Soudan and retain his kingdom until his death in 1918.

Bargains of Collaboration, Bricolage, and African Intermediaries in Colonial French West Africa

Mademba benefitted from early colonial efforts to build colonial rule on improvisation and expediency. So did many thousands of other Africans.

---

[31] Mamoudou Sy, "Capitaine Mamadou Racine Sy (1838–1902)," unpublished paper, Dakar, 2010.
[32] Johnson, "William Ponty," 127–156.

Nearly fifty years ago, the Cambridge imperial historian Ronald Robinson argued that there could be no colonialism without the active or passive acceptance of colonialism by subject people. Colonial states were just too weak and metropolitan powers too parsimonious to invest in repressing subject people all of the time. Robinson challenged historians to examine the "bargains of collaboration" that lay at the heart of the engagement between subject people and the colonial state. By "bargains of collaboration" Robinson meant how subject people exploited new opportunities unleashed by colonialism to accumulate wealth, power, and prestige.[33] Such benefits depended upon the roles that Africans played within colonial administrations and they could include colonial support for "traditional" officeholders, steady income for employees, patronage from powerful officials, and access to cultural resources. Some became, in Henri Brunschwig's terms, "black whites."[34] Others, however, "straddled" the colonial and "traditional" worlds by using the resources of the colonial state to pursue customary goals within local communities.[35]

In his important study of the "thin white line" of European district administrators in colonial Africa overseeing tens of thousands of Africans, Anthony Kirk-Greene argued that "Without the manpower and machinery of the native administration or similar local government bodies, all the way from paramount chiefs, district headman, and treasury staff to dispensers, foremen of works, and forestry agents ... the colonial administrator could never have functioned or even survived in his job."[36] Reflecting on the French colonial experience, Brunschwig wrote that "colonization brought forth an abundant gaggle of voluntary collaborators. The Whites, incapable of fending for themselves, have always and everywhere found agents: militia, police, boys, cooks, porters, etc, [who] constituted a proletariat recruited from among the less

[33] Ronald Robinson, "Non-European Foundations of European Imperialism: Sketch for a Theory of Collaboration," in *Studies in the Theory of Imperialism*, eds. Roger Owen and Bob Sutcliffe (London: Longman, 1972), 117–142; Colin Newbury, *Patrons, Clients, and Empire: Chieftaincy and Over-rule in Asia, Africa, and the Pacific* (Oxford: Oxford University Press, 2003).

[34] Henri Brunschwig, *Noirs et Blancs dans l'Afrique noire française: Comment le colonisé deviant colonisateur, 1870–1914* (Paris: Flammarion, 1983).

[35] On straddling, see Andreas Eckert "Cultural Commuters: African Employees in Late Colonial Tanzania," in *Intermediaries, Interpreters, and Clerks: African Employees in the Making of Colonial Africa*, eds. Benjamin Lawrance, Emily Osborn, and Richard Roberts (Madison: University of Wisconsin Press, 2006), 248–269; on pursuing local goals, see Jean-Hervé Jézéquel, "'Collecting Customary Law': Educated Africans, Ethnographic Writing, and Colonial Justice in French West Africa," in *Intermediaries*, 139–158, and Jamie Monson, "Claims to History and the Politics of Memory in Southern Tanzania, 1940–1960," *International Journal of African Historical Studies* 33 (3) 2000, 543–565.

[36] Anthony H. M. Kirk-Greene, "Thin White Line: The Size of the British Colonial Service in Africa," *African Affairs* 79 1980, 26, 41.

privileged groups in traditional societies."[37] In her study of Anglo-Egyptian Sudan, Heather Sharkey notes that "colonialism was a day-to-day performance of power in which petty employees took part by presenting the face of government to the general populace in their capacity as inspectors, collectors, law enforcers, teachers, and clerks."[38]

Colonial states often brought immense power to suppress revolts, but they could rarely sustain such expression of control.[39] Far from establishing an "iron rule," colonial officials ruled with precarious authority. Emily Osborn has reversed this notion of an "iron rule"; instead, French colonial administers in Upper Guinea were surrounded by a "circle of iron" formed by their complete dependency on interpreters and local chiefs.[40] During this period, as Robert Delavignette described, "the interpreters kept the [commandant] turning in a narrow circle of intrigues," out of which he had no escape because he was dependent upon them for information, for translation, for mediation, and often also for the basic necessities for daily life, such as food, labor, and sexual services.[41]

Africans who learned European languages in order to translate Europeans' commands to African subjects and to translate African words and concepts into European languages also learned to parse European concepts.[42] Throughout the continent, African employees, teachers, and missionaries produced ethnographies and local histories, many of them having a distinctively self-interested character.[43] Many of these interpreters used their roles as cross-cultural brokers to bolster their own families' claims to traditional power and access to economic resources, such as land and labor. A more careful focus on what intermediaries did and what they gained from working for the colonial authority offers new insights into the practice of colonialism. Such bargains of collaboration were unstable and needed to be periodically renegotiated as colonialism itself changed over time. Those formed during these

---

[37] Brunschwig, *Noirs et Blancs*, 213.

[38] Heather Sharkey, *Living with Colonialism: Nationalism and Culture in Anglo-Egyptian Sudan* (Berkeley: University of California Press, 2003), 138.

[39] Bruce Berman and John Lonsdale, *Unhappy Valley: Conflict in Kenya and Africa* (Athens: Ohio University Press, 1992).

[40] Emily Osborn, "'Circle of Iron': African Colonial Employees and the Interpretation of Colonial Rule in French West Africa," *JAH* 44 (1) 2003: 29–50.

[41] Robert L. Delavignette, *Freedom and Authority in French West Africa* (London: Cass, 1968), 41. See also Tamba Mbayo, *Muslim Interpreters in Colonial Senegal, 1850–1920: Mediations of Knowledge and Power in the Lower and Middle Senegal River Valley* (Lanham, MD: Lexington Books, 2016).

[42] William Worger, "Parsing God: Conversations about the Meaning of Words and Metaphors in Nineteenth-Century Southern Africa," *JAH* 42 (3) 2001, 417–447.

[43] See esp. Jézéquel, "Collecting Customary Law."

moments differed from those formed two or three decades later as colonial rule gradually matured.

Despite the recognition of the importance of indigenous employees to the colonial state, we know very little about the Africans who worked for it.[44] African colonial employees were not simply lackeys of the colonial state. Instead, African colonial employees used the new opportunities created by colonial conquest and colonial rule to pursue their own agendas, even as they served their employers.[45] During the early phase of conquest and establishing colonial rule, many of these African intermediaries moved easily between still fragile colonial spaces and gradually transforming precolonial spaces. Jeffrey Herbst captured this process with his concept of the uneven ways in which colonial states broadcast their power.[46] Broadcasting power was a dynamic process and it waxed and waned over time. As it varied, the spaces African intermediaries inhabited changed, thus opening and foreclosing opportunities. Inhabiting these transitional spaces that would eventually lead toward fuller integration with a colonial system permitted precolonial practices to cohabitate with colonial ones. These transitional spaces also gave rise to what Richard White termed "creative misunderstandings."[47] Such creative misunderstandings were evident in Archinard's policies of reviving African polities that had been defeated by subsequent African conquerors and by appointing new rulers, few of whom had local legitimacy. On the other side, Mademba, one of Archinard's new kings, used the revised space to invent his own legitimacy and to remake himself periodically.

---

[44] Studies of African soldiers and African police provide exceptions to this general statement. See, for example, Myron Echenberg, *Colonial Conscripts: The Tirailleurs Sénégalais in French West Africa, 1857–1960* (Portsmourth, NH: Heinemann, 1991); Timothy Parsons, *The African Rank-and-File: Social Implications of Colonial Military Service in the King's African Rifles, 1902–1964* (Portsmourth, NH: Heinemann, 1999); Gregory Mann, *Native Sons: West African Veterans and France in the Twentieth Century* (Durham, NC: Duke University Press, 2006); and Michelle Moyd, *Violent Intermediaries: African Soldiers, Conquest, and Everyday Colonialism in German East Africa* (Athens: Ohio University Press, 2014). On African police, see Joël Glasman, *Les corps habillés au Togo: Genèse colonial des métiers de police* (Paris: Karthala, 2014). Babacar Fall and I are engaged in a collaboration with FASTEF of UCAD, the Senegal National Archives, and Stanford University in the study of colonial employees of the West African Federation using personnel files.

[45] For a wonderful example of this situation, see Amadou Hampaté Bâ's brilliant autobiographical novel, *The Fortunes of Wangrin*, translated by Aina Pagolini Taylor (Bloomington: Indiana University Press, 1999).

[46] Jeffrey Herbst, *States and Power in Africa: Comparative Lessons in Authority and Control* (Princeton, NJ: Princeton University Press, 2000).

[47] Richard White, *The Middle Ground: Indians, Empires, and Republics in the Great Lakes Region, 1650–1815*, twentieth anniversary edition (New York: Cambridge University Press, 2011), 50, 68.

In periodically remaking himself, Mademba drew on cultural symbols and practices from the multiple worlds that he inhabited in the transitional space that was early colonial Soudan. In drawing on such a diverse array of different symbols and practices, Mademba acted as a *bricoleur*, made famous by Claude Lévi-Strauss. Lévi-Strauss juxtaposes the *bricoleur*, who uses "whatever is at hand," to the engineer, "who is always trying to make his way out of and go beyond the constraints imposed by a particular state of civilization."[48] Building on Lévi-Strauss, Jack Goody defines the *bricoleur* as a "cultural handy-man," who learns by doing and by improvisation rather than from recipes or book-knowledge.[49] Throughout his career, Mademba was an African *bricoleur* who navigated the profoundly unstable and changing worlds of late precolonial and early colonial French West Africa. The thing that Mademba made – his *bricolage* – was himself. As colonialism matured, Mademba periodically remade himself each time with a slightly different combination of elements at hand. Born into a Muslim family in the French colonial town of Saint Louis du Sénégal in 1852, Mademba attended the French school reinvigorated by Governor Faidherbe that was designed for sons of chiefs and interpreters. At a time of increasing Muslim militancy and anticolonial resistance, Mademba joined the young Senegalese Post and Telegraph Department. As he rose through the ranks of the department, Mademba added to his social stature by becoming a Freemason. His career took off as he was recruited to help build the telegraph for the decade-long military conquest of the vast interior of the Soudan and served in the process as interpreter and political agent for the French military command. To reflect his new stature, Mademba wanted a uniform, but as a civilian agent of the telegraph service, no such uniform was available. Nonetheless, as a reward for his loyal service, the military command agreed to provide Mademba with a special uniform. Armed with his new uniform, Mademba enhanced his authority and command over his telegraph crew and over Africans living along the expanding telegraph lines. As conquest accelerated, so did Mademba's authority. The French military command increasingly placed Mademba at the head of ranks of African auxiliaries fighting for the French, but also themselves. Mademba proved again and again both his capacity to command and his loyalty to the French. In the aftermath of conquest, the French rewarded Mademba by making him king (*faama*) over the territories of Sinsani. This was a kingdom fashioned under French colonialism and France's Third Republic, and thus Mademba was bound by the fluid meanings of the French civilizing mission.

[48] Claude Lévi-Strauss, *Savage Mind* (Chicago: University of Chicago Press, 1966), 13–16.
[49] Jack Goody, *The Domestication of the Savage Mind* (Cambridge: Cambridge University Press, 1977), 24, 140, 144.

In making himself king, Mademba drew on the available material and social elements around him. Félix Dubois, who visited Mademba in his kingdom in late 1894 or early 1895, remarked that Mademba attired himself as king in a manner of the *bricoleur*.

> The king's wardrobe remains local. He has avoided dressing himself in European clothing, but he has adopted a red fez and a long cape in the form of a medieval shroud, green in color, and heavily decorated with gold embroidery and bedecked with diverse medals of which one is the medal of the Legion of Honor. I admit that he has, just a small resemblance, to a king of the theater who appears to have just left the storeroom of the accessories. At the very least, however, he avoids looking ridiculous in vest and jacket.[50]

Following a near catastrophic fall from grace in 1899–1900, during which he was held under house arrest in the capital city of the French Soudan, Mademba remade himself yet again. Mademba did not hesitate to wear a vest and jacket during his visit to France in 1906 to promote himself as the economic modernizer of the Soudan and the promoter of colonial cotton for the metropolitan textile industry. In Paris, Mademba presented himself as a modest man rather than a king; a man who opened his own doors and allowed others to pass first. At the same time, the textile industry vetted him as a precious collaborator in making the Soudanese economy useful to French manufacturing. Mademba used his time in France to meet with journalists in order to narrate the story of his rise to become king and in the process to remake himself yet again. Mademba was an efficient *bricoleur* of his own image during a period of transition in the Soudan from a precolonial to colonial space. His capacity to remake himself diminished as the colonial state strengthened and as it asserted a rule of law.

Rules of Law

What was the significance of the minister of colonies' decision in March 1900 to deny Mademba's request to bring the evidence against him before a French court? Under what conditions of the law did Mademba even have the right to assume that he could request to have his case heard by a French court? What rules governed and empowered the minister to deny Mademba's request? And what did the investigation into Mademba's alleged abuses of power and crimes and the decisions surrounding these allegation tell us about the rule of law in early colonial French West Africa?

Let us begin with the "rights" Mademba had to request a trial by a French judge in order to clear his name. During the revolutionary zeal of 1848 that

---

[50] Félix Dubois, *Tombouctou la mystérieuse* (Paris: Flammarion, 1897), 91.

overthrew the constitutional monarchy of Louis Philippe and established the Second Republic, the republican advocates for the abolition of slavery prevailed. On April 27, 1848, the provisional government abolished slavery throughout the French empire and immediately granted former slaves who lived in the old French slaveholding colonies of Guadalupe, Martinique, Guiana, and Réunion rights of citizenship. The 1848 decree abolished slavery throughout the French empire, but did not uniformly extend citizenship to all of its inhabitants. Victor Schoelcher, ardent abolitionist, served as president of the commission charged with developing the abolition decree and with defining the status of the freed slaves. The commission recommended freedom and citizenship for the slaves of the old slaveholding colonies, but hesitated to grant citizenship to the indigenous subjects of the newest colony, Algeria. Slaves in the old French establishments of Gorée and Saint Louis were freed, but the freed slaves and the indigenous inhabitants of these towns did not gain full citizenship but "partial" citizenship. They gained the right to vote for representatives to the French national assembly and the municipal council and the right to bring their legal disputes before French courts – both of which were rights of citizenship – but because these inhabitants were largely Muslim, they retained their rights to bring disputes regarding family issues before qadis and eventually the Muslim Tribunal established in Saint Louis. Within the French empire, the right of these inhabitants to retain their personal status as Muslim and thus to bring their disputes before Muslim judicial authorities was exceptional and thus placed them in a situation of legal ambiguity: they were neither citizens nor subjects, although they exercised the rights of citizenship without being French citizens.[51] Everywhere in the French empire, there existed a route to French citizenship, but only for those who as individuals convinced French officials that they had renounced their personal status, agreed to abide by the French civil code regarding family and inheritance issues, and demonstrated that they had lived by French norms. In contrast, the legally gray areas in which the inhabitants of Gorée and Saint Louis and their descendants (referred to as *originaires*) lived became a subject of significant struggles as French officials sought to clarify the limits on their rights and as these *originaires* demanded full recognition of their rights. Their legal situation was resolved only in 1916, largely in response to claims being made by the *originaires* to have their

---

[51] According to Yerri Urban's research into decrees and case law, French citizenship was "fragmented" by gender, nationality, and religious status, yielding a bewildering array of partial citizenships and incomplete rights. Yerri Urban, "La citoyennité dans l'Empire colonial français est-elle spécifique," *Jus Politicum: Review de droit politique* 14 (2017), 151–187; Yerri Urban, *L'indigène dans le droit colonial français, 1865–1955* (Clement-Ferrand: Fondation Verenne, 2010). See also the distinction between citizenship and subjecthood in Emmanuelle Saada, *Empire's Children: Race, Filiation, and Citizenship in the French Colonies*, translated by Arthur Goldhammer (Chicago: University of Chicago Press, 2012).

status clarified before being recruited to the French military to fight for the motherland.[52] Mademba, who was born in Saint Louis in 1852, was subject to these legal ambiguities regarding his status. At times, the colonial administration labeled him an indigenous subject and at other times as a French citizen.[53] This gray area that Mademba inhabited provided both challenges and opportunities as he traversed different roles throughout his long career serving the French. But when he wrote to the governor-general requesting that he be permitted to clear his name before a French judge, Mademba was invoking the rights granted to him as an *originaire* of Saint Louis and thus as someone who had French-like citizenship. Mademba was thus claiming the rule of law.

When the minister of colonies denied Mademba's right to bring his case before a French judge, he was acting within his authority as a head of the relevant government department charged with overseeing the conduct of employees. The minister's authority stemmed from the jurisdiction of administrative law (*doit administratif*), which in France served as separate body of law and courts dealing with government employees in the course of their formal activities. The separation of public from private disputes was formalized in the immediate aftermath of the French Revolution of 1789 and modified by successive constitutions, but legal principles of jurisdictional separation remained. In effect, private law regulates the relationships between citizens as individual actors; administrative law is concerned with "rules, procedures, and remedies applying to the relations of individuals via-à-vis public authorities."[54] The legal principle behind administrative law in France was that when acting as a public authority, the state and its official employees enjoy "a legal

---

[52] See G. Wesley Johnson, *The Emergence of Black Politics in Senegal: The Struggle for Power in the Four Communes, 1900–1920* (Stanford, CA: Stanford University Press, 1971); Dominique Sarr and Richard Roberts, "The Jurisdiction of Muslim Tribunals in Colonial Senegal, 1857–1932," in *Law in Colonial Africa*, eds. Kristin Mann and Richard Roberts (Portsmouth, NH: Heinemann, 1991), 131–145; Conklin, *A Mission to Civilize*, 103–105; Catherine Coquery-Vidrovitch, "Nationalité et citoyenneté en Afrique occidentale français: Originaires et citoyens dans le Sénégal colonial," *JAH* 42 (2) (2001), 285–305; Larissa Kopytoff, "French Citizens and Muslim Law: The Tensions of Citizenship in Early Twentieth-Century Senegal," in *The Meaning of Citizenship*, eds. Richard Marback and Marc W. Kruman (Detroit: Wayne State University Press, 2011), 320–337; Emmanuelle Saada, "The Republic and the *Indigènes*," in *The French Republic: History, Values, Debates*, eds. Edward Berenson, Vincent Duclert, and Christophe Prochasson (Ithaca, NY: Cornell University Press, 2011), 224–225; Frederick Cooper, *Citizenship between Empire and Nation: Remaking France and French Africa, 1945–1960* (Princeton, NJ: Princeton University Press, 2014), 6.

[53] According to a census taken in 1904, Mademba was a "naturalized" citizen, one of four French citizens residing in Sinsani. État nominative des Européens présent à Sansanding, July 31, 1904, Correspondance Affaires administratives, Cercle de Segu, 1891–1917, ANM 2 D 102.

[54] Eva Steiner, *French Law: A Comparative Approach* (Oxford: Oxford University Press, 2018), 247.

personality so as to enable its representatives ... to take and enforce unilateral administrative acts in the performance of their duties."[55] Under French administrative law, its courts deal with ordinary citizen's grievances with public authorities and with the conduct of government officials accused of misgovernment or misrule. Although administrative law shielded public employees from most legal suits when they acted in their official capacities, public officials were culpable when they acted in an unlawful or reprehensible manner in their official capacity. An 1873 decree opened the administrative courts to hear actions brought by individuals who were seeking damages from actions caused by "persons employed in the public service." The 1873 decree and subsequent case law developed an important distinction between harm done through *faute de service* (wrongful actions due to the operation of regular administrative actions such as being run over by an official vehicle) and *voie de fait* (acts of flagrant irregularity), which occurred when an administrator took the law into his own hands and/or abused official powers. The distinction between *faute de service* and *voie de fait* is important for determining whether or not the state is liable for damages and which court is competent to hear the claim.[56] Thus, if the administrator's actions amounts to a *faute personnelle* rather than an administrative act, then the public officer is considered personally liable and the case proceeds in civil courts. Especially in cases where alleged criminal conduct occurred, individual citizens harmed could seek a formal exception from the administrative court to pursue criminal cases.[57]

Mademba's alleged malfeasance and crimes that almost led to his downfall emerged out of reports collected from the Segu district administrator and most significantly from a formal review of Soudanese colonial administrators and administrative functions ordered by the minister of colonies in 1899. The charge fell to the office of the inspector-general within the Ministry of Colonies, who in turn charged Inspector-general Danel to lead the review. As I shall examine in Chapter 7, Danel collected testimony from Mademba's

---

[55] Ibid., 255.

[56] Duncan Fairgrieve and Françoise Lichere, "The Liability of Public Authorities in France," in *The Liability of Public Authorities in Comparative Perspective*, ed. Ken Oliphant (Cambridge: Intersentia, 2016), 156–175; Bernard Pacteau, *Contentieux administratif* (Paris: Presses Universitaires de France, 1985), 15–28; Bernard Schwartz, *French Administrative Law and the Common-Law World* (New York: New York University Press, 1954), 72–73; Steiner, *French Law*, 254–255, 264–272.

[57] Schwartz, *French Administrative Law*, 258–262; Eva Steiner, "Administrative Law," in *French Law*, 260–272; George A. Bermann and Étienne Picard, "Administrative Law," in *Introduction to French Law*, eds. George A. Bermann and Étienne Picard (Alphen aan den Rijn: Kluwer Law International, 2012), 57–102. Several forms of administrative courts were established, including the ones in French West Africa that heard disputes and grievances brought by citizens and even African subjects. Many of these can be found in the National Archives of Senegal in the files dealing with *affaires contentieux*.

subjects regarding his administrative acts that fell within the scope of *voie de fait* and other actions that were criminal in nature. In forwarding his dossier on Mademba to the newly arrived delegate of the governor-general in the Soudan and to the governor-general himself, Danel concluded that Mademba's role as *faama* of Sansanding should be terminated and that he be subject to further punitive action. Acting in his official capacity, Danel also forwarded his dossier of alleged crimes to the attorney-general of the French West Africa Federation.[58]

Gouvernor-general Chaudié, himself a former inspector-general, nonetheless rejected Danel's assessment and suggestions. Chaudié wrote to the minister of colonies that "The Mademba affair is at once more delicate and more serious than [Danel] describes. If this colony were a colony constituted in the normal way, nothing would be easier than to suppress the functions of a functionary. But is Mademba really a functionary when he exercises the authority of *faama* of Sansanding?"[59] The period 1899–1900 was a tumultuous time for the political organization of French West Africa, with a major reorganization of the Soudan underway. As the head of the administrative agency involved, the minister of colonies had the authority to decide the validity of the case brought against Mademba. In deciding as he did not to pursue either legal or administrative sanctions against Mademba, the minister was making a clear statement that the rule of law as it prevailed in metropolitan France was certainly not or not yet operative in French West African colonies. So what was the rule of law and what did its presumed absence mean within the context of the turn of the century in the French Soudan?

Gouvernor-general Chaudié's statement to the minister of colonies that the Soudan was not constituted as an "ordinary colony" underscores the transitional nature of colonialism that prevailed there and the fact that different ideas of colonialism overlapped. Within this transitional world, different rules of law also prevailed. Without venturing into the more complex plural legal world that provided opportunities for African disputants, I want to concentrate on the rules of law linked to the two competing models of colonialism: the rule of law for the French military that still dominated the administrative structures in the Soudan and the civilian rule of law being promoted by the reformists in France. Central to the French military command was the obligation to obey, which was the cornerstone of hierarchy and authority. Enshrined in the 1857 Code of Military Justice, the military's rule of law provided "legal containment" for the application of swift and terrible punishment for military-specific infractions that included disrespect for superiors, insubordination, laziness, and "bad will." French soldiers were also subject to ordinary penal

---

[58] Inspector-gen. Danel, Rapport: Inspection générale concernant la verification du service de Mademba, Fama Sansanding, Jan. 14, 1900, ANS-AOF 15 G 176.

[59] Gouv.-gen. Chaudié, Notes attached to Danel, Rapport, Feb. 1, 1900, ANS-AOF 15 G 176.

law. Although the 1857 Code established a set of military tribunals, superiors were permitted to apply exemplary punishments to assure authority and obedience.[60] In many ways, Mademba's application of justice in his kingdom resembled the military rule of law in which any challenges to his authority demanded swift and terrible punishments. Competing with the military's rule of law in the Soudan was a civilian rule of law.

Since the French Revolution, one of the driving forces of republicanism has been the struggle against tyranny and judicial arbitrariness. Taming the monarch and controlling the magistrates in the quest of uniform application of the law lay behind the Napoléonic Code and many of the periodic reforms of the judiciary over successive French constitutions and republics. Ending arbitrariness is one of the hallmarks of the rule of law.[61] In reflecting on the rule of law, Léon Duguit, one of France's most prominent jurists of the early twentieth century, drew on Rousseau's concept of social solidarities and social contract but argued that with the proliferation of government functions, rules – that is, positive law – must govern not only relations among men but also relations between men and the state. In Duguit's conception, the state is bound, just like individual, to the rule of law. "Rulers, who are individuals like the ruled . . . should act in conformity with objective law and can only act within the limits which it fixes."[62] No one is above the law and the law must be applied equally.

Closely linked to the ideal of equality before the law was the principle of protection against arbitrariness in the application of the law. These two principles lie at the heart of the United Nations Rule of Law indicators.

> It refers to a principle of governance in which all persons, institutions and entities, public and private, including the state itself, are accountable to the law that are publicly promulgated, equally enforced and

---

[60] See Jorg Gerkrath, "Military Law in France," in *European Military Law Systems*, ed. Georg Nolte (Berlin: De Gruyter Recht, 2003); Charles Herbert Hammond, Jr., "Neither Lenient nor Draconian: The Evolution of French Military Justice during the Early Third Republic," unpublished PhD dissertation (University of California, Davis, 2005); John Cerullo, *Minotaur: French Military Justice and the Aernoult-Rousset Affair* (Dekalb: Northern Illinois University Press, 2011). I thank Wallace Teska for prompting this issue.

[61] Paul Jankowski, "The Republic and Justice," in *The French Republic*, 154–155. For a more detailed analysis of the various controversies and reforms regarding arbitrariness, see the magisterial study by Jean-Pierre Royer, Nicolas Derasse, Jean-Pierre Allinne, Bernard Durand, and Jean-Paul Jean, *Histoire de la justice in France du XVIIIe siècle à nos jours* (Paris: Presses Universitaires de France, 1995).

[62] Léon Duguit, "The Rule of Law," in *Modern French Legal Philosophy*, eds. Alfred Jule Émile Fouillée, Joseph Charmont, René Demogue, and Léon Duguit, translated Franklin Scott and Joseph P. Chamberlain (Boston: The Boston Book Co., 1916), 324; Léon Duguit, "The State and the Law, as Concrete Facts Rather Than Abstract Considerations," in *Modern French Legal Philosophy*, 342.

independently adjudicated . . . [and] requires, as well, measures to ensure adherence to the principles of the supremacy of law, equality before the law, accountability to the law, fairness in the application of the law, separation of powers, participation in decision-making, legal certainty, avoidance of arbitrariness and procedural and legal transparency.[63]

Legal scholars and political scientists draw distinctions between the rule of law and rule by law.[64] In the Nazi regime in Germany and among many autocratic states, parliaments make laws often in the direct service of the state. As such, they rule by law, but not necessarily in the broader sense of rule of law. Building on this distinction, Martin Krygier further distinguishes between what he terms a "thin" or "formal" cluster of legal institutions from a "thick" or "substantive" cluster of traits that form a more expansive vision of the rule of law.[65] Krygier's invocation of thick and thin helps explain the significance of Gouvernor-general Chaudié's remark cited earlier: "If this colony were a colony constituted in the normal way, nothing would be easier than to suppress the functions of a functionary." Chaudié's remark, merely a decade after the French captured Segu from the Umarians and less than two years since the French captured the last major independent state-builder Samory Turé, came at a moment of significant transition in the nature of colonialism in French West Africa that pitted Archinard's model of indirect rule against a more robust republican vision of colonialism. Chaudié's remark links to this discussion of the rule of law in at least three ways. First, by suggesting that the French Soudan was not a colony constituted in the "normal" way, its presumes that there was an understanding of what a normal colony was. I do not know exactly what Chaudié was pointing to when he cited a normal colony. Perhaps he had in mind the "old colonies" of the Caribbean and the Indian Ocean where the Second Republic's abolition of slavery and extension of metropolitan rights of citizenship prevailed. Perhaps he had in mind Algeria,

---

[63] United Nations Department of Peacekeeping Operations and Office of the High Commissioner for Human Rights, *The United Nations Rule of Law Indications: Implementation Guide and Project Tools* (New York: United Nations Publications, 2011), v–vi, 1. See also Tom Bingham, *The Rule of Law* (London: Penguin Books, 2010); Stephen Humphrys, *Theatre of the Rule of Law: Transnational Legal Intervention in Theory and Practice* (Cambridge: Cambridge University Press, 2010).

[64] Barry R. Weingast, "The Political Foundations of Democracy and the Rule of Law," *American Political Science Review* 91 (2) 1997, 245–263; Steven Levitsky and Daniel Ziblatt, *How Democracies Die* (New York: Crown, 2018); Larry Diamond, *Ill Winds: Saving Democracy from Russian Rage, Chinese Ambition, and American Complacency* (New York: Penguin, 2019).

[65] Martin Krygier, "The Rule of Law (and Rechtstaat)," *International Encyclopedia of the Social and Behavioral Sciences* 20 (2015), 783, second edition. Krygier elaborates these issues in Martin Krygier, "Four Puzzles about the Rule of Law: Why, What, Where? And Who Cares?," in *Getting to the Rule of Law*, ed. James E. Fleming (New York: New York University Press, 2011), 64–104.

which had integrated the northern districts into metropolitan government practices following the 1881 reorganization.[66] Second, the idea of a normal colony was linked to the idea of the civilizing mission, which formed at least an ideological justification for late nineteenth–century colonialism. And third, how could a civilian rule of law operate in the context of plural legal systems organized by the principles of the protectorate where the maintenance of difference was enshrined in customary law?

Robust debates in metropolitan France regarding colonization during the late nineteenth century reflected different interests and interest groups. There was little agreement among these groups and even less capacity to deliver metropolitan visions into diverse colonial contexts.[67] Enthusiasm for colonialism and empire waned in the face of the challenges of actually implementing them. France's parliamentarians balked in the face of the huge costs not only of colonial conquest but of the potential costs of implementing colonial rule itself. The reluctance of the metropolitan government to pay for the costs of establishing a system of metropolitan courts and staffing them with trained magistrates yielded only "modest achievements on the ground . . . and disappointment for republican ideals."[68] Despite changing ideals concerning colonialism, the lack of investment in courts and magistrates had a perverse feedback loop that limited the possibilities of the rule of law. Establishing colonial "hegemony on a shoestring" more often than not led not to the rule of law but to persistent conflicts about what the law was.[69] Moreover, harmonizing the metropolitan legal system with what prevailed in the colonies might be the magistrates' vision, but it did not necessarily accord to the prevailing practices of "the politics of difference" based on ideas of racial and civilizational distinctions.[70]

---

[66] See Alice L. Conklin, Sarah Fishman, and Robert Zaretsky, *France and Its Empire since 1870* (New York: Oxford University Press, second edition, 2015), 70. Significantly, the 1881 reorganization and the extension of citizenship in Algeria to Jews in 1870 and to the Spanish, Maltese, and Italian immigrants in 1889 deepened the distinctions between citizens and subjects. For more detail, see Sophie B. Roberts, *Citizenship and Antisemitism in Colonial Algeria, 1870–1962* (Cambridge: Cambridge University Press, 2018) and Lewis, *Divided Rule*.

[67] See among others, Kanya-Forstner, *The Conquest of the Western Sudan*; Conklin, *A Mission to Civilize*; Christopher Maurice Andrew and Alexander Sydney Kanya-Forstner, "The French 'Colonial Party': Its Composition, Aims and Influence, 1885–1914," *Historical Journal* 14 (1) 1971, 99–128; Martin Evans, ed., *Empire and Culture: The French Experience, 1830–1940* (London: Palgrave, 2004); Martin Evans, ed., *The French Colonial Mind*, two vols. (Lincoln: University of Nebraska Press, 2011).

[68] Royer et al., *Histoire de la justice in France*, 753. For more detail on how budgetary constraints and limited personnel influenced colonial justice, see the larger section in this volume, 752–834.

[69] Berry, *No Condition Is Permanent*, 29.

[70] "Politics of difference" is a core concept in Jane Burbank and Frederick Cooper, *Empires in World History: Power and the Politics of Difference* (Princeton, NJ: Princeton University Press, 2010).

Senior colonial officials including Governor Grodet, Lieutenant-governor Trentinian, and Lieutenant-governor Ponty issued persistent condemnations of corporal punishment, regular circulars admonishing administrators about the proportionality of crimes and punishments, and constant calls for regularity, which were ideological cornerstones of the civilian rule of law. These condemnations were also useful in the effort by civilian administrators to undermine the military's rule of law and their claims for continued dominance of the colonial state. In this sense, the call for the rule of law was a weapon in the struggle between competing models of colonialism rather than an achievable goal. Martin Chanock captured this situation well, not just for French West Africa but for all of colonial Africa. "Other myths have arisen from the legal colonization of Africa. There is that of the colonisers, perhaps their last surviving myth, that the legacy of legality, the rule of law, and equal and uncorrupt justice was an important benefit conferred by colonization."[71]

---

[71] Martin Chanock, *Law, Custom, and Social Order: The Colonial Experience in Malawi and Zambia* (Cambridge: Cambridge University Press, 1985), 5.

1

Mademba and the Foundations of the Bargains of Collaboration, 1852–1888

Mademba Sèye was born on March 3, 1852, in Saint Louis du Sénégal near the mouth of the Senegal River bordering on the Atlantic Ocean. The Wolof-speaking residents of the town referred to it as Ndar, which was a fishing village before the Portuguese and other Europeans first came to the mouth of the river in 1444. When the Europeans first reached the Senegal River, they did not linger long in Ndar on their voyages, preferring settlements further south and deeper into the Atlantic, especially the uninhabited Cabo Verde archipelago discovered by the Portuguese in 1456, who founded the first European settlement in the Atlantic tropics in 1462. The Portuguese built a chapel on the island of Gorée, but did not establish a permanent settlement there. In 1588, the Dutch began using Gorée as a base. The deepening of the Atlantic economy and the transatlantic slave trade brought the inhabitants of the Senegal River valley more fully within the reach of these new encounters and ushered in political, economic, and cultural pressures that accelerated changes already underway in Senegambian societies.[1]

European settlements in Senegambia were few and fragile, subject to intra-European rivalries as well pressures from African polities. In 1659, the French established their presence on the island near the mouth of the Senegal River that would become Saint Louis. The British established themselves on James Island in the mouth of the Gambia River. In 1677, a French fleet seized Gorée. Increasing European presence contributed to the expansion of commerce and the exchange of culture. Commerce and the cultural exchange moved in many directions as Europeans adapted to African commercial and political practices and as Africans adapted to European ones.[2] In the course of the eighteenth

---

[1] Toby Green, *The Rise of the Trans-Atlantic Slave Trade in Western Africa, 1300–1589* (Cambridge: Cambridge University Press, 2012).

[2] Philip Curtin, *Economic Change in Precolonial Africa: Senegambia in the Era of the Slave Trade* (Madison: University of Wisconsin Press, 1975); Boubacar Barry, *Senegambia and the Atlantic Slave Trade*, translated by Ayi Kwei Armah (Cambridge: Cambridge University Press, 1998); Peter Mark and José da Silva Horta, *The Forgotten Diaspora: Jewish Communities in West Africa and the Making of the Atlantic World* (Cambridge: Cambridge University Press, 2011).

century, European rivalries led to the periodic changes in European overrule along the Senegambian coast: the Dutch displaced the Portuguese only to be displaced by the French and British, who then displaced each other periodically. None, however, could exert significant control over Africans and African polities. All the while, trade in African commodities including slaves, gold, gum arabic, and foodstuff flowed to sustain the tiny European presence as Africans imported European guns, textiles, hardware, metals, and other consumables. African polities linked to the coast and to the expanding commerce of the Sahara strengthened. Islam spread and periodically erupted into militant reform movements. During the French Revolution, free and property-owning residents of Saint Louis sent a letter of grievances to the National Assembly protesting the role of the chartered companies in dominating trade and demanding that the monopoly over the gum trade be abrogated in favor of freer trade. In 1789, the value in the gum trade, widely used in the metropolitan textile industries, exceeded the value of slave exports. Britain again seized Saint Louis and Gorée in 1809. France regained possession of Saint Louis and Gorée from the British following the end of the Napoléonic wars in 1817 (see Map 1.1).

At least four changes swirled through Saint Louis during the mid century when Mademba Sèye was born in 1852. The first was the gradual ending of the transatlantic slave trade and the change in the economic and political foundations of the wider regional economy of the Senegal River valley, which involved increased demand for gum arabic and groundnuts – each commodity was associated with different economic and political practices. The second was the resurgence of militant Islam associated with Al Hajj Umar Tal. Umar's preaching put into stark relief the meaning of Dar al-Islam and forced Muslims to articulate their practices and their politics in relationship to these debates. The third was the revolution of 1848 that toppled the monarchy of Louis-Philippe in favor of new democratic ideologies, free trade, and the abolition of slavery. The year 1848 left a profound legacy in Saint Louis that persisted beyond the collapse of that revolution. And the fourth was the arrival of Louis Léon César Faidherbe as the new governor, ushering in a newly aggressive French presence that led to French colonial expansion. Faidherbe is credited with establishing three colonial institutions that contributed to the foundations of French colonial authority.[3]

Even though Senegambia had become significantly less important to the overall transatlantic slave trade in the course of the eighteenth century, the slave trade still exerted an enormous influence on the region and on the interactions between Africans and Europeans. After the British abolished the slave trade in 1807, they pursued an aggressive diplomatic strategy of

---

[3] For background, see Yves-Jean Saint-Martin, *Le Sénégal sous le Second Empire: Naissance d'un empire colonial (1850–1871)* (Paris: Kathala, 1989) and Régine Bonnardel, *Saint-Louis du Sénégal: Mort ou naissance?* (Paris: L'Harmattan, 1992).

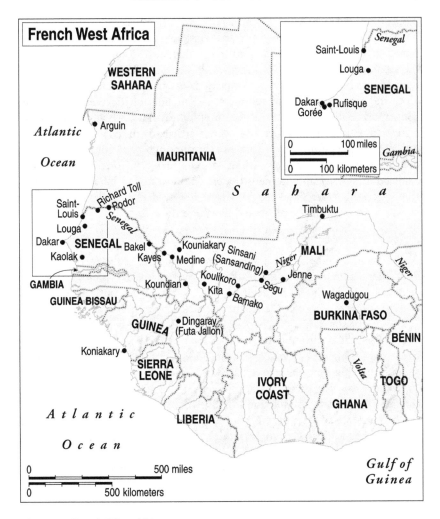

Map 1.1   French West Africa

pressuring other European and non-European carriers in both the Atlantic and Indian Oceans to also suppress it. The British managed to pressure France to abolish the slave trade in 1815 as part of the treaty to end the Napoléonic wars.[4] Britain, which had seized Gorée and Saint Louis, agreed to return these

---

[4] Suzanne Miers, *Britain and the Ending of the Slave Trade* (New York: Africana Publishing Co., 1975); Trevor Getz, *Slavery and Reform in West Africa: Toward Emancipation in Nineteenth Century Senegal and the Gold Coast* (Athens: Ohio University Press, 2004).

outposts to the French. The French returned to Saint Louis with a commitment to nurture both commerce and agriculture, including bold plans to
establish plantations using the local labor that was no longer exported into
the Atlantic world.[5] By 1826, these ambitious agricultural plans were abandoned and commercial interests of Saint Louisian merchants predominated.
Since the abrogation of the commercial monopoly of the French chartered
companies in the late eighteenth century, metropolitan wholesale merchants
competed with métis and African traders, particularly in the gum trade. Given
the complex commercial practices surrounding the gum trade along
the Senegal River, the expansion of commerce favored locally based
Saint Louisian African and métis traders who invested in long-term relationships with the Trarza and the Brakna. These traders invested in boats and
crews to move commodities up and down the river. By the 1830s, a quarter of
the 12,000 inhabitants of Saint Louis earned their livelihoods from the gum
trade.[6]

The boom in the gum trade was fragile. During the 1830s and 1840s, price
fluctuations of gum and *guinée* cloth led to oversupply, and increasing debt of
Saint Louisian merchants left few local merchants able to continue in the gum
trade. Moreover, by the 1850s, the prominence of the gum trade in the
economy of Saint Louis declined as better financed metropolitan merchants
invested heavily to promote the trade in groundnuts, which expanded rapidly
in the coastal plains south of the Senegal River and into the Siin and Saalum
regions and along the Gambia River. Groundnuts, according to Martin Klein,
"transformed Senegal from a stagnant relic of the slave trade into a bustling
colony."[7] By 1850, the population of Saint Louis had swelled to 15,000 and the
city had become a "place of opportunity" for African traders, freed slaves, and
African refugees fleeing from political and religious ferment in neighboring
African polities.[8]

Islamic revival, reform, and revolution periodically convulsed what David
Robinson refers to as the Senegalo-Mauritanian zone since at least the

[5] Richard Roberts, *Two Worlds of Cotton: Colonial and the Regional Economy in the French Soudan, 1800–1949* (Stanford, CA: Stanford University Press, 1996), chapter 3.
[6] James L. A. Webb, Jr., *Desert Frontier: Ecological and Economic Change along the Western Sahel, 1600–1850* (Madison: University of Wisconsin Press, 1995); Hilary Jones, *The Métis of Senegal: Urban Life and Politics in French West Africa* (Bloomington: Indiana University Press, 2013), 40–44.
[7] Martin A. Klein, *Islam and Imperialism in Senegal: Sin-Saloum, 1847–1914* (Stanford, CA: Stanford University Press, 1968), 38; Bernard Moitt, "Slavery and Emancipation in Senegal's Peanut Basin: The Nineteenth and Twentieth Centuries," *International Journal of African Historical Studies* 22 (1) 1989, 27–50.
[8] See Curtin, *Economic Change in Precolonial Africa*; Barry, *Senegambia*; David Robinson, *Paths of Accommodation: Muslim Societies and French Colonial Authorities in Senegal and Mauritania, 1880–1920* (Athens: Ohio University Press, 2000), 31–33.

seventeenth century. Another wave of Islamic militancy in the eighteenth century led to the establishment of the Islamic polities of Futa Toro, Bundu, and Futa Jallon.[9] The militant preaching by Al Hajj Umar Tal in the 1840s further roiled African polities and Muslim communities in this region, many of which were already suffering from changes in the regional and Atlantic economies.[10] During his pilgrimage, Umar deepened his affiliation with the Tijaniyya sufi brotherhood and returned to West Africa as *khalifya* (deputy) of the order. Umar preached a more "exclusivist interpretation" of this order's teachings, which contributed to Umar's eventual call for *hijra* (withdrawal) and jihad. Umar's more militant message urged believers to maintain religious and political distance from European authority. Not all Muslims followed Umar, but his preaching encouraged a wider debate among the Muslim community about the meaning of Dar al-Islam. In 1846, Umar established a settlement in Dinguiray, near Futa Jallon, where he recruited followers and launched his first jihad against the kingdom of Tamba. In the 1850s, Umar recruited heavily in the Futa Toro region and renewed his call for Muslims to withdraw from French authority. In 1855, his army defeated the Bambara kingdom of Kaarta and he clashed militarily with the French at their fort at Médine. Umar's militant message caused deep rivalries within Futa Toro communities. Blocked by an increasingly expansionist French colonization, Umar turned eastward to wage jihad against the Bambara of Segu. Umar also waged jihad against the Muslim theocratic state of Masina, where his actions resulted in claims that he caused *fitna* or civil strife. Widespread rebellions against Umarian overrule shook the region.[11]

The third variable in the rapidly changing environment of Saint Louis was the French Revolution of 1848.[12] The provisional government in Paris decreed on April 27, 1848, that slavery in all French territories was abolished and reasserted the long-standing French legal concept that French soil liberates (*sol libérateur*) all slaves who touch it. In the plantation colonies of the

[9] See David Robinson, *Chiefs and Clerics: Abdul Bokar Kan and Futa Toro, 1853–1891* (Oxford: Clarendon Press, 1975); Michael A. Gomez, *Pragmatism in the Age of Jihad: The Precolonial State of Bundu* (Cambridge: Cambridge University Press, 1992); Rudolph T. Ware III, *The Walking Qur'an: Islamic Education, Embodied Knowledge, and History in West Africa* (Chapel Hill: University of North Carolina Press, 2014).

[10] Martin A. Klein, "Social and Economic Factors in the Muslin Revolution in Senegambia," *JAH* 13 (4) 1972: 419–441; David Robinson, *The Holy War of Umar Tall: The Western Sudan in the Mid-Nineteenth Century* (Oxford: Clarendon Press, 1985); Robinson, *Paths of Accommodation*, 16–25.

[11] Robinson, *The Holy War of Umar Tall*; Robinson, *Paths of Accommodation*, 21–22.

[12] For background on the 1848 revolution, see John M. Merriman, *The Agony of the Republic: The Repression of the Left in Revolutionary France, 1848-1851* (New Haven, CT: Yale University Press, 1978) and Christopher Guyver, *The Second French Republic, 1848-1852: A Political Reinterpretation* (London: Palgrave Macmillon, 2016).

Caribbean and the Indian Ocean, freed slaves become citizens and together with other free citizens had the right to elect representatives to the French National Assembly. Slaves were also freed in Saint Louis and Gorée, but ambiguity surrounded their status as citizens persisted. The 1848 decree nonetheless had significant impact on France's two Senegalese outposts. In 1845, slaves constituted fully 50 percent of the population of Saint Louis and nearly 65 percent of that of Gorée.[13] Slaves were freed, but because of a severe housing shortage on Gorée and Saint Louis, many of those newly freed continued to work for their former masters for wages. New forms of unfreedom emerged; unfree people continued to reside in these two towns, and streams of unfree children continued to arrive. Many were recognized as "wards" and placed as apprentices with urban notables.[14] French administrators and magistrates sought to limit the definition of "French soil" in order not to destabilize Saint Louis and its neighboring African communities.[15] Runaway slaves from African communities deemed friendly to the French were returned to their masters, while runaway slaves from enemies were freed. Coinciding with Umar's call for Muslims to leave the areas of French authority, thousands of Fulbe and their slaves migrated away from the region around Saint Louis.[16]

By 1852, the Second Republic gave way to the Second Empire under Louis Napoléon, who was eager to reassert power through empire. The architect of a more expansionist French colonialism in Senegal was Louis Léon César Faidherbe, who served in Algeria during the crucial phase of conquest and expansion. Faidherbe first arrived in Senegal as military director of engineering from 1852 to 1854; he was promoted to governor in 1854. Faidherbe served as governor from 1854 to 1861 and then again from 1863 to 1865. Faidherbe's success as governor benefitted from the profound changes in the colony's economy as it transitioned from the gum trade toward the trade in groundnuts. This period witnessed the expansion of Bordeaux-based merchant houses into Senegal together with a business-friendly metropolitan government under the Second Empire.[17] Faidherbe also benefitted from the

---

[13] Martin A. Klein, *Slavery and French Colonial Rule in French West Africa* (New York: Cambridge University Press, 1998), 23; Kopytoff, "French Citizens and Muslim Law," 325.

[14] Kelly Duke Bryant, "Changing Childhood: 'Liberated Minors', Guardianship, and the Colonial State in Senegal, 1895–1911," *JAH* 60 (2) 2019: 209–228.

[15] On the meanings of free soil, see Robert Harms, *The Diligent: A Voyage through the Worlds of the Slave Trade* (New York: Basic Books, 2002) and Sue Peabody and Keila Grinberg, eds., *Free Soil in the Atlantic World* (London: Routledge, 2015).

[16] Klein, *Islam and Imperialism in Senegal*, 165–166; Jones, *The Métis of Senegal*, 59–60. See Klein, *Slavery and French Colonial Rule*, 19–36 for the fullest discussion of this period.

[17] Saint-Martin, *Le Sénégal sous le Second Empire*, chapters 20–21; Dominque Barjot, Éric Anceau, Isabelle Lescent-Giles, and Bruno Marnot, eds., *Les Entrepreneurs du Second Empire* (Paris: Presse Université Paris-Sorbonne, 2003).

fact that he survived much longer than most previous governors of Senegal.[18] Faidherbe was also an ambitious military officer eager to secure the commerce so crucial to the colony by conquest and annexation.

During this relatively long administrative reign, Faidherbe created or transformed several key institutions that helped transform the French colony of Senegal into a major force in West Africa. In 1857, Faidherbe created the *Tirailleurs Sénégalais*, modeled loosely on the Algerian *Tirailleurs indigènes*, which was a volunteer force of indigenous soldiers who received relatively good pay, good rations, and a uniform. The *tirailleurs* were also promised a share of the booty captured in wars. Founded close on the heels of the abolition of slavery, it is not surprising that many new recruits were former slaves. As Faidherbe launched aggressive territorial expansion, he increased the *Tirailleurs Sénégalais* from two companies in 1857 to six in 1860.[19]

Recognizing the need to augment the administrative side of the colony, Faidherbe founded the *école des otages* in 1856. Faidherbe's decision was part of a wider strategy to promote accommodations with the Muslim majority in Saint Louis, especially after his order to expel Tijaniyya clerics from Saint Louis.[20] He created the *école des otages* as a way to provide secular French education to Muslim boys. Since 1817, Saint Louis had a series of lay and clerical French schools. The first was an elementary school, which experimented with various metropolitan and mixed Wolof–French curricula. In the early 1840s, the Brothers of Ploërmel, a Catholic teaching order, established a series of elementary schools. While the schools were designed to promote French civilization, they also provided practical subjects – such as bookkeeping. But they also encouraged conversion. Promoting conversion, however, threatened to alienate the Muslim population of Saint Louis. Most Muslim children in Saint Louis attended Qur'anic schools. In 1857, Faidherbe ordered that marabouts operating Qur'anic schools be licenced. All boys twelve and older were also required to attend evening classes in French at the Ploërmel schools.[21] Faidherbe also consolidated power in the Directorate of Political Affairs, which managed both internal and external relations of the colony. In order for the French officers of the directorate to engage with the affairs of

---

[18] Leland Barrows, "Louis Léon César Faidherbe (1818–1889)," in *African Proconsuls*, 58. For analysis of the Second Empire's imperial interests, see David Todd, "A French Imperial Meridian, 1814–1870," *Past and Present* 210 Feb. 2011, 155–186.

[19] Echenberg, *Colonial Conscripts*; Barrows, "Faidherbe," 61–62.

[20] Barrows, "Faidherbe," 64.

[21] Joseph Gaucher, *Les débuts de l'enseignement en Afrique francophone: Jean Dard et l'École Mutuelle de Saint-Louis du Sénégal* (Paris: Le Livre Africain, 1968); Denise Bouche, "L'école française et les musulmans au Sénégal de 1850 à 1920," *Revue française d'histoire d'outre-mer* 61 (223) 1974, 218–235; Kelly M. Duke Bryant, *Education as Politics: Colonial Schooling and Political Debate in Senegal, 1850s–1914* (Madison: University Wisconsin Press, 2015), 14–15, 56.

Africans, they needed reliable interpreters. Faidherbe's decision to create the *école des otages* was designed in part to help expand the pool of Africans willing and capable of serving as intermediaries in the expanding colonial state without pressure to convert.[22]

The third significant innovation designed to help transform France into what David Robinson terms a "Muslim power," was the establishment in 1857 of a Muslim tribunal recognized by the colonial state as a central part of the colonial judicial apparatus. The Muslim tribunal was the result of nearly a quarter century of political pressure by the Muslim population of Saint Louis to have the colonial state recognize shariʿa law as a means of adjudicating civil disputes among Muslims. The authorization of the Muslim tribunal coincided with increased tension and conflicts with more militant Muslims along the Senegal River valley and the interior, and helped solidify support of Muslims for the French colonial project in Senegal.[23] The recognition of Saint Louis's Muslim inhabitants' right to adjudicate their civil disputes in a religious court bumped up against French tradition of the separation of church and state, especially in the legal sphere, and raised questions about the content of rights granted to residents of French territories in 1848.[24]

The Beginning of Mademba's Narrative

I know virtually nothing about Mademba's childhood. According to Abd-el-Kader Mademba's biography of his father, and the only written source for this period of Mademba's life, Mademba's father fled the unrest initiated by Al Hajj Umar's preaching and recruitment in Futa Toro and settled in Saint Louis. "M'Baye-Sy, father of Mademba, of the Torodo tribe, did not want to admit that there was any other prophet other than Mohammad. After entering into conflict with El Hadj Omar, he preferred to seek refuge in Saint Louis next to Faidherbe, who had proclaimed in the name of France the respect for all religions."[25] By these two sentences, Abd-el-Kader Mademba signaled that Mademba was from a clerical family and a member of the Sy lineage.

---

[22] Robinson, *Paths of Accommodation*, 81–85; Mbayo, *Muslim Interpreters in Colonial Senegal.*

[23] Robinson, *Paths of Accommodation*, 79–85; Ghislaine Lydon, "Obtaining Freedom at the Muslims' Tribunal: Colonial Kadijustiz and Women's Divorce Litigation in Ndar (Senegal)," in *Muslim Family Law in Sub-Saharan Africa: Colonial Legacies and Post-colonial Challenges*, eds. Shamil Jeppie, Ebrahim Moosa, and Richard Roberts (Amsterdam: Amsterdam University Press, 2010), 136–139.

[24] Sarr and Roberts, 'The Jurisdiction of Muslim Tribunals in Colonial Senegal"; Mamadou Diouf, "The French Colonial Policy of Assimilation and the Civility of the Originaires of the Four Communes (Senegal): A Nineteenth Century Globalization Project," *Development and Change* 29 (1998): 671–696.

[25] Abd-el Kader Mademba, *Au Sénégal et au Soudan Français* (Paris: Larose, 1931), 9.

According to Mademba's personnel dossier, Mademba's patronym was not Sy but Sèye.[26] Even at his funeral in 1918, Lieutenant-governor Brunet's eulogy referred to Mademba as Sèye.[27] The shift in patronym from Sèye to Sy was highly significant in laying claim to a prestigious clerical lineage that was linked to the Fulbe cleric Malik Sy, the founder of the theocratic Muslim state of Bundu in the early eighteenth century.[28] Another Malik Sy rose to prominence in the late nineteenth century as the grand marabout of Tivaouane in Senegal and one of the key figures who chartered paths of accommodation with the French colonial state.[29]

Oral histories recorded in and around Sinsani, where Mademba would rule as *faama*, present a very different version of Mademba's origins. Mademba was not well-loved by the inhabitants of Sinsani and this legacy no doubt influenced my informants' recollections. According to Binke Baba Kuma, a wonderful informant who was a descendant of Sinsani's chief when Mademba arrived in 1891. "The faama of Sansanding arrived here [in Sinsani] thanks to the French. He was born in Senegal and went to school together with the son of his master, [Mamadou] Racine [Sy], who when he entered the army, requested that the French take care of Mademba."[30] In all of his responses, Binke Baba Kuma was usually careful in how he used words in order not to tarnish an elder's reputation. Thus, his reference to Mademba's "master" remains undefined. Several other informants were not as differential. Alamake Togora of Sinsani stated that Mademba "was a slave of the Peuls and it was due to his master that he was able to accomplish what he did. In compensation, he gave his first born son the first name of his master."[31] Mademba's first-born son was Racine. Togora's statement thus supports Kuma's assertation that Mamadou Racine Sy was either the son of his master or his master directly. I want to quote one final informant, Al Hajj Soumaila Fane of Tesserela. Fane notes in his recitation of oral history that "[Mademba] was born in Fouta [Toro], but he grew up together with Captain Racine." When I asked Soumaila Fane how Mademba came to be *faama* of Sinsani when he was not from a family of chiefs or kings, Fane replied that "Mademba was a bastard. In the Fouta, one throws bastards into the bush. It was Racine who discovered him in the bush. He was a bastard. Racine placed him in the

---

[26] ANOM Dossiers personnels (Mademba) 2862.
[27] "Les obsèques du Fama Mademba, Discours du Lieutentant-Gouverneur," *JOHSN*, Sept. 1, 1918, 414.
[28] Gomez, *Pragmatism*, 25–51. I owe this interpretation of the shift of patronym from Sèye to Sy to Babacar Fall.
[29] Robinson, *Paths of Accommodation*, chapter 10.
[30] Interview with Binke Baba Kuma, Sinsani, July 7, 1992. For more information on Mamadou Racine Sy, see Seydou Madani Sy, *Le capitaine Mamadou Racine Sy (1838–1902): Une figure sénégalaise au temps des Tirailleurs* (Paris: Karthala, 2014).
[31] Interview, Alamake Togora, Sinsani, July 12, 1992.

school ... [Mademba] never spoke the names of his father or his mother."[32] There is much I do not know about Mademba's origins and the various and conflicting interpretations of his origins have much to do with the ways in which the narrative of Mademba's life was periodically remade. Such ambiguities are empowering to the historian because divergent interpretations suggest that there were several sides to Mademba's life and that different groups of actors experienced him differently.

According to his colonial employment personnel file, Mademba was indeed born in Saint Louis in March 1852, the year Faidherbe first arrived as director of military engineering and before he became governor.[33] Similar to most Muslim children, Mademba attended Qur'anic school in Saint Louis. Beginning when they were around seven years old, children attended schools run by Muslim teachers. Many students remained with their teachers for five or six years. Learning in these West African Qur'anic schools involved significant bodily discipline, labor to support the teacher and his community, and recitation during which pupils learned not only to the recite the Qur'an but also how to be good Muslims.[34] Under Governor Faidherbe, the colonial state sought to surveil and control Qur'anic schools in French territory, fearing that they might be sites for anti-French propaganda. In Saint Louis alone in the mid 1850s, there were at least twenty Qur'anic schools, but probably many more.[35] Beyond the foundations of learning the Qur'an, Arabic, and the embodiment of Islam, students often went on to learn religious sciences, geography, mathematics, and law, especially from scholars with regional reputations. It is not clear how far Mademba pursued his Islamic education. All I know is that Abd-el-Kader Mademba noted in passing that "After solid Qur'anic studies, [Mademba] was admitted in to the school of hostages that Faidherbe created in Saint Louis in 1855."[36] The idea of a school for hostages was not new to Faidherbe, who institutionalized the practice and provided ministerial funds for the operation of the school. Under Faidherbe, the school promoted a secular education in French, mathematics, geography, and Arabic, and it became a boarding school, where students were taught, fed, and housed. Almost all of the students received scholarships. Between its founding and its temporary closing in 1871, the *école des otages* had some 103 students over

---

[32] Interview, Al Hajj Soumaila Fane, Tesserela, July 15, 1992.

[33] ANOM Dossiers personnels (Mademba) 2862.

[34] Ware, *The Walking Qur'an*, introduction and chapter 1.

[35] Denise Bouche, "L'enseigement dans les Territoires français de l'Afrique Occidentale de 1817 à 1920: Mission civilisatrice ou formation d'une élite?," Unpublished PhD dissertation, Université Paris I, June 8, 1974 (Lille: Atelier Reproductiion des Theses, 1975), 286–294; Duke Bryant, *Education as Politics*, chapter 2; Octave Homberg, *L'École des colonies* (Paris: Plon, 1929), 192.

[36] Mademba, *Au Sénégal*, 9. Abd-el-Kader Mademba may have used Homberg as his source, since Homberg also cites the 1855 date, Homberg, *L'École des colonies*, 192.

fifteen years.[37] Among them were "sons of chiefs who subsequently became the best auxiliaries of our African penetration."[38] Abd-el-Kader Mademba elaborated on this theme. "From this school of hostages exited those who became provincial chiefs, interpreters, military officers, teachers, bookkeepers, employees. Many returned to their places of origin to become farmers. During the first expeditions to the Soudan, the former pupils of the school of hostages rendered large services to the chiefs of the columns." Given that Mademba's father was not a chief and that the family was already living in Saint Louis, the conditions of Mademba's entry into the *école des otages* remain unclear. Abd-el-Kader went on to state that "Mademba's scholarly success brought the attention of the Governor."[39] In an interview with *Le Petit Parisien* in 1906, Mademba reflected on his experience at the *école des otages* and with Faidherbe.

> Raised by General Faidherbe in Saint Louis du Sénégal, I was among the first negroes sent to the French School founded by that officer. That institution had the name "School of the Sons of Chiefs and Hostages" and only enrolled the children of those who had made their submission and who were given as a guarantee of their loyalty to the metropole in order for their children to be educated *à la française*. General Faidherbe personally occupied himself with me. He enhanced not only my instruction, but also my education.[40]

The last two sentences here are important: "General Faidherbe personally occupied himself with me. He enhanced not only my instruction, but also my education." In her study of letters from students at the reopened and renamed *école des otages*, Kelly Duke Bryant argues insightfully that in the course of providing students with basic necessities such as food, clothing, and shelter the school became a surrogate family. "In approaching the school and its associated officials and personnel as 'family,' students both situated themselves as dependents within a colonial hierarchy and also sought colonial patronage." Duke Bryant further argues that in invoking French officials as "fictive fathers and patrons," African graduates of these boarding schools "used the school and the knowledge, status, and connections it provided for their own ends."[41] Fathers provided for their children and "accordingly, such fictive fathers also faced social obligations." Faidherbe in particular took a "keen interest" in the pupils at his new school, which was located near the

---

[37] I want to thank Kelly Duke Bryant for sharing with me digital images of the existing pages of the school's roster. I was not, however, able to determine definitively which student was Mademba.

[38] Homberg, *L'École des colonies*, 192.

[39] Mademba, *Au Sénégal*, 9.

[40] *Le Petit Parisien*, Oct. 27, 1906.

[41] Duke Bryant, *Education as Politics*, 94–100.

colonial government offices in Saint Louis. Faidherbe not only visited the school twice a week but every Sunday morning, Faidherbe had the students visit him so that he could encourage and reward them. Invoking such fictive kinship expressed dependence and submission, but also an expectation of patronage.[42] I do not know when Mademba entered the *école des otages*, but I do know that just before he turned seventeen, he entered the colonial Post and Telegraph Department as an auxiliary clerk.

Working for the Colonial Telegraph Service

By 1869, when Mademba joined the telegraph service, the Senegalese colonial state was emerging from its chrysalis into an aggressive conquest machine. Conquest depended on military superiority, which in turn depended upon a host of provisioning services. Just as essential as bullets and food, reliable intelligence was crucial to military victories. Intelligence was often gathered by scouts, but few European military men had adequate knowledge of African languages. They depended on African interpreters, who controlled the flow of information and interceded between French military and African chiefs, whether allied or belligerent. African interpreters parsed complex African realities into European conceptual and strategic categories.[43] No matter how dependent the French were on African sources of information, they could not rely unquestioningly on self-interested interpreters. Instead, they sought to create a "moral community" of indigenous intermediaries, whose interests lay in supporting the colonial endeavor and in their bargains of collaboration.[44] Many of these intermediaries were of originally of low social status and participation in the colonial endeavor provided significant social mobility.

French military leaders in French West Africa stood at the head of fairly compact armies composed of a handful of European officers, a small number of noncommissioned European soldiers, a sizeable number of locally recruited *Tirailleurs Sénégalais*, and often a larger number of more or less irregular African auxiliaries. This army had to be provisioned, which generated another army of porters, many of whom were recruited from *villages de liberté*, where slaves liberated from enemy lands were settled, often with the intention of providing a pool of coercible labor for the myriad tasks of conquest: building

---

[42] Ibid., 106–107.

[43] Worger, "Parsing God"; Benjamin Lawrance, Emily Osborn, and Richard Roberts, "Introduction: African Intermediaries and the 'Bargain' of Collaboration," in *Intermediaries*; Mbayo, *Muslim Interpreters in Colonial Senegal*.

[44] The concept of creating "moral communities" of intermediaries essential to the colonial project was originally framed by Christopher Alan Bayly, *Empire and Information: Intelligence Gathering and Social Communication in India, 1780–1870* (Cambridge: Cambridge University Press, 1996), 6–7, 61–66.

forts, roads, railways, telegraph lines, and eventually railways. And this army of porters and builders also had to be fed. Provisioning, thus, was a central mission of both the military and the colonial state.[45]

European military leaders also needed means of quick communication between units, and between men in the field and those at central command. European military expansion in West Africa coincided with new military and communication technologies, especially the telegraph.[46] The use of telegraphy increased rapidly in Europe and the United States following converging discoveries regarding transmission of electromagnetic impulses along wires and the development of the Morse code between 1831 and 1836. By the late 1840s, telegraph wires crisscrossed both Europe and the United States.[47] The challenge was linking different regions, especially those separated by water. The development of insulated submarine cables in 1850 permitted faster communication across channels and oceans, linking England to mainland Europe, but also France to Algeria, which in the 1850s saw the massive use of French troops to suppress Algerian resistance to French colonialism. The first submarine cable linking Europe with West Africa was completed in 1874 and one linking Saint Louis to Europe was completed in 1885.[48] Mademba's career in the telegraph service of colonial Senegal coincided with the dramatic increase in telegraphy and conquest in French West Africa.

Telegraph in Senegal began with Faidherbe's territorial expansion in 1855. The first telegraph line linking Saint Louis with recently conquered Kajoor was built in 1859. A marine cable linking Gorée and Dakar was originally established in 1861, but it failed almost immediately. By 1862, Saint Louis and Dakar were in constant communication. The conquest and pacification of Waalo in 1868 led to the linking of Saint Louis and the French posts at Richard Toll and Dagana and southward to Gandiole and Louga. The outbreak of hostilities with the Umarians in 1869 fed the pressure to push the telegraph toward Podor. African adversaries of French expansion understood the power of the telegraph and strategically cut the wires whenever they could, as the

---

[45] Denise Bouche, *Les Villages de liberté en Afrique noire française, 1887–1910* (Paris: Mouton, 1968); Richard Roberts, "The Emergence of a Grain Market in Bamako, 1883–1908," *Canadian Journal of African Studies* 14 (1) 1980: 37–54; Klein, *Slavery and French Colonial Rule*.

[46] Daniel R. Headrick, *The Tools of Empire: Technology and European Imperialism in the Nineteenth Century* (New York: Oxford University Press, 1981); Daniel R. Headrick, *The Invisible Weapon: Telecommunications and International Politics, 1851–1945* (New York: Oxford University Press, 1991).

[47] George Shiers, ed., *The Electric Telegraph: An Historical Anthology* (New York: Arno Press, 1977).

[48] Headrick, *The Tools of Empire*, chapter 11; Headrick, *The Invisible Weapon*; Jean-Claude Allain, "L'Indépendance câblière de la France au début du XXè siècle," *Guerres mondiales et conflits contemporains* 166 (April) 1992: 115–131.

Damel of Waalo and Lat Dior did during their resistance. With the intensification of expansion under Colonel Brière d'Isle in 1877, increased pressure was put on expanding telegraphy along the Senegal River to Bakel and from Dakar to Kaolak and on to Siné near the Gambia River. Depending on terrain and supply of materials, the fifty men crews building the telegraph averaged four kilometers per day.[49]

By the time the telegraph entered the Soudan in 1878, the work of laying the telegraph had become routinized.[50] Several crews often worked simultaneously on different lines or on different stretches of the same line. A European agent usually directed each crew. By 1893, however, given the paucity of trained Europeans in Senegal and the Soudan, only one European agent supervised several crews. The European supervisor oversaw the distribution of the equipment, the clearing of the trees for the telegraph lines, the proper height and alignment of the lines, and the provisioning of his crew. He was assisted by four or five African supervisors. The crew was divided into five units. The first team was charged with identifying which trees to cut and which to select for use as poles. Some trees served as better telegraph poles than others because they resisted termites and water damage. The second team, consisting of twenty workers, cut the trees and dug the holes to support the poles. The third team prepared the trees selected as poles by cutting the branches and moving them close to the holes. This team also hardened the poles by burning the surface. A fourth team installed the poles and the isolators on each pole. The fifth team, consisting of three workers, installed the telegraph wire. This was a critical part of the work of the telegraph crews and had to be done with care. And finally, two or three workers were assigned the task of providing water to the rest of the crew, "who drank copiously." The work of building the telegraph did not stop during the "bad season," but continued throughout the year. Flooding during the rainy season necessitated constant repair work on the line. Every October, crews checked the existing lines, replaced poles that had deteriorated, replaced broken isolators, tested the tension of the wires, and cleared the bush under the telegraph lines. Even the best hardwood trees selected as poles had to be replaced every four to six years.[51]

A central part of the work of the European supervisor was to manage the material necessary for construction. The telegraph service experimented with using metal pylons, particularly along the flood-prone banks of the Senegal

---

[49] Gouvernement Général de l'AOF, *Les Postes et Télégraphes en Afrique Occidentale* (Corbeil: Éditions Crété, 1907), 198.

[50] Our ability to reconstruct the detail of the telegraph service in the French Soudan is limited by a fire in 1896 that destroyed the archives of telegraph post in Kayes, which was the headquarters of the colony until 1908. Ibid., 177.

[51] Ibid., 190–201; Jacques Méniaud, ed., *Les Pionniers du Soudan: Avant, avec, et après Archinard, 1879–1894* (Paris: Société des Publications Modernes, 1931), vol. 1, 38–39.

River from Bakel to Kayes, but these pylons had to be imported from France and were cumbersome to transport. Indeed, each pylon had to be divided into three parts in order to be head-loaded by African porters. Telegraph wire and isolators rounded out the requirements. In French West Africa, the telegraph service chose the three millimeter galvanized iron wire rather than the heavier four millimeter gauge used in France. The telegraph wire arrived in Senegal in 500 meter rolls, each weighing twenty-eight kilograms and capable of being head-loaded by an African porter. The isolators arrived by ship in cases of 100, which had to be repacked into smaller bundles. Along some routes, animals were used to carry the equipment, but most of it was head-loaded. The telegraph crews also constructed telegraph depots every 100 kilometers.[52]

In 1887–1888, the telegraph service in the Upper River was reorganized into two linked but separate divisions with headquarters in Kayes: the provision of services of telegraph crews and posts and the technical division charged with construction and repair of lines and posts, and provision of the construction materials. With the expansion of conquest and the militarization of the colony, the telegraph became an indispensable tool of governance. A central part of Mademba's work was repairing the telegraph lines damaged by France's African enemies, the distrustful local population, the rainy season, and occasionally by giraffes. Archinard, who took over the military command in 1888, and who wanted more resources for the telegraph service, wrote to the governor of Senegal, that it was impossible "to govern the land if the [military] posts cannot communicate with each other through the means of the telegraph."[53] By 1885, telegraph linked Bamako on the Niger with Paris; in 1889, a cable sent from mainland France arrived in Bamako eight hours later, closely tying together the empire.[54]

Workers in the telegraph service of colonial French West Africa were divided into three cadres with different responsibilities and commensurate salaries. In the French Soudan at the beginning of the twentieth century these were the metropolitan cadre, which was reserved for Europeans and consisted of a single inspector or subinspector, senior clerks (of which there were none appointed), ordinary clerks (of which there were twenty-two), and supervisors (none appointed). The second cadre consisted of local employees divided into receivers (zero), senior clerks (four), ordinary clerks (twenty-two), auxiliary clerks (eight), mechanics (one), head agents (four), local agents (nine), head

[52] Gouvernement Général l'AOF, *Les Postes et Télégraphes*, 188–195.

[53] Martine Cuttier, *Portrait du colonialisme triumphant: Louis Archinard (1850–1932)* (Panazol: Lavauzelle, 2006), 277–284, fn 164, 283 citing Archinard, Situation des Postes et Télégraphes, Jan. 23, 1890, ANS K series.

[54] Paul Butel, ed., *Un officier et la conquête colonial: Emmanuel Ruault (1878–1896)* (Bordeaux: Presses Universitaires de Bordeaux, 2007), 190; see also Méniaud, *Pionniers*, I, 37.

supervisors (one), and in a world dominated by males, one female employee, whose tasks were not specified. The third cadre was the military telegraphers, of which there were twenty-five. The workers of the telegraph service were thus divided into military and civilian branches, even if at the beginning of the telegraph service it served almost exclusively the needs of the military. Of the 906 employees in the French West African telegraph service in 1906, 9 percent were Europeans, 3 percent held military appointments, and 88 percent were Africans.[55] In addition, daily construction workers were recruited locally, whether by choice or force. Free porters, for example, could receive as much as one meter of *guinée* cloth and one liter of rice per day; others, especially those recruited from the official *villages de liberté*, received only subsistence.[56] The racial boundaries separating these cadres were relatively inflexible, even in the fluid world of the nascent colonial state. Nonetheless, Mademba was formally placed in charge of the technical division.

Mademba Sèye: Building Colonialism and the Bargains of Collaboration

With Faidherbe's departure from Senegal in 1865, his aggressive agenda of conquest faded. Paris instructed subsequent governors to cease new military adventures and to consolidate their control over territory already conquered.[57] Groundnuts were expanding rapidly in the plains of Kajoor and into Siin and Saalum further south. Pressure was building in Saint Louis to link better this region to the export markets, to build the railway connecting Saint Louis and Dakar, and to connect these regions through telegraph lines. By the mid 1860s, however, the groundnut regions of western Senegal were caught up in civil wars that pitted the monarchies against insurgent Muslims, rivalries that were intensified by militant Islamic preaching, by increased French territorial conquest, and by challenges borne of new economies.[58] On February 1, 1869, Mademba joined the colonial telegraph service as an entry-level local employee. The curriculum at the *école des otages* did not prepare Mademba for the technical duties of building and maintaining a telegraph system.

---

[55] Gouvernement Général, *Les Postes et Télégraphes*, 19–20.

[56] On daily wage and provisions, see Bouche, *Villages de liberté*, 58–64, 87–88, 146–153; Roberts, *Warriors*, 143–146; and Klein, *Slavery and Colonial Rule*, 87–88; on *guinée* cloth, see Richard Roberts, "Guinée Cloth: Linked Transformations within France's Empire in the Nineteenth Century," *Cahiers d'études africaines* 32 (128) 1992: 597–627.

[57] Kanya-Forstner, *The Conquest of the Western Sudan*, 43.

[58] See Yves-Jean Saint-Martin, *Le Sénégal sous le Second Empire* for the most comprehensive discussion. See also Mamadou Diouf, *Le Kajoor au XIXè siècle: Pouvoir ceddo et conquête colonial* (Paris: Kathala, 1990) and James F. Searing, *"God Alone Is King": Islam and Emancipation in Senegal: Two Wolof Kingdoms of Kajoor and Bawol, 1859–1914* (Portsmouth, NH: Heinemann, 2002).

Presumably, Mademba spent the first few months on the job learning about the telegraphy and the construction of the lines.

As part of a global pandemic, cholera struck Saint Louis in November 1868 and again in June 1869.[59] Among the casualties was Governor Pinet-Laprade; Colonel Valière assumed command of the colony. Valière ordered the September 1869 march to Louga in the center of the raging civil Kajoor civil war in which Lat Joor was mobilizing one faction. Mademba was part of the contingent of civilian employees of the telegraph service seconded to the military to assist in the construction of the telegraph lines. The telegraph group went about its business when Lat Joor's forces attacked and besieged the smaller telegraph group. Mademba faced his first military confrontation. According to his son, Mademba wanted to take up arms and join his military comrades in an effort to push back against Lat Joor and reunite the French forces. The commander of his contingent, Lieutenant Frey, rejected Mademba's request and ordered him to race to the main column and alert them to the critical situation Frey's forces faced. Mademba succeeded and reinforcements arrived.[60]

In 1870, the Franco-Prussian War (1870–1871) led to the fall of the Second Empire and the emergence of the Third Republic; Mademba was posted to the telegraph bureau in Betet, Senegal.[61] I know virtually nothing about Mademba during the 1870s. Mademba was still at the telegraph post at Betet in early April 1878 when the French explorer Paul Soleillet stopped there. Betet, which is no longer identifiable on maps, was not far from Rufisque, where Soleillet had disembarked a few days before.

> From three o'clock the land becomes sandy and uninhabited. At four-thirty Soleillet arrives at Bettet's post where he is received by Masemba (sic), a black Muslim from St. Louis, [an] employee of the telegraph and already a respected marabout. [Soleillet] leaves [the post] the next day Sunday, April 7, at five o'clock in the morning, crosses a cool oasis and follows the edge of the sea all day long.[62]

Soleillet's brief description suggests that Mademba's long tour of duty in Betet was rather dreary, being merely a backwater of the colony. Soleillet indirectly suggests that Mademba may have spent some of his leisure time running a Qur'anic school or at least deepening his knowledge of Islam. The 1870s was a

---

[59] Myron Echenberg, *Africa in the Time of Cholera: A History of Pandemics from 1817 to the Present* (New York: Cambridge University, 2012), 46–47.

[60] Mademba, *Au Sénégal*, 11–12; Diouf, *Le Kajoor au XIXè siècle*, 239–240.

[61] Archinard noted that Mademba was the district officer of Betet, not merely the telegraphist, between 1870 and 1871. Archinard, letter to Étienne, under sec. of state for colonies, Nioro, Jan. 9, 1891, ANOM Soudan I-1a.

[62] Paul Soleillet, *Voyage à Ségou, 1878–1879, rédigé d'aprés les notes et journaux de Soleillet par Gabriel Gravier* (Paris: Challamel, 1887), 18.

fraught time for West African Muslims caught between Islamic reform and revolution and a range of accommodations with expanding French colonialism. If Mademba was actually deepening his knowledge of Islam while in Betet, it was part of an emerging quest for his identity and place in a rapidly changing world. It may also have been part of Mademba's ongoing efforts to periodically remake himself.

Abd-el-Kader Mademba suggests that the one evening Mademba spent with Soleillet in Betet was a crucial turning point in Mademba's life. "His Soudanese career, [Mademba] recounted by himself forty years later, was born of a conversation with the explorer Soleillet, who during his visit to Betté in 1879 (sic), spoke of all the hopes [the French] pin on the still unknown land along the Niger."[63] Except for notations regarding his regular promotions up the employment ladder in the telegraph service – from fifth class clerk to fourth class to third class – the archival record regarding Mademba is relatively silent from 1870 to 1879.[64] His regular promotions indicate that he was a diligent employee fully capable of the tasks he was assigned. But nothing in the record indicated that he was prepared to renegotiate his original bargain of collaboration, which was regular pay for government service. On that fateful evening of April 6, 1878, Soleillet may well have planted in Mademba the seeds of imagining adventure, wealth, and prestige along the Niger River. Not long thereafter, Mademba was given the opportunity to take part in the French military expansion into the Soudan. Mademba's career suddenly took off.

The appointment of Colonel Louis-Alexandre Brière d'Isle as governor of Senegal in 1876 signaled a return to a more expansionist policy in West Africa. In 1879, the appointment of former governor of Senegal Jean Jauréguiberry as minister of the Navy gave a further boost to plans for territorial expansion. In anticipation of further military conquest, preparations needed to be made. Additional explorations of the Upper River region, which was seen as the launching pad for conquest of the interior, were needed. With the approval of the minister, Brière sent Captain Joseph Simon Gallieni on a mission in 1879 to map and generate treaties with the chiefs and polities of the Bafoulabe region. The Bafoulabe region was just to the south of the Umarian state of Kaarta and Segu, which had fallen to Al Hajj Umar in the 1860s. Gallieni's mission was so successful that Brière next sent him on a mission to Segu to assess the context of future French expansion. Gallieni's mission to Segu was not as productive of treaties as his Bafoulabe mission, but it did redouble French resolve to conquer the Soudan.[65]

---

[63] Mademba, *Au Sénégal*, 12–13.

[64] ANOM Dossiers personnels (Mademba) 2862; Mademba at Betet, see *Moniteur du Sénégal*, Mar. 1, 1870.

[65] Joseph Simon Gallieni, *Voyage au Soudan Français (Haut-Sénégal et pays de Ségou), 1879–1881* (Paris: Hachette, 1885); Kanya-Forstner, *The Conquest of the Western Sudan*, 55–112.

The second prerequisite for military expansion was to extend telegraph communication from Saint Louis to the Upper River region. Since 1877, the telegraph was making its way eastward along the Senegal River. But as it did, telegraph construction bumped up against the civil war raging in Futa Toro. By 1880, the telegraph was mostly completed except for a portion between Saldé and Bakel. This gap coincided with the region controlled by Abdul Bokar Kane, who refused the French permission to construct the telegraph line through his territory. The Saldé–Bakel line was finally completed in 1885.[66] In 1879, Mademba was reassigned to the Upper River division of the telegraph service. And the third piece of the foundation for French expansion into the Soudan was the creation of the new position of the commandant supérieur du haut-fleuve, the supreme military commander with full powers of all operations in the Upper River area, including command of a new battalion of *Tirailleurs Sénégalais*. The supreme military commander was to report to the governor of Senegal, who also maintained the budget over his activities.[67]

In his new position, Mademba was actively engaged in constructing the telegraph from Bakel to Médine. Mademba was still at this task in 1880 as Lieutenant-colonel Gustave Borgnis-Desbordes, newly appointed as the supreme military commander, prepared to move boldly into the French Soudan. Desbordes's plans were disrupted, however, by the outbreak of two yellow fever epidemics in Saint Louis in 1880 and 1881 that led to the deaths of considerable numbers of Europeans, including the newly arrived Governor Lanneau. Yellow fever epidemics sowed not only death but also massive supply disruptions since public health efforts to contain the disease involved quarantine. The 1881 epidemic was particularly deadly to the newly arrived contingent of European soldiers and civilian employees, including the European cadre for the telegraph service.[68] Even with the shortage of material, Mademba pushed on with his limited equipment. A frustrated Desbordes complained about the general disarray in the telegraph service, with few agents capable of any tasks with the exception of Mademba. "Arriving at Médine," Desbordes wrote, "I found a native telegraph employee, named Mademba, who was well instructed in his work, intelligent, active, and ready to assist me. He also has significant experience constructing telegraph lines." Desbordes recognized that he was overstepping the racial hierarchy in the telegraph service, but stated simply that he had two choices: either to abandon

---

[66] Robinson, *Chiefs and Clerics*, 124–138; Robinson, *Paths of Accommodation*, 131–132.

[67] Kanya-Forstner, *The Conquest of the Western Sudan*, 72, 87–94.

[68] Gouv. Sén, p.i., letter to Min. Marine, Saint-Louis, Aug. 8, 1881, ANOM Sénégal et dépendances XII-117: travaux de PTT. See also Capitaine Pietri, *Les Français au Niger: Voyages et combats* (Paris: Hachette, 1885), 260; Kalala Ngalamulume, *Colonial Pathologies, Environment, and Western Medicine in Saint-Louis-du- Sénégal, 1867–1920* (New York: Peter Lang, 2012), 50–81.

construction altogether until new European supervisors arrived or push ahead under Mademba's leadership. Desbordes appointed Mademba head of the construction crew, hired two or three additional native supervisors, and instructed that all the necessary material and means of transport be put at Mademba's disposal. Mademba was quickly promoted to second class clerk and then to first class clerk because of his "exceptional services." Mademba's crew laid the 121 kilometer line linking Bafoulabe with Toukoto, which was "superior" in all respects despite the paucity of material. Mademba, Desbordes noted, acquitted this task with "intelligence and devotion."[69]

Desbordes's experience with Mademba and several African interpreters convinced him that trusted and devoted African intermediaries were absolutely essential to the success of the French military mission of conquest. Desbordes also reflected on Europeans' dependence on these intermediaries and the ease to which Europeans could be misled.

> We rely on the interpreters to describe the wealth of the country, the number of herds, the supplies of grain, the numbers of guns, etc. They can easily deceive us if they are not honest and have some other interests. It is therefore essential that we choose interpreters with great care since they can do us great harm and bring about general disaffection [with our mission of conquest].[70]

Captain Ruault, who served as administrator of Bamako during the conquest, noted the power of the interpreter.

> The selection of a good interpreter is of utmost importance for a commander of a post, which has both military and administrative functions ... Most are conscientious. Some interpreters, however, alter the meaning of the speech that they translate by favoring whoever will offer them a pot of wine. Others exploit our influence for their own gain ... We must identify those interpreters who have tendencies to flatter local chiefs and who give to them information that they find agreeable even if it is not the truth.[71]

To help with conquest, Desbordes established a military intelligence division for the Upper River campaign, which had military as well as political tasks.

---

[69] Desbordes, cmdt. sup., letter to gouv. Sén., Médine, Dec. 23, 1880, ANS-AOF 1 D 56; cmdt. sup., Rapport sur la Campagne 1880–1881 dans le Soudan, np, nd [1881] ANS-AOF 1 D 59.

[70] Lt. Col. Borgnis-Desbordes, Campagne de 1880–1881 dans le Soudan, Saint-Louis, July 6, 1881, ANOM Sénégal et dépendances IV-73 bis. On the dependence of European soldiers and administrators on African intermediaries, see Osborn, "Circle of Iron" and Emily Osborn, *Our New Husbands Are Here: Households, Gender, and Politics in a West African State from the Slave Trade to Colonial Rule* (Athens: Ohio University Press, 2011), 127–128.

[71] Paul Butel, ed. *Un Officer et la conquête colonial*, 165–166, 201.

This service eventually was absorbed into the Political Bureau of the central command.[72]

Mademba did not disappoint Desbordes. He pushed the construction of the telegraph forward into the interior of the Soudan despite irregular supplies of construction material.[73] Mademba also used every opportunity to provide additional intelligence to the French. In January 1882, for example, he noted in a letter to the military commander that he discovered traces of horses in the area of Griogolla, where his crew was working. Given how the tracks were made, Mademba assumed that these horses were evidence of African enemies spying on the French military column.[74] France's enemies had begun to realize the importance of the telegraph and took every opportunity to cut the lines and to steal the telegraph wire, the isolators, and the other material.[75] On April 3, 1883, a band of Samory's troops raided Mademba's encampment at Dialocoro on the route between Kita and Bamako and made off with three reels of telegraph wire and a herd of cattle destined to support the French column.[76] Mademba retreated with his crew to Bamako, where he persuaded Desbordes to permit his crew of fourteen men to accompany a retaliatory raid against Samory. According to his son, Mademba had his first serious military encounter that tested his ability to command during fighting. "A few days later, during a very heated encounter with the Malinke warriors, Mademba and his men penetrated the enemy camp, retrieved the telegraph wire, and continued to construct the line that reached Bamako shortly thereafter."[77]

The year 1883 marked a significant turning point in Mademba's bargains of collaboration. He had proven himself an able manager of his telegraph crew, and with his first taste of military adventure, he successfully tested his capacity to command. The French military leadership was keenly attentive to these successes. Even before the April 1883 military raid, Desbordes had written to the governor of Senegal requesting that he send Mademba to Mont Valérien, just outside of Paris, for advanced training in telegraphy. "Mademba," Desbordes wrote, "is a dedicated native employee of the telegraph service of the Upper River, who is performing all the difficult tasks with great zeal,

[72] Cuttier, *Portrait du colonialisme triumphant*, 270–271.

[73] Mademba, letter to cmdt. sup., Guinina, Mar. 2, 1883, ANM J 43.

[74] Mademba letter to cmdt. sup., Toukato, Jan. 4, 1882, ANM J 1.

[75] Chef de service télégraphe, letter to cmdt. sup., Kayes, Oct. 23, 1882, ANM J 1.

[76] Archinard avec la collaboration du Lt. L. Levasseur, Historique succinct des nos rélations avec Samory et Tieba, np, July–Aug. 1889, ANOM Sénégal et dépendances IV-93.

[77] Mademba, *Au Sénégal*, 23–24. For supporting evidence. see Col. Desbordes, Rapport sur les affaires avec l'armée de Samory, commandé par Fabou, du 19 à 27 Avril 1883, np, nd, ANOM Sénégal et dépendances IV-77. The attack on the Dialocoro telegraph camp is noted in États de Service de M. Mademba Sèye, Bafoulabe, May 3, 1888, ANOM Dossiers personnels (Mademba) 2862. See also Lieutenant de Vaisseau Hourst, *Sur le Niger et au Pays des Touaregs: La Mission Hourst* (Paris: Plon, 1898), 63–65.

intelligence, and dedication despite significant impediments. I know that this employee would benefit from a trip to France to see the progress being made in telegraphy." Desbordes underscored the importance of nurturing the dedication of natives like Mademba to the French mission in Africa.

> Colonization of Senegal will only be accomplished by the means of natives who we attract to our goals, which are primarily the work of civilization, not conquest and exploitation. In this regard, nothing can replace a voyage to France, which then becomes like an open book that the Blacks can read and comprehend ... Over the past years, I have often raised the issue about how useful it is for the most intelligent and dedicated natives to improve their skills through a tour of our arsenals for two or three months. I urge you, M. Governor, to approve this request that M. Mademba be sent to France for advanced telegraphy training.[78]

The governor agreed and Mademba sailed to Bordeaux at the end of July 1883. Mademba spent nearly three months at Mont Valérien on the outskirts of Paris. His annual salary was raised to 3300 francs, he received an extra stipend of 10 francs per day while in France, and he was promoted to "native" clerk first class in colonial telegraph service with the title of "chief of construction of the telegraph line in the Upper River." On Desbordes's recommendation, the governor of Senegal wrote to the Minister of the Navy recommending that Mademba be awarded the honorary rank of the cross of the Legion of Honor. In forwarding his approval to this recommendation, the Director of Colonies argued that not only had Mademba rendered "exceptional services" to France, but that "bestowing this honor has the power to produce the best results" for those who receive it.[79]

Created in 1802 by Napoléon Bonaparte, the Legion of Honor recognized outstanding service to France in peacetime as well as in wartime, regardless of the social status. By 1805, Napoléon extended these awards to foreigners who had demonstrated their service to France. The numbers of legionnaires for each rank was fixed by law and the nomination of individuals had to pass several administrative layers.[80] These awards were manifested in ceremonies

---

[78] Borgnis Desbordes, letter to gouv. Sén., Bamako, Mar. 2, 1883, ANOM Dossiers personnels (Mademba) 2862.

[79] Direction des colonies, Min. Marine, Note pour le Min., Paris, Aug. 16, 1883 and Note pour le cabinet du Ministre, Paris, Aug. 22, 1883, ANOM Dossiers personnels (Mademba) 2862.

[80] On the Legion of Honor, see Jean Daniel, *La Légion d'Honneur: Histoire et organisation de L'Ordre National* (Paris: Éditions André Bonne, 1948); Jean Tulard, François Monnier, and Olivier Echappé, eds., *La Légion d'honneur: Deux siècles d'histoire* (Paris: Perrin, 2004); Michel Wattel and Béatrice Wattel, *Les Grand-Croix de la Légion d'Honneur de 1805 à nos jours: Titulaires français et étrangers* (Paris: Archives et culture, 2009).

and medals, which Mademba proudly wore. As Lieutenant-colonel Gallieni explained in 1887, for France's mission in the Soudan to succeed, "France has to rely increasingly on natives to promote our civilization and commerce, and we must do all we can to encourage the natives in this task ... This nomination of Mademba will have a positive influence on the natives we employ all around us, in our construction, our schools, our telegraph system, etc."[81]

We do not know much about Mademba's experiences in France in 1883. We do know, however, that Desbordes was absolutely right about how significant such visits were to nurturing African loyalty to France's mission. Paris in the early 1880s must have astonished the young African telegraphist. With more than two million inhabitants, Paris dwarfed anything that Mademba had experienced. Baron Hausmann, credited with the major urban renovations of the Second Empire, continued his efforts to remake Paris into a bourgeois capital of Europe. He used the collapse of the Paris Commune to exile the working classes to the suburbs and to transform the inner city into a cosmopolitan center of the arts, business, and government. We can imagine Mademba during his free time promenading along the new boulevards of the central districts in awe of the scale of building and the ongoing electrification. During these early years of the Third Republic, France was becoming more prosperous, more bourgeois, and more imperial.[82] Walking those streets in Paris in 1883, Mademba would likely have attracted stares of Parisians unaccustomed to seeing African men. Mademba was certainly in awe of the progress and excitement that France exuded during the Belle Époque.

In his study of Freemasons and French imperialism, Owen White discovered that Mademba most likely became a Mason during or shortly after this visit to France in 1883. Freemasonry in France in the nineteenth century involved a relatively decentralized and plastic ideology that articulated local interests within generally agreed commitments to progress, anticlericalism, liberty of consciousness, the brotherhood of all mankind, and mutual support of its members. Central to the organizational structure of Freemasonry were the lodges, which were in many ways "republics in miniature" and committed to the promotion of science, individual progress, free thought, and fraternity.[83]

---

[81] Extract of a letter from Lt.-col. Gallieni to gouv. Sén., Kayes, May 12, 1887, ANOM Dossiers personnels (Mademba) 2862.

[82] Raymond Rudorff, *Belle Époque: Paris in the Nineties* (London: Hamish Hamilton, 1972), 27–30; Johannes Willms, *Paris: Capital of Europe: From the Revolution to the Belle Époque* (New York: Homes and Meier, 1997), 334–339. See also Mary McAuliffe, *Dawn of the Belle Époque: The Paris of Monet, Zola, Bernhardt, Eiffel, Debussy, Clemenceau, and Their Friends* (Lanham, MD: Rowman and Littlefield, 2011), especially chapter 12 on 1883.

[83] Sudhir Hazareesingh and Vincent Wright, *Francs-Maçons sous le Second Empire: Les loges provincials du Grand-Orient à la veille de la Troisième République* (Rennes: Presses Universitaires de Rennes, 2001), 26–27, 156.

Freemason lodges became crucibles for the development of a new form of sociability and strove to create "an enlightened universalism" in which there was a "pure brotherhood of men."[84] In France, Masonic lodges were simultaneously social clubs, incubators for republican political thought, and generators of professional networks. To achieve these goals required a practical commitment: Masons were encouraged to acquire positions of power in government and other sectors of society.[85]

Different lodges in France and in the empire had different commitments to these principles. White points out that despite the relatively small number of Masons in French West Africa, the portability of their ideas "served to connect them to a highly organized network that spanned the divide between metropole and overseas France."[86] Saint Louis already had a Masonic lodge in 1781 that included Frenchmen and members of the influential métis community. Few black Africans were admitted, in part because the Masons worried about their lack of formal French education and commitment to Masonic ideals. As a graduate of the *école des otages* and as a member of the Legion of Honor, Mademba certainly qualified and had proven his loyalty, and he was initiated into the relatively new Union Sénégalaise lodge, which was established in 1874.[87] In the 1880s, when Mademba was a member, the Union Sénégalaise lodge promoted a new school for "apprentices, *hommes de couleur*, and former slaves."[88] As a Mason, Mademba joined what Bayly has called a "moral community" of intermediaries so essential to colonialism. All colonial lodges were deeply committed to the "emancipatory action" of the French civilizing mission.[89]

Membership in the Masons thus brought with it brotherhood and a community of like-minded gentlemen. Membership also had an instrumental quality in linking members to powerful patrons. White describes several cases where Masons in West Africa appealed to more powerful members for

---

[84] Stefan-Ludwig Hoffmann, *The Politics of Sociability: Freemasonry and German Civil Society, 1840–1918* (Ann Arbor: University of Michigan Press, 2007), 5–13.

[85] André Combes, *Histoire de la Franc-Maçonnerie au XIXè siècle* (Monaco: Éditions du Rocher, 1999), vol. 2, 158–163; Hazareesingh and Wright, *Francs-Maçons*, 32, 187–219; Maurice Larkin, "Fraternité, solidarité et sociabilité: Les racines herbeuses du Grand Orient de France (1900–1920)," in *L'héritage jacobin dans la France d'aujourd'hui: Essais en l'honneur de Vincent Wright*, ed. Sudhir Hazareesingh (Oxford: Oxford University Press, 2002), 93.

[86] Owen White, "Networking: Freemasons and the Colonial State in French West Africa, 1895–1914," *French History* 19 (1) 2005: 94–95.

[87] Ibid., 98–99, fn 32. By the late 1890s, a new racialism eroded this sense of equality and fewer black Africans were initiated or sought initiation. Ibid., 99. See also Georges Odo, *La Franc-Maçonnerie dans les colonies, 1738–1960* (Paris: Éditions Maçonniques de France, 2001), 60.

[88] Jones, *The Métis of Senegal*, 110–112. See also Robinson, *Paths of Accommodation*, 103.

[89] Combes, *Histoire de la Franc-Maçonnerie*, II, 399.

assistance with employment requests. We have no records of Mademba appealing to more powerful fellow Masons, but the sense of fellowship no doubt contributed to Mademba's abilities to renegotiate the bargains of collaboration after his return from France and later in his career.[90] This was especially true since William Ponty, as a fellow Mason, would emerge as Mademba's patron during the challenging period when he was under investigation for crimes and abuses of power. One of the leaders of the Colonial Lobby in the Third Republic and the under-secretary for state for colonial affairs when Colonel Archinard proposed that Mademba be made king of Sinsani was Eugène Etienne, who was also a Mason.[91]

Mademba and the Work of the Military's Political Bureau

Upon his return from France in late 1883, Mademba rapidly took over the telegraph construction and pushed aggressively to link Kayes with Bamako and to repair the damaged line. Colonel Boilève, the new supreme military commander, placed Mademba directly under the authority of the central command, and thus no longer subject to the civilian telegraph service. Exactly why this occurred is not clear from the archival record, although we can assume that it was because Mademba had broken the racial ceiling in the telegraph service by being named chief of telegraph construction for the Upper River and thus encountered the hostility of M. Dabadie, the European director of the telegraph service of the Upper River based in Kayes. Boilève complained about how difficult it was to recruit and retain competent Africans for the many tasks of supporting the military campaign. He urged the governor of Senegal to double the salary of the best native employees, including Mademba, whose work has made the telegraph perfectly operable.[92] Being directly under the central command placed Mademba close to the center of political power in the nascent colonial conquest state. In 1883–1884, the nascent conquest state was besieged by rebellions in Beledugu and was increasinglu threatened by Samory's forces, which had even marched to the gates of Bamako, before retreating.[93]

Paris was not pleased with the military's rapid territorial advance during the aggressive campaigns of 1883–1884. The ministry of the Navy instructed the

---

[90] White, "Networking," 100–101. See also Combes, *Histoire de la Franc-Maçonnerie*, II, 397–398, fn 13. Robinson, *Paths of Accommodation*, 103 notes that William Ponty was a member of the Union Sénégalaise lodge. According to Combes, Mademba rejoined the Cosmos lodge in 1907, likely following his 1906 visit to France, *Histoire de la Franc-Maçonnerie*, II, 404. See also Larkin, "Fraternité, solidarité et sociabilité."

[91] Combes, *Histoire de la Franc-Maçonnerie*, II, 397–398.

[92] Col. Boilève, cmdt. sup., Campagne 1883–1884 dans le Soudan, Saint Louis, Aug. 8, 1884, ANOM Sénégal et dépendances IV-79 bis.

[93] Méniaud, *Pionniers*, I, 198.

governor of Senegal to reign in the military leadership and instructed the military to consolidate their conquests before engaging the two major African states in the region: the Umarian state at Segu and Samory Ture's state on the Milo River. Between 1884 and 1886, Mademba was posted in Senegal, where he led the construction of the telegraph linking Rufisque and Joal and Saldé and Bakel, and thus away from the center of military and political power in the Soudan.[94] During this period, Mademba developed good relations with M. Hübler, the head of the Post and Telegraph Department in Senegal. Hübler was affiliated with the Alliance Française and committed to promoting instruction in French. The Freemasons were also deeply committed to promoting secular instruction in French. Exactly when Mademba and Hübler cooperated in expanding French instruction is not clear, but according to General Faidherbe's memoire,

> Colonel Gallieni was also concerned with developing instruction in French among the Blacks. To that end, he ordered the creation of school in each post. Under the authority of the commandant of the post, the under officers and soldiers of the garrison offered preliminary instruction in the French language as a means to divert the youth from the teachings of the marabouts. The costs of the instruction books were covered by the Alliance Française, whose task is conducted through the entire world.
>
> It was not only in the posts of the Upper River where these schools were established. M. Hübler ... aided by M. Mademba-Sèye, one of the most intelligent natives who is also the most devoted to the national cause, pursue with indefatigable ardor the same goal in the posts along the coast, in Saloum, Casamance, etc.[95]

The shift from leading a Qur'anic school in Betet in the 1870s to promoting instruction in French at military posts marked yet another phase in Mademba's periodic efforts to remake himself.

Mademba's fortunes changed dramatically with the appointment of Lieutenant-colonel Gallieni as supreme military commander for the 1886–1887 military campaign and with a change in Paris that supported increased military activity.[96] The political and military situation in the Upper River and in the Soudan had changed from 1884 when the French National Assembly pushed back against increased military expenditures: the

---

[94] États de Service de M. Mademba Sèye, commis principal colonial des PT faisant fonction de contrôleur du Service technique, May 3, 1888, Bafoulabe, ANOM Dossiers personnels (Mademba) 2862.

[95] Général Faidherbe, *Le Sénégal; La France dans l'Afrique occidentale* (Paris: Hachette, 1889), 474–475. This was the only reference to Mademba in Faidherbe's entire memoire.

[96] For background, see Marc Michel, *Gallieni* (Paris: Fayard, 1989); on the military conquest, see Méniaud, *Pionniers*, I, 275–307 and Kanya-Forstner, *The Conquest of the Western Sudan*.

French had established a loose agreement with Samory regarding spheres of influence and Amadu had reasserted his authority over his brother in Nioro. In the meantime, however, Al Hajj Mamadu Lamine Drame, a Soninke Tijaniyya scholar, had resettled near Médine and began preaching and recruiting followers. His arrival in Médine in 1885 further enflamed the multiple and conflicting regional movements invoking Islam, reform, and resistance to the French. In January 1886, Mamadu Lamine led his forces into the Muslim state of Bundu, where he sacked villages and forced the Sy dynasty to flee. Mamadu Lamine then laid siege to the French fort of Bakel in April 1886. Forming a temporary alliance with forces in Futa opposed to Mamadu Lamine, Commandant Supérieur Frey pushed Mamadu Lamine's forces out of Bakel and into the Upper Gambia. Mamadu Lamine regrouped in the Upper Gambia and returned to the Bundu area the next year, where he again threatened French forts along the Upper River. When Gallieni was appointed supreme military commander in November 1886, he was instructed to subdue Mamadu Lamine, which he accomplished in the Spring 1887.[97] Mademba participated in the 1887 campaign against Mamadu Lamine. Battlefield victories regularly led to the division of the booty captured from the enemy, especially prominent was the division of Mamadu Lamine's wives, concubines, and slaves.[98] Gallieni seemed little bothered by this division of human booty.

> I did not know what to do with the seventeen women brought to me. I asked them, through Alassane [Gallieni's interpreter], if they would not marry my *tirailleurs*. We know how easy it is for native women in Senegambia to change their masters. These [women] came from all the points of the Soudan; they had been given to the marabout as soon as he arrived in the country. What does it matter to them to change their slavery? . . . Our blacks from Senegal admire success. Women do not escape this rule, and, in the end, our prisoners are perhaps very satisfied to pass in the hands of [our] brave soldiers. I ordered the women to stand in a line. I also ordered the seventeen *tirailleurs* who had most distinguished themselves in the campaign to come to attention. I then called number 1, who made his choice, then number 2, and so on, until the last tirailleur. There was then only one woman left, and naturally only the oldest and the ugliest was left. So it is in the midst of the laughter and the joy of the whole camp, gathered to enjoy this spectacle, that the last tirailleur was called, a beautiful and robust Bambara, and he took possession of his [new] wife.[99]

---

[97] Lieutenant-colonel Gallieni, *Deux campagnes au Soudan Français, 1886–88* (Paris: Hachette, 1891), 8–17; Méniaud, *Pionniers*, I, 288–293; Abdoulaye Bathily, "Mamadou Lamine Dramé et la Résistance antiimperialiste dans le Haut-Sénégal (1885–1887)," *Notes Africaines* 125 1970: 20–32; Robinson, *Chiefs and Clerics*, 145–149; Gomez, *Pragmatism*, 152–169.

[98] Gallieni, *Deux campagnes*, 79.

[99] Gallieni, *Deux campagnes*, 121–122; Bathily, "Mamadou Lamine," 27.

During a similar event later in the campaign, Mademba likely chose Mariam Aidara, one of Mamadu Lamine's elite wives, and her two daughters for himself.[100] This was how Mademba began building both his prestige and his household.

As Gallieni pacified the Upper Senegal and turned eastward into the Soudan, he confronted a still rebellious Beledugu, the Umarian state at Segu, Samory along the Milo River, and Tieba in Sikasso. Gallieni described the French presence in the Soudan as a "thin line from Kayes to Bamako," supported by a few military posts and villagers fearful of their powerful neighboring African states.[101] Because of Mademba's effectiveness as head of the telegraph crew, in leading his men into a battle in 1883, and for his provision of intelligence whenever he could, Gallieni requested in 1886 that Mademba be seconded to the military command, even as he still pursued construction and repairs on the telegraph. The same year, Mademba was awarded the rank of "chevalier" in the Legion of Honor. Gallieni also pursued an aggressive policy of securing treaties with African chiefs willing to side with the French. Mademba certainly participated in several of these treaty missions through his role in Gallieni's Political Bureau, where Mademba served as interpreter.[102]

In moving ever closer into the center of the military command, Mademba sought more recognition for his dual work as director of telegraph construction and as a member of the Political Bureau. He requested a new uniform reflecting his rank, which in the civilian administrative service was parallel to that of a lieutenant. Mademba understood well how important uniforms were for commanding respect (see Figure 1.1).[103] As a career soldier, Gallieni also recognized the power of uniforms and supported Mademba's request for one.

> I strongly support Mr. Sèye Mademba's request to be named deputy chief of military telegraphy in the French Soudan. This rank will not change his salary, but it will give him the right to wear the uniform. As you well know, the uniform is necessary in our colony and in the Soudan in particular, for the prestige it offers our staff in the midst of the native population . . . I would add that this native, because of his deep knowledge

---

[100] Abdoul Drame, letter to Gouv.-gen., Saint Louis, Aug. 17, 1899, ANS-AOF 15 G 176.

[101] Gallieni, Rapport du Lt.-col. Gallieni, cmdt. sup. du Soudan Français sur la situation politique du Soudan Français à la fin de la campagne 1887–1888, May 10, 1888, Bafoulabe, ANS-AOF 1 D 92.

[102] Chef de Bataillon, Rapport sur le Colonne du Niger, [Nango], May 28, 1887, ANS-AOF 1 D 90. Mademba is also listed as an employee in the Post and Telegraph Department. This report includes Mademba under the heading of "European," which may reflect the ambiguities surrounding the status of the *originaires* of the Four Communes of Senegal holding rights of French citizenship.

[103] Osborn, "Circle of Iron."

Figure 1.1 Mademba and his telegraph construction crew, ca. 1880s.
(Source: Borgnis-Desbordes Collection, Bibliothèque nationale de France: Société de Géographie, with permission)

of the countries [and people] of the Soudan has often been employed by me in several very important political missions, especially since the death of my loyal interpreter, Alassane Dia. Without M. Mademba's assistance, I would have faced significant difficulties from a political point of view.[104]

Mademba's rise to the inner circle of the military command was facilitated by the death of Gallieni's trusted interpreter Alassane Dia in February 1887. Alassane had been Gallieni's guide and interpreter since his mission to Segu in 1880.[105] In his eulogy, Gallieni stated that "the life of this valiant servant can be captured in a few words: absolute devotion to the French cause, courage beyond proof, and pushed often towards heroism. For this native, his adapted

[104] Gallieni, letter to gouv. Sén., Kayes, May 12, 1887, ANOM Sénégal et dépendances XII-117. See also Mademba's letter requesting this uniform, Mademba, letter to Gallieni, Kayes, May 10, 1887, ANOM Sénégal et dépendances XII-117.
[105] Aristide Auguste François Pérignon, *Haut-Sénégal et Moyen-Niger: Kita et Ségou* (Paris: J. Andre, 1901), 122.

country was a veritable cult ... Alassane gave blind devotion to all the French officers who used his services."[106] Gallieni promoted Mademba as chargé des affaires in his Political Bureau and nominated him for the Legion's "Cross of Cambodia."[107]

It is not clear what the title chargé des affaires meant in the context of the tenuous French presence in the Soudan. Normally used to refer to an official in a diplomatic role, Mademba's portfolio was much larger. Gallieni sent Mademba on missions to outlying villages and regions that were simultaneously diplomatic and practical. Villages that accepted French protection were in turn obliged to provide millet and rice to feed the French column and to supply labor to build the newest forts. When persuasion did not work, Gallieni dispatched a section of *tirailleurs* under the command of Under-lieutenant Saba Maram to help Mademba with these requisitions. Requisitions were a central part of the meaning of French protection.[108]

Indeed, Gallieni described Mademba as "charged with the political affairs of the column" and instructed Mademba to assist a troop of *tirailleurs* to scout the region and secure supplies of rice and millet for the colonial army. Gallieni eventually appointed Mademba director of his Political Bureau, which was charged with coordinating the information received from various informants and military sources and negotiating with African chiefs and notables.[109] In his memoire of his appointment as supreme military conmmander, Gallieni recalled that at a reception for him in Kayes in November 1887, chiefs of surrounding villages, African officers of the *Tirailleurs Sénégalais*, "outfitted in their splendid oriental uniforms," and the interpreters attached to the column attended. "They were presented to me by Mademba Sèye, the head of the political bureau."[110] Mademba's request for a military uniform was ultimately denied because he was not a formal member of the military telegraph service. After significant back and forth, the Ministry of Navy eventually recognized the power of uniforms and authorized Mademba to wear a newly designed uniform of the civilian telegraph service.[111]

[106] Gallieni, Paroles pronouncées sur la tombe de l'interprète Alassane Dia, Kayes, Feb. 14, 1887, ANS-AOF 15 G 29.

[107] Le chef du 4ème Bureau, letter to gouv. Sén., Paris, Oct. 4, 1886; gouv. Sén., letter to min. Marine, Saint Louis, Oct. 7, 1887; Gallieni, letter to sous-sec d'État, au bord du "Sénégal," Oct. 21, 1887, ANOM Dossiers personnels (Mademba) 2862.

[108] Order #58, Gallieni to Mademba, Kita, Jan. 10, 1888, ANS-AOF 1 D 93.

[109] Cuttier, *Portrait du colonialisme triumphant*, 272–273.

[110] Gallieni, *Deux campagnes*, 326–327.

[111] Arrêt no. 258, 5ème bureau, Paris, Sept. 9, 1887, ANOM Sénégal et dépendances XII-117. See also le chef de la 2ème division, rapport au sous sec d'État, Paris, Sept. 9, 1887, ANOM Sénégal et dépendances XII-117.

During this period, Mademba increasingly came into conflict with the director of the civilian telegraph service in which Mademba was still employed. Gallieni weighed into this conflict with strong support for Mademba and accused M. Cartier, the new director of the telegraph service, of "bad will" toward Mademba, whom he accused of a poor work ethic and lack of attention to his tasks. Gallieni's support for Mademba represented the flip side of the bargains of collaboration, in that French patrons protected their loyal African servants.[112] Gallieni also requested that Mademba receive a salary supplement of 500 francs for his devotion and service.[113]

At the end of the 1887–1888 military campaign, Gallieni stated in self-satisfied terms that the "political situation in the French Soudan is actually very good. There is no obvious danger on the horizon." But he warned that the interior of French West Africa remained a "land of surprises" and only the foresight and perseverance of the military chief can keep small problems from developing into major challenges. Gallieni was pleased that his Gambia column had routed Mamadou Lamine and his followers. Mamadou Lamine and his son were executed. The villages of the Upper Senegal that Mamadou Lamine had burned have been rebuilt and commerce has returned to the region. Nonetheless, Gallieni urged continued vigilance against the "false prophets" (Amadu, Samory, and Aguibu), whose propaganda may still sway chiefs and populations who have not fully supported the French presence.[114] In 1888, Gallieni returned to France and passed on both the military command and Mademba to Lieutenant-colonel Archinard.

In 1888, after nearly two decades in the French colonial telegraph service, Mademba Sèye had demonstrated his deep commitment to France and to France's mission in West Africa. He had also demonstrated through his technical skills and his political acumen that France's promotion of his education, his employment, and his training had amply returned their investment. Mademba had clearly become a core member of the "moral community" of intermediaries that had become so essential to the working of late nineteenth–century empire. Mademba had proven that he was able to manage people as well as technology. As Mademba moved closer to the inner circle of

---

[112] Letter, Gallieni to cmdt., Kayes, Boungourou, Jan. 22, 1887, ANM J 1. See also Gallieni's eulogy for the interpreter Alassane Dia, Gallieni, Paroles prononcées sur la tombe de l'interprète Alassane Dia, Kayes, Feb. 14, 1887, ANS-AOF 15 G 29 and Gallieni's remarks on Alassane Dia in his *Deux campagnes*, 28, 147–148.

[113] Administration des colonies, 3ème bureau, rapport au sous sec d'État, Paris, July 26, 1888, ANOM Dossiers personnels (Mademba) 2862.

[114] Gallieni, Rapport du cmdt. sup. du Soudan Français sur la situation politique du Soudan Français à la fin de la campagne 1887–1888, Bafoulabe, May 10, 1888, ANS-AOF 1 D 92.

political and military decision-making, he proved yet again that he understood how to command authority when needed and how to defer to authority as well. These two sides – commanding authority and deferring to authority – were to become even more pronounced as Mademba entered the more aggressive phase of conquest with the appointment of Lieutenant-colonel Louis Archinard as supreme military commander in 1888.

2

Conquest and Construction of Indirect Rule in the French Soudan, 1886–1891

Despite various and continued forms of African resistance, conquest was often the easiest phase of the colonial project. Transforming conquered space into colonial territory was a protracted, uneven, and contradictory process. French military leaders in the Western Soudan often read voraciously in the archives of the region. Louis Archinard, for example, studied Eugène Mage's 1865 report on the design and layout of Segu city in advance of his storming that city twenty-five years later.[1] Each newly appointed military leader studied the previous military commander's reports with an eye toward strategies and enemy positions. All set their goals on conquest. In his memoire, Emile Thiriet wrote that "It is interesting and occasionally poignant to peruse the archives of a Soudanese post. This is the best means to get a good sense of the organization of the land and its history since the planting of the French flag."[2] Few, however, paid much attention to the organization of the postconquest administration.

Had they wanted to plan what postconquest colonial administration would be like, military commanders could draw on models established by Faidherbe, the governor of Senegal during the mid-century phase of expansion. And Faidherbe certainly drew on French experience in Algeria, where he had served before being posted to Senegal. Algerian postconquest administration drew in its turn on Napoléon's brief experience with colonization of Egypt. The model of the "enlightened" protectorate, in which the superior power sought to use modern science to revive the ancient glory of the weaker power found significant resonance with French efforts to revive African kingdoms along the Niger River in the last decade of the nineteenth century.[3]

Western imperial powers of the late eighteenth and early nineteenth centuries laid the foundations for the emerging legal category of the

[1] Lieutenant-colonel Archinard, *Le Soudan Français en 1889–1890: Rapport militaire du Commandant Supérieur* (Paris: Imprimerie Nationale, 1891), 21–22.
[2] Emile Thiriet, *Au Soudan Français: Souvenirs 1892–1894, Macina–Tombouctou* (Paris: Imprimerie André Lesot, 1932), 56.
[3] Jean-Loup Amselle, *Vers un multiculturalisme français: L'empire de la coutume* (Paris: Aubier, 1996).

protectorate through elaborations of the idea of "protection." Under what they term as a "global reordering project," Lauren Benton and Lisa Ford examine British legal thinking about how to engineer legal order in a loosely organized emerging empire. British "rage for order" involved making legible legal practices throughout this diverse space. Protection emerged as a catchall concept to help this process. "The connections are nowhere more apparent than in the deployment of protection as an incorporative legal strategy in places of growing British jurisdictional ambition," they argue. The problem, Benton and Ford admit, was that the "meanings of protection were notoriously unstable."[4] Regardless of its ambiguity, the utility of the legal category of the protectorate became a means to intervene more fully in a colonial context.

The protectorate thus emerged as the predominant international legal instrument that furthered late nineteenth–century imperial expansion. At its most basic, the protectorate was an arrangement "whereby one state, while retaining to some extent its separate identity as a state, is subject to a kind of guardianship by another state."[5] The protectorate usually came into being through military conquest or a treaty ceding a certain degree of sovereignty to the superior power. The modern form of the protectorate gained its legal character most explicitly during the nineteenth century.[6] In all cases, significant ambiguities existed surrounding the legal authority that the parties had to enter into these protection agreements and the conditions that ensued from them. Lewis Tupper in 1907 praised these agreements for their "elasticity" in permitting the application of protection with "discretion."[7] "Protectorates are of many kinds and degrees and each one is more or less a law until itself," wrote Malcolm McIlwraith in 1917.[8] The practice of protectorates, however, was legally messy. Paul Dislère, a leading French scholar of colonial legislation, argued that

> [o]nce a state is placed under the protectorate of another power, it abdicates completely its external sovereignty and abandons entirely its foreign policy. But, in terms of its administration of its internal affairs, the protected state in general reserves more or less full independence to run its local government . . . This regime varies from country to country and it is impossible to establish a precise formula for the operation of the protectorate.[9]

---

[4] Lauren Benton and Lisa Ford, *Rage for Order: The British Empire and the Origins of International Law, 1800–1850* (Cambridge, MA: Harvard University Press, 2016), 12, 84.

[5] Jennings and Watts, *Oppenheim's International Law*, vol. 1, 278.

[6] John P. Grant and J. Craig Barker, eds., *Parry and Grant Encyclopedic Dictionary of International Law* (Dobbs Ferry, NY: Oceana Publications, second edition, 2004), 404.

[7] Lewis Tupper, "Customary and Other Law in the East Africa Protectorate," *Journal of the Society of Comparative Legislation* 8 (2) 1907: 173.

[8] Malcolm McIlwraith, "The Declaration of a Protectorate over Egypt and Its Legal Effects," *Journal of the Society of Comparative Legislation* 17 (1–2) 1917: 240.

[9] Paul Dislère, *Traité de législation coloniale* (Paris: P. Dupont, 1914), 214–215.

Frantz Despagnet agreed with Dislère on the legal complexity of the protectorate but shifted the emphasis between old and new protectorates, which
differed in the degree of internal sovereignty practiced by traditional rulers.
With the "modern" establishment of protectorates, Despagnet wrote, "the
protector nation is required to assist the protected on the road towards
civilization."[10]

The archival record is fairly silent on how deeply Lieutenant-colonel
Gallieni thought about the postconquest administration of the Soudan.
Gallieni was skeptical about the African rulers' willingness to serve France's
interests in promoting commerce. Gallieni cautioned against investing too
much power with one chief or one group. Rather than siding with strong
chiefs, Gallieni preferred to support the "weaker ones," but in the end he
argued the only policy that would transform the Soudan was to found French
influence through "our justice and encourage the workers [to promote com-
merce] and weaken the 'exactions of the chiefs.'" In order to assure this
outcome, Gallieni was convinced that the French military needed to be on
the ground for a long time to come.[11]

A rudimentary notion of how the French military in the Soudan conceived
of the protectorate is found in the language that Gallieni embedded into a
treaty signed in 1880 with the chiefs of the Upper River region of Fouladugu.
Gallieni's treaty seemed a ready-made template for the protectorate in that the
subordinate group or groups declared that they wanted to live free of any other
external power and by their own free will sought the exclusive protection of
France, the superior power. Article 2 was a crucial part of the protectorate.
"The French Government agrees never to involve itself in the interior affairs of
the land, to leave to each chief to govern and administer his people following
their customs, practices, or religion; and never to alter the constitution of the
land under its protection." France reserved the right to build forts if such
construction was deemed by all parties to be in their mutual interests. The
chiefs agreed in turn to impose no restrictions on commerce and to provide
materials and workers to help with the construction of forts if the parties
agreed to their construction. Article 5 of the Gallieni treaty laid out the
principles of extraterritoriality for French nationals. "In the case where a
controversy emerged between a French national and a chief or one of his
subjects, this dispute will be judged by a representative of the [Senegalese]
governor with an appeal to the head of the colony."[12] The legal principles of

---

[10] Despagnet, "Les protectorats," 53–54.
[11] Gallieni, Note relative au programme de la Campagne 1887–88 dans le Soudan Français,
St. Raphael, Sept. 24, 1887, ANOM Sénégal et dépendances IV-90; Procès verbal, commission du Haut Fleuve, première session, Paris, Jan. 15, 1890, ANOM Soudan VII-1.
[12] "Traité avec le Fouladougou," Goniokori, Apr. 16, 1880, reproduced in Pérignon, Haut-
Sénégal et Moyen-Niger, 196–197.

these articles remained more or less the same in treaties signed by the French military commanders, although the numbering and extent of internal and external sovereignty changed.[13] Whereas existing chiefs signed the treaty of protection, the conquering French held "palabres" with chiefs they sought to install following military victories. When they could, the French sought to restore chiefs with legitimate claims on political office. Sometimes, Africans who had proven their loyalty to the French were appointed as chiefs and kings even if they had no legitimate claim on political office. In this way, the treaty of protectorate sowed the seeds of French policy of indirect rule. But first, French military presence had to be extended.

In 1888, Gallieni, together with former supreme military commanders Brière and Desbordes, pushed for Louis Archinard to become the next military commander in the Soudan. Archinard already had considerable Soudanese experience. In 1880, Captain Archinard had been posted to the Soudan following a tour in Indochina and charged with military construction, a position not unlike the one Faidherbe first held in Senegal. During Archinard's first tour in the Upper River region from 1880 to 1883, he became part of the inner circle of French officers closely associated with Colonel Borgnis-Desbordes. Archinard thus arrived in the Soudan during its early triumphant waves of conquest and as it pushed forward relatively easily until they reached Bamako in 1883. Then, given changes in French metropolitan politics, conquest seemed to stop. Between 1883 and 1886, the military command of the Upper River was held by a series of relatively undistinguished one-year appointments. Metropolitan political forces resisted further conquest and the French military did not advance significantly until Gallieni assumed the leadership in 1886. The ever wider reach of conquest raised the costs of supporting the military. Flashy military successes were important in fueling political support for military conquest. The Berlin West African Conference (November 15, 1884–February 26, 1885) provided momentum for the Scramble for Africa and put extra pressure on the French military to move their agenda forward. Archinard, however, left the Soudan in 1884 and spent nearly four years back in France, where he moved steadily up the military leadership hierarchy.[14]

Conquest Accelerated

If the military in French West Africa remained convinced of its glorious role as conqueror and pacifier of the Western Sudan, Paris did not. The ministers of

[13] I thank Tom Bassett, who has studied numerous treaties, for this suggestion.

[14] For detail on Archinard's career and especially for this period from 1880 to 1888, see Kanya-Forstner, *The Conquest of the Western Sudan*, 84–147; Cuttier, *Portrait du colonialisme triumphant*, 104–228.

the Navy, most of whom were military men in their own right, assumed the dominant republican ideologies of progress and free trade. They also understood, even if they did not condone, the military's agenda, and while they could accept the need to maintain a militant posture, they stressed that the underlining objectives of French occupation were not simply conquest. "Vis-à-vis the Futanke in general," Minister Rousseau wrote to the governor of Senegal in the summer of 1885, "observe an attitude that is defiant but not hostile." He went on to develop what he took to be the objectives of the French endeavor:

> Time, foresight, consistency, and above all equity are the arms with which we will triumph effectively against all resistance that we encounter at the beginning of our influence. [Our] loyal partisans, who might now be small in number, will rapidly increase once they recognize that far from exploiting them, we want only to establish a situation in which they can tranquilly cultivate their land, profit from the progress of our industry in refining their [techniques of] production, permit the free exchange of their products for ours, and help them appreciate the value of [our products].[15]

This vision, replete with its paternalist assumptions, did not exclude force as a tool for the advancement of French influence. It merely subordinated its importance. Paris drew the fine line between preserving security and gratuitous adventure. This was clear in the 1884 instructions Minister Peyron sent to Colonel Frey, the new military commander. "Only in the case of direct attack by Amadu, or in the case of his ravaging the land that furnishes us with subsistence for our garrisons and other indispensable resources, only then push Amadu beyond Beledugu, without going too far."[16]

Louis Archinard, military commander during the conquest of the Middle Niger valley from 1888 to 1891 and 1892 to 1893, pushed to the limit the implications of "security."

> To respond to an aggression by pushing directly back to the old line will not produce success for us. The enemy will return, he will have with him the booty taken from our villages, and he will not wait for us. Amadu's lands and ours share too large a space for our small number of soldiers and partisans not to see that by attacking only in self-defense [we] will not stop the ruin of our people ... The necessity of one day taking Segu is recognized everywhere ... I am talking of an eventuality, and I am not asking for an order to take Segu, I am asking only to conserve some liberty of action with all the responsibility it implies for a military leader on campaign, but I ask for permission to decline all responsibility if my freedom of action is taken away.[17]

[15] Rousseau, min. Marine, to gouv. sén., Paris, July 4, 1885, ANM B 165.
[16] Vice Admiral Peyron, min. Marine, to gouv. sén., Paris, Apr. 19, 1884, ANM B 165.
[17] Archinard, letter to gouv. sén., Kayes, Jan. 9, 1890, ANM B 83.

Upon assuming the military command in late 1888, Archinard absorbed Gallieni's inner circle of trusted staff of interpreters and political agents, including Mademba. Archinard did as other military commanders had done: he read voraciously earlier dispatches and reports from the region.

Following the French capture of the Futanke fortress of Koundian in February 1889, Mademba writing from his role within the Political Bureau advised Archinard to redouble his diplomatic outreach to the Bambara of Beledugu. "Now would be an excellent opportunity to affirm our influence in this region" and undermine Amadu's propaganda that he is an ally of the French and thus an ally of the Bambara.[18] As Archinard began planning his march against Segu, his "diplomatic" corps increased their efforts to bring the enemies of the Futanke closer to the French. Mademba played a central role in gathering and synthesizing information collected from a diffuse group of French officers, interpreters, and informants. Only when referring to French officers did Mademba attribute the source. All of his other informants remained anonymous. In July 1889, Archinard returned to France for a short leave. Paris was not pleased with his flaunting of instructions not to engage in aggressive military actions and there was some uncertainty about whether he would return to the Soudan.[19] During his absence, Mademba sent Archinard regular updates on the political situation in the Soudan, especially focusing on Amadu and the wider Futanke empire, Samory, and Tieba. This was the rainy season when most military activities ceased, but not political intrigues. The rainy season especially in Kayes was also a period of precarious health and Mademba informed Archinard about the French officers who had died or were incapacitated because of illness.[20]

Mademba's letters to Archinard during this period were quite long and detailed. These letters were largely filled with information about France's major enemies in the region. Mademba provided detail about Samory's campaign against Tieba in Sikasso and the various intrigues and revolts against his rule. Mademba suggested that the problems Samory faced would likely make for a favorable campaign against him, but Mademba also warned that conditions were still dangerous for French troops and advised that they should not venture too far from their forts.[21] Given Archinard's focus on the Umarian state at Segu, Mademba kept him informed about the state of the Bambara resistance. In a subsequent letter, Mademba informed Archinard about rumors of Karamoko Jara's death. Karamoko was the heir to the Ngolossi

---

[18] Mademba, letter to cmdt. sup. (Archinard), Affaires politiques, Koundian, Feb. 19, 1889, ANS-AOF 1 D 95.
[19] Méniaud, *Pionniers*, vol. 1, 415; Kayes, Sept. 19, 1889, SHD Papiers Réquin (Mademba letters to Archinard) 1 K 108.
[20] Kayes, Aug. 31, 1889, SHD Papiers Réquin (Mademba letters to Archinard) 1 K 108.
[21] Kayes, Aug. 19, 1889, SHD Papiers Réquin (Mademba letters to Archinard) 1 K 108.

dynasty in Segu and a major leader of the Bambara resistance against the Futanke. Within a few weeks, Mademba confirmed Karamoko's death. Mademba wrote that it was not yet clear who would succeed Karamoko, but Mademba hoped that "Karamoko's partisans would rally to N'To and thus form a homogeneous party to sustain the Bambara cause [against the Futanke] which has been weakened by the civil war between Karamoko and N'To."[22] In contrast to these conflicts in neighboring African polities, Mademba assured Archinard that "tranquility reigns everywhere where we have direct administration of the land."[23]

Even as Mademba served as Archinard's political affairs officer, he continued his role as director of telegraph construction. Indeed, several of his political informants were members of his telegraph construction crew.[24] Part of Mademba's expanded portfolio was rather more delicate and revealed an extraordinary level of trust between Mademba and Archinard. It seems that Archinard put Mademba in charge of his household in Kayes. Mademba reported that the package of cloth that Archinard had sent from Saint Louis had arrived and that he had divided the cloth among members of Archinard's household: Bintou received four pieces, Ramata received two, and Dieynaba and Soumba – "the mistress" of the household – each received one piece. Mademba also informed Archinard that Bintou desired a cloth being sold by a local merchant and wanted to pay for that herself, but Mademba bought it for her. Upon learning that Archinard was indeed returning to Kayes, Mademba wrote that "I told Bintou and she was very happy to hear the news. She asked me to tell you of her joy at this news and that all the members of the household are waiting impatiently for your return."[25] Archinard was a bachelor, but notwithstanding this status, it was very common for French officers to have female companions.[26]

Archinard's thinking about a postconquest administration was also spiked by a letter the governor of Senegal received from Under-secretary of State Étienne in February 1890. The supreme military commander of the Soudan reported to the governor of Senegal until 1892, when the Soudan was separated from Senegal administratively.[27] Paris was so worried about cost overruns from military excursions that Étienne was charged with chairing a commission

---

[22] Kayes, Aug. 31, 1889 and Sept. 19, 1889, SHD Papiers Réquin (Mademba letters to Archinard) 1 K 108.

[23] Kayes, Aug. 19, 1889, SHD Papiers Réquin (Mademba letters to Archinard) 1 K 108.

[24] Kayes, Aug. 31, 1889, SHD Papiers Réquin (Mademba letters to Archinard) 1 K 108.

[25] Kayes, Aug. 19, 1889 and Sept. 19, 1889, SHD Papiers Réquin (Mademba letters to Archinard) 1 K 108.

[26] See for example, Michal Tymowski, "Les esclaves du Commandant Quinquandon," Cahiers d'études africaines 158 2000: 351–361.

[27] Minister du commerce, de l'industries et des colonies, Rapport au Président de la République, Paris, Nov. 21, 1893, ANOM Soudan VII-1. Upon Archinard's departure

to examine France's policy in the Soudan.[28] Étienne provided the governor and Archinard a framework for thinking about how the budget debate was shaping policy: there were one-time expenses linked to military expansion and there were recurring costs of administration. Without framing what Paris had in mind, Étienne effectively gave Archinard leeway on one-time military expenses in exchange for planning how to reduce long-term administrative costs.[29] The conquest of Segu gave Archinard the opportunity to put into place his plan for limiting administrative costs.

In conquering Segu in April 1890, Archinard clearly exceeded his ministerial orders, but dismantling the Umarian state had become his overpowering objective. For almost a year in advance, Archinard made secret arrangements for the march to Segu. Stores of munitions and food had to be on hand, bridges built along the proposed route, auxiliaries recruited, and negotiations pursued with the Bambara rebels. Captain Marchand reported from his mission in 1889 to Farako, the headquarters of Jara resistance on the left bank opposite Segu, that the Futanke capital was heavily fortified, and that any attack on the city would require considerable firepower.[30]

The actual march to Segu began nearly two months in advance of the actual storming of the city. Archinard left Kayes, the usual staging point for the annual military campaign, and followed the supply route to Bamako. Along the route, Archinard recruited additional auxiliaries. The two French gunboats, berthed at Koulikoro, joined the procession as it departed for Farako opposite Segu. A flotilla of canoes from Somono villages on the left bank joined to make this expedition a colorful affair and a logistical nightmare (see Map 2.1).

Archinard's army consisted of 720 regular African soldiers, 32 French officers and enlisted men, and 1,500 African auxiliaries who were eager for battle and the plunder that was their reward.[31] Twenty-five years earlier, Mage had reported on the fabulous treasure captured from the Bambara and hoarded by the Futanke.[32] Early on the morning of April 6, 1890, Archinard's troops and artillery were ferried across the Niger on canoes

---

as military commander in 1893, Louis Alphonse Grodet, a civilian functionary, become governor of the Soudan.

[28] Procès verbal, commission du Haut-Fleuve, première session, Paris, Jan. 15, 1890, ANOM Soudan VII-1.

[29] Étienne to gouv. sén., Note relative à notre situation actuelle et à notre avenir dans le Soudan Français, Paris, Feb. 4, 1890, ANM B 165.

[30] Méniaud, *Pionniers*, vol. 1, 459; Lt. Marchand, Mission Marchand, 1889, ANS-AOF 1 G 115. For more detail on the diplomatic engagements between France and the Bambara, see Jennifer Ward, "The French–Bambara Relationship, 1880–1915," University of California, Los Angeles (unpublished PhD dissertation, 1976).

[31] Méniaud, *Pionniers*, 1, 450–451, for a detailed breakdown of the numbers involved.

[32] Ibid., 1, 455; also Lt. Mage, letter to gouv., Segu-Sikoro, Mar. 5, 1864, ANS-AOF 1 G 32.

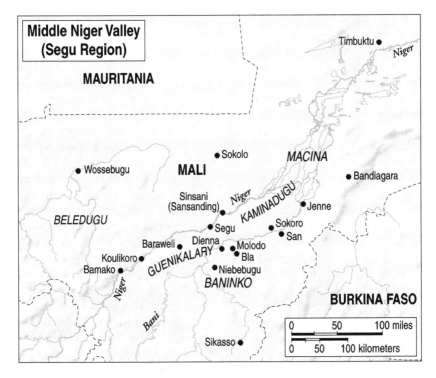

Map 2.1 Middle Niger region

supplied by the Somono from Nyamina and Farako. By early afternoon, Futanke resistance had evaporated and Segu belonged to the French. Although Amadu had managed to strengthen his position within the Umarian leadership in 1884, Segu remained a weak link. In 1887, Lieutenant Caron had reported that Segu was suffering from drought, and that her former enemy, Sinsani, was supplying her with grain.[33] By 1890, the situation had worsened. The Futanke controlled Segu and little else.

Segu fell without resistance, much as it had fallen to the Umarians nearly thirty years earlier. Indeed, Mandani, Amadu's son and the ruler of Segu, had fled the night before, leaving behind a large number of women belonging to senior Futanke leaders.[34] Lieutenant Sensarric quickly occupied the treasury,

---

[33] Caron, letter to cmdt. sup., np, Oct. 31, 1887, ANS-AOF 1 G 83; Lieutenant de Vaisseau E. Caron, *De Saint-Louis au Port de Tombouctou: Voyage d'une canonnière française* (Paris: Augustin Challamel, 1891), 330–331.
[34] Archinard, *Le Soudan Français en 1889–1890*.

but it proved to be almost bare. To halt the auxiliaries' wild scramble for booty, Archinard ordered the *tirailleurs* to chase them out of Segu.[35]

Heady from the military triumph at Segu, Archinard ordered a quick march to the Futanke fortress at Wossebugu in Beledugu. Wossebugu sat astride the important Nioro to Nyamina route that was crucial to the Umarian flow of goods and personnel. As described by Mage, Wossebugu was an "immense village well-fortified with walls" and it remained an important citadel containing 3,000–3,500 inhabitants of whom one-third were warriors and cavalry.[36] Archinard argued that the fall of Wossebugu would fundamentally weaken Amadu's control over Beledugu and thus encourage Bambara support for the French. With a small column of 27 European, 265 African troops, and his Political Bureau including Mademba, Archinard marched on Wossebugu, expecting that it would fall as easily as Segu. Archinard was unprepared for the fierce resistance he found. The French were forced to fight house by house. Mademba joined the battle fighting side-by-side with Lieutenants Alakamessa and Bonnier. During the battle, a Futanke marksman shot Mademba in the stomach. His wound could have been life-threatening, but he was saved by the holster of his pistol and a heavy brass button on his tunic, which deflected the bullet.[37] In many ways, the battle of Wossebugu was a pivotal moment for Mademba. He was already a trusted intermediary. But having been wounded on the field of battle together with his French companions solidified his standing among the French officers of this era of conquest. Although the French prevailed, they and their troops suffered significant losses.[38] Wossebugu was a reminder that the Futanke were not yet ready to acquiesce to French rule. With Wossebugu in French hands, Archinard declared that "I have formally returned Ouossebougou to its former owner, the chief of Digna."[39] This was another indication of Archinard's emerging policy of reviving African political authorities, which had fallen to the "foreign" Muslim conquerors.

Building on Faidherbe and Gallieni's practices, Archinard sought legitimacy for the new colonial state in what he understood to be traditional African political forms. This was particularly so in the case of Segu, which had a long tradition of kinship prior to Futanke conquest. Since 1889, Captain Underberg in Bamako had been following Archinard's instructions to entice the Jara rebel leader to join the French cause. Archinard's goal was to restore the Ngolossi,

---

[35] Archinard, Rapport militaire, Campagne 1889–1890, ANS-AOF 1 D 105.

[36] Eugène Mage, *Voyage dans le Soudan occidental* (Paris: Hachette, 1868), 290–291; Archinard, *Le Soudan Français en 1889–1890*, 35–36.

[37] Archinard, *Le Soudan Français en 1889–90*, 43–44; Méniaud, *Pionniers*, I, 476–448.

[38] Archinard, *Le Soudan Français en 1889–90*, 54. Bonnier would rescue Mademba during the revolt of 1891–1892.

[39] Ibid., 54.

the former Bambara rulers of Segu, to power. The vision of a revived Segu Bambara state was appealing to both the Jara and the French. For the Jara, an alliance with the French might provide a means of rising above the competing loyalties of the resistance movement; for the French, a Jara leader in Segu would provide legitimacy to a French protectorate without the costs of direct administration.[40] Karamoko Jara's death in the summer 1889 muddied considerably Archinard's efforts to revive the Segu Bambara state.

In his effort to identify a single leader to whom he could return the "sovereignty" of the former Segu state, Archinard vastly simplified a highly complex array of factions within the loosely organized Bambara resistance. The Umarian conquest of Segu in 1861 fractured the tenuous unity of the Segu Bambara state and unleashed the centrifugal forces the led to the dispersal of Bambara political and military leaders. The predominant characteristics of Bambara resistance to the Umarians were its small scale, decentralized command, and fluid alliances. No warlord exerted sufficient legitimacy or power to lead. At times, the warlords would fight on the same side, only to become bitter enemies shortly thereafter. It was not uncommon for one faction to leave the battle because it found another opportunity to pillage.

In reflecting on the history of Bambara resistance to the Futanke, the "Resident of Segu" in 1891 noted that "the slave warriors, captives of the *faama* of Segu, were for the Jaras less for reasons of real attachment than because of a community of tastes resulting from long years of pillaging and exactions accomplished together."[41] During the thirty years of Umarian rule, there was no consistent or coherent unity among the Bambara of Segu nor widespread loyalty to the Jara family. According to Al Hajj Soumaila Fane, the Umarian conquest of Segu led to the collapse of whatever unity there may have been among the Bambara of Segu. The Bambara forces separated into four groups, each following different warlords; each fought on their own, for themselves, and for their followers. When I asked why these groups did not form a common front to combat the Futanke, Fane responded "because of their ignorance and rivalries, they did not know how to reconcile each other. If they did briefly unite, they quickly abandoned their friends. The Futanke could never vanquish them, but they could not vanquish the Futanke either."[42] Captain Underberg put the feuding among the Bambara into perspective. "After a short period of apparent submission [to the conquering Futanke in 1861], the resistance broke out forcefully." Mansa Toma was the heir of the N'Golossi. N'To was Mansa Toma's chief *tonjon* warrior. Karamoko

---

[40] For more detail, see Ward, "Bambara–French Relationship."

[41] Briquelot, Rapport sur la situation politique des territoires dépendants de la Résidence de Segou, Segu, Sept. 15, 1891, ANM 1 E 71.

[42] Interview with Al Hajj Soumaila Fane, Tesserela, Jan. 24, 1984.

Jara, however, resented Mansa Toma, who was his brother, and killed him.[43] "An internecine war then broke out among the Bambara. One party, under the orders of N'To, continued to fight against the Tokolors, but refused to obey the orders of Karamoko Jara, the author of the fratricide ... The hate between these two is too violent to seek a peaceful solution."[44]

According to Al Hajj Fane, Karamoko conspired to kill N'To but he escaped and declared himself "neither a partisan of the N'Golossi nor the Futanke. He was only for himself."[45] N'To fled with his followers to the left bank, where he established his base. From Farako and Markadugu, N'To raided Umarian caravans that crossed Beledugu from Nioro to Nyamina. He also led raids northward into Macina and other Futanke strongholds. Never strong enough to defeat the Umarians, N'To led his band in continuous small-scale raids that contributed to the overall insecurity of the region. In 1883, N'To agreed to French protection. In 1887, Lieutenant Caron described the constant feuding among Barbara warlords as feudalism. "Nothing reminds me more of feudalism than the parceling of the land among Karamoko [Jara], N'To, and Mafafa."[46] Captain Underberg called the alliance France had with N'To "purely platonic" and whatever relations the French claimed with N'To were "insignificant."[47] Lieutenant Jaime, who passed through the left bank in 1889, noted that the partisans for N'To and Karamoko Jara were evenly divided, although N'To, "the oldest and the bravest," retained the loyalty of almost all of the *tonjonw* warriors.[48]

Since the Umarian capture of Kaarta in 1855, several Massassi Bambara warlords of Kaarta had drifted eastward to the left bank of the Niger, complicating even further the rivalries and political factions there. Chief among them was Bojan, who had sided with the French and provided auxiliaries for military missions. In 1889, Archinard nonetheless identified Karamoko Jara as the rightful heir to the Segu throne, but with Karamoko's death, his younger brother, Mari Jara, took over the contested leadership among the N'Golossi Jara resistance only on the eve of French conquest.[49] In September 1889,

---

[43] *Fadewnkèlè* is the Bamana term that signifies war among brothers of the same father but usually of different mothers. For more detail, see Roberts, *Warriors*, chapter 2.

[44] Capt. Underberg, letter to Marchand, Bamako, Aug. 24, 1889, ANS-AOF 1 G 115.

[45] Interview with Al Hajj Soumaila Fane, Tesserela, Jan. 24, 1984.

[46] Caron, *De Saint-Louis*, 330.

[47] Capt. Underberg, letter to Marchand, Bamako, Aug. 24, 1889, ANS-AOF 1 G 115.

[48] Lieutenant de Vaisseau Jaime, *De Koulikoro à Tombouctou à bord du "Mage," 1889–1890* (Paris: E. Edentu, 1892), 317.

[49] Archinard, instruction pour l'Ensigne de Vaisseau Jaime, cmdt. le flotilla du Niger, July 2, 1889, Senegal, ANOM Sénégal et dépendances IV-95; Capt. Delaneau, Canonnière Niger, Mission politique, np, Apr. 19, 1886, ANOM Sénégal et dépendances IV-84. Méniaud, *Pionniers*, I, 431; Samba Lamine Traoré, *La saga de la ville historique de Ségou* (Paris: L'Harmattan, 2011), 108, 112.

Captain Marchand began to negotiate with Mari Jara and promised that with the force of French arms and in the name of the French military commander, he would see Mari Jara repossess Segu and the Jara's "ancient patrimony."[50]

Despite the divisions and rivalries among the Bambara, Archinard crowned Mari Jara king of Segu soon after the French conquest. I have no way of knowing whether Archinard saw the coronation as a long-term commitment to African institutions of state or as a temporary expedient. He did, at any rate, crown three additional Africans kings during the next three years, although each had somewhat dubious claims on the offices' political legitimacy.[51] Clearly, Archinard imagined a generic form of African kingship as an adequate solution to the problems of building a new state on the ashes of Futanke rule, of inserting French power in strategic sectors of the new polity, and of reigning in the costs of administering colonial territory.

On April 11, 1890, just after the fall of Segu, Archinard negotiated with Mari Jara about the return of the Jara to the kingdom of Segu. In these deliberations, Archinard was assisted by Mademba and Amadu Coumba, both of whom served in Archinard's political affairs division and both served as interpreters and advisors. Mari Jara was assisted by four of his closest military leaders. Archinard told the assembled chiefs of the larger villages of the Segu heartland that

> Frenchmen have not come to Segu to take the land and to govern themselves, but with the intention of giving to the Bambara that which was stolen by the Futanke. One of the reasons that influenced the French to come is that the Futanke were insolent bandits [and] barriers to free trade. But I know that the Bambara are bandits too, and that they pillaged not only the city but also the goods of other Bambara. This is not good. I will give Segu to the son of your previous kings: your *faama* will be, beginning today, Mari Jara, but under certain conditions that will guarantee that the happiness of the land will be assured, that trade will be free, and that the Bambara of the right bank will not pillage those of the left bank ... To that end, the Commandant Superieur will leave a white officer with his troops here. This Resident will reside in the *Diomfutu* [Amadu's palace]. The French Resident will not occupy himself with the administrative affairs between the *faama* and his neighboring villages. The *faama* will fully exercise his rights and nominate or change his chiefs according to his views, but the Resident has the right to be informed of all that takes place.[52]

[50] Marchand, letter to Capt. Underberg, Nyamina, Sept. 10, 1889, ANS-AOF 1 G 115.

[51] For an important engagement with the invention of tradition debate, see Spear, "Neo-traditionalism and the Limits of Invention in British Colonial Africa."

[52] Archinard, palabre of Apr. 11, 1890 with Mari Jara, Nyamina, Apr. 19, 1890, ANS-AOF 15 G 172; Méniaud, *Pionniers*, 1, 517–519.

Archinard built guarantees for commerce into this contract for a new state. He could do no less since promoting free trade was part of France's justification for conquest. Archinard also stated that the French troops stationed in Segu would be at Mari Jara's disposition, thus lending French military support to the refurbished Segu state.

The *faama*, Archinard further explained, had the right to collect all taxes and revenue that was customarily his to collect. The only exception, Archinard insisted, was that revenue from market taxes, charges from ferrying across the Niger, and fees paid by caravans would be divided into two portions, with one portion going to the French. Archinard separated out two enclaves on the left bank of the Niger – Nango and Sinsani – from Mari Jara's territorial control. "Nango is inhabited above all by the Bambara from Kaarta. This town and its surrounding villages will remain under direct French authority and be administered by one of our most loyal servants." Archinard did not mention him directly, but he gave Bojan the keys to Nango. Bojan had been a principal leader of the largely Beledugu auxiliary troops during the recent Soudanese campaigns, he had served the French well, and Archinard wanted to reward him. But placing Bojan at Nango, only forty kilometers from Segu, made him a direct threat to whatever legitimacy Mari Jara had.

In the April 1890 negotiations, Archinard had not yet decided on what to do with Sinsani. He left it as an autonomous city under the direct authority of the French and dispatched a small contingent of *tirailleurs* to defend it.[53] "Similar to Nango, Sansanding, where there is today almost nothing, the French want to return this town to its former prosperity. Sansanding will remain under direct French authority." At the conclusion of the palabre, Archinard asked Mari Jara if he had any objections to France's stipulations regarding his return to power. Mari Jara responded that he understood well these conditions and that he had no objections.[54]

The day after Segu fell to Archinard, the military commander wrote to the governor of Senegal describing the ease with which the French captured the city. Chiefs from all over the region streamed to Segu to make their submission to him.

> All thank us for having removed the tyranny of the Toucouleur and the return of their liberty. I will remain here for several more days in order to return order to the column, organize the land, and install the Bambara

---

[53] Capt. Menvielle, Notice historique du Royaume et du cercle de Segou, 2ème partie, 1895, Segu. Menvielle's history was reproduced in a brochure by the Commissariat de direction des affaires économiques for the Exposition de Marseille, Paris, June 17, 1922, ANS-AOF 1 G 209.

[54] Palabre, signed by Archinard, Mamadou Racine, Mademba, Amadou Coumba (in Arabic), Bonnier, Underberg, and Quinquadon, Nyamina, Apr. 19, 1890, ANS-AOF 15 G 172.

faama of Segu. I will also install a Resident, who will be the true king and will sign all the treaties that I will authorize in regard to Macina, Timbuktu, and the neighboring lands.[55]

In calling the French "Resident" the true king, Archinard was clearly invoking the asymmetrical dual sovereignty inherent in the protectorate model. France would remain the dominant authority. Although N'To was nominally aligned with the French, Archinard also promised Mari Jara that he would suppress N'To, who remained in revolt against the new *faama*, in order to end the incessant civil wars among the Bambara.

Kanya-Forstner has argued that Archinard's model of returning indigenous rulers to power in regions conquered from the Umarians was "not the product of any firm belief in the principles of 'Indirect Rule.'" Rather, Kanya-Forstner believed that Archinard saw such restitution as a temporary expedient in order to free the French military from the burdens of territorial administration. "In conquered territories, Archinard's principal objective was to maintain sufficient order and security for his columns to concentrate on their military tasks without being distracted by 'petty [administrative] problems.'" He further argued that Archinard understood these polities to be temporary and once conquest was completed, they would fall under direct French administration.[56] In a revealing report written to the under-secretary of colonies in Paris at the end of his 1893 campaign, during which Archinard captured Macina from the Umarians and installed Aguibu as *faama*, Archinard stated that "in Macina, which is a protectorate under the authority of Aguibu and Sansanding and its dependencies, where Mademba rules, our authority is absolute. [My decision to apply the protectorate] is due to political considerations, the desire not to increase the number of European personnel necessary for administration, and to retain a certain degree of autonomy." Archinard was purposefully vague here about the meaning of the protectorate and the place of French direct administration, although he was clearly pushing back against the Ministry of Colonies about the need to control costs. Archinard did not specify what "absolute authority" meant in the context of these protectorates, nor what the protectorate meant in practice.[57] Archinard gave no indication that he understood the terms of precolonial political legitimacy in the African kingdoms he created or recreated.

The state as conceived by Archinard was instrumentalist. He offered no evidence of planning for a state with a distinctive colonial character.[58] Indeed,

[55] Archinard, telegraph to gouv. sén., Bamako, Apr. 12, 1890, ANOM Sénégal et dépendances IV-95.

[56] Kanya-Forstner, *The Conquest of the Western Sudan*, 196–197.

[57] Rapport du Col. Archinard à la fin de mon dernier séjour au Soudan to under-secretary of colonies, Paris, Nov. 1893, ANS-AOF 1 D 137.

[58] Archinard, letter to gouv. sén., Kayes, Jan. 9, 1890, ANM B 83.

the revived Bambara state Archinard created in Segu in 1890 rested on a basic contradiction: warfare was central to the political economy of the precolonial Bambara state and the only warfare the French tolerated was on their own terms.[59] Mari Jara, however, did not or could not control his *tonjonw* followers, who continued to pillage both sides of the river.[60]

On May 29, 1890, only after six weeks as *faama*, Captain Underberg, the Resident at Segu, summoned Mari Jara and his leading councilors to a meeting. Underberg had also ordered Bojan to attend. Underberg accused Mari Jara and his advisers of conspiring to assassinate the French Resident and his troops and declare themselves independent of French overrule. Underberg ordered Mari Jara and his advisors summarily executed.[61] Nowhere in the existing archives is there evidence of Underberg's accusations of Mari Jara's alleged plot.[62]

Archinard had been worried about Mari Jara's weaknesses even before he left Segu in mid April 1890 for Wossebugu. Archinard worried that Mari Jara and the Bambara of Segu could not manage their own affairs and he anticipated that France's long-time ally, Bojan, would eventually sit on the Segu throne.[63] Captain Pérignon, who served as district officer of Segu in 1900, provided a retrospective justification of Underberg's actions.

> Without strength, Mari let his warriors devastate that land and paid no heed to the commitments he entered into during the palabre of 11 April. He also concealed everything from the Resident. On 9 May 1890, his warriors, who wanted to free themselves from our over-rule, organized a plot to massacre the officers of our garrison. Being always indecisive, the Bambara did not quickly act, which permitted the Resident to discover the plot.[64]

The executions of May 29 revealed the weakness in Archinard's generic model of revived traditional African states, for state power among the Segu Bambara depended on a complex relationship between the king and his

---

[59] See Roberts, *Warriors*, chapter 2.

[60] Pérignon, *Haut-Sénégal et Moyen-Niger*, 167; Capt. M. Menvielle, Notice historique du Royaume et du cercle de Segou, 2ème partie, Segu, 1895, ANS-AOF 1 G 209.

[61] Rapport annuel, Notice géographique, historique, topographique et statistique, Segu, 1902, ANM 1 D 127. It is clear that the author has combed the archives for this report.

[62] For more detail, see Sundiata A. Djata, *The Bamana Empire by the Niger: Kingdom, Jihad and Colonization, 1712–1920* (Princeton, NJ: Markus Weiner Publisher, 1997), 125–126.

[63] Archinard, Rapport militaire, campagne 1889–90, ANS-AOF 1 D 105; Capt. M. Menvielle, Notice historique du Royaume et du cercle de Segou, 2ème partie, Segu, 1895, ANS-AOF 1 G 209.

[64] Pérignon, *Haut-Sénégal et Moyen-Niger*, 167. Pérignon will play a central role in protecting Mademba in 1900.

warriors. Immediately following the May 29 executions, Archinard appointed Bojan *faama* of Segu.[65] Archinard had confidence in Bojan's loyalty and ability to command, although Bojan has no legitimate claim on Segu's kingship. Bojan was a chief of the quite separate Beledugu branch of the Bambara, who had established a kingdom in Kaarta. Once he secured his position in Segu, Archinard also ordered Bojan to undertake a mission to Sikasso to negotiate the border between Segu and Sikasso.

Following the executions of May 29, the surviving *tonjonw* and their followers fled Segu into the Baninko region to the southeast that spanned both banks of the Bani River. This was part of the former heartland of the Segu Bambara state and had remained a center of resistance to the Umarians for three decades. Within a few months, the Baninko region was in general revolt against the French. The tiny squadron that Archinard had left behind at Segu was thinly stretched. Bojan was forced to make a hasty return from his mission to Sikasso. Bojan's departure from Segu so soon after his coronation as *faama*, according to Pérignon, "had a bad effect" on the strength of the rebellion.[66]

In May or June 1890, Archinard sent Mademba, now fully recovered from the wound he received at Wossebugu, on a mission to Bandiagara, which was the third of the three linked polities of the Umarian empire. Amadu's brother, Mouniru, ruled there. Nioro remained the capital of the Umarian empire after Amadu's move from Segu to Nioro in 1884, although Nioro exerted little influence on these two other Futanke capitals. Mademba believed that he had established good relations with Mouniru during the latter's visits to Kita and Bamako. However, increased French aggression against the Umarians and the fall of Segu soured whatever good will existed between them. Mademba was not even allowed to meet with Mouniru when he arrived in Mopti and was forced to retreat quickly. Mademba wrote to Archinard that under these conditions any treaty of friendship would be impossible to secure.[67]

Upon Mademba's return from Mopti in August, Archinard ordered him to assemble a column of several thousand African auxiliaries and march into the Baninko.[68] This was a major command for Mademba, who had no formal military training except what he had gained participating in the annual military campaigns after 1883. Never before had Mademba been placed at the head of a major army. Nonetheless, Mademba's army moved boldly into the Bani region, forcing the submission of rebellious villages. By the end of

[65] Capt. Menvielle, Notice historique du Royaume et du cercle de Segou, 2ème partie, 1895, Segu, ANS-AOF 1 G 209; see also Pérignon, *Haut-Sénégal et Moyen-Niger,* 168.

[66] Pérignon, *Haut-Sénégal et Moyen-Niger,* 170.

[67] Mademba, dispatch to Archinard and telegram to gouv. sén., Kayes, July 27, 1890, ANOM Sénégal et dépendances IV-95; Cmdt. Sup. Humbert, Situation du Soudan à la date du Aug. 27, 1890, Kayes, ANS-AOF 15 G 33; Méniaud, *Pionniers,* I, 526.

[68] Méniaud, *Pionniers,* II, 75.

August, Bojan's army of some 4,000 auxiliaries joined Mademba. Overwhelming force helped Mademba and Bojan pacify the region. By early September, Mademba reported that he had captured and summarily executed two of Mari Jara's brothers and captured a third, who had fled deeper into the Baninko. Mademba executed the third brother shortly thereafter.[69] No further news from Mademba arrived and rumors circulated that Mademba had been killed in the Baninko.

Colonel Humbert, who remained in Kayes while Archinard was on the march toward the Futanke fortress of Koniakary, barely repressed his pleasure when Mademba finally arrived there in mid November. Humbert telegrammed the governor of Senegal that Mademba has returned from his mission to the outlying regions of the Bani River in complete health. "Noise of his death has been discredited. Please praise Mademba's highly successful mission at the head of three thousand fighters in the Baninko region in the official journal of the colony."[70] Between being wounded in battle at Wossebugu and his command of African auxiliaries in the Baninko campaign, Mademba had proven his capacity to command and deepened his ties with his fellow French officers.

Mademba arrived in Kayes just in time to prepare for the French march on Nioro. Besides Mademba, Mamadou Racine Sy and William Ponty, serving as Archinard's personal secretary, participated in Archinard's column.[71] On New Year's eve, Archinard marched triumphantly into Nioro without facing any significant resistance. Amadu and the remaining Futanke leadership had fled to Bandiagara, leaving behind members of the leadership's families and those Umarian troops unwilling to follow Amadu eastward. Archinard remained in Nioro accepting delegations from Futanke troops and neighboring villages seeking to make peace with the new conquerors. Archinard did not linger in Nioro, but set out in pursuit of Amadu, seeking to cut off his escape to Macina. Archinard telegrammed Segu to order N'To and his followers to block Amadu from crossing the Niger. Despite their doubts about N'To's loyalty, the French still had confidence in their alliance with him. Unfortunately for the French strategy, the rebellion in the Baninko region roared to life again in mid December and continued well into the new year.[72] By mid February 1891, the combined forces of Archinard's column, N'To's warriors, and Mademba's forces, newly assembled in Nyamina, moved back into the Baninko and squashed the rebellion.[73]

---

[69] Cmdt. Humbert, Situation au Soudan français à la date du Oct. 16, 1890, Kayes, Oct. 17, 1890, ANS-AOF 15 G 33; Cmdt. sup., telegram to gouv. sén., Kayes, Oct. 5, 1890, ANOM Sénégal et dépendances IV-9; Pérignon, *Haut-Sénégal et Moyen-Niger*, 170.

[70] Cmdt. sup., telegram to gouv. sén., Kayes, Nov. 16, 1890, ANOM Soudan I-1.

[71] Sy, "Capitaine Mamadou Racine Sy," 35.

[72] Méniaud, *Pionniers*, II, 16–49.

[73] Capt. Briquelot, Rapport sur la situation politique du territoire dépendant de la residence de Segou, Sept. 15, 1891, ANM 1 E 71; Capt. Underberg, letter to cmdt. sup., Segu, Feb. 10, 1891, ANM 2 D 102. See also Djata, *The Bamana Empire by the Niger*, 126–130.

French conquest of Segu in April 1890 and Nioro in January 1891 sent signals that the French were the new rulers of the land. Village chiefs streamed to Archinard to make their formal obeisance. "Almost all the Blacks," Méniaud wrote, "request nothing more than to be under our direct command without having native chiefs serve as intermediaries." Méniaud's comment that Africans did not want to be ruled by native chiefs, few of whom had the best interests of their communities at heart, is telling. Such direct rule may only have been possible only close to the headquarters of the district officer. Archinard, however, cautioned his district officers, all military men, "to avoid the loss of time needed to intervene in all the little disputes that are particular in nature and instead to direct all disputes between masters and slaves, husbands and wives, landowners in the same villages to the judges of the land who are widely respected: marabouts, elders, even sorcerers." Even though district officers should not intervene in small disputes, they should learn local customs, no matter how rudimentary, in order to improve them, albeit gradually. Archinard instructed his district officers to intervene only in situations where there are conflicts between members of different ethnic groups or religions.[74] As refugees from Futanke rule streamed back to their former homes, they sought to reconstitute their former communities. Archinard believed in "local royalty," whether the imam, another religious leader, or the notable elders, but none should be the "king." "Do not," Archinard cautioned, "constitute kingdoms or powers that are too extended or too considerable in order to avoid difficulties in the future."[75] Archinard did not, however, heed his own cautions regarding reconstituting African kingdoms with powerful kings.

The Baninko rebellion in May 1890 and its revival in December sobered Archinard, for it revealed the immediate weakness of his version of indirect rule. Although his commitment to African kingship as a form of indirect rule was unshaken, he would now only appoint Africans who had proven themselves loyal collaborators, regardless of their traditional claims on kingship. Thus, following the execution of Mari Jara in May 1890, he crowned Bojan *faama* in Segu, but worried about future rebellions. The Segu Bambara, he argued, did not want to be ruled by a Massassi Bambara from Kaarta regardless of his claim to high office. Following the capture of Nioro, Archinard wrote to Eugène Étienne, the powerful undersecretary of state for colonies, on January 9, 1891 that Bojan's kingdom was much too large and unstable for Africans to govern. They constantly produced revolts, and revolts, Archinard did not have to say, raised ever greater financial demands on the ministry

---

[74] Méniaud, *Pionniers*, II, 54–55. See also Col. Trentinian's similar remarks to French military serving as district officers in 1896, Lt.-gouv. col. Trentinian, Note circular, Bamako, Feb. 3, 1896, ANM 2 M 4.

[75] Méniaud, *Pionniers*, II, 56.

because of the costs of pacification. "I have thought," he reported, "that it will be good to establish a second kingdom next to that of Segu, a kingdom that will be powerful and devoted and that could extend toward Jenne, where it will eventually place its capital. This kingdom will be formed out of the land of the left bank of the Niger ... The new chief will reside in Sinsani." Archinard concluded that the only problem with this model of the state was to find a suitable candidate. He then proposed Mademba Sèye, whose devotion and leadership were clearly proven.[76] He waited, however, until early March 1891 before acting on his idea of a new African kingdom carved out of Segu.

On January 29, 1891, while still in Nioro, Mademba was put in charge of 2,000 of Amadu's former warriors who had surrendered to the French in Nioro and whose submission had been accepted by Archinard. Most of these former Umarian warriors were originally from the Middle Niger valley.

> After Amadu's escape from Nioro, all the slave soldiers came to me requesting a new master. Almost all of these were Bambara, who had gotten rewards from serving Amadu. I have given these prisoners to Mademba, just as I gave the prisoners of Segu to Bojan. Here is a good army of some 2,000 professional warriors, who in the hands of an able leader, can further our goals in the region and especially help to rid the land of dangerous looters.[77]

The status of these prisoners of war (*sofa*) remained ambiguous. On the one hand, they were prisoners. On the other, they remained armed soldiers. The best analogy was probably something akin to the slave soldiers of the old Segu Bambara kingdom. These *tonjonw* were simultaneously slaves and soldiers, who were loyal to their masters only as long as their masters provided for their material well-being through successful warfare and the sharing of the booty. The French military in the Soudan had long used such prisoners of war as part of their auxiliary troops. Exactly what the conditions were of Amadu's former troops surrender and subsequent assignment to Mademba remains unclear, although they recognized that they were Mademba's men and obliged to serve him.[78] As part of their service, these *sofa* owed Mademba both military service and labor service.[79] One of my informants in Sinsani captured the ambiguity of the *sofa*'s status. "Some say that the *sofa* were slaves. That is both true and

---

[76] Archinard, letter to under secretary for colonies, Nioro, Jan. 9, 1891, ANOM Soudan I a.

[77] Méniaud, *Pionniers*, II, 77, 82.

[78] In 1899, these *sofa* of Mademba petitioned the French district officer in Segu for their unconditional freedom and end of their service to Mademba. See Chapter 8 for further discussion.

[79] Capt. Pérignon noted that Mademba's *sofa* "owed him a certain amount of labor each month," which meant either a labor obligation or a share of the harvest. Capt. Pérignon, Rapport à gouv.-gen. sur les faits attribués à M. Mademba, Segu, Mar. 15, 1900, ANS-AOF 15 G 176.

false. Some of our ancestors sided with Seku Omar [Tal] because of religion and continued with him until they encountered the French." When I asked why the *sofa* remained with Mademba if they were not slaves, Alassane Togora responded that "The *faama* allowed them to do whatever they wished. They pillaged the people in order to sell [their looted goods]. They were feared."[80] Gausu Cisse reiterated this point when he said that "when the *sofa* were installed in Sinsani, they pillaged everyone. That is the reason why the villages did not want anything to do with the *sofa* because the *faama* gave them the power to abuse the people."[81] Binke Baba Kuma had a slightly different sense of the *sofa*'s relationship with Mademba. He referred to them as "*suruka*" or seasonal workers who worked for a *jatigi* [Bambara: host, employer] three or four days a week. The rest of the time they worked for themselves. "The *suruka*, the Bambara, the Maraka, everyone worked for [Mademba]."[82] According to Al Hajj Soumaila Fane, "The *sofa* were under the authority of the *faama*, but they considered themselves superior to all the others. The *sofa* were the chiefs of the others, but they were Mademba's people. They were like our current soldiers. They were not slaves, but they could not do anything without their chief telling them what to do."[83]

Contemporary French observers shared the sense of ambiguities in the status of the *sofa*. Lieutenant Hourst defined *sofa* as prisoners of war (*captifs militaires*).[84] During his tour of Sinsani in 1900, Lieutenant Veil defined the *sofa* as "not merely the men with arms, but all slaves of the crown."[85] We actually have testimony from one of Mademba's *sofa* who was interviewed in Sinsani in 1899. Canouba Jara, who served Mademba as one of his main guards, described his status "We are all slaves by order of the French and now belong to the *Fama*."[86] In addition to military service, the *sofa* worked on Mademba's fields five days a week. They were also obliged to give Mademba a third of the harvests on their own fields, which they worked during their free time.[87] In addition to the 2,000 slave soldiers, their families, and their slaves, Somono who had been resettled in Nioro, and other original inhabitants of the Niger River region also received permission to accompany Mademba on his march back to the Middle Niger valley. In total,

[80] Interview with Alassane Togora, Sinsani, July 12, 1992.
[81] Interview with Gausu Cisse, Sinsani, July 12, 1992.
[82] Interview with Binke Baba Kuma, Sinsani, July 7, 1992.
[83] Interview with Soumaila Fane, Tesserela, July 15, 1992.
[84] Hourst, *Sur le Niger et au Pays des Touaregs*, 265.
[85] Lt. Veil, Rapport au sujet de son séjour à Sansanding du 16 au 19 Janvier, Segu, Jan. 21, 1900, ANS-AOF 15 G 176.
[86] Deposition, Canouba Jara, in Capt. Lambert letter to lt.-gouv. pi, Segu, Nov. 28, 1899, ANS-AOF 15 G 176.
[87] Cmdt. Segu, letter to Resident at Sinsani, Segu, July 29, 1904, ANM 2 D 102.

Mademba's column consisted of around 7,000. In Binke Baba Kuma's telling, Mademba's entourage was 7,700.[88]

Méniaud's description of Mademba's column as it entered Nyamina in early February 1891, drawn from Archinard's writings, is worth presenting.

> It is truly curious, the parade of Mademba's column, which was a pleasure to see. There was indeed a certain regularity to this parade, which Mademba has organized into smaller groups. Women were especially numerous. Many were on horseback carrying themselves happily and proudly. Taking turns, the warriors led the horses and children followed . . .

> With his Cross of the Legion of Honor displayed on his boubou, Mademba followed closely the griots and flute players who led the parade. To understand how one must lead the blacks, one must emulate their ways of being and one can no longer find in [Mademba] the Black from Saint Louis, who was strong physically and emotionally like our gradu- ates, and who when he walked along the boulevards of Paris in 1883, could be mistaken for an African king. "I am only an employee of the telegraph service," he responded, "and at the service of France." He has always been at the service of France and he remains, admired and loved by all who have had him under their orders and who have seen him in battle.[89]

Méniaud's reconstruction of Archinard's description of Mademba should have given pause when Archinard noted that the once cosmopolitan African employee of the colonial Post and Telegraph Department had morphed into an African king.

Arriving in Nyamina, Mademba was ordered to leave the women and children in that city and lead his soldiers across the river and into the Baninko region once again. The news Archinard had received was that the situation in Baninko was deteriorating. At the end of February, Mademba's troops joined French troops and N'To's auxiliaries outside of the rebel center of Dougoutiguila. After a fierce battle, Mademba and his troops participated in further pacification, including another battle for Diena, before returning to Nyamina.

Once back in Nyamina, Archinard made Mademba king, *faama* of Sansanding. On March 7, 1891, Archinard crafted a letter of investiture that created a new kingdom and crowned Mademba king of Sinsani.

> In the name of France, which I represent here [in the Soudan] and awaiting final approval by the Minister of Colonies, I hereby grant you the suzerainty over the territories of the left bank of the Niger that actually

---

[88] Méniaud, *Pionniers,* II, 79. Interview with Binke Baba Kuma, Sinsani, Dec. 19, 1976. In Bambara cosmology, 7,700 is a magic number.

[89] Méniaud, *Pionniers,* II, 88.

are part of the land of Segu and are not part of the district of Bamako; over the region of Sarro; over the region of Monimpe; and over the cities of Sansanding and Sokolo.

Archinard's choice of the term "suzerainty" is telling. The term was not sovereignty, which would have implied self-rule; instead, the term referred to a level of authority over indigenous rulers in these areas.[90] It signified a form of superordinancy. But it was a form of superordinancy constrained by its dependency upon France. Archinard's use of "suzerainty" may not have been self-conscious in invoking the presumed superior supremacy of France over Mademba's new kingdom, but this is clearly what he meant. In so doing, Archinard created a protectorate in which Mademba ruled.

> You have agreed with me and by extension with France to accept the task of governing these provinces as the Blacks prefer to be governed, but also in the spirit of justice, humanity, and disinterestedness that places the wellbeing of your subordinates above the personal gratifications of those who govern ... All the populations [of your new kingdom] hope to see arrive, with your effort and with the help of France, an era of peace and prosperity, which has been out of reach for so long.

Archinard's instructions here reflected the model of a senior bureaucrat rather than a suzerain, who works disinterestedly for the good of the community.

> Confident in the devotion you have shown in the past and until this day to France, I have put in your hands all the resources that I control after the submission of Kaarta and you command today a large army that you will build even stronger by recruiting from your villages ... You agree to work with all your capacity for the development of the lands of the blacks under French influence and to further our ideas of civilization and our commerce.

Later in the letter of investiture, Archinard further circumscribed the new kingdom's suzerainty.

> In return for the power, the resources, and the assistance we have given you, you agree to always recognize the suzerainty of France over the lands you command. Moreover, you agree to furnish the French garrisons in your lands with provisions from the region ... and an annual obligation to furnish twenty good war horses to the Commandant Superieur of the Soudan. Once you have fulfilled these conditions, you are entitled to keep all the charges you will levy from your provinces and towns.

---

[90] See, for example, Luise White and Douglas Howland, eds., *State of Sovereignty: State, Laws, Populations* (Bloomington: Indiana University Press, 2009); Steven Press, "Sovereignty at Guantánamo: New Evidence and a Comparative Historical Interpretation," *Journal of Modern History* 85 (3) 2013: 592–631; Benton and Ford, *Rage for Order*.

By recognizing France's suzerainty, Mademba also agreed not to enter into any treaties without the formal consent of the supreme military commander. Moreover, Mademba had no legal authority over any Europeans who may reside, voyage, or conduct commerce in his kingdom. "The French Resident at Segu represents France throughout this region. It is therefore foremost that you will have relations with him and will conform to his plans for the region." This line underscored Archinard's understanding already in Mari Jara's investiture of April 1890 that the French Resident was the real "king" of the region.

Archinard placed Mademba and his new army in Sinsani to serve as an advanced sentinel on the route to Macina. Indeed, Archinard anticipated that once France conquered Macina, which was the last bastion of Futanke power, Mademba would become *faama* over a kingdom that extended up to Timbuktu. Archinard envisioned that once Mademba became ruler over Macina, he would renounce his claims over the Bambara lands of the left bank, resettle in Macina, and concern himself with extending French influence and authority northward and eastward into the vast Niger Bend region (see Figure 2.1).

Archinard did not consider Mademba's kingdom transitory. Instead, he wrote that although the moment was not quite right to discuss the issue of dynastic succession, he promised that the French government would do so eventually. Archinard stated that he spoke for the French government in assuring Mademba that the kingship would be "transmissible from father to son with special agreement for each of your descendants who may be called upon to succeed you." Archinard then promised to send one or several of Mademba's sons to France with the goal of preparing them to succeed Mademba and to continue the work of promoting "our ideas of civilization."[91]

In a letter to Captain Briquelot, who was newly appointed Resident of Segu in March 1891, Archinard further circumscribed his model of indirect rule and the role of African kings, especially Bojan, recently named *faama* of Segu. "You are in regard to the empire of Segu a virtual commandant de cercle. *Faama* Bojan is your intermediary to permit you to govern without us having to impose too quickly our European ideas." Archinard further argued that relying on African kings offered significant cost advantages. "At the same time, the authority given to Bojan permits us to minimize the use of our personnel that would require significant resources and reassures our black souverains, who are our neighbors. They will understand that far from supplanting them, on the contrary, our goal is to provide them with stable authority over the long

---

[91] Lettre de investiture de M. Mademba, in Pérignon, Généralités sur Haut Sénégal Moyen Niger, 1900, ANS-AOF 1 G 248; see also Méniaud, *Pionniers*, II, 117–120 for a copy of this letter of investiture.

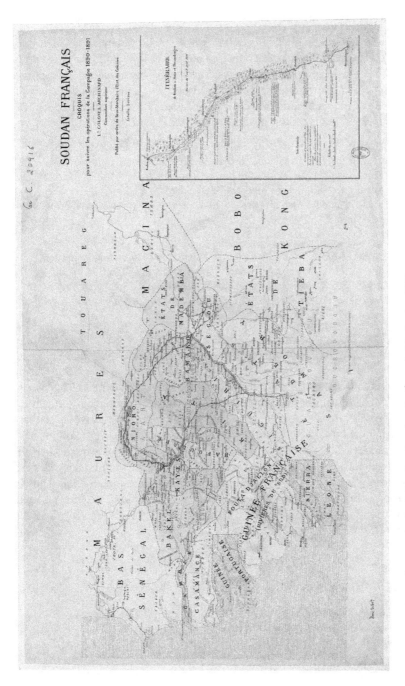

Figure 2.1 Archinard, map of *French Soudan* showing the États de Mademba, 1891.
(Source: Louis Archinard, *Soudan français: Croquis pour suivre les opérations de la campagne 1890–1891* [Paris: Sous-secrétariat d'État des colonies, ca. 1891].
Note États de Mademba. Reproduced with Permission from the Bibliothèque Nationale de France)

term."[92] The year 1891 marked a significant moment in Archinard's thinking about African kingship and the French model of indirect rule. Archinard's ideas were not influenced by the classic British thinking along these lines, since in 1891, Frederick Lugard was only just beginning to reorder the kingdom of Buganda, which served as his original canvass for his model of indirect rule later articulated most fully for Northern Nigeria. In a letter to his sweetheart in June 1891, Briquelot described how he understood Archinard's model of the protectorate and his task in governing the land.

> I am very satisfied to be in Segu because I am well installed here and because there is so much for me to do and so much is interesting. At Segu, I find myself at the forefront of our march towards the interior of Africa. I also direct the internal and above all external administration of three black kingdoms that are tied to us by treaties of protectorate or by other means.

> Here at Segu, where we last year returned the land to the former chiefs dispossessed by Amadu's father. The [kingdom] at Sansanding we created this year. We have placed there one of our most intelligent and faithful servants. It is here that shepherds become kings! The [kingdom] of Kenedugu has existed before we arrived and we have not yet attached it to us.[93]

Elsewhere in his instructions to Briquelot, Archinard anticipated that Mademba may have some trouble with his prisoners of war, those given to him by Archinard following the fall of Nioro. "Avoid with great care any actions that may be used by these warriors against Mademba. That would place Mademba in an impossible situation, which would remain difficult for considerable time."[94] Archinard suggested rounding up the wives of these former Futanke soldiers who might still be in Segu, and who may not have been remarried by the French Resident or Bojan as spoils of war, and permitting Mademba the opportunity of redistributing them in Sinsani. Archinard was keenly aware of how conquest bequeathed to the conqueror the rights to distribute captured booty, of which women were among the most prized. Redistributing the booty was a core principle of the relationship between warriors and rulers in West Africa.[95]

---

[92] Extrait des instructions remises par le cmdt. sup. au Résident de Segu, Nyamina, Mar. 9, 1891, quoted in Méniaud, *Pionniers*, II, 123.

[93] Cmdt. Briquelot, letter to Pauline, Segu, June 7, 1891, in *Lettres et carnets de route du Commandant Briquelot de 1871 à 1896: Correspondances*, ed. André Audbry (Paris: Manuscrit.com, 2003), 211–212.

[94] Extrait des instructions remises par le cmdt. sup. au Résident de Segu, Nyamina, Mar. 9, 1891, quoted in Méniaud, *Pionniers*, II, 125–126.

[95] Roberts, *Warriors*, chapter 2.

Early in March 1891, Mademba reassembled his huge entourage of soldiers, their wives and children, and their herds in Nyamina. Mademba marched toward Sinsani, most likely with his griots and flute players leading his "parade" as they had done upon entry to Nyamina in February. On March 15, 1891, just a week after Archinard has crowned him king, Mademba entered Sinsani. "I have the honor to inform you," Mademba wrote to Captain Briquelot, the current Resident of Segu, "that I have arrived at Sansanding and I have assumed the functions of *faama* conforming to the customs of the country. The village of Sansanding has received me with great enthusiasm. I received the same reception from all the villages along my route." Once settled in Sinsani, Mademba sent our runners to alert all of the villages in his new kingdom to his arrival and to make their submission to him. "The chiefs and elders come to me in Sansanding," Mademba wrote, "to hear how I will administer the country."[96] Among the paradoxes of Mademba's rise to king was that the paper he used to write to Captain Briquelot still had the letterhead of his former job, "Controleur chef du Service technique des Postes et Télégraphes du Soudan." Mademba had merely crossed out his former title. But this was no mere use of an old letter head for his new title. Under the authority of the governor of Senegal and the under-secretary of state for colonies, Mademba was formally seconded to his new position as king and was permitted to retain his salary and "advantages stemming from his functions as controller of posts and telegraphs in the Upper River."[97] Mademba was simultaneously an African king and employee of the colonial state.

More concerning, however, was Mademba's statement that "he had assumed the functions of *faama* conforming to the customs of the land." Sinsani had never had a king, so there was no obvious customs to draw on. As a child of the French colonial city of Saint Louis, Mademba had little if any direct experience with African customs of kingship. Mademba's only exposure to African kingship was through his treaty-making experience or on the battlefield. Nor was Archinard overly concerned with the customs or even legitimacy of his newly created kingdoms. Instead, Archinard empowered Mademba to invent the customs of kingship. And this Mademba set out to do in his new kingdom and in the process remake himself yet again.

---

[96] Mademba, Fama de Sansanding et Dépendances to M. le Résident de Segou, Sinsani, 16 Mar 1891, ANM 1 E 220.

[97] Chef du 1ère Bureau, note pour le Bureau technique, Paris, Mar. 31, 1891, ANOM Dossiers personnels (Mademba) 2862.

3

"A World of Deception and Defection"

Misrule, Rebellion, and Indirect Rule Revisited, 1891–1895

The capital of Mademba's new kingdom in March 1891 was a mere shadow of its former grandeur. Thirty years of Futanke overrule in the region and three decades of rebellion and resistance had led to the decline of the once flourishing entrepôt on the left bank of the Niger River. During his tour of Sinsani in 1886, Captain Delanneau of the gunboat "Niger" described the town as "a mass of ruins ... without the importance it once had." Despite their periodic campaigns, the Umarians were unable to seize the town and suppress resistance on the left bank. The cost of incessant war to the economic life of Sinsani was high. Futanke leaders' efforts to block commercial movement along the Niger toward Timbuktu and upstream to the southern trade routes had reduced Sinsani's market to mere local transactions. "The inhabitants," Delanneau wrote, "have retired to interior villages, where they more easily conduct their affairs," leaving Sinsani an empty shell.[1] In recognition of Sinsani's long resistance against the Futanke, immediately after the fall of Segu in April 1890, Archinard agreed "to protect" Sinsani and to leave that city outside of a newly reconstituted Segu Bambara kingdom in exchange for an annual payment.[2] Archinard, however, expected that once Segu fell to the French, the riverine cities of Nyamina, Sinsani, Jenne, and Timbuktu would once again become major commercial centers and rebuild their wealth and influence.[3]

This chapter examines Archinard's model of indirect rule in practice. Despite Archinard's efforts to respect African customs of political rule, few of the Africans he chose to be rulers had legitimate claims on the positions that they were to hold. Instead, Archinard chose them because they had proven themselves loyal to the French and capable of commanding warriors. In the

---

[1] Capt. Delanneau, Canonnière "Niger" mission politique, rapport du commissaire du gouv., np, Apr. 19, 1886, ANOM Sénégal et dépendances IV-84; Jaime, *De Koulikoro*, 155.

[2] Archinard, telegram to gouv. sén., Bamako, Apr. 12, 1890, ANOM Sénégal et dépendances IV-95.

[3] Archinard, letter to sous sec. d'État, Kayes, Jan. 20, 1890, ANOM Sénégal et dépendances IV-95; see also Colonel Archinard, *Le Soudan en 1893* (Le Havre: Imprimerie de la Société des Anciens Courtiers, 1895), 18–19.

case of Sinsani, where Archinard installed Mademba as *faama*, the inhabitants of the city had never had nor sought political sovereignty. The Maraka, Bambara, and Bozo inhabitants of Sinsani had been content to leave the political kingdom to the ruling dynasties of nearby Segu and devote themselves to their commercial, clerical, agricultural, and fishing endeavors. Archinard's model of indirect rule and the individuals he chose to lead these kingdoms quickly came to haunt the French as overlapping rebellions against these French-imposed rulers erupted in several regions of the Middle Niger valley. Far from reducing the costs of administration, as Archinard had peddled to the Ministry of the Navy as the solution to the challenges of administering a huge new territory, these failed experiments in indirect rule led to massive new costs as the French were obliged to repress the rebellions. Far from transforming conquered territory into colonial spaces and conquered Africans into loyal subjects, French conquest unleashed new expressions of deep-seated enmity and grievances (see Map 3.1).

Old Rivalries and Indirect Rule in the Middle Niger

Upon their arrival, Mademba's large retinue swelled Sinsani's sparse population. Mademba's *sofa* and their families needed to be housed amid the ruins and fed. Mid March also signaled the beginning of the agricultural cycle. The arrival of several thousand men, women, and children stressed Sinsani's already shattered landscape. Mademba chose a central location in Sinsani for the construction of his palace – chasing off the current village chief, Kami Kuma, from the choice parcel of over one hectare. According to Binke Baba Kuma, Mademba appropriated everything he wanted, including 400 hectares of land upon which "everybody worked for him: Bamana, Bozo, Maraka, *sofa*. The Bozo fished for him." Mademba's *sofa* occupied "the empty spaces" among the ruins, which eventually became the quarter of the *sofa*.[4] Arriving late in the dry season "without provisions and without resources was particularly hard on the *sofa*" wrote a French officer in a historical perspective penned in 1896. The *sofa* were forced to live in huts built of straw until they could construct more durable residences and many feared being "isolated and abandoned in Sansanding with a chief they did not know."[5]

  Binke Baba Kuma also noted that Mademba's *sofa* were far from being a coherent group. "It was Archinard who gave these *sofa* to Mademba. They

---

[4] Collective interview with Binke Baba Kuma and Kuma elders, Sinsani, July 17, 1992. Binke Baba added that this appropriation of urban land for Mademba and for his *sofa* was the cause of the current conflict over land in Sinsani – over a hundred years later.

[5] No author, Notices historiques du Royaume de Segou, 2ème partie, np, 1896, ANM 1 D 55-2.

Map 3.1   Sinsani and Middle Niger region

were composed of people from Nioro, from Fouta, from Samory Turé."[6] French sources put the number of *sofa* at just over two thousand with four hundred horses. Many *sofa* felt disappointed to have been separated from the main French column headed by Archinard because they believed that they would be auxiliaries of the great French commander and thus likely recipients of significant booty. "Great was their disappointment when they separated from the column and took the route to Sansanding." Not surprisingly, a number of *sofa* deserted with the onset of the insurrection later that year.[7]

---

[6] Interview with Binke Baba Kuma, Sinsani, 19 December 1976.
[7] No author, Notices historiques du Royaume de Segou, 2ème partie, np, 1896, ANM 1 D 55-2.

The *sofa* were effectively prisoners of war and thus reluctantly Mademba's people.

In response to my question about why the French made Mademba *faama* of Sinsani, Binke Baba Kuma pointed to the bargains of collaboration.

> The French brought Mademba to Sinsani. After their victories one after the other, they arrived at Segu, where they found that the Peuls of Fouta and Amadu had fled. Having discovered that they did not have a chief who pleased them, they installed Mademba as *faama*. They had confidence in him. They came from Senegal together with Mademba and he was their man of confidence. They did not know anyone here in Sinsani. They gave Mademba also the regions of Sana and Kala. Mademba commanded the Bamana. I will tell you that it was due to [Mamadou] Racine, who recommended Mademba originally to the French. They installed Bojan in Segu. They installed men they had confidence in.

Binke Baba went on to say that while Mademba was in Nyamina, even before Archinard made him *faama*, one of Sinsani's notables visited Mademba and urged him to come to Sinsani. When I pressed Binke Baba to elaborate whether this notable was a member of the chiefly family of Sinsani, he deferred from identifying the person except to say that "there were people among us who wanted new power ... Mademba finally installed one of them as chief." Three months after Mademba arrived in Sinsani, Binke Baba's grandfather, the village chief, died and Mademba appointed Boua Cisse as chief.[8]

What Mademba probably did not know was that the Kuma and the Cisse had long been rivals in Sinsani and had long struggled over the chieftaincy. This rivalry goes back at least to the Bambara civil war of 1790 and resumed every time a new *faama* was installed in Segu. Lamine Cisse served as Sinsani's chief on the eve of Al Hajj Umar's march to the Middle Niger valley in 1860 and remained loyal to the Segu Bambara until the Umarian conquest. As Umar approached Nyamina, Koromama Kuma secretly promised that the gates of Sinsani would be open to him and his army. Lamine urged resistance, but capitulated just before Umar's arrival at Sinsani. Umar removed Lamine and appointed Koromama Kuma as the new chief. Because of excessive demands on Sinsani for revenue, in 1863, Sinsani's inhabitants joined the widespread regional revolt against the Umarians. Between 1863 and 1865, the Umarians laid siege to Sinsani and nearly decimated the town. Sinsani continued its resistance against the Umarians until the arrival of Archinard.[9] Boua Cisse wasted little time in seeking a new patron and in promoting his interests in becoming chief.

---

[8] Interview with Binke Baba Kuma, Sinsani, July 17, 1992.
[9] For more detail, see Roberts, *Warriors*, 84–89, 97–99.

The Kuma–Cisse rivalry in the heart of Mademba's new capital was only a small part of a patchwork of wider and deeper rivalries throughout his new kingdom. Archinard forged the State of Sansanding and Dependencies out of areas that had long fought against the Futanke in Segu and Macina and consisted of groups that had moved in and out of alliances with the Futanke and with the rebels. Each village and regional chief had long-standing grievances against neighbors, local rivals, and overlords. Three decades of resistance to the Futanke had instilled a sense of political and territorial autonomy that flew in the face of France's goal of creating strong, loyal, and stable African kingdoms. In 1893, fresh from his victory over the Futanke of Macina and his suppression of the revolts in the Segu and Sinsani kingdoms, Archinard admitted that "it was difficult to organize definitely the territory that we did not completely understand and the people who did not understand France's goals; recent revolts challenged and disrupted our authority. This situation made more difficult the bright goals we had for *Fama* Mademba, who found himself amid more deception and defections than we had expected."[10] What role, however, did Mademba play in events of 1891 and 1892 that necessitated a French column to rescue him? What did the revolt against Mademba mean for Archinard's indirect rule policy?

Mademba and the Sinsani Revolt

Among Mademba's first tasks in his new role as *faama* was to expect the ritual submission of neighboring and regional chiefs and to lay claim to boundaries of his new kingdom only vaguely defined by Archinard's letter of investiture. Within two days of his arrival in Sinsani, Mademba wrote to the Resident of Segu, to whom he was obliged to report regularly, that

> the village of Sansanding has received me with enthusiasm. It was the same through all the villages I passed since Ganguie, located to the west. I have not yet seen all the territory [of my kingdom] in order to report on the spirits of the population. I have also sent runners to all the important villages and cantons [to summon] the chiefs and notables to see me in Sansanding in order to hear about my plans to administer the land.[11]

Mademba expected these chiefs and notables to make their formal submission to his authority. Mademba drew on a Mande ritual *ka kaliya*, which was to entrust or to give oneself to another, usually a superior power.[12] Mademba demanded this act of submission and harbored grievances when it was not

---

[10] Archinard, Rapport sur la campagne 1892–93, Paris, Nov. 1893, ANS-AOF 1 D 137.

[11] Mademba, letter to the Resident of Segu, Sinsani, Mar. 16, 1891, ANM 1 E 220.

[12] Many thanks to Jan Jansen for explaining this term, personal communication, May 1, 2014.

performed. Mademba also alerted the Resident that he was sending spies throughout his kingdom to gather intelligence, especially about Amadu, whose flight from Nioro brought him to the northern reaches of Mademba's kingdom. In another letter, Mademba requested that Captain Underberg, the Resident of Segu, send him several loads of kola nuts, which he wanted to give to his spies in order to disguise them as merchants.[13] Throughout his long tenure, Mademba relied on spies to provide him with information not only about threats to French control but also about any dissent against his rule.

Mademba lost no time in staking claim to the sovereignty of his kingdom by establishing customs collectors. Customs, or the 10 percent *wusuru* collected on all goods entering a kingdom, was a major source of revenue for African and colonial states alike. But one kingdom's customs bumped up against another polity's revenue. And collecting the *wusuru* several times on the same merchant would cut deeply into the merchant's profits and discourage commerce. When a merchant first crossed Mademba's kingdom and paid customs at one of the three villages along the major caravan routes, he would often have to pay a second time when he crossed into Bojan's kingdom a few days later. Mademba wrote to Underberg that this situation was detrimental to commerce and that Underberg should discuss this with Bojan and arrange that traders should not be taxed twice. Mademba did not volunteer, however, to share his customs revenue with Bojan.[14]

Mademba was quite concerned about maximizing revenue for his new state. He had significant responsibilities as *faama*, including his obligation to provide food for his *sofa* as well as his extended household. He also had to provide food for the workers who were building his palace and rebuilding the town's outer walls. Even if such labor was unpaid, Mademba nonetheless was obliged to provide subsistence to the workers. Thus, when the townspeople of Sinsani protested the order to pay head taxes in French coin, Mademba readily agreed to accept cowries and payment in kind.[15] Mademba was also responsible for providing subsistence whenever he hosted an official visitor or a contingent of troops. Tax payments in the form of commodities could be used to feed his workers and visitors. Townspeople in Sinsani complained about the nearly continuous demands Mademba made on their stores of food.[16]

Part of Mademba's strategy in maximizing his revenue and his authority was to push the boundaries of the ill-defined territory of the États de Sansanding as far as possible, thus increasing the sources of tax revenue. But it also meant a larger potential number of political problems to resolve. Within

---

[13] Mademba, letter to the Resident of Segu, Sinsani, Mar. 18, 1891, ANM 1 E 220.

[14] Mademba, letter to the Resident of Segu, Sinsani, Mar. 21, 1891, ANM 1 E 220. For more on the French debates about the *wusuru*, see Roberts, *Warriors*, 58–61, 68.

[15] Mademba, letter to the Resident of Segu, Sinsani, Apr. 30, 1891, ANM 1 E 220.

[16] See Chapter 7 for more detail drawn from townspeople's depositions.

a month in his new office, Mademba enacted a judgment issued by Underberg in Segu regarding a dispute between N'To and the Kabankao, a group residing to the northwest of Sinsani. Both fell within Mademba's kingdom. Apparently this dispute dealt with a set of reciprocal raids between these two groups. Both groups had long relied on raids as part of their political and economic resistance to the Futanke, and French conquest did not end their activities. The tension between N'To and the Kabankao, however, started when Karamoko Jara poisoned Mansa Toma. The Kabankao remained loyal to the Jara dynasty. N'To, who was loyal to Mansa Toma, refused to recognize Karamoko as *faama* and revolted. Following Underberg's instructions, Mademba oversaw the return of livestock and slaves captured by each group but this did not end the hostility between these groups. As Captain Briquelot retrospectively noted, "It was only by misunderstanding the Bambara that we could have thought that this act would end the dispute. New grievances emerged within the year."[17]

By the end of April 1891, barely two months into his rule, Mademba was able to extend his authority however briefly into the Sahel north of Sokolo. A combined group of Mademba's *sofa*, N'To's warriors, and men from Sokolo arrested the marabout Hanine, a Maure closely associated with Amadu. The supreme military commander had ordered Hanine's arrest. Mademba was obviously pleased with the success of this mission, which tested the military prowess of his new kingdom: he redistributed the booty from Hanine's capture, including livestock and slaves, to the forces that captured Hanine. Mademba's redistribution of the booty was a signal part of the social contract between the ruler and his warriors in precolonial Western Sudan. Mademba wasted no time before executing Hanine in Sinsani.[18] Hanine's execution was the first recorded execution in the new state of Sansanding, but it was not Mademba's first execution. He had already bloodied his hands executing the Jara rebels in the Baninko rebellion of 1890–1891. Nor would it be the last execution in Sinsani. Mademba understood the right to execute a prisoner as a core component of his sovereignty and he did not hesitate to use this authority when he felt challenged. In May, Mademba executed Birama Couilibaly, likely one of his *sofa*, who had deserted with a rifle.[19] Such executions, however, blurred the lines between internal and external sovereignty inherent in the

---

[17] Capt. Briquelot, Rap. sur la révolte du Royaume de Sansanding, Segu, Apr. 1, 1892, ANS-AOF 15 G 172; Mademba, letter to the Resident of Segu, Sinsani, Apr. 14, 1891, ANM 1 E 220.

[18] Briquelot, Résident Segu, letter to cmdt. sup. p.i., Segu, Aug. 26, 1891, ANM 1 E 219; Mademba, letter to the Resident of Segu, Sinsani, Apr. 28, 1891, ANM 1 E 220. For more detail on the political economy of distributing the booty, see Roberts, *Warriors*.

[19] Mademba, letter to Mon Capitaine [Briquelot], Sinsani, May 17, 1891, ANM 1 E 220.

protectorate agreement and bumped up against Mademba's commitment to promote French civilization.

The theme of Mademba's preoccupation with his many wives runs throughout his story. It was common French practice during the conquest phase to reward loyal troops with shares of the booty, especially captured women.[20] The wives of conquered rulers were especially prized as they conveyed status to the receiver. This was especially true of the royal and elite women of the Futanke capitals of Segu and Nioro, which fell to the French in April 1890 and January 1891. Archinard presented Sokna Fofana to Mademba during the division of the booty. These gifts were rarely challenged; the distributed women who found themselves with stronger, more elite protectors probably counted themselves fortunate.[21] Later in 1891, however, Aguibu, a half-brother of Amadu who had sided with the French since 1887, requested the return of Sokna Fofana. It is not at all clear if Sokna was Aguibu's wife or relative but the request made its way through the French command and to Mademba. Mademba's own words in this incident, which seems to have been resolved in his favor, are nonetheless telling.

> In response to your letter numbered 24, I want to inform you that Sokna Fofana is in effect my wife for the past year. In May, she had a child who died but I nonetheless very much like her. She is to me a wife and everybody here knows this. If she is returned to Aguibu that would be in the eyes of the natives a considerable affront to me. In this world of the blacks, it is only from servants [i.e., slaves] that one removes a woman to give to another without their agreement. I request that you relay to the commandant supérieur these reasons and request that I keep my wife.[22]

This passage is highly revealing of the Mademba's anxieties over his authority as king. But it also reveals Mademba's assumptions about how his status as king was deeply linked to his stature as household head. To take away his wife would be to challenge and weaken his authority both as household head and king. This notion of the household as a model of state power and statecraft has been raised by Marie Perinbam regarding the political organization of the chieftaincy of Bamako and as a general model for the Segu Bambara. Emily Osborn deepens the analysis of the relationship between the household and

---

[20] Klein, *Slavery and Colonial Rule in French West Africa*, 82–84.

[21] See Marcia Wright, *Strategies of Slaves and Women: Life-stories from East/Central Africa* (New York: L. Barber Press, 1993) and Steven Feierman's reinterpretation of the case of Narwimba in "African Histories and the Dissolving of World History," in *Africa and the Disciplines: The Contributions of Research in Africa to the Social Sciences and Humanities*, eds. Robert H. Bates, Valentin-Yves Mudimbe, and Jean O'Barr (Chicago: University of Chicago Press, 1993): 167–211.

[22] Mademba, letter to the Resident of Segu, Sinsani, nd [but between June 3 and 6] 1891, ANM 1 E 220.

the state in her longitudinal study of the state and power in Kankan.[23] As we shall see, as Mademba's power and authority over his kingdom waned, he invested more in his control over his household. As his household increased, so too did his anxieties about his authority.

Challenges to Mademba's power and authority multiplied in the months after his arrival in Sinsani. Not all regional chiefs arrived at Sinsani's gates to proclaim their submission to Mademba's new authority. Villages and towns to the north and northeast, where resistance to the Futanke was strong, were especially reluctant to accept Mademba's authority or recognize French over-rule. In his swing through the region following the pacification of the revolt of 1891–1892, Archinard described the situation in which Mademba found himself commanding as extremely difficult. According to Archinard, the Kabankao, who had sided early with the rebels against Mademba, were "among the most difficult and intransigent groups I have ever encountered." Moreover, Mademba found himself among "very bad neighbors including Tiama of Monimpe, Demba of Segala, and N'To of Markadugu."[24] Archinard could also have included Abderahman of Sokolo, who also sided with the rebels. But what made these chiefs "bad neighbors" varied considerably.

Of Tiama of Monimpe and Demba of Segala I know relatively little. Monimpe had signed a protectorate treaty with the French in the late 1880s, but Tiama held a grievance against Mademba, who had fined him a horse for some alleged disobedience early in Mademba's reign.[25] I know a bit more about Abderahman of Sokolo and N'To of Markadugu. Sokolo was a town along the Sahel that suffered during the second half of the nineteenth century due to incessant political instability in the region and the decline of commer-cial routes from the Niger River further inland. Sokolo's economy, composed of a mix of farmers, mostly Bambara, but also some Maraka, and Fulbe herders, waxed and waned in relationship to the strength or weakness of Futanke rule in Macina. By the time the French arrived, Sokolo was a mass of "ruins ... different wars since Al Hajj Umar have devastated this land."[26] No matter how devastated his town, Abderahman, chief of Sokolo, valued his political autonomy. The French had actually guaranteed his political auton-omy in a protectorate treaty that they had signed in 1887. Abderahman

---

[23] B. Marie Perinbam, *Family Identity and the State in the Bamako Kafu, c. 1800–c. 1900* (Boulder, CO: Westview Press, 1997); Osborn, *Our New Husbands Are Here.*

[24] Archinard, Rap. de campagne 1892–93, Paris, Nov. 1893, ANS-AOF 1 D 137.

[25] Monimpe and Sarro had signed protectorate treaties with the French in the late 1880s. No author, Notices historiques du Royaume de Segou, 2ème partie, np, 1896, ANM 1 D 55-2; see also Chef d'Escadron Bonnier, *Mission au Pays de Segou: Campagne dans le Gueniekalary et le Sansanding en 1892* (Paris: Imprimerie Nationale, 1897), 70.

[26] Chef d'Escadron Brisse, commandant du cercle, Rap. pol., Sokolo, Aug. 16, 1893, ANM 1 E 74.

honored this treaty when he refused safe passage to Mandani, the Futanke ruler at Segu, when he fled the advancing French army in April 1890. Unsurprising, Abderahman was furious that Sokolo was placed under the authority of Mademba in Sinsani and thus refused the formal act of *ka kaliya*, submission. Captain Briquelot captured Abderahman's anger in his report of April 1891. "With the treaty in his hand, the chief of Sokolo demands to know why he has been placed under the authority of the *faama* of Sansanding and why the *faama* has sent a tax collector to his town. The formation of the kingdom of Sansanding has broken everything." Briquelot was therefore not surprised when Abderahman gave hospitality to Amadu after fleeing Nioro and then sided with Al Hajj Bouguni in the revolt against Mademba later in 1891.[27] French policy of signing protectorates with African allies regardless of their stature and power during the early phase of conquest when any ally was better than an enemy would later limit their abilities to forge more coherent postconquest political entities.

But local rivalries in Sokolo further inflamed the situation and contributed to Abderahman's decision to resist Mademba. Abderahman's brother, Mamady Coulibaly, had contacted Mademba through the village chief Boua Cisse when his brother refused to make submission. Mamady told Mademba that the town was equally divided, with half following him and the other half Abderahman and sought Mademba's assistance in securing the chieftaincy for himself in exchange for his loyalty to Mademba.[28] This was a political language that Mademba understood. In his correspondence with the Resident of Segu throughout 1891 and well into 1892, Mademba excoriated Abderahman and exposed his "alliance" with Al Hajj Bouguni, the alleged rebel leader, all the while suggesting that this alliance was anti-French and not anti-Mademba. Although I do not know the exact relationship between Mamady and Abderahman, rivalries between brothers (Bamanakan: *fadenw kèlè*), especially brothers of different mothers in polygynous households, is a common trope in Bamana and Malinke oral traditions.[29] Major Bonnier, who led the pacification of this rebellion in 1892, noted that Mamady "hated Abderahman" and that Mademba "found a partisan with Mamady." Abderahman, in turn, accused Mademba of "plotting to kill him in order to replace him with

---

[27] Capt. Briquelot, Résident Segou, letter to cmdt. sup., Segu, Apr. 27, 1891, ANM 1 E 219.
[28] Mademba, letter to the Resident of Segu, Sinsani, nd [probably May 30, 1891], ANM 1 E 220.
[29] Maurice Delafosse, *Haut-Sénégal-Niger* (original Paris: Champion, 1912; republished Paris: Larose, 1972), vol. 2, 289–290; Capt. Pérignon, Généralités sur Haut Sénégal et Moyen Niger, 1900, ANS-AOF 1 G 248; interviews with Ce-Baba Kuma, Sinsani, Dec. 28. 1976; Al Hajj Ismaila Fane, Tesserela, Mar. 15, 1977; Binke Baba Kuma, Sinsani, Mar. 21, 1977; Cekoro Kulubali, Segu, Feb. 26, 1977.

Mamady as chief."[30] Such local rivalries compounded the challenges of establishing stable and enduring polities in this region.

In this world of deceit and defection, N'To stands out for special attention. N'To first came to French attention in 1883, as we saw in Chapter 3, when the French had begun to establish their beachhead along the Niger at Bamako. The French first noticed N'To because of his unrelenting but rarely successful fight against the Futanke. With few allies in the vicinity of the Bamako, the French entered into a "pact" with N'To to support in principle each other's security, since both were opposed to Amadu and the Futanke. Certainly, in 1883, the French were not ready to tackle the Futanke head on, which N'To did more or less continuously. This "pact" was called into question in 1884, when N'To requested that the French come to his assistance during his assault on Amadu, who was in Nyamina, which he used as a way station when crossing Beledugu from Nioro. "All of Beledugu," wrote Colonel Boilève in 1884, "listens to the advice of the commander of the Bamako fort to have patience [before attacking the Futanke], except N'To." The French did not aid N'To, whose forces were routed. In 1889, Captain Underberg in Bamako described the French alliance with N'To "as purely platonic and the relationship between us is insignificant."[31] Captain Marchand, who spent time with N'To in Farako in 1889 in preparation for the upcoming campaign against Segu, had a very different opinion of the rebel leader. "N'To is a brave and energetic leader, who makes decisions on his own and knows how to implement them. He is beloved by those who follow him in his revolt and his enemies fear him equally." Now that Karamoko was dead, Marchand believed that N'To would be loyal to Mari Jara, who was not implicated in Karamoko's murder of Mansa Toma, N'To's *faama*. Marchand warned, however, that the other *tonjown* chiefs, who had sided with Karamoko, would be "mortally opposed" to any reconciliation with N'To.[32] Given the hostility of the other *tonjown* chiefs to N'To, he probably did not have a major role in Mari Jara's brief reign and almost certainly no role in the rebellion that broke out less than two months later. In any case, French estimation of N'To increased considerably when N'To and his contingent of 150 warriors played a prominent role in the suppression of the Baninko rebellion of 1891.[33]

[30] Bonnier, *Mission au Pays de Ségou*, 76.
[31] Underberg, cmdt. le forte de Bamako, letter to Marchand, chef de la mission du Segu, Bamako, Aug. 24, 1889, ANS-AOF 1 G 115.
[32] Marchand, Notice sur le Royaume Bambara de Segou, Nyamina, 1889, ANM 1 D 55-5.
[33] Capt. Briquelot, rap. sur la situation politique du territoire dépendant de la résidence de Segou, Segu, Sept. 15, 1891, ANM 1 E 71; Rap. du Capt. d'artillerie du Marine Klobb, chef d'état major de la colonne sur la part prise par cet officer au combat de Dienna, Souba, Mar. 5, 1891, ANS-AOF 1 D 117.

Fresh from battles in Baninko, N'To returned to his villages of Markadugu just beyond Farako. His return coincided with Mademba's triumphant march into Sinsani. N'To's Markadugu villages fell within the boundaries of Mademba's new state. Mademba was consistently annoyed that N'To did not come to Sinsani to formally submit to him. In the course of Mademba's first year and throughout the rebellion, N'To studiously stayed on the side lines. By doing so, N'To challenged Mademba's authority ever so subtly without rising against him. Captain Demafer, who served as Resident of Segu during Briquelot's home leave, wrote that "since the installation of the *faama* [in Sinsani], N'To has displayed an intelligence superior to the majority of blacks . . . He very adroitly recognized the difficulties of negotiating between Al Hajj Bouguni and *Fama* Mademba, but he never fully committed to either side."[34] N'To's decision not to act during the Sinsani revolt in support of either side was more complex than Demafer realized. The French officer who penned the December 1893 report captured N'To's reluctance. "Today, N'To is completely devoted to the French, but he will never submit to another indigenous ruler."[35] In N'To's eyes as well as others in 1891 and 1892, Mademba did not have a legitimate claim on high political office in the wider Segu region. At the core of the subsequent rebellions was French indirect rule policy that created African kingdoms without understanding local debates regarding the legitimacy of political rule.

The Sinsani Revolt, 1891–1892

The revolt that imperiled Mademba's kingdom was part of a wider rebellion against French conquest that persisted in some areas well into 1893. Indeed, there were at least four different strands to the rebellion that shook the confidence of the new colonial order; they converged in time and threatened Archinard's model of indirect rule. French conquest of Segu in April 1890 had not arrested the centrifugal tendencies that had long dominated the region and rendered efforts at political centralization challenging. The French had thought that they had contained these forces when they squashed the Baninko uprising that followed the execution of Mari Jara in May 1890. On the contrary, within six months after the initial pacification, Baninko was again in turmoil, fueled by a different alignment of local forces. Almost immediately, the right bank of the Niger rose in rebellion followed by an uprising on the left bank and another among the Minianka east of the Bani River. The Sinsani revolt was the fourth strand. Each of these four strands reflected local and regional grievances. Together, however, they threatened

---

[34] Capt. Demafer, Résident Segou, Situation pol des Royaumes de Segou et Sansanding en Septembre 1892, Segu, Sept. 23, 1892, ANM 1 E 71.

[35] Rap. sur le cercle de Segou, Segu, Dec. 18, 1893, ANS-AOF 15 G 175.

France's tenuous hold on conquered territory at the center of the new colony of the French Soudan and challenged Archinard's model of indirect rule.

The French saw conspiracy in the coordination of these revolts, orchestrated by the Futanke and radical marabouts, if not by orders of Amadu directly. French belief in conspiracy was comforting in part because it glossed over the need for more careful analysis into local grievances. Typical is a 1902 retrospective report from Segu's district officer.

> We should recall that Amadu, son of Al Hajj Umar, had returned to Nioro in 1884. After our capture of that city, he fled to Bandiagara in Macina. There he organized with two Maure marabouts, Badi Thalet Mahmoud and Baya, and succeeded in rising the inhabitants of the left bank, particularly those of Sokolo, in revolt against us. These rebels attracted the Bambara of Kaarta and marched under the orders of the chief of the Fulbe, Al Hajj Bouguni.[36]

En route to Bandiagara from Nioro, Amadu sought hospitality along the way from village chiefs including Al Hajj Bouguni in the region of Nampala. Captain Underberg in Segu dispatched one of his agents to inform Bouguni that "anyone who welcomes Amadu will be considered our enemy."[37] Bouguni was chief of the Bouaro-Nampala Fulbe, a relatively small band, located north of Sokolo along the Sahel. Despite Underberg's warning, Bouguni offered Amadu hospitality during the eight days he rested in Nampala. Bouguni's honorific title, al hajj, indicated that he had made the pilgrimage. As a notable Muslim, it was only fitting that he provide respectful hospitality to Amadu, the titular head of the Umarian branch of the Tijaniyya brotherhood. Upon Amadu's departure from Nampala, Bouguni accompanied him along the route with fifteen horsemen and perhaps one hundred warriors.[38] This may have been the total force Bouguni commanded. Bouguni eventually became the face of the revolt against Mademba, at least in French versions, even though he had no specific grievances against Mademba. The degree to which Bouguni actually instigated and led the revolt is unclear. A 1906 archival report included an oral account that offered a very different explanation. Tiembele Coulibaly, chief of Kolodugu, accompanied Mademba on a tour of the northern frontier of his kingdom in November 1891. Two days march outside Kolodugu, Tiembele left the column. When Mademba's column arrived at Kolodugu, Tiembele closed the town's gates and fired shots at Mademba. "Tiembele was

---

[36] Rap. annuel, Notice géographique, historique, topographique et statistique, Segu, 1902, ANM 1 D 127.
[37] Underberg, letter to cmdt. sup., Segu, Feb. 23, 1891, ANM 2 D 102.
[38] Capt. Briquelot, letter to cmdt. sup., [Segu], nd [but probably Apr. 1891], ANM 1 E 219.

the first to revolt against the authority of *Fama* Mademba ... This was the beginning of the revolt in which Al Hajj Bouguni become involved."[39]

Tiembele Coulibaly's actions against Mademba in November 1891 may have been the spark, but the fuel of revolt had been building for months. Already in April 1891, Abderahman of Sokolo protested Mademba's imposition of his suzerainty over Sokolo, which he claimed contravened the protectorate the that the French established with him in 1887. Captain Briquelot feared that if Mademba insisted on his mandate, this would push Abderahman into Amadu's camp despite Abderahman's history of resistance to the Futanke.[40] In June 1891, Mademba set out with a column of *sofa* to inspect his territory and to recruit commitments from his subjects to support him in case of war. Mademba complained that N'To did not welcome him, claiming that he was ill.[41] In August, Mademba reported increased pillaging throughout the northern and eastern limits of his kingdom, areas that bordered on Futanke-controlled Macina. Mademba did not respond forcefully to these challenges to his sovereignty and his authority. Village chiefs requested his assistance in quelling these raids but Mademba instead urged patience.[42] At the time, Mademba was deeply engaged with overseeing the construction of his palace and Sinsani's city walls, yet his inaction may have signaled weakness.

No matter how busy he was with construction, Mademba invested time in the formalities of his office, including a formal visit to Segu to celebrate Bastille Day. Mademba sent ahead by land his entourage of warriors and their horses and by canoe his wives and griots. Mademba left a few days later by one of the few Niger River steamers operated by the French. He joined his entourage a few miles outside of Segu, where he mounted his horse in order to make a regal entry.[43] Mademba also wrote letters of condolences upon the death of French officers with whom he had served. He sent his condolences to Bojan on the death of his son and heir. Mademba used his literacy to maintain contact with his former patrons, including the governor of Senegal, who wrote to Colonel Humbert, the supreme military commander who replaced Archinard, asking the latter to let Mademba know that he "has fond memories of [Mademba] from twenty years ago and wishes Mademba success and prosperity" in his new kingdom.[44]

---

[39] Rap. pol. Segu, July 1906, ANM 1 E 72. This report provided the historical perspective because Tiembele Coulibaly was again involved in a protest involving paying taxes to Mademba in 1906.

[40] Capt. Briquelot, letter to cmdt. sup., Segu, Apr. 27, 1891, ANM 1 E 219.

[41] Mademba, letter to Resident, Sinsani, June 3, 1891, ANM 1 E 220.

[42] Mademba, letters to Resident, Sinsani, Aug. 12 and 13, 1891, ANM 1 E 220.

[43] Mademba, letter to Resident, Sinsani, July 7, 1891, ANM 1 E 220.

[44] Gouv. sén., telegram to cmdt. sup., np, May 15, 1891, ANM 1 B 172; Mademba, letters to Resident, Sinsani, Aug. 17, 1891 and Oct. 4, 1891, ANM 1 E 220.

By October 1891, Humbert became increasingly concerned that Mademba was preoccupied with his domestic household and local construction and not projecting authority in his kingdom. "I believe that Mademba has been too long inactive in Sansanding ... His enemies will attribute his prolonged inaction to weakness and will make the goals of his kingdom more difficult to achieve."[45] Humbert's warning was already too late. In late October, Mademba dispatched a contingent of sixty *sofa* to Sokolo in order to establish a garrison there and to assert his authority. Abderahman refused it entry, in part because Abderahman's brother Mamady had become part of Mademba's political circle. Briquelot ordered Mademba to lead a tour of the rebellious regions. Mademba again approached N'To for assistance, but N'To declined, claiming that he was still sick. During his mid November tour, Mademba and his force found that villages along the way, including Niebebugu and Molodo, closed their gates to him. Without fresh water and food, Mademba abandoned his tour and returned to Sinsani.[46] "This situation," Mademba wrote to the Briquelot, "is very serious and merits punishment ... If I don't get permission to do so, I will risk losing my prestige and my enemies will be encouraged to attempt a coup." Briquelot could not sanction such punishment against Sokolo without contravening the principles of protection. So he passed the issue up the administrative ladder. With still no authorization forthcoming from the French, Mademba fumed "I must be given authority to take action against the rebel villages of Kala," he wrote in late November. "Everyone," he added, "is deceitful" referring no doubt to Tiembele Coulibaly's decision to join the rebels and N'To's refusal to assist him.[47] In late November, Mademba received permission to punish the rebel town of Serouala, which was affiliated with Sokolo. Mademba mobilized his warriors and set out to punish Serouala. As his forces camped for the night outside the town, a barrel of gunpowder exploded, which spooked Mademba's forces, who hastily retreated back to Sinsani. Mademba did not attempt to punish Sokolo again. Lieutenant-colonel Bonnier put the blame for this ignominious retreat squarely on Mademba, who "had failed miserably" in leading his troops.[48]

Fearing the start of a major rebellion, Briquelot encouraged Mademba to finish work on the city's walls and on his palace. Briquelot also worried that Mademba's authority over his *sofa* was weakening. He ordered Bojan to send a column of his forces to Sinsani to defend the city. Bojan put a force of 600 cavalry and 1,700 warriors under the command of his cousin, Donkoro,

[45] Col. Humbert, letter to Capt. Briquelot, Kayes, Oct. 24, 1891, ANM B 150.
[46] Capt. Briquelot, Rap. sur la révolte du royaume de Sansanding, Segu, Apr. 1, 1892, ANS-AOF 15 G 172.
[47] Mademba, letters to Resident, Sinsani, Nov. 1 and 28, 1891, ANM 1 E 220.
[48] Bonnier, *Mission au Pays de Ségou*, 69.

and it marched to Sinsani in mid December.[49] Mademba was no doubt happy to have these extra troops and wrote to Briquelot that "I have rarely seen an African column march with such order."[50] Mademba did not complain that the maintenance of Donkoro's column fell upon him and the residents of Sinsani, although this many new mouths to feed challenged the food stores in the region. Mademba added that work on the city's walls was complete with battlements and that his palace was "built with high walls to withstand assaults." Following Briquelot's instructions, Mademba divided Sinsani's forces into three divisions; in addition, his own palace guard composed of "free men in my service," including former *tirailleurs*, and several Wolof, and workers from Saint Louis formed a mobile company prepared to assist where needed.[51] As Mademba was consolidating his defenses, the rebels were holding a "grand palabre" in Molodo at which chiefs of a dozen towns attended. Following the trope of Islamic conspiracy, Mademba reported that Sidi Bekay Kunta, a leading cleric of the Qadriyya brotherhood, instigated the rebels.[52] It was highly unlikely, however, that the leaders of the Kunta would be aligned with any movement affiliated with the Futanke's Tijaniyya brotherhood.[53] Mademba explained to Briquelot that any stranger entering Sinsani during this period of heightened anxiety had to present himself to the *faama*. While Mademba welcomed Muslim clerics and permitted them to preach their religion, he would not tolerate any who challenged France's influence and his authority.[54]

Just as the rebels within Mademba's kingdom were meeting in Molodo in mid December, another rebellion started in Baninko. Whereas the first Baninko rebellion against French conquest of Segu was led by Mari Jara's kin and *tonjown* warriors in direct response to the French execution of the *faama*, the second Baninko rebellion was more diffuse. *Tonjown*, radical Muslim clerics, "benighted" Bambara farmers, Maraka, and Fulbe were all involved. In 1891, the Baninko region was in the midst of a raging cattle disease that threatened the Fulbe's herds. Moreover, Bojan's efforts to impose his sovereignty through new chiefs and reimposed taxes were widely resented. Briquelot reported that a "grand palabre" was held at Kamunu under the leadership of several surviving *tonjown* leaders and "two marabouts." One was a Maure, self-styled as the "Mahdi" who claimed to have made the pilgrimage

---

[49] Capt. Briquelot, Rap. sur la révolte du royaume de Sansanding, Segu, Apr. 1, 1892, ANS-AOF 15 G 172.

[50] Mademba, letter to Resident, Sinsani, Dec. 28, 1891, ANM 1 E 220.

[51] Mademba, letter to Resident, Sinsani, Dec. 22, 1891, ANM 1 E 220.

[52] Mademba, letter to Resident, Sinsani, Dec. 17, 1891, ANM 1 E 220

[53] For background, see Robinson, *The Holy War of Umar Tall* and Christopher Harrison, *France and Islam in West Africa 1860–1960* (Cambridge: Cambridge University Press, 1988).

[54] Mademba, letter to Resident, Sinsani, Dec. 22, 1891, ANM 1 E 220.

and would not reveal his real name until after the success of the uprising. The other was Hamidu, his Bambara "milk brother," which refers to brothers from the same mother. Both had arrived in the Baninko a year or so earlier and attracted a clientele for their juggling and for their provision of magical grisgris or amulets.[55] "Manufacturers of amulets, these marabouts quickly came to dominate the population of traditionalists and to have them blindly obey [the marabouts]. The Mahdi preached that the rifles and cannons of the whites would only shoot water."[56] Briquelot's report reflected the comforting notion that radical Muslims were at the center of all of the unrest in the new colony and that traditionalist Africans were easily misled by unscrupulous preachers.

The second Baninko revolt thus had several different strands. The surviving *tonjown* leaders resented the imposition of Bojan's authority and they were prominent at the Kamunu palabre. But the Fulbe pastoralists and Bambara and Maraka farmers also had grievances. During the early phase of Bojan's rule in Segu, the Fulbe of Baninko regularly provided warriors to support Bojan's forces. By the middle of January 1892, noise of increasing rebelliousness was coming from the left bank of the Bani and even closer to Segu itself. A number of Bojan's *sofa* deserted, thus weakening the *faama*'s power and authority. The Fulbe warriors from Baninko who had joined Bojan's forces also began to desert. Fearing the spread of the uprising to the Segu heartland, Briquelot ordered Donkoro's column of Bojan's *sofa* to leave Sinsani and head back to the capital. At the beginning of February, Lieutenant Hourst led a small column against the rebel town of Touna. As soon as the column arrived, the rebels fled. Several neighboring villages came to Hourst's camp to make their submission.[57]

The assassination of Lieutenant Huillard on April 19, 1892, while on a mission in the region to determine the boundaries of the Segu and Sikasso kingdoms, seems to have been the catalyst for the next phase of the rebellion. Huillard had stopped for the night at the Bambara village of Souba, where a group of rebels killed him while he slept. Murdering French officers could not easily be tolerated. Captain Briquelot, the Resident of Segu, immediately set out to punish the village where the event occurred and burned Souba and the Fulbe cattle encampments nearby. Briquelot next led his force to rescue Baraweli, the major commercial center of the region, which was besieged by

---

[55] Juggling (*jonglerie*)was simultaneously a sport, a spectacle, and a religious rite. Exactly what it meant in the Baninko is not clear.

[56] Capt. Briquelot, Rap. sur la situation pol. du territoire dépendant de la résidence de Segu, Segu, Sept. 15, 1891, ANM 1 E 71; see also the 1902 report, which follows Briquelot's 1891 report closely, Rap. annuel, Notice géographique, historique, topographique et statistique, Segu, 1902, ANM 1 D 127.

[57] Capt. Briquelot, Rap. sur la situation pol. du territoire dépendant de la résidence de Segu, Segu, Sept. 15, 1891, ANM 1 E 71; Bonnier, *Mission au Pays de Ségou*, 14–15.

the rebels. Briquelot's forces entered the town after a short battle, but on their route back to Segu, they were ambushed by a "mass of cavalry and fighters." Briquelot and two other French officers were wounded, but the French forces routed the rebels.[58] Bonnier, who led the major force that quelled the second Baninko revolt in May 1892, placed the blame for the rebellion on the "Fulbe and their Bambara allies who want to rid the land of the French."[59]

The Minianka part of the uprisings of 1891–1893 is least well documented. The Minianka, an acephalous Senufo speaking group, was situated in an arc running north and south of Sikasso, Tieba's capital. In 1890, Captain Underberg had already secured a treaty with Tieba and in 1891 the French sought to determine the boundaries between Bojan's and Tieba's kingdoms. During one of these tours, Briquelot had installed new chiefs in the region who would be loyal to Bojan.[60] The northern Minianka region had long been a contested boundary between Segu and Sikasso. Bonnier attributed the Minianka revolt to their resistance to Bojan and his efforts to impose his authority in the region.[61] The revolt in Minianka persisted well into spring 1893, when Archinard moved his column into the region and suppressed this revolt before turning north for the final conquest of the Futanke empire in Bandiagara.[62]

The revolts in Kaminiadugu, which broke out in late March 1892, and in Gueniekalary, which started in April, were linked to the revolts in Sinsani and Baninko, respectively (see map 2.1). Gueniekalary was the region southwest of Segu and bordered on Baninko. Here the revolt was explicitly against Bojan's overrule and sparked by the mobilization of the Fulbe groups in the region. Briquelot feared that this new front would block the flow of French reinforcements from Bamako on the left bank of the Niger and together with the revolt in Baninko threaten Segu itself. During the suppression of the Gueniekalary revolt, Bonnier repeatedly heard complaints that the residents were "exhausted" by the insistent demands from Bojan for troops to man his army, laborers to keep the roads open, and taxes. The Kaminiadugu revolt also spread to Sarro, which was on the right bank opposite Sinsani. Bonnier attributed the spread of the Sinsani revolt to the right bank to the leadership of Al Hajj Bouguni and the chief of Sarro, whose authority was threatened by Mademba, and the influence of the "macinakés." Several of the villages in this

---

[58] Rap. annuel, Notice géographique, historique, topographique et statistique, Segu, 1902, ANM 1 D 127.

[59] Bonnier, *Mission au Pays de Ségou*, 14–17.

[60] Rap. annuel, Notice géographique, historique, topographique et statistique, Segu, 1902, ANM 1 D 127.

[61] Bonnier, *Mission au Pays de Ségou*, 4.

[62] Archinard, Rap. de campagne 1892–93, Paris, Nov. 1893, ANS-AOF 1 D 137; Capt. Briquolet, Notes sur l'histoire et la situation actuelle au Macina, Segu, Mar. 1892, ANS-AOF 1 G 158.

region remained loyal to N'To, who was studiously standing on the sidelines as the revolt erupted. The spread of these four revolts was by no means coordinated, but their convergence stretched Briquelot's tiny garrison in Segu and the ragtag forces of Bojan and Mademba.[63]

In early January 1892, Mademba wrote to Briquelot that the "enemy gains new partisans daily." Mademba launched a nighttime raid on the "enemy," which he termed a "great success." Mademba's cavalry returned with a number of captured horses and two prisoners, who were summarily executed in Sinsani. Before they were executed, the prisoners told Mademba that Al Hajj Bouguni had preached that God had promised to deliver Sinsani into the rebels' hands. Mademba complained that the rebels let themselves be "misled by impostors and marabouts who offer only deceptions."[64] After another successful engagement with Bouguni's forces, Mademba's allies were caught in an ambush and most of his troops fled back to Sinsani in disarray. After the departure of Donkoro's column to aid the suppression of the Baninko rebellion, Sinsani was left with weakened defenses and an exhausted store of food.[65]

How serious a threat Al Hajj Bouguni's forces was to Mademba is not clear. In late January 1892, the core of Bouguni's force consisted of 160 cavalry and some 300 warriors. By early March, Bouguni's force had swelled to 300–400 cavalry and an undetermined number of warriors.[66] In late February, a forward column of Bouguni's forces reached Sinsani's walls, but Mademba's forces easily repulsed them. Bouguni camped in Sanamadugu, where he assembled his force for the threatened assault on Sinsani. Perhaps the most serious threat to Mademba was not the military one but the loss of his prestige and authority in the face of generalized rebellion. The rebels effectively blockaded Sinsani, where food was becoming scarce, and fear of the impending assault gnawed at the defenders' resolve. One by one, Mademba's *sofa* deserted Sinsani. Mademba was forced to buy food on credit from Segu to provide for his troops. By the time Bonnier arrived in Sinsani in late June, only 400–500 *sofa* remained of the 2,000 given to Mademba after the fall of Nioro. The majority had fled or were in hiding in Segu. Of the 400 horses Mademba received from Archinard before his initial entrance into Sinsani, most were so emaciated that only forty or so could be ridden into battle.[67] From his

[63] Bonnier, *Mission au Pays de Ségou*, 4–5, 11–12, 47–55. Bonnier noted that a Futanke column arrived in Kaminiadugu to aid the rebels, but was easily routed by his troops.

[64] Mademba, letters to Resident, Sinsani, Jan. 2 and 9, 1892, ANM 1 E 220.

[65] Mademba, letters to Resident, Sinsani, nd [but both mid to late Jan. 1892], ANM 1 E 220.

[66] Mademba, letters to Resident, Sinsani, nd [late Jan. 1892 and Mar. 10, 1892], ANM 1 E 220.

[67] Bonnier, *Mission au Pays de Ségou*, 53–54.

weakened position, Mademba continued to assert to the Resident of Segu that "we must be forceful in our response to the treachery of the old chiefs in order to assure our domination." In mid March, Colonel Humbert, the supreme military commander, and no loyal friend of Archinard, argued that "these kingdoms [created by Archinard], too large and too hastily formed, have produced serious dangers." In terms of Mademba, Humbert concluded that "*fama* Mademba is titular head of a beautiful and grand kingdom, but he is far from being its master."[68]

On March 5, Bouguni led his 400 cavalry into the attack on Sinsani from three sides. Mademba's forces, although depleted, still had sufficient firepower to halt the advance before the city's walls, and after three hours of fighting, Bouguni's forces retreated. Along the way, they raided smaller villages.[69] Bouguni reassembled his force and crossed the Niger into Kaminiadugu, where they joined the rebels on the right bank. Around this time, Bonnier reported that Bouguni asked Amadu for assistance in the rebellion. Amadu in turn asked his talibes but their response was "feeble." By the end of May, some 700 Futanke warriors led by Oumarel Samba Doromdel left Bandiagara to join the rebel armies. Using this information about reinforcements, Bouguni decided to lay siege again on Sinsani. Bonnier was especially worried that a band of Minianka rebels had crossed the Bani and were preparing to join the rebels in Kaminiadugu, which would yield a combined rebel army that would be hard to stop. By mid June, Bonnier had quelled the rebellion in Baninko and Gueniakalary. He reassembled the French forces in Segu and marched into Kaminiadugu.[70]

In late May or early June 1892, Bouguni's forces recrossed the Niger to lay siege again on Sinsani. Mademba reported that Bouguni's forces were camped just outside Sinsani's walls, tightening the blockade and skirmishing with Mademba's forces. One of the Niger flotilla's gunboats arrived at Sinsani with some much needed food and a French officer, who Mademba installed in the yet unfinished barracks he was constructing. Bonnier ordered the French officer to train Mademba's *sofa* and to cloth them in blue uniforms, made from local cloth. They were to become "the blue cavalry of Sansanding." During this time, Mademba was effectively a prisoner in his *Diomfutu*, or palace, which when it was finally completed measured 150 by 100 meters and was surrounded by walls five meters high (see Figure 3.1).

---

[68] Col. Humbert, Rap. sur la situation actuelle du Soudan, Kerouane, Mar. 18, 1892, ANOM Soudan I-2. See also Méniaud, *Pionniers*, I, 278.

[69] Mademba, letters to Resident, Sinsani, Mar. 10, 1892 and Apr. 6, 1892, ANM 1 E 220.

[70] Mademba, letters to Resident, Sinsani, May 19, 20 and 21, 1892, ANM 1 E 220; Bonnier, *Mission au Pays de Ségou*, 41–42, 50–51.

Figure 3.1   Mademba's palace, ca. 1900.
(Source: Pérignon collection, Bibliothèque nationale de France, ca. 1899–1900, SGE SG WE-513, with permission)

Briquelot argued that Mademba's retreat into his palace actually encouraged the rebels, who saw this as a sign of weakness.[71] Conditions in Sinsani deteriorated to the point that groups of residents risked swimming across the Niger rather than remain in the city.

In late June, Bonnier decided to quash the Kaminiadugu rebellion. He launched a major attack on Koila on June 22, which fell easily to the French forces. Bonnier left the mopping up operations to Donkoro, the chief of the auxiliary forces and left "urgently" for Sinsani. Bonnier feared that with the deepening of the rainy season, travel and battle would be much harder. Bouguni continued to amass his troops at Dosseguela, a village about twenty kilometers outside of Sinsani. Bouguni claimed that his next assault would be

---

[71] Briquelot, letter to cmdt. sup., Segu, April 5, 1892, ANM 1 E 220; Bonnier, *Mission au Pays de Ségou,* 51, 57. Sinsani was one of the leading centers of indigo-dyed cloth production in the region.

the victorious battle for that town. Bonnier arrived at Sinsani on June 24 with his small force of European officers, *tirailleurs*, and battle-hardened auxiliaries. Bonnier ordered N'To to assemble his forces at Sinsani for the upcoming battle, but N'To demurred. Mademba worried that he could not feed Bonnier's troops even with the support of Segu grain stocks.[72] As Bonnier's column approached Dosseguela, Bouguni departed, announcing that he had to begin cultivation of his fields, leaving his son and the Futanke warrior, Oumarel, in command. Bonnier estimated Bouguni's forces to consist of 1,500 cavalry and warriors. Once the battle was engaged, the Futanke cavalry quickly fled, but the rebels in general fought hard, leaving some 300 dead when the fighting was over. The French lost eight *tirailleurs* and had three dozen wounded.[73] Bouguni's rebel army disbanded and Bouguni fled eastward into the Sahel.

N'To, who claimed to be sick, finally arrived at Dosseguela with the troops Bonnier had requested, but only after the fighting had ended. Bonnier was furious at N'To's behavior, but in front of the victorious French commander, N'To requested his pardon. Mademba continued to insist that N'To be punished for his "duplicitous behavior toward me, which merits definitive correction because it will diminish my authority in this land."[74] Given his services to the French, Bonnier was reluctant to take action against N'To or to let Mademba punish N'To.[75] Instead, he passed this problem up the ladder to the supreme military commander. Humbert's disastrous stint as the supreme military commander led to his recall in the fall of 1892, so he too passed the problem of how to deal with N'To to his successor. After recovering in France, Archinard returned to the Soudan and led the 1892–1893 annual military campaign.

Before his departure from the left bank, Bonnier sought to resolve the outstanding disputes and punish the remaining rebels. Abderahman was on top of Bonnier's list precisely because he was one of the first to rebel against Mademba. In a letter to Bonnier, Abderahman professed his deep and abiding loyalty to the French and claimed that his dispute was with Mademba, who was "his personal enemy." "Everything bad," Abderahman stated, "came from Boua Cisse, the Maraka chief of Sansanding and from the *fama* of Sansanding." Bonnier demanded that Abderahman submit to him personally and gave Abderahman two days to arrive at the town of Molodo or else Bonnier's column would march directly against Sokolo. Abderahman capitulated and came to Bonnier, where he explained that his enmity toward

---

[72] Mademba, letter to Resident, Sinsani, June 14, 1892, ANM 1 E 220.

[73] Bonnier, *Mission au Pays de Ségou*, 51–65.

[74] Mademba, letter to Resident, Sinsani, nd [but late summer or early fall 1892], ANM 1 E 220.

[75] Pérignon, Généralités sur le Haut Sénégal et Moyen Niger, Segu, 1900, ANS-AOF 1 G 248.

Mademba and Boua Cisse stemmed from their alliance with his brother, Mamady, who wanted to kill Abderahman and take over the chieftaincy. Bonnier initiated a meeting in which Mademba and Abderahman reconciled their differences. Abderahman accepted Mademba's offer of hospitality and "they became delighted with each other." By early December 1892, Mademba signaled that Abderahman had "spontaneously sent me his daughter in marriage. I believe that this act guarantees the fidelity of the chief of Sokolo who also attaches his lands to mine."[76]

Back in Sinsani, Mademba's remaining *sofa* complained bitterly to Bonnier about Mademba's treatment of them. Mori, the chief of the *sofa*, explained that they followed Mademba to Sinsani because they were the slaves of the French and remained devoted to the French, but they requested that they be moved elsewhere, anywhere away from Mademba. "We fight and we kill" for Mademba, Mori stated, "but when we get back, the *fama* cuts our throats." Mademba responded to these accusations by admitting that he had indeed executed several *sofa*, especially those who deserted. Mademba justified his actions: "it is the custom of black kings [and] it would be dishonorable in the eyes of all if he did not deal harshly with the guilty ones." Mademba here invoked Archinard's letter of investiture that Mademba was to rule as the blacks like to be ruled, but Mademba clearly exceeded his mandate by relying on violence to command respect. Bonnier counseled Mademba to desist from executing any additional *sofa* without first securing the express permission of the white officer whom he installed in Sinsani. Bonnier assigned Captain Guittard and Lieutenant Szymanski to head a small garrison stationed in Sinsani in the yet to be completed barracks and European quarters. Bonnier also convened a palabre at Sinsani of all of the major rebel leaders as well as N'To and Boua Cisse. Bonnier oversaw the *ka kalifa*, the formal submission to Mademba, which included a solemn swearing on an "amulet" N'To had specially ordered for this event. In addition, fearing that Mademba would "impose too heavy a hand because he was now the strongest," Bonnier decided to levy the fines on the rebels himself. These were conspicuously mild.[77] Bonnier's actions – installing a French officer in Sinsani, curtailing Mademba's authority to engage in capital punishment, and taking away from Mademba the right to punish those who challenged his power – eroded Mademba's authority at exactly the moment when the Mademba overcame the challenges of widespread rebellion.

Bonnier's actions in curtailing Mademba's authority spoke louder than his written criticism. Bonnier wrote that Mademba "had certainly committed several blunders, which were considerable but not sufficient to have been the

---

[76] Mademba, letter to Resident, Sinsani, Dec. 5, 1892, ANM 1 E 220; Bonnier, *Mission au Pays de Ségou*, 72–77.
[77] Bonnier, *Mission au Pays de Ségou*, 79–80.

dominant cause of the Sansanding revolt, which spread without such cause and which must be attributed principally to Amadu's incitement."[78] Captain Demafer, serving as Resident of Segu during Briquelot's convalescence in France, noted the double utility of having the French garrison posted to Sinsani.

> It would demonstrate to everyone the devotion we have towards the *Fama*. In addition, I do not have complete confidence in his abilities to resolve certain questions of political order. He has demonstrated too often that he has a very heavy hand in repressing certain faults committed and in levying fines. These practices have alienated a certain number of his subjects. He must learn to have patience in certain situations or risk again another revolt.[79]

What Bonnier and Demafer described as Mademba's heavy hand was in fact the very instruments of power and authority that Mademba had to use precisely because he had no traditional legitimacy for his position as *faama* of Sinsani. Archinard's return from his year's leave of absence led to the final conquest of the Middle Niger valley with the French capture of Jenne and Bandiagara. Archinard also set out to reorganize the region administratively, which had paradoxical implications for his model of indirect rule.

Indirect Rule Revisited

Archinard resumed his position as supreme military commander with ministerial agreement to secure the interior of France's new colony along the Niger River, but with clear orders from Paris not to engage in any additional military expeditions. Archinard's orders were to lay enduring administrative foundations to the new colony and to promote commerce and the peaceful penetration of French interests.[80] Archinard's brilliance as the architect of French conquest was to ignore orders from Paris, secure military victories, and present those to Paris as *faits accomplis*. Colonel Humbert had tried to move more gradually by securing treaties and building security, but events on the ground forced him to respond. He was not successful in any of these areas. In late 1892, Archinard gave Lieutenant Combes orders to pursue the conquest of Samory and in early 1893 Archinard was ready to bring closure to the conquest of the Middle Niger region. Kayes along the upper Senegal River remained the military's staging ground and there Archinard assembled his

---

[78] Ibid., 55.

[79] Capt. Demafer, Situation pol. des Royaumes de Segou et Sansanding en September 1892, Segu, Sept. 23, 1892, ANM 1 E 71.

[80] Méniaud, *Pionniers*, II, 286–287; Kanya-Forstner, *The Conquest of the Western Sudan*, 194.

column for the 1892–1893 campaign. In Kayes, Aguibu, one of Al Hajj Umar's sons, who had sided with the French since 1887, when they recognized him as "king of Dinguiray," joined Archinard's column with a small contingent of twenty cavalry. Archinard included Aguibu in his column as a tool of diplomacy in negotiating a peaceful solution to the remaining pieces of the Futanke empire in Bandiagara because of Aguibu's "significant prestige among the Futanke."[81] This year's military column had a somewhat later start than usual; Archinard's forces left Kayes only in late February 1893 and made their way along the Sahel toward Gumbu, where an isolated rebellion had started. Archinard was uncertain of the causes of this rebellion, but he wondered if the actions of the chief of the garrison, the *tirailleur* Lieutenant Sadioka, had perhaps engendered malcontentment among the residents through his administrative actions. Archinard had dispatched Lieutenant Canrobert to investigate the situation in Gumbu. Canrobert's mission "utterly failed" and he was forced to flee with his cavalry. Shortly thereafter Lieutenant Sadioka also fled Gumbu, leaving behind baggage, which was subsequently pillaged.[82] Instead of pursuing the idea that Sadioka's actions may have precipitated the rebellion, Archinard fell back to the comforting theory of Islamic conspiracy. He accused Amadu or his agents of fomenting Islamic "fanaticism." Archinard arrived in Gumbu to receive the town's submission and impose the new order. After a palabre with the town's residents, all of whom declared themselves friends of the French, Archinard reestablished the customs house and the garrison, imposed a fine on the town, an annual tax of 6,000 francs, and the obligation to provide subsistence to the newly installed garrison.[83]

From Gumbu, Archinard headed toward Segu to assemble a larger column for the main military goals of pacifying Minianka and quashing the remaining Futanke strongholds at Jenne and Bandiagara. Archinard's stop in Segu involved far more than pursuing his military agenda. Archinard used his Segu visit to reframe his model of indirect rule. *Faama* Bojan organized a royal welcome.

> On each side, the population assembled to see us pass, the tambourines and the drums produced an infernal noise. We were able to distinguish in the crowd Bojan's wives, who because Bojan is less severe than Muslim rulers, permitted his wives to attend the ceremony. They were dressed in small cloths ... and each carried proudly an umbrella in the national colors.

---

[81] Méniaud, *Pionniers*, II, 315.
[82] Ibid., 344.
[83] Archinard left Lt. Mamadou Racine in charge of the small Gumbu garrison. Archinard, *Le Soudan en 1893*, 9–12; see also Méniaud, *Pionniers*, II, 344–349.

Archinard was pleased with this welcome, but did not want to delay the major business at hand and did not want to leave Bojan in any uncertainty about his intentions. In a private meeting with Bojan, Archinard stated

> I praised [Bojan] for his devotion to our cause and I thanked him for his obedience to the orders of the commandant superieur and to those of the Residents who resided in Segu and who unanimously had only positive words about him. In addition, we discussed the situation in the Segu kingdom, the rebellions, the revolts, the wars on all sides. Moreover, his representatives in the various parts of this immense territory were men of questionable quality and not disinterested [in their administration], whose actions provoked more revolts, his warriors were vanquished in almost all battles, all of this contributes to the fact that he cannot continue to exercise power without having us continue to intervene and fight for him. This will be war without end ... Given the diverse populations composed of different races with vastly different interests that makes the territory so difficult to govern, I have been persuaded by recent experiences that only whites can successfully govern.[84]

Archinard promised to pay public homage to Bojan and offered him the consolation prize of the chieftaincy of a number of abandoned Futanke villages near Nioro, which was also close to his old father, Dama, and near the ancestral home of the Massassi Bambara.

Bojan accepted his demotion with equanimity and perhaps relief. Archinard's report quoted Bojan's reply. Bojan responded to Archinard:

> You have given me Segou and I have done what I could. I have expected your arrival in order to discuss the situation with me. What you have said is justified and I thank you. You have always treated me with respect. Indeed, you have treated no other black with more respect. My family remains duly honored and I will remain devoted to the French. If there is ever anything I can do for the French, I will rush to offer them assistance.[85]

Within six days of being dethroned, Bojan and his large entourage of family, advisors, and warriors crossed the Niger en route to his homeland. On March 15, 1893, Segu became an administrative district with a French military officer as district commander. Aware that his actions in dethroning Bojan may further unsettle the situation in Sinsani, Archinard sought to reassure Mademba that his intentions were to keep Mademba in power.[86]

In the meantime, Archinard rested his troops and assembled the auxiliary forces. These included Mademba's blue cavalry, other auxiliary troops trained

---

[84] Archinard, Rap. de campagne 1892–93, Paris, Nov. 1893, ANS-AOF 1 G 137.
[85] Ibid.
[86] Méniaud, *Pionniers*, II, 365–368.

by French officers, and the *tirailleurs* dispatched from Kayes, Bamako, and Segu. By the beginning of April, Archinard set out for Minianka. As Archinard moved through Minianka, he accepted the submission of village chiefs and learned that perhaps only twenty villages remained hostile to the French. Even those reputedly hostile villages greeted Archinard warmly, except Kenitieri where Archinard's forces had a taste of battle.[87] Archinard then met with the almamy of San, which had emerged over the past decades as the most significant market in the region. The almamy pledged his support to the French and complained only of the incessant pillaging of caravans moving through the Minianka region. Archinard's mopping up operations obviously left much to be desired because the very next year, Captain Quinquandon wrote that "we remain incapable of effectively protecting caravans that pass through Minianka. If we want to impose our order in this region, it will only be through our *tirailleurs* and cannons. As we have already experienced, it is very difficult to punish each and every village."[88] Archinard obviously did not have the patience of such village by village operations. He was eager to claim the bigger prize.

As the column moved closer to Jenne, Aguibu began to play a more significant role in the diplomatic effort to have the Futanke concede to the French. Aguibu sent trusted envoys to Jenne to see if the city would submit peacefully to the French. They returned without success. Aguibu pleaded for some extra time to negotiate, but the third envoy returned with the news that there were "no means to peacefully resolve the situation." Méniaud noted that "obviously, Aguibu wanted to avoid the destruction of Jenne, which would be his fief with all the town's riches."[89] Once outside the city's gates, Archinard let fire his cannons. Later that day, an escaped slave from inside Jenne sought out Aguibu to tell him that the townspeople of Jenne had agreed to submit to the French, but the Futanke commander, Alpha Moussa, refused to capitulate. The battle for Jenne required street-by-street urban fighting made more difficult because so many of Jenne's houses had several stories. After three days, Jenne was in French hands. "The chief of the Diavandos, the chief of the Peul, and the merchants of Jenne flock to me, out of breath, and fell to my feet: 'Stop the fighting! Stop the *tirailleurs*! There is nothing stopping you from entering the city. Everything is yours. We will do whatever you want." Archinard called off the fighting. The French forces assembled the booty, including weapons and captured women. Archinard also confiscated all of the horses in the city and all of the large cargo canoes so central to the commerce along the Bani and Niger.

---

[87] Ibid., 370–383.
[88] Commandant de cercle Quinquandon, Rap. au sujet de fonctionnement de la justice administrative dans le cercle de Segou, Segu, April 1, 1894, ANM 2 M 9; Archinard, *Le Soudan en 1893*, 17–20.
[89] Méniaud, *Pionniers*, II, 395.

With two French officers and eleven *tirailleurs* casualties of the battle, Archinard imposed war reparations of 1,000 bars of salt upon the city. He also ordered an annual tax of 2,000 francs.[90]

Archinard claimed a section of the city to house the French garrison and ordered the town chief to maintain the buildings and provide subsistence for the troops without cost to the French. Archinard also described in detail what probably happened frequently, but was rarely discussed. The city's notables were instructed to bring 200 female slaves, who were being held to trade in Timbuktu, to exchange for the female hostages. "These women will be married to our *tirailleurs*, most of whom are auxiliaries and who have not yet received any booty from either Minianka or Jenne." According to Archinard, the female slaves clapped their hands in joy once they realized that they would not be sold into the desert, but would remain in the Soudan as free people. Archinard also insisted that each husband pay him a token thirty francs bridewealth payment, as was the local custom. Following his own interpretation of custom (which emerged as a reinvented French custom), Archinard then promised to give the thirty francs to each woman in order to buy cloth to form her "trousseau."[91]

Archinard reassembled his troops and marched to Mopti and Bandiagara, the major Futanke centers. Additional French forces with significant firepower arrived by gunboat at Mopti. Mopti fell to the French without a fight. The battle for Bandiagara was tepid compared to Jenne and the French captured Bandiagara on the April 29.[92] Amadu and a small band of loyal followers fled eastward, eventually to arrive at the borders of the Sokoto Caliphate.

After resting his troops and tending to the wounded, on May 4, 1893 Archinard held a long meeting with Aguibu and then handed him a letter in investiture making him king of Macina.

> By virtue of the powers that the government of France has given me, I make you king of Macina and I install you in Bandiagara, the capital of Macina.
>
> Our interests are the same; France does not wish to invade all of Africa. For her, it is sufficient to have friends and when they are certain of each other, they will come to each other's aid ... In giving Macina to you and to permit you to command all the Toucouleurs who are in the region, I do not want you to transform Bandiagara into a Toucouleur empire and I will not permit new immigration from Fouta. You have declared publicly – and I am very happy you did – that you have relied on God and France [to accomplish your goals] and that you have promised to cut the neck of anyone who sows discord among us.[93]

---

[90] Archinard, *Le Soudan en 1893*, 25–37, quote on 35–36.
[91] Ibid., 38.
[92] Méniaud, *Pionniers,* II, 420–425.
[93] Archinard, letter to Aguibu, Bandiagara, May 4, 1893, ANS-AOF 1 D 137.

Archinard went on to define ever so vaguely the boundaries between Macina and Segu and expected Aguibu to control the border to the north and east. Archinard also promised to expedite the transfer of Aguibu's family and his "people" from Dinguiray to Bandiagara.[94]

Archinard left Bandiagara and headed to Sinsani. Before reaching Sinsani, Archinard sent Mademba a letter providing more details about his plan to reorganize Mademba's domain. Mademba had been expecting some significant change, given Archinard's decisive action in dethroning Bojan, but he was confident that he would not fall to the same fate as Bojan.

> The weakness of your *sofa*, their desertions, and the harsh measures you have used to maintain your authority have made me think that I have imposed on a you a task too heavy to accomplish ... I have abandoned the idea that I have long held to see you one day command in Bandiagara. The diverse populations of Bandiagara have for thirty years voluntarily obeyed representatives of Al Hajj Umar's family, so I have given Macina to a member of that family, Aguibu ... For the past two years, you have occupied one of our furthest frontier posts and on behalf of all of the Soudan, you deserve the recognition for this task ...
>
> You will thus remain *Fama* of Sansanding and Dependencies, but the territories under your command will be less extensive and will be surrounded by districts under French command. Wisely administered, Sansanding and Dependencies will no longer oblige us to intervene with our *tirailleurs* as in the past. In this new situation, your personal situation will be much improved because your will no longer have to support such a large army of *sofa*, griots, and functionaries that have cost you heavily and have not contributed to the security and prosperity of the land.[95]

Archinard also imposed on Mademba an annual tax of 1,000 francs staring in 1895, when he expected prosperity to return to Sinsani. In his report on the 1892–1893 military campaign, Archinard reflected on what seemed contradictory actions in dethroning Bojan because of his failures to command Segu, enthroning Aguibu as *faama* in Bandiagara, and in keeping Mademba in office despite his failures to command. In keeping Mademba in power, Archinard returned to the bargains of collaboration that Mademba had rendered to France and to the military command generally. "*Fama* Mademba has rendered all kinds of services to the diverse supreme military commanders who had succeeded in that position since 1880 and especially to Colonel Gallieni. He has served valiantly as an interpreter as well as a soldier and it pained me to have to impose measures that may pain him." In a special note in his 1892–1893 report, Archinard described Mademba's tenure as king as a "period

---

[94] Méniaud, *Pionniers*, II, 437.
[95] Archinard, letter to Mademba, np, May 14, 1893, ANS-AOF 1 D 137.

of transition" through which he will emerge with a status of wisdom and respectability. "He was *fama* yesterday and he will retain his title." Archinard added what may be the crucial aspect of Mademba's long investment in the bargains of collaboration: reciprocity on France's part. "It would be undignified on our part and cruel to him to demote him when he in fact has treated us with the highest respect and most goodwill possible." Archinard's assessment of the bargains of collaboration clearly privileged loyalty over competence. Bojan has been loyal as well, but perhaps not quite as deeply invested in the colonial bargains of collaboration. Archinard went on to describe the population of Mademba's domains as being among the "most difficult and ungrateful" in the region, with chiefs who "acted with malice and created a world [milieu] of deception and defections that neither he nor us had been able to imagine."[96] Archinard expected Mademba to manage fairly easily the transition from his former position as *faama* over an extended territory to his new situation as ruler over a much diminished domain.

Equally intriguing, Archinard also noted that even though Mademba was not a devout Muslim, he had gained the respect of the Muslim inhabitants of Sinsani. Mademba could command the Muslims because "they respected him, his race, his family, and his education." And, Archinard added, among non-Muslim blacks, "Mademba conducts himself just as we conduct ourselves."[97] Four aspects of these remarks are worth contemplating. First, Archinard referred to Mademba as a native. Ambiguity continued to surround Mademba's legal status as an *originaire* of the Four Communes and thus as someone who exercised some rights of French citizens. But in making Mademba a "king" in his model of indirect rule, he could hardly have appointed a French citizen. Second, it remains unclear what Mademba's identity actually was. In a world where religious identity established status, who was Mademba? Was he antireligious or at least anticlerical as most Freemasons were? Or did he invent his own syncretic practices? And what did Archinard mean by citing his "race" and family as sources of Mademba's attributions of respect? It could be that this was a moment of the gradual transition of Mademba Sèye into Mademba Sy, thus claiming authority from the Sy lineage, which was a leading Muslim clerical family.[98]

Third, Mademba's education at the *école des otages* and his literacy in French certainly helped him navigate the nascent French colonial state. In an interview with Binke Sadiki Traoré, BaKoroba Kuma, and Binke Baba Kuma, they suggested that Archinard kept Mademba in power because he

---

[96] Archinard, Rap. sur la campagne 1892–93, Paris, Nov. 1893, ANS-AOF 1 D 137. The aside on Mademba in the report is entitled "Nota."

[97] Ibid.

[98] Mademba, *Au Sénégal*, 9, where his son formally enshrines the Sy lineage.

was literate in French and therefore communicated easily with the French leadership in the Soudan.[99] Dahou Traore has a different explanation when I asked why the French retained Mademba as *faama* when they revoked others. Traore responded that "Mademba served as Archinard's right hand," suggesting that loyalty trumped ability.[100]

And fourth, despite the evidence that his model of indirect rule was deeply flawed, Archinard did not hesitate to disavow his commitment to put the administration of conquered territories into the hands of trusted intermediaries regardless of their political legitimacy to rule. These actions underscored Archinard's rather inchoate notion of what constituted political legitimacy in these African kingdoms, which fell to European scholar-administrators like Maurice Delafosse and his cadre of unacknowledged African informants to determine.[101]

When he finally arrived in Sinsani at the head of his army in May 1893, Archinard was greeted by Mademba and Captain Bellat, the Resident posted to that town. Archinard publicly thanked Mademba for his "noble attitude in administering in our name the territory so extensive and filled with jealous and greedy chiefs who have betrayed him overtly and who have sought to undermine his authority." Archinard was nonetheless "very pleased to see [Mademba] in such good health" and he commended Mademba for "always being a faithful and devoted servant of the French cause."[102] Archinard sent out runners to summon chiefs of the region to a palabre the following day. N'To, who was "covered with grisgris and proceeded by a large group of musicians," arrived already on the May 17, but Archinard ignored him as he continued his long discussion with Mademba.[103]

By the May 18, a large throng of chiefs and notables had arrived to greet Archinard and to submit to his authority. The palabre lasted well into the night and reconvened the next day. To the assembled crowd, Archinard thanked Mademba for his services and the chiefs for coming. He singled out N'To for his refusal to come to the aid of Mademba and Abderahman for his actions during the rebellion, and that he had heard their excuses, but was not persuaded. He told the chiefs that he had come "not to punish, but to reorganize the land to avoid future troubles." But he warned them that should any group rebel in the future, he would return and demolish their villages. He told the assembled group that France retained confidence in Mademba, but that Sokolo and the surrounding region would henceforth become a separate

---

[99]   Interview with Binke Sadiki Traoré, BaKoroba Kuma, and Binke Baba Kuma, Sinsani, 17 July 1992.
[100] Interview with Dahou Traore, Sibila, July 19, 1992.
[101] For example, Delafosse, *Haut-Sénégal-Niger*.
[102] Archinard, Rap. sur la campagne 1892–93, Paris, Nov. 1893, ANS-AOF 1 D 137.
[103] Méniaud, *Pionniers*, II, 440.

district under the command of a French officer and that because he did not believe that the deep rift between Mademba and N'To could ever be breached and that he recognized the long support N'To had offered France, he separated N'To's villages around Markadugu from Mademba's kingdom and placed them directly under the authority of the Segu district officer. Archinard further diminished Mademba's domain of Kaminiadugu on the right bank of the Niger, which he also placed under Segu's authority. He also charged Captain Bellat with the task of defining more carefully the exact boundaries of Mademba's rump kingdom.[104] Archinard left Sinsani the next day for Segu, then headed back to Kayes and onward to France. It was fitting that the reinscribing of the bargains of collaboration in the reorganization of the kingdom of Sansanding and dependencies should be among Archinard's final acts as supreme military commander of the Soudan.

The Beginning of the End of Military Rule in the Soudan: Governor Grodet, 1893–1895

During the 1892–1893 military campaign, Archinard suffered from serious dysentery or other gastrointestinal diseases referred to as "bilious fever." Before his departure, Archinard appointed Colonel Combes as interim supreme military commander, but Combes fell ill in July 1893.[105] Lieutenant-colonel Bonnier took over as another interim supreme military commander as the under-secretary of state in the Ministry of the Navy Delcassé pondered the future of the Soudan and its leadership. Paris was unhappy with the continuous budgetary overruns caused by these seemingly unending military adventures as well as costly operations to quell rebellions in the Soudan, and equally unhappy with the military leadership's blatant disregard of ministerial instructions to stabilize the colony and stimulate its economy and not to pursue further military conquests. Moreover, the National Assembly continued to harbor deep suspicions about the loyalty of military officers, if not the entire military establishment, following the crisis of 1886–1889, which involved a right-wing antirepublican movement led by General Boulanger.[106] In a surprise move, Delcassé separated Soudan from Senegal and appointed a civilian, Louis Alfonse Grodet, as governor of the Soudan in November 1893. The National Assembly also created a new Ministry of Colonies out of the Ministry of the Navy in 1894.

---

[104] Archinard, Rap. sur la campagne 1892–93, Paris, Nov. 1893, ANS-AOF 1 D 137.

[105] William Ponty was on hand in Saint Louis to bid farewell to Archinard. Ponty was Archinard's "secretary," and as a civilian he nonetheless had very close relations with the military leadership. Méniaud, *Pionniers*, I, 449.

[106] See Conklin, Fishman, and Zaretsky, *France and Its Empire since 1870*, 83–86 and Chapter 6 this book for more detail.

Grodet was a strong-willed administrator with experience as governor in the Antilles and French Guyana. Grodet also had pronounced antimilitary leanings, which probably made him a leading candidate in the eyes of Delcassé and the National Assembly, but he was probably not the best choice to lead a still restless military administration in the Soudan. Many French military men in the field, many of whom administered large districts, resented his intrusion into their freedom of action and often resisted his policies. Grodet could never be sure if his orders would be implemented. Nonetheless, Grodet introduced legislation and polices that began the contested construction of the civilian rule of law, which was to have significant consequences for Mademba and Archinard's model of indirect rule.

Grodet was quick to feel the military's resentment against his efforts to constrain their agenda of combat and conquest. French officers disregarded or circumvented Grodet's orders, particularly those orders that seemed to countermand the district officers' expression of their authority. The application of justice quickly became a site for the struggle between Grodet's vision (supported by the civilian politicians of the Third Republic) of a society ruled by law and by a commitment to basic human rights and the military's commitment to its own rule of law, its autonomy, and its authority. In January 1894, Grodet wrote to Colonel Etienne Bonnier, the supreme military commander, regarding the issue of corporal punishment. "I am absolutely opposed to this type of repression of natives. In my opinion, it undermines [our] prestige in the eyes of the Blacks." Corporal punishment, the military countered, was the logical expression of power and authority even as French officers' replaced African kings as commanders of districts. To military officers, the power to punish was central to maintaining discipline and order. Grodet persisted "In regard to the weak nature of our authority, I believe that using brutal coercion will have no success. It will reduce our authority to their level of morality. It is necessary to treat the native with firm resolve, but also with humanity. In a word, do not confuse resolve with rudeness, energy with brutality."[107] In a circular of February 26, 1894 Grodet formally prohibited the use of corporal punishment in the Soudan. There was undisguised frustration in Grodet's letter of July 19, 1894, when he wrote to the senior military commander of the Eastern region that "I have prohibited [corporal punishment] in the most formal and absolute manner ... I prohibit yet again in the most absolute fashion this type of punishment, which is unworthy of our civilization. Please make certain to bring this letter to the attention of all the district commanders in your region."[108]

[107] Gouv. Grodet, letter to cmdt. sup., Région Nord-Est (Segu), Kayes, Jan. 26, 1894, ANM B 150.

[108] Gouv. Grodet, letter to cmdt. sup., Région Est (Bamako), Kayes, July 19, 1894, ANM 2 M 59.

Grodet used the struggle over corporal punishment as a lever to try to impose a greater administrative order and oversight over the activities of the district officers, most of whom were military officers. To provide a more coherent picture of the administration of justice – and to control better against the abuses – Grodet ordered each district officer to report on the application of justice in his district. "There does not exist in the Soudan a code of administrative justice applicable to the lands placed in our dependence. At this time, I believe, one renders justice by inspiration to prevailing customs whenever possible." While Grodet recognized that in a land populated by different "races" it would be wrong to impose uniformity in judgments, he was concerned that "for identical misdemeanors, the punishment varies according to the temperament of the one who imposes the verdict." Grodet wanted a "guide to the principle offenses" in order to assist the commandants when rendering justice.[109] The reports written in 1894 are of uneven quality, but they are the first of a successive series of questionnaires about the administration of justice and about customs. The very effort of collection of information lay at the heart of the colonial effort to control – over both administrators and Africans.[110] Grodet's efforts also constituted a nascent effort to promote the civilian rule of law.

The Segu administrator's report, written by Lieutenant Quinquandon, is particularly thoughtful. It also reveals both the haphazard dispensation of colonial justice and the underlying struggles over the rule of law.

> At the post of Segu, an officer, usually one of the commandant's assistants, is designated to render justice. The natives of the district present themselves successively at the office of that officer without fear and expose freely their complaints or their requests. Everyone has access to the post and is presented in his turn by an old African chief, who is an aged native of the land and admirably knowledgeable about justice. He is an excellent auxiliary to the officer, who consults him. Many of the cases presented are absolutely local in the land and often quite obscure; it would be very difficult to define a wrong in this or that sense, if one did not have recourse to an ancient of the country.
>
> Judgment is always rendered in the presence of the two parties. In effect, the natives who have a dispute, explain each in his turn and as fully as he wishes, and when the officer is assured that the two have nothing more to add, he pronounces the sentence, which is usually perfectly accepted.[111]

---

[109] Gouv. Grodet, letter to cmdt. sup., Région Nord-Est (Segu), Kayes, Jan. 26, 1894, ANM B 150.

[110] For an Indian example, see especially Nicholas Dirks, "'From Little King to Landlord': Colonial Discourse and Colonial Rule," in *Colonialism and Culture*, ed. Nicolas Dirks (Ann Arbor: University of Michigan Press, 1992).

[111] Cmdt. Quinquandon, Rap. sur le fonctionnement de la justice administrative dans le cercle de Segu, Segu, Apr. 1, 1894, ANM 2 M 92.

Later in this report, Quinquandon raised two additional points. The first is that there was no uniformity to punishments, such that when "two natives commit the same fault, they will likely see two different punishments applied." This was the case because "custom" varied from region to region, among the different "races," and according to extenuating circumstances. Quinquandon was certainly neither the first nor the only one to articulate a concern about the "regularity" of justice, which was a core principle of the civil code in France. This concern with regularity lay at the heart of the tensions between the two models of colonial jostling for prominence in the Soudan.

In his second point, Quinquandon took a forceful stand against Grodet's prohibition against corporal punishment.

> It is regrettable that we cannot apply the usages of the land in all the range of punishments which we inflict, because our humanity opposes some. I speak primarily of corporal punishments. These are the only ones in certain instances which produce the desired effect in the Blacks: corporal punishment is widely used among the natives and they accept it completely. It is part of their morals.

Quinquandon raised an important issue regarding inconsistency in French colonial justice policy: How was it possible on the one hand to respect custom (no matter how arcane and difficult it was to interpret) and not to respect customary punishment?[112] A similar situation prevailed in British Central Africa. Martin Chanock has argued that the terror of precolonial punishments were deeply enmeshed with the maintenance of political authority. Once the ordeal, for example, was removed, the authority of the indigenous rulers, which the British were attempting to foster, weakened. In place of the terror of punishment, Chanock writes, came a "routine oppression."[113]

Already in 1891, Archinard had feared that in establishing French authority, he was inviting Africans to turn to his French officers as judges for their ordinary disputes. "The district officers should not judge disputes except in very exceptional cases and particularly when there are disputes between different villages or cantons or in cases dealing with strangers."[114] It was abundantly clear to Captain Porion in 1894, commandant of Bamako, that he was spending a considerable amount of his time adjudicating local disputes. "Justice," he wrote to Grodet, "is rendered in the headquarters of the district every Monday, Wednesday, and Friday. After listening to the contradictory

---

[112] See similar concerns in Capt. Porion, Étude sur la justice administrative indigène dans le cercle de Bamako, Bamako, July 19, 1894, ANM 2 M 54. Porion was careful to underline that even though corporal punishment was a precolonial practice and widely accepted by Africans, it was no longer applied in his district.

[113] Chanock, *Law, Custom, and Social Order*, 125.

[114] Archinard, letter no. 149, np, Apr. 23, 1891, cited in Lt. Sargols, Notice sur la justice indigène et la justice musulmane au Soudan, np, Mar. 1896, ANM 1 D 15.

statement of the parties, translated by the official interpreter, the commandant gives his verdict." From this passage, it would seem that Porion moved fairly expeditiously through the disputes, but later in his report, he stressed that he consulted with individual notables of the three leading families of the district in his efforts to rendering justice "conforming to the custom of the Bambara and the Maures." Porion also noted that he had charged a group of ten notables to assemble a compendium of the district's customs. This group spent six hours a week on the task and had already distilled the customs relating to marriage, property, and inheritance. This compendium, Porion stated, will shortly serve as a guide for officers charged with rendering justice in the district.[115]

In response to Grodet's suggestion to staff the local tribunals with three French officers, Porion argued that such a plan was both impossible and impractical. Some districts, he reminded Grodet, did not even have three French officers; those that did, the burden of participating in the thrice weekly court would overwhelm the already overburdened administrators. Porion stressed that the power and authority of the commandant was intimately tied to rendering judgments. "Judgments are pronounced by the commandant alone, and to alter that practice would result in the complete destruction of the prestige of the commandant. From the point of view of Bambara law, the commandant replaces the former *faama* and exercises an absolute power."[116] Although Porion had not followed Archinard's advice to avoid entanglement in local disputes, he nonetheless clearly articulated Archinard's instrumentalist position that rendering justice was a clear expression authority. Porion's statements also provide evidence that the district officers were already becoming what Robert Delavignette has described as the *"vrais chefs d'empire."*[117] Porion saw himself as the unquestioned ruler of his district. This is exactly what Grodet was worried about. For Grodet, the power and authority of the French district officers should flow from their prestige as representatives of France and from their reputation for humanity and evenhandedness.

Because of his close ties to the French military, Mademba was certainly aware of the struggles raging through the colonial administration. After his 1893 reorganization of Mademba's kingdom, Archinard ordered Mademba to report regularly about the state of his kingdom to the commandant of Segu. Mademba's monthly reports in 1893 and 1894 were usually mundane and repetitive. At times, he was testy, as when he responded to the commandant of Segu's rebuke that Mademba did not keep him informed about the events happening to the northeast of his kingdom. Mademba wrote back "I have not

---

[115] Capt. Porion, Étude sur la justice administrative indigène dans le cercle de Bamako, Bamako, July 19, 1894, ANM 2 M 54. I have not, however, seen this guide.
[116] Ibid.
[117] Robert Delavignette, *Les vrais chefs de l'empire* (Paris: Gaillmard, 1939).

forgotten [to inform you of this region], but due to the new reorganization, I was not instructed to report on this region." As for Sinsani, Mademba stated that ever since the arrival of Al Hajj Umar more than thirty years ago, he had never seen such extensive and flourishing fields. "Even the *sofa*," Mademba added, "have begun to cultivate seriously this season despite the scarcity of food here."[118] A bit more unusual in his correspondence was his request for a monthly shipment of flour. Mademba reported to Segu that his cook was also a baker. Fresh bread, Mademba promised, would be waiting for any Europeans who made the journey to Sinsani.[119] By the beginning of 1895, Mademba reported to Segu that he had started experimenting with growing wheat in order to avoid relying on shipments from France through Segu.[120]

Governor Grodet visited Mademba in Sinsani during a tour of the Niger River in April 1895, but I do not seem to have any archival records of this visit.[121] Later that month Grodet was forced from office by the military he could not control and by his own failure to adapt to the peculiar pressures of building a new colony in the heart of the West African interior with inadequate financial resources. With the exception of the major catastrophe of Lieutenant-colonel Bonnier's march on Timbuktu in early 1894, which underestimated the Tuareg capacity for resistance and resulted in the nighttime raid on the French camp that left seventeen French soldiers dead, no significant rebellions shook the relative calm along the Middle Niger valley. Mademba's wheat experiment was part of the transformation of his public persona from *faama* and loyal intermediary into an agricultural innovator and champion of promoting economic development in the new colony. This effort to burnish the image of a progressive, enlightened rule bumped up against Mademba's increasingly erratic, despotic, paranoid behavior. Grodet's rule-of-law seedling grew steadily after 1895 and brought new and uncomfortable attention to Mademba's rule in Sinsani.

[118] Mademba, letter to cmdt., Segu, Sinsani, Aug. 25, 1893, ANM 1 E 220.
[119] Mademba, letter to cmdt., Segu, Sinsani, May 27, 1893, ANM 1 E 220.
[120] Mademba, letter to cmdt., Segu, Sinsani, Jan. 1, 1895, ANM 1 E 220.
[121] Gouv. Soudan (Grodet), telegram to Min. Col., Mopti, Apr. 9, 1895, ANOM Soudan I-7.

4

"A Curious and Very Engaging Mixture of European and Native Customs"*
Republican Traditions and African Kings, 1895–1899

Mademba could not have but felt unmoored by the Archinard's 1893 reprimand and his redefinition of Mademba's place within the military's agenda for the French Soudan. He certainly felt relieved that Archinard did not dismiss him as king as he had Bojan. Even though Archinard was battling serious health problems in 1893, his rapid departure from the Soudan for convalescence in France only disguised the more fundamental changes facing the military. Any change to the military's prominence in the Soudan had significant implications for Mademba, since his bargains of collaboration were made with the French military.

By the time of Archinard's departure in 1893, the practice of administration in the Soudan was founded upon a broad and fairly loose application of the concept of protectorate administered by indigenous rulers mixed together with areas administered directly by French officers. The day-to-day activities of rule were to be left to Africans operating within reconstituted African kingdoms, chosen more for their loyalty to France than for their intrinsic legitimacy. French officers were to spend their time winning battles and gaining glory. However, even as Archinard tried hard to deflect Paris's efforts to establish civilian authority, he put French officers in a position where they were obliged to spend more of their time with the ordinary business of empire than with the exciting prospects of conquest. Paradoxically, Archinard's model of the reconstituted African kingdom served only to increase the burden of the French officers' daily activities because the lack of legitimacy often fueled rebellions.

Archinard's model of colonial rule did not long remain unchallenged. Despite the rapid forward march of conquest, the French National Assembly was running out of patience with military rule in West Africa. Minister of Navy Théophile Delcassé dismissed Archinard, who was both popular among the French officers eager for combat opportunities and among the French masses eager for stories of conquests, and appointed Louis Alphonse Grodet as civilian governor in 1893.[1] Mademba, who increasingly saw

---

* Dubois, *Tombouctou la mystérieuse*, 92.

[1] William Schneider, *An Empire for the Masses: The French Popular Image of Africa, 1870–1900* (Westport, CN: Greenwood Press, 1982); Tony Chafer and Amanda Sackur,

conspiracies through the opaque haze of incomplete information and his own insecurities, no doubt worried about Grodet's intentions in regard to his own position.

The Ministry of Colonies soon realized that its appointment of Grodet was not yielding the results it anticipated. Grodet was recalled in June 1895 and Lieutenant-Colonel Louis Edgar de Trentinian was named interim governor and supreme military commander of native troops, thus promising the return of the military to prominence in the Soudan. But Trentinian's appointment was not an unalloyed victory for the military. Grodet's recall and Trentinian's appointment coincided with the creation of l'Afrique Occidentale Française (AOF) under Governor-general Jean-Baptiste Chaudié. The Ministry of Colonies expected the creation of the AOF to introduce new institutions guiding policy and budgetary oversight for all the member colonies.[2]

Even though Trentinian's appointment provided some stability to Mademba's bargains of collaboration with the military, Mademba's sense of isolation and fears for his status increased. He maintained ties with his old patrons and nurtured new ones whenever he could, especially with those who shared Mademba's sense of his mission to promote French interests even as he promoted his own. During the period 1895–1899, Mademba increasingly withdrew into his palace, where he surrounded himself with his many wives and his own sense of royal vocation and splendor. He actively increased his "harem" during this period, often taking whichever girl or woman he wanted regardless of their consent or marital status. Although Mademba's control over his women had been a source of anxiety since at least 1891, when he was first appointed king, his obsessions increased during this period. This chapter explores how the wider changes in the landscapes of colonial power influenced Mademba and his kingdom during this crucial period of institutional change in the Soudan.

Mademba's Bargains of Collaboration under Pressure: Grodet and Trentinian

Mademba did not feel comfortable with Governor Grodet. They did not share the same intimate experience of military comradery, the thrill of battle, the challenges of strategy, and the exuberance of conquest. Mademba worried about Grodet's efforts to weaken the military and in particular to weaken his patron, Colonel Archinard. William Ponty, Archinard's personal secretary, who would eventually be appointed lieutenant-governor of the Soudan, had

---

Promoting the Colonial Idea: Propaganda and Visions of Empire in France (New York: Palgrave, 2002).

[2] Newbury, "The Formation of the French West Africa Federation"; Conklin, *A Mission to Civilize.*

already in 1894 been charged with recovering Archinard's personal papers.[3] These were likely papers relating to the administration and organization of the newly conquered Soudan and the military's complicity in the slave trade referred to in the following letter. In January 1896, Mademba wrote to Archinard about his encounters with Grodet some eight months before.

> Our friends who are seriously concerned about me have in effect written to warn me about Mr. Grodet's intentions when passing through Sansanding while on tour. They warned me to be on guard because Mr. Grodet is interested in certain personal papers that I may have that could be used against you. I awaited his visit with firm resolution that I will act officially correct with him as necessitated by our formal relations [but will not divulge anything to him]. In effect, he camped within a kilometer upstream from Sansanding without stopping to stay here. The next day he continued his route to Mopti, although I did see him from the banks of the river. He told me that we will return in a month.
>
> On his return from Timbuktu, he had a short visit with me in Sansanding, but he did not discuss the papers in question. We only spoke about the proposed boundary dispute with Sokolo. I was relieved that he left my territory intact, under the same conditions that you had made with the interim commandant of Sokolo [back in 1893] ... I am glad that this affair was resolved without incident. I had prepared arguments that invoked your name in order to provide context to this affair. You must know, my Colonel, that I could not do otherwise because your name remains always attached to all [administrative] questions in the Soudan and you were the author of all the texts that form the law of the land.
>
> Mr. Grodet must have known my opinion in advance of his departure from Kayes. I have never concealed my opinions from his friends who have come here. Each time they initiated discussion about [the events of] Timbuktu, I cut them short and declared clearly that General Desbordes and the colonels Archinard and Bonnier are my friends and it pains me to hear at my home these inexact accusations leveled against them.
>
> These friends of Mr. Grodet also wanted me to discuss how the Commandant Superieur tolerated the trade in slaves, but I answered that on the contrary, he made serious efforts to suppress this trade. I reminded them that it has been less than fifteen years that we have begun to transform a land as large as the Soudan.[4]

---

[3] Gouv. Grodet, letter to min. col., Kayes, Apr. 6, 1894, ANOM Soudan I-6a. In this letter, Grodet authorized Ponty to search for Archinard's papers, but that he was to decide with the archivist of the squadron which papers were personal and which were administrative and should be retained in the archives.

[4] Mademba, letter to Archinard, Sansanding, Jan. 15, 1896, SHD Papiers Réquin (Mademba letters to Archinard) 1 K 108.

I have virtually nothing from Grodet's side on this visit to Mademba. On April 9, 1895, Grodet telegrammed the minister of colonies that he had arrived in Mopti having spent five days in Segu. Grodet added that he planned a visit to the *faama* of Sansanding on his return.[5]

Grodet's departure from the Soudan in 1895 reflected a change in the Ministry of Colonies' approach to its French West African colonies. By then, the ministry must have realized that Grodet was given the task of taming the military that was well beyond his abilities given the weak institutions of colonial rule and the lack of trained civilian personnel who could replace military officers in local administrative roles. Lieutenant Hourst, who had fought under Archinard, captured the sentiment of many French officers of the relief that they felt when he wrote that "Colonel du Trentinian, who has – finally! – replaced M. Grodet in the government of the Soudan."[6]

In his next letter to Archinard, Mademba wrote how much he appreciated Archinard's nomination for his advancement in the Legion of Honor to the rank of officer despite the setbacks of 1891–1892. "I have not for one single instant forgotten," Mademba wrote, "that you have always and in all circumstances supported me ever since I had the good fortune and honor to meet you."[7] Mademba also reported to Archinard that he recently had the honor to meet the new lieutenant-governor, Lieutenant-Colonel Trentinian, who replaced Grodet. Trentinian visited Mademba in Sinsani for two days during a tour of the Niger River from Koulikoro to Timbuktu.[8] Although Mademba did not know Trentinian before, his relief in having a new military patron was palpable. "I have found with Colonel de Trentinian that same sympathy that I have from you." Trentinian explained to Mademba how much he also appreciated Archinard's support and promotion of his own career.[9]

Even though they were patron and client, Archinard and Mademba expressed interest in each other's well-being that persisted even after Archinard left the Soudan. Mademba updated Archinard that his young son, Cheikh Mahmoudou, who was born in Kayes in 1888 during Archinard's first tour as supreme military commander, was now attending the White Fathers' school in Segu, and that his two eldest sons were pursuing advanced schooling in Saint Louis. Gustave was in school with the Brothers of Ploërmel and, thanks to Governor Lamothe of Senegal, Mamadou Racine, the eldest, was in

[5] Grodet, telegram to min. col., Apr. 9, 1895, Mopti, ANOM Soudan I-7.

[6] Hourst, *Sur le Niger et au Pays des Touaregs*, 33.

[7] Mademba, letter to Archinard, Feb. 23, 1896, Sansanding, SHD Papiers Réquin (Mademba letters to Archinard) 1 K 108.

[8] Gouv.-gen., letter to min. col., Mar. 16, 1896, Saint Louis, ANOM Soudan I-7.

[9] Mademba, letter to Archinard, Feb. 23, 1896, Sansanding, SHD Papiers Réquin (Mademba letters to Archinard) 1 K 108.

the *collège des fils de chefs.* "All my family" Mademba wrote, "has charged me with sending you their fondest memories and I send you my most sympathetic wishes for your good health."[10]

Mademba's sense of a reemerging stability in the changing political order of the Soudan probably grew in response to requests by the Segu district commander in 1895 that he, as a fellow king, should reach out to Babemba in Sikasso and encourage him to rally to the French cause. Mademba informed the commander that he had indeed received a response to his letter to Babemba, in which the *faama* of Sikasso replied that he would be happy to agree to the French demands if the French would provide him with firearms.[11] Babemba was not only engaged in securing his own power in Kenedugu but he was increasingly worried about Samory's designs on his kingdom.[12]

Within this context of shifting colonialism, Félix Dubois, a French adventurer, reporter, and entrepreneur, helped promote the image of Mademba as a "progressive" African king. Working as a reporter for the French newspapers *Figaro* and *L'Illustration,* Dubois was on a voyage to Timbuktu when he passed through Sinsani in late 1894 and again on his return in February 1895.[13] On his return, he was delirious with fever and recuperated in Mademba's palace. Dubois compressed his two visits into one section of his memoire, *Tombouctou la mystérieuse,* published first in 1897. Dubois was clearly impressed with Mademba. Mademba also took advantage of Dubois's visit to begin to present a revised version of his life that included allusions to his royal heritage. Dubois's version of Mademba's origins as a son of a Wolof chief may be the first recorded instance of this version of Mademba's efforts to lay claim to the "traditional" legitimacy of his position as *faama.*

> Twelve hours from Segu by boat along the Niger River lies Sansanding, on the left bank. Here there is neither a soldier nor a white. Nor is the city and territory governed by a native chief. After direct administration and the protectorate, we have a new form of our domination, and I might add one of the most interesting variants. This is the initiative of Colonel Archinard. This is not a government by blacks who have not yet been in contact with western civilization, but by a Europeanized black.[14]

Dubois described the *école des otages* as one of the "wise institutions" created by Governor Faidherbe. At this school were sons of kings and major chiefs of

---

[10] Ibid.

[11] Cmdt. du Région Nord Est, letter to lt.-gouv., Segu, Oct. 20, 1895, ANS-AOF 15 G 174.

[12] Yves Person, *Samori: Une Révolution Dyula,* three vols. (Dakar: IFAN, 1968–1974); Soumaïla Sanoko, *Le royaume du Kénédougou, 1825–1898* (Bamako: Nouvelle Imprimerie Bamakoise, 2010).

[13] Yves-Jean Saint-Martin, *Félix Dubois, 1862–1945: Grand reporter et explorateur de Panama à Tamanrasset* (Paris: L'Harmattan, 1999), 66–83.

[14] Dubois, *Tombouctou la mystérieuse,* 87.

Senegal, who were exposed to French civilization and "impregnated" with our ideas, who then became part of a "cult of France." Many of these students succeeded their fathers as chiefs; others entered the Senegalese or Soudanese military or civilian bureaucracies. Some rose to ranks of officers while others took on the important tasks of interpreters and others entered into administrative functions, including the telegraph service.

> And such was the case with Mademba, son of a Waalo chief with considerable religious and political authority. Around 1869, he entered into the Telegraph service. During twenty years, he aided the cause of French penetration with the most devoted services having served successively Colonel Borgnis-Desbordes as well as Colonel Archinard on the long march to the Niger. After the capture of Segu, the latter believed that it was time to reward such a worthy servant and he created on the left bank a little kingdom with Sansanding as its capital.

> This government of blacks along the Niger by a black of Senegal fashioned and affiliated with us, impregnated with our manner of living and thinking, entirely devoted to us and our ideas, in one word, this is a government of a Black Frenchman and it is a happy discovery. Here among the people who only yesterday surrendered, is a lively and daily teacher, who encourages them to change so they will become devoted to us as well. When we remember just how modest are both the resources and personnel to effect these changes in the Soudan, one would be very hard pressed to find a more precious or worthy moral force.[15]

Dubois felt no need to authenticate Mademba's claim to be the son of a Waalo chief. Afterall, Mademba attended the *école des otages*, which was the school for sons of chiefs. Not all chiefs sent their sons to the *école*; some sent their slaves or other "hostages" instead.[16] Dubois considered Mademba a black Frenchman, without even reflecting on the ambiguities of his *originaire* status.[17] Dubois's description of Mademba echoed Thiriet's 1893 comments about Mademba's hospitality.

> Mademba wears native dress, but his language and his manners are those of a European and his hospitality is royal. The lunch he offered us was generous, well prepared and served and the meats were tender … The table was covered with fine linen and crystal from the best stores in France, the water was fresh and excellent wine and Champagne accompanied the desserts and pastries made by a very able black cook. At the conclusion of the meal, we had coffee and liqueurs as we listened to a varied and interesting conversation by the fama, who also offered us

---

[15] Ibid., 88–89.
[16] Bouche, "L'enseigement," 328–341; Duke Bryant, *Education as Politics*, 6, 33.
[17] As discussed in the Introduction, exactly what these rights were remained somewhat unclear.

excellent cigars. We could almost forget that we were in the middle of the
Soudan, in a lost corner of Africa thousands of kilometers from civilization.[18]

Thiriet nicely captured Mademba's method of winning the affections of
Europeans in the Soudan, who were most often deprived of the comforts of
home. But Mademba's method was not merely instrumental. He believed that
he represented "civilization" in this isolated corner of the Soudan, even though
his persona was far more complicated than being merely a black Frenchman.
Dubois captured well this complex bricolage of Mademba's persona.

> Every white who passes through Sansanding, whether his position is
> important or not, finds a warm welcome of a friend. Even if you only
> meet him once … you will never forget him. This black is the small
> Manteu-Bleu of Europeans in the Soudan. Having appreciated all the
> benefits that he has received from his European education and although
> he is a Muslim, he sends his two eldest sons to the Catholic mission
> schools in Saint Louis. Subscribing to our journals and newspapers,
> Mademba is current with all the politics and events in France, and
> especially those of the colonial movement.[19]

Being conversant with the debates about colonization in France, Mademba
knew that the current idioms involved *la mise en valeur* or economic development. Dubois was very interested in this area, both as a reporter but also as
budding entrepreneur. Dubois would over the next decade promote aggressively a scheme to develop roads and import trucks to carry goods and
passengers from the glacially advancing railhead to Bamako.[20] Before his
arrival in Sinsani, Dubois had seen from his perch in a Niger canoe the
expansive cotton fields that covered both banks of the Niger around
Nyamina and Segu, which he described as "vast fields dedicated to this
precious textile."[21] Dubois listened carefully as Mademba discussed his various
agricultural experiments including wheat, cotton, and rice as well as his
orchards of plum and peach trees. Mademba was eager to try out different
varieties of food and industrial crops. He was especially eager to promote
cotton. In 1897, Mademba wrote to Archinard that the future of local cotton
for the French market was limited because "our cotton, which has very short
fibers, has no value in France." Mademba requested that Archinard send him
long staple cotton seeds for his experimental fields.[22] In September 1897,
Mademba wrote that his experiments with long staple Georgia cotton were

---

[18] Thiriet, *Au Soudan Français*, 177–178.
[19] Dubois, *Tombouctou la mystérieuse*, 89.
[20] Saint-Martin, *Félix Dubois*, 107–136. Dubois's enterprise failed by the early 1900s.
[21] Dubois, *Tombouctou la mystérieuse*, 78–80.
[22] Mademba, letter to Archinard, Sinsani, Mar. 1, 1897, SHD Papiers Réquin (Mademba
      letters to Archinard) 1 K 108.

already yielding "remarkable" results, with these varieties much further developed than native cotton planted at the same time.[23] During these years, Mademba actively promoted his kingdom as a site for agricultural innovation as he sought to refashion his identity into that of a progressive agent of economic development in the Soudan. Dubois described Mademba's agricultural experimentation as evidence of "practical colonization."[24] Dubois did not mention and Mademba certainly did not volunteer information about who worked on Mademba's experimental fields and under what conditions. This was to become a major issue in 1898 as Mademba came under increasing attention from the French colonial administration.

As Dubois toured Mademba's experimental fields and Sinsani itself, he often heard the natives say that "Mademba is not a black, he is a *toubab* (European)." Dubois interpreted this as praise, noting that this appellation had nothing to do with race, but with the high esteem that the natives have for Europeans and the progress that they have brought to the land. Calling Mademba a *toubab* may well have been high praise, but it was not without irony that the term also reflected the alien nature of Mademba's status in Sinsani. Dubois also noted that Europeans shared this general sense of high esteem when discussing Mademba and stressed that the Europeans "do not *tutoie* Mademba ... [but] treat him as a white."[25]

Dubois's visit to Mademba revealed part of the complex persona Mademba had developed since his enthronement in 1891, if not since he joined the colonial Post and Telegraph Department in 1869. As I examine Dubois's discussion of Mademba's clothing choices, we need to be mindful of Mademba's efforts barely ten years earlier when he pressed his military patrons to help him acquire a uniform reflecting his rank and stature in the Post and Telegraph Department. Clothing reflected status in the Soudan.[26] Dubois noted that Mademba was "knowledgeable of the multiple native idioms, having traveled across the Soudan for many years," suggesting that Mademba knew well the statements he was making both in words and attire.

> The king's wardrobe remains local. He has avoided dressing himself in European clothing, but he has adopted a red fez and a long cape in the form of a medieval shroud, green in color, and heavily decorated with gold embroidery and bedecked with diverse medals of which one is the medal of the Legion of Honor. I admit that he has, just a small resemblance, to a king of the theater who appears to have just left the storeroom of the accessories. At the very least, however, he avoids looking ridiculous in vest and jacket.[27]

---

[23] Mademba, letter to cmdt. Segu, Sinsani, Sept. 1, 1897, ANM 1 E 220.
[24] Dubois, *Tombouctou la mystérieuse*, 80.
[25] Ibid., 80.
[26] Roberts, *Two Worlds of Cotton*, chapter 2; Osborn, "Circle of Iron."
[27] Dubois, *Tombouctou la mystérieuse*, 91.

Figure 4.1   Mademba Sy, ca. 1900.
(Source: Pérignon Collection, Bibliothèque nationale de France, ca. 1895–1900, with permission)

Figure 4.1, taken by Lieutentant Pérignon probably around 1900, captures well Dubois's description of Mademba's royal attire. Figure 4.2 was taken by the great colonial photographer of French West Africa, Edmond Fortier, also captured Mademba in his regal splendor. Although by the time Fortier staged this photograph in late 1905 or 1906, Mademba had even more medals and

Figure 4.2   Mademba surrounded by his courtiers and praise singer, ca. 1905.
(Source: Fortier Image of Mademba, ca. 1905–1906)

may have modified his attire just a bit.[28] Absent was the red fez that Dubois has remarked. And it is not clear if Mademba's cape was still green, but green was not a local dye in the color pallet of the Soudanese textile industry.

Dubois further elaborated Mademba's affinity for bricolage. He remarked that in Mademba's kingdom as in his household "there reigned a curious but quite engaging mixture of European and native customs." This *mélange*, as Dubois put it, was most noticeable in Mademba's palace and at his dinner table.

> Mademba's residence is composed of a series of grand courtyards, which are divided by numerous buildings, all of which are enclosed by walls. His residence is simultaneously a farm, a military barracks, houses of commerce, and the palace, which is like those of the kings of Homer. To reach the last courtyard where the monarch dwells, one has to pass groups of horses, women, sheep, children, chicken and ducks, groups of servants some of whom are armed while others measure rice or millet, prepare bars of salt, tobacco, and kola nuts for sale. Once in Mademba's apartments, next to the skins of cattle and panthers that cover the floor for the native

---

[28] Philippe David, *Inventaire général des cartes postals Fortier* (St. Julien au Sault: self-published, 1986), vol. 1, 3.

audiences one finds comfortable tables and chairs, lamps, clocks as well as thousands of European objects that are in themselves of little interest, but become remarkable when found in a native's flat.[29]

As an expert reporter, Dubois made much of these juxtapositions, which he knew would also interest his readers. And his publishers certainly agreed. *Tombouctou la mystérieuse* was republished in 1897 and an English edition was published that year with Heinemann in London. Dubois's next passage elaborates further these juxtapositions as he described Mademba's Muslim practices and the meal service that he obviously enjoyed.

> Mademba retains the faith of his parents as do a number of his subjects who practice Islam. He voluntarily practices polygamy, but not all the other required practices. Towards the end of the day, under the watchful eyes of the chickens and cocks, who devour their ration of millet, talking and sitting next to Mademba, I drain my glass of absinth or whatever he served me from his many bottles as I looked melancholically at his undefiled glass. Full of tact and unwilling to scandalize, his glass contained pure water. Nor did he dally as the sun set as he prostrated himself in the prayers of a good Muslim. Shortly thereafter we were at dinner, surrounded by his intimate servants, most of them Senegalese as their master. And suddenly, there was another glass before me filled with red wine or champagne from the royal cellars, not least the final glass of Chartreuse. In addition, the meal was served in the European style with plates and utensils changed with every course, a small luxury that one rarely finds even among the Whites of the Soudan.[30]

After dinner, Mademba regaled his guest with stories of Sinsani's lost splendor, its heroic resistance against the Futanke, and its subsequent decline. Mademba described Sinsani's gradual recovery and the path to the future that he envisioned for the city. Dubois was impressed with Mademba's detailed information about colonial conquest and the pacification of the region. Mademba also arranged for Dubois to chat with Boua Cisse, the old village chief, who Mademba appointed as chief upon his arrival and whom we shall encounter again shortly. Boua Cisse explained how before the Futanke conquest of the Middle Niger, almost all of the freight canoes that traversed the Niger between Sinsani and Timbuktu belonged to his family carrying commodities and slaves by the hundreds. Not long after this interview Boua Cisse fled Sinsani fearful for his life.

Lieutenant Hourst, who fought side by side with Mademba during the Baninko revolt and who called Mademba his friend, also noticed the curious *mélange* of cultures that was Mademba during his visit in December 1895 en

---

[29] Dubois, *Tombouctou la mystérieuse*, 90.
[30] Ibid., 90–91.

route to Timbuktu and down the Niger to Sarafere. Alerted as to his arrival, Mademba greeted the mission on the banks of the Niger, "surrounded by his griots and his guards, wearing his superb green cape on which shines the Legion of Honor medal so valiantly won." As Hourst's party of European officers entered Mademba's palace, Mademba

> removed his cape, the black chief disappeared and we rediscovered the former Mademba, the learned, the intelligent, the fine conversationalist, who was well-informed of European events, and the man who all French travelers in the Soudan have come to appreciate. He offered us the honors of an excellent meal, very European, and we drank together glasses of champagne, which he did not disdain because he does not belong to the foolish fanaticism of so many of his co-religionists.[31]

While Mademba did not drink alcohol together with Dubois, he apparently did not hesitate to do so with his French officer friend.

As Hourst described Mademba's palace, he noticed not only the guards at the entrance but the large number of women and children in the various vestibules leading deeper into the core of the palace. Hourst thought that there was "something irregular" about these women and children who served Mademba. Hourst, however, noted that "Mademba was in general pleased with the choice of his servants, not the least because nowhere in the Soudan did I see any comparable collection of pretty girls."[32] This collection of pretty girls was separate from the inner rooms where his wives lived, which even Hourst did not enter.

Hourst's party of European officers and African sailors remained in Sinsani for three days before continuing on their mission. As a crude marine, Hourst gave his African crew two months advance salary, shore leave, and a cautionary speech. "My friends," he began, "we will be shortly be passing Timbuktu; at no point will you woo the women you will meet. This will only result in disputes and possibly fights with the natives. I advise you to take your advance and enjoy Sansanding, because for the next year, once we are finished with Sansanding, we are finished with women." Tongue in cheek, Hourst added that if such a thing as birth statistics existed in Mademba's kingdom, he would not be surprised if nine months later there appeared a significant increase in births.[33] It was not clear what Hourst was implying by suggesting that the women of Sinsani were somehow more available than in other possibly stricter Muslim towns along the Niger. Clearly, however, Mademba's large entourage

[31] Hourst, *Sur la Mission Hourst*, 66.

[32] Ibid., 65. Hourst called them *korosiguis*, which he translated as "those who stand to the side."

[33] Ibid., 66–67.

of women in his palace made a statement about how the *faama* exhibited his power.

Conflict of Colonialisms: The Third Republic's Antimilitarism and the Founding of the AOF

Disappointed with Grodet and realizing that far stronger measures were needed to tame the military in the Soudan, Minister of Colonies Chautemps established the AOF in 1895 and appointed Jean-Baptiste Chaudié as governor-general. The establishment of the AOF was but another stage in the ongoing conflicts over colonialism, which pitted Archinard's model of indirect rule against the centralized, uniform, and regularized program of the republican civilizing mission.[34] It was not until 1899, at the end of Trentinian's appointment, that the minister of Colonies again sought to impose a civilian order on the Soudan. In 1899, William Ponty, born Amédée William Merlaud-Ponty but preferring the shortened version of his name, was appointed the "permanent delegate of the governor-general in the Soudan." This was effect-ively the governorship, and his title was so changed in 1904. Ponty would play an increasingly important role in the events of 1899 and 1900 when Mademba was under formal investigation for alleged abuses of power, which is the subject of the next chapter. Ponty had been a civilian appointee to the administrative office of the supreme military commander since 1890, inter-rupted only briefly by a tour of duty in Madagascar. As a civilian, Ponty had considerable combat experience – he was actually wounded in action against Samory's forces – and both understood and respected the military agenda in the Soudan. This helps to account for his success as governor. His tenure in office was central to the elaboration of both the administrative structure of the colony and many of its economic, political, and social policies. He remained in office until 1908, when he became governor-general.[35]

The Third Republic's deep ambivalence to the French military had its roots in the general antimilitarism of the 1880s. Throughout the nineteenth century, the republican tradition viewed the military as a monarchist and royalist bastion of privilege, power, and patronage. Republicans saw the military as opposed to their concepts of civil society. Antimilitary tendencies were enflamed by the Boulanger affair from 1886 to 1889. General Georges Boulanger had been a highly popular minister of War in one of Georges Clemenceau's short-lived ministries. Although he was in office a mere eighteen months, General Boulanger quickly rose to be a commanding political figure

---

[34] The best source for a critical interpretation of the republican principles of France's civilizing mission in West Africa is Conklin, *A Mission to Civilize*. The program of republican civilizing mission was never fully realized.

[35] Johnson, "William Ponty," 127–156.

with a belligerent anti-German nationalist message. His political ideology was inconsistent and became increasingly demagogic and rightist. Boulanger's pretensions to authoritarian political role frightened republican sentiment in France, which associated Boulanger with the old fears of military power and privilege. The Boulanger affair contributed to the Third Republic's increasing intolerance of the military's insubordination in the Soudan.[36]

The Third Republic's attack on the military's autonomy in the Soudan also had its roots in the predominance of lawyers as both deputies in the National Assembly and in the civil service. By the mid nineteenth century, the study of the law had become one of the most popular choices for a liberal education.[37] Philip Nord has aptly termed the late nineteenth century the "republic of lawyers."[38] These newly empowered lawyers also engaged in a major assault upon the metropolitan judiciary. Between 1879 and 1883, hundreds of judge-ships dating from the Second Empire were abolished, well over a thousand justices quit or were forced to leave office in what has been termed a "judicial revolution." The new organization of justice in France was to be founded upon the new commitment to republican principles of increased attention to per-sonal and public freedoms and increased involvement of the citizenry in its operations. Jury trials became more common.[39] Civil servants and elected officials with legal backgrounds who were willing to reform existing insti-tutions in order to bring them more in line with contemporary policy and republican ideals were also eager to reach deeply into the colonies.

What is of consequence for our story is that the French military officers in the field experienced the pressures of antimilitarism and institutional reform. Some of these pressures were felt through efforts to directly change the order of command by placing a civilian at the head of the newly conquered regions of the Soudan in 1893. But they were also felt by the increasing pressures to regularize administrative actions. Such regularization played itself out clearly in the application of justice in the Soudan and the promotion of the civilian rule of law.

Changes in the place of law within the program of colonialism reflected the struggles among the French over competing models of colonialism. Shifting administrative practice therefore reflected debates about the meaning of

---

[36] James Harding, *The Astonishing Adventure of General Boulanger* (New York: Scribner, 1971); William D. Irvine, *The Boulanger Affair Reconsidered: Royalism, Boulangism, and the Origins of the Radical Rights in France* (New York: Oxford University Press, 1989); Jean Garrigues, *Le Général Boulanger* (Paris: O. Orban, 1991).

[37] Theodore Zeldin, *France 1848–1945* (Oxford: Clarendon Press, 1973), vol. 1, 483–484.

[38] Philip Nord, *The Republican Moment: Struggles for Democracy in Nineteenth-Century France* (Cambridge, MA: Harvard University Press, 1995), chapter 6, esp. pp. 136–137.

[39] Jean-Louis Debré, *La justice au XIXè siècle: Les magistrats* (Paris: Librarie Académique Perrin, 1981); Jean-Pierre Royer, Renée Martinage, and Pierre Lecocq, *Juges et notables au XIXè siècle* (Paris: Presses Universitaires de France, 1982), pp. 359–370.

colonialism.[40] As discussed in Chapter 4, the application of justice and the issue of corporal punishment quickly became a site for the struggle between Grodet's vision (supported by the civilian politicians of the Third Republic) of a society ruled by law and by a commitment to basic human rights and the military's commitment to its autonomy, its authority, and its own sense of the rule of law. Appointed to replace Grodet, Lieutenant-Colonel Louis Edgar de Trentinian was an old military hand, but astute enough to recognize the waning of military rule in the Soudan. Trentinian pushed for the establishment of a more formal native tribunal system in order to remove the bulk of "little affairs" from the shoulders of the French commandants. The natives, Trentinian noted, have become accustomed to bring even their smallest dispute before the jurisdiction of the commandant, who is reduced to the role of a simple justice of the peace. "Do not," Trentinian cautioned his administrators, "get mixed up in the many disputes without significance, which demand understanding of the morals and traditions of the population. Give instead additional prestige and authority to the native leaders, who are our indispensable intermediaries."[41] Depending upon the status of the litigants, the task of rendering justice should fall upon the elders, the notables, the village chiefs, and the marabouts. Commandants were to judge only in cases involving disputes between villages, those involving strangers, and cases of serious offenses. In so doing, Trentinian began to articulate a structure for the administration of native justice and to regularize it. Regularization flowed logically from the desire to spare the commandants these tasks, but also to provide a means of controlling for abuses and arbitrariness. Regularization led inexorably toward codification and inevitably toward a resolution of the struggle between the two colonialisms of the Soudan. Trentinian's governorship coincided with the formation and formative years of the AOF.

The creation of a separate Ministry of Colonies in 1894 further strengthened the hand of those wishing to impose the civilian agenda over that of the soldiers in French West Africa. In June 1895, Minister of Colonies Chautemps drew up the constitution of the French West African government-general. Despite its little success until 1897, the Indochinese model lay at the heart of the efforts to establish the government-general.[42]

---

[40] Richard Roberts, *Litigants and Households: African Disputes and Colonial Courts in the French Soudan, 1895–1912* (Portsmouth, NH: Heineman, 2005), chapter 2.

[41] Lt.-gouv. Trentinian, Note circular, Bamako, Feb. 3, 1896, ANM 2 M 4.

[42] The regulations of the government-general of Indochina are part of the file dealing with the constitution of the AOF. Exposé sommaire de la reglementation concernant l'organisation administrative de l'Indo-Chine française, nd, np, ANOM AOF VII-2. Arthur Girault, *Principes de colonisation et de législation coloniale* (Paris: L. Tenin, fourth edition, 1921–1923), vol. 1, 277; Jacques Thobie, "La France coloniale de 1870 à 1914," in *Histoire de la France coloniale: Des origines à 1914*, eds. Jean Meyer, Jean Tarrade, Annie Rey-Goldzeiguer, and Jacques Thobie (Paris: Armand Colin, 1991), 685–697, 706.

In appointing Jean-Baptiste Chaudié governor-general of French West Africa, Chautemps hoped to impose a clear order of command over the newly created colonies of French West Africa and to insure that the minister's program would prevail.

> In appointing you to the high functions that are invested in your office, the government of the Republic does not under-estimate the difficulty nor the importance of the tasks delegated to you. You are to be the artisan of a program whose success will bring prosperity to the lands united under your command. Thanks to the powers you have, the government expects you to imbue our colonial policies in these regions with a method and a spirit that they have been all too often lacking.[43]

Chautemps chose Chaudié as governor-general because of the latter's proven record as an inspector within the Ministry of Navy. The role of the colonial inspector changed over the course of the nineteenth century; with the creation of a separate Ministry of Colonies, the corps of colonial inspectors was given a fuller mandate and a higher degree of autonomy.[44] Chaudié, who had been a naval commissioner and inspector in the Ministry of Navy, was promoted to the senior position of inspector-general in the Ministry of Colonies. Chautemps thus expected Chaudié to impose a greater regularization of colonial rule.

The governor-general of the AOF was simultaneously the head of the newly federated colonies and the governor of Senegal. As governor-general, Chaudié struggled to impose his will on the lieutenant-governors, who, much like their counterparts in Indochina, retained a wide degree of autonomy. This was especially true in terms of financial autonomy. Colonial budgets were approved by the minister of Colonies; Côte d'Ivoire and Dahomey retained an even more tenuous relationship to the government-general. The only direct control the governor-general actually had was over Senegalese affairs and over military operations in the Soudan. Without the power of the purse or clear authority over decisions in each colony, the government-general of French West Africa was, in Girault's terms, "a useless facade."[45]

Chaudié was generally unable to restrain the military from pursuing its goals. This was particularly the case of their goals to conquer Samory and Babemba. As Grodet had tried, Chaudié used the regularization of justice as an instrument for grafting the "spirit" of civilian rule onto the military's view of

---

[43] Min. Col., confidential instructions to Gouv.-gen. Chaudié, Paris, Oct. 11, 1895, ANOM AOF I-1.

[44] For a general history of inspections in France, see Cédric Glineur, *Histoire des Institutions adminstratives, Xè–XIXè siècle* (Paris: Économica, 2017); Girault, *Principes,* part 2, vol. 1, 352–371.

[45] Girault, *Principes,* part 2, vol. 1, 297. See also Newbury, "The Formation of the French West Africa Federation."

colonialism. Chaudié continued Grodet's the attack on corporal punishment and added his concerns about the lack of proportionality in judgments. Evidence of corporal punishment may have disappeared from the archival record after Grodet's instructions in 1894, but it certainly did not disappear from the district officers' tool kit of powers.[46] Governor-general Chaudié had been pursuing the issue of proportionality between crimes and punishment since his early tenure. Following another tour of the Soudan in 1900, he wrote an angry letter to the minister of Colonies. "Regarding the administration of justice, my tour revealed an unacceptable situation ... The fundamental principles upon which rests the entire judicial edifice of the land where civilization exerts its influence is often not understood by district administrators." Chaudié was especially concerned with widespread "irregularities," which he did not explain, and with the lack of "proportionality." Chaudié railed against district officers who inflicted punishments wholly out of character with the offense, such that even minor offenses resulted in long prison sentences; in some cases, even life imprisonment. Too often, Chaudié argued, the commandants continued to render justice themselves, without recourse to local elders and thus without a sense of local customs. Too often, Chaudié wrote, "commandants have a disdain for the life and liberty [of the natives], which I believe must characterize justice in regard to the natives."[47] For Chaudié, the regularization of the native legal system was an unambiguous effort to control the French military officers and the remaining African kings in protectorates. Yet, as we shall see, Chaudié's commitment to regularization had its limits. Chaudié, who pinned another Legion of Honor medal on Mademba at a ceremony in Kati in December 1896, did not hesitate to quash the investigation into Mademba's alleged abuses of power in 1900.[48]

Of Regularity and Madness: Mademba's Downward Spiral, 1897–1898

Colonel Trentinian navigated the changing landscape of authority in the Soudan by being attentive to both the policy directives from the new government-general and the needs of his military officers in the front lines

---

[46] William Ponty, the délégué to the government-general (effectively the lieutenant-govenor of the Soudan), chastised the commandant of Nioro for inflicting forty lashes as punishment. Ponty reminded the commandant that corporal punishment was no longer recognized in the colony and that it was reprehensible in the eyes of humanity and civilization. Ponty, letter to cmdt., Nioro [Kayes], Sept. 26, 1900, ANS-AOF 15 G 58.

[47] Gouv.-gen. Chaudié, letter to min. Col. with copies to 1ère Direction, 1ère Bureau, and Sec-gen 3ème Bureau, Saint Louis, Mar. 21, 1900, ANOM Soudan VIII-2. An even stronger letter in the same vein was sent to Chaudié's lieutenant-govenors under his authority: Chaudié, letter to govs. of Guinée Française, Côte D'Ivoire, and Dahomey, Saint Louis, Mar. 19, 1900, ANOM Soudan VIII-2.

[48] The ceremony was held Dec. 23–25, 1896. *JOAOF*, Jan. 2, 1897, #64.

as well as those stuck in district headquarters. Continued French military pressure on Samory has forced him to move eastward into the northern Côte d'Ivoire and southern Soudan where he engaged a long siege of Sikasso. Trentinian sensed that the time was approaching for a final assault on Samory and Sikasso. Trentinian was also mindful of the challenges raised by Governor-general Chaudié regarding irregularities in the administration of justice and corporal punishment. He also recognized that more and more Africans were bringing their disputes to district officers and that their involvement in adjudicating these disputes was becoming increasingly burdensome.[49] By 1897, the Segu administrator noted that over the last month, "there has been a huge increase in the legal disputes brought before the commandant, which takes a vast amount of time especially when we are obliged to examine the dispute and consult with native chiefs." These consultations required patience, since they were often long and tedious, having to parse divergent interpretations of customs and traditions. The commandant of Segu noted that many Bambara of the region would not accept the judgments of a qadi and many chefs de canton, who were appointed by the French, exercised little influence and were often venal. He hoped for the eventual establishment of a tribunal of elders whose judgments would be "dignified and certain."[50]

Given these pressures from above and below, Trentinian responded with enthusiasm when he received from the governor-general the request that he order his administrators to complete a survey on legal customs in the colony. The governor-general, in turn, had likely received the request from the Ministry of Colonies in Paris, but he too saw in this survey an opportunity to establish an empirical foundation to his interests in the regular application of justice. The survey on legal customs originated with the Union international de droit et d'économie politique, based in Berlin. Trentinian wrote to his administrators

> I attach great significance to this work not only for its scientific value that emerges from our cooperation with the goal of the Union international, but because this work will be of great utility for those of us who serve and will serve in the colony. I therefore urge you to pay very careful attention to this questionnaire. Never generalize, note the local differences in practices, and give only absolutely correct, complete, and authentic responses.[51]

Few of the completed questionnaires were detailed as Trentinian hoped. Some were produced with care, others were done in haste. Most generalized, even if

---

[49] Lt.-gouv. Trentinian, Note circulaire, Bamako, Feb. 3, 1896, ANM 2 M 4.
[50] Rap. pol., Segu, Feb. 1897 and Rap. pol., Segu, Apr. 1897, ANM 1 E 71.
[51] Lt.-gouv. Trentinian, Note circulaire to cmdts. de cercles, Kayes, Dec. 19, 1896, ANS-AOF 1 G 138.

they noted how customs differed among the different "races" of their districts.[52] None, as far as I can tell, explained how the commandants collected
their information or who their African informants were. The 1897 surveys of
custom constituted a more or less uniform body of evidence regarding the
diversity of African customs in French West Africa and was compiled into a
massive distillation by 1900, which formed part of a "library" on native
customs.[53]

Mademba compiled one of these questionnaires for his États de Sansanding.
The questionnaire laid out the general areas of inquiry: relations within the
family; marriage; death of a spouse; divorce; domestic life; inheritance; political
organization; justice; punishment and fines; land tenure and property rights;
and commercial practices. Mademba's responses to the questionnaire ran to
forty-two pages, which was one of the lengthier reports in the series. Mademba
framed his responses in terms of the four prominent ethnic groups in his
domain: Bambara, Maraka, Fulbe (Peul), and Bozo. He explored differences in
customs in only a few of these general areas. Most of the differences Mademba
discussed related to inheritance among those who did and did not practice
Islam. Mademba's discussion of the family took nearly half of the report
(twenty out of forty-two pages), reflecting both the survey's concerns with
domestic disputes and Mademba's growing obsessions with his own household. Mademba wrote that

> The head of the family has the duty to ensure the well-being and provide
> for the needs of his subordinates drawn from the results of the work done
> by all in support of the community [family]. He is charged with providing
> the food, order, and corporal punishments for all members, free and slave
> alike when they are guilty of acts that merit punishment. He does not,
> however, have the right of life and death because the law and customs
> reserve this power only to the chief or king of the land. He does have the
> right to sell the slaves of the households, who are considered part of the
> family's patrimony. He does not have the right to sell any blood relative,
> but he may pawn a relative in order to guarantee a debt if it is in the
> interests of the family during imperious conditions. The head of the
> family is also responsible for all debts incurred by subordinate members
> of his community ...
>
> The head of the family has incontestable rights over the men, over the
> women, and over the girls who are not yet married. When they leave their
> family home for the home of their husbands, the guardianship over them

---

[52] The French term *race* is best translated as nationality or ethnic group.

[53] Études de Barat, commis des Affaires indigènes à Nioro, 1897–1900, ANS-AOF 1 G 229.
In 1908–1909, Lieutenant-governor Clozel sent out another request for a more compre-
hensive survey of native customs that Delafosse relied on in preparing his magisterial
Haut-Sénégal-Niger. See also Roberts, *Litigants and Households*, chapter 3.

is transferred from the head of the family to the head of their husband's family ... The dignity of the head of the family does not change.[54]

Despite Trentinian's instructions to guard against generalizations, Mademba's discussion of the authority of the household head is framed as general rules. The household head is dignified and his power over the "subordinates" in his community is incontestable. On the flip side of the household head's authority, he is obliged to feed his household members and is responsible for any debts or misdeeds that his subordinates may have incurred. The household head alone can render corporal punishments on his subordinates.

I elaborate some of the sections on marriage in Mademba's report, since we may find clues in how he framed these issues for his relationship to his own household. Marriage, Mademba wrote, was purely a civil contract in which the man is considered superior to the woman. The Maraka, Mademba wrote, were bound by Islamic law and could only marry four free wives at any one time. Maraka household heads, Mademba added, could however marry as many slave wives as they could manage as long as they did not jeopardize the subsistence obligations that they had to their free wives. In contrast, Mademba noted that for the traditionalist Bambara, the household head could have as many free and slaves wives as he wanted. Among the Bambara, all wives were considered "slaves" insofar as they form part of the family patrimony. The eldest son in line to succeed him acquired all of his father's wives as wives except for his proper mother, who was not inherited as a wife. Later in the report, Mademba noted that extramarital sex "constituted an act of fornication that is condemned by law and custom." Children born of these unions are considered strangers by the father's kin and as such can neither carry the name of father nor inherit from him.[55]

The section of Mademba's report on "political organization" was surprisingly short, especially on the authority of kings. I would have anticipated that Mademba would have used this opportunity to lay claim to a vast array of real or invented powers of African kings. Indeed, Mademba did lay claim to vast and uncontested authority, but his justification was quite simple.

> The political organization of black lands is generally composed of villages organized into cantons or districts under the authority of a superior chief, who usually carried the title of king. Each canton or district is administered under the name of the king by chiefs appointed by the king. At the village level, chiefs are chosen from among those families that have lived in the village the longest. The canton chiefs reside in the capital, where they form part of the council to the king that deals with all issues relating

[54] Mademba, Réponse au questionnaire sur les coutumiers juridiques des naturels de l'Afrique, Sinsani, Mar. 30, 1897, ANOM Comité Française pour l'Outre-Mer 183.
[55] Ibid.

to political affairs, administration, and justice in the land. Canton chiefs have representatives in their districts who transmit all affairs concerning their districts to the chiefs. Next to each king is another official called the war chief. His task is to organize the contingents of troops in case of war. He is like the canton chiefs and participates in the king's council ... The superior chief or king alone had the right to take a life conforming to the laws and only in cases of murder, high treason, etc. He also has the right to impose taxes. The *sofa* form royal guard and serve as police as well. People regard the king as sacred in the sense that he represents God who has chosen him from all his creatures to be his representative on earth. The dignity of the king is hereditary.[56]

The boldest statement in this passage is the claim that African kings are God's representative on earth. With this statement, nothing more probably needed to be said about the king's authority or power. This statement also points to Mademba's growing megalomania. Megalomania is often expressed in terms of delusional fantasies of power, inflated self-esteem, and narcissistic personality traits. But it is also linked to paranoia and especially fears of challenges to power or status. The positions of household head and *faama* are dignified statuses, worthy of unquestioned respect. Indeed, both the king's authority and that of the household head are uncontestable in their own domains. So any contestation of this authority is a challenge to the overall sense of power and status. Megalomania – now referred to as nnarcissistic personality disorder – and paranoia are often conjoined traits signaling personality instability. When power is part of the equation and when the person experiencing decomposition feels threatened, danger lurks close at hand.[57] A paranoid person tends to see intention in accidents. A common feature in paranoia is a belief in conspiracies concerned with those wishing to harm that individual.[58]

Mademba's paranoia accelerated into the spring and summer of 1897. For some time, Mademba had been building up his harem. How he did so is not completely clear, although a formal complaint against Mademba by Faba Diabakate in 1898 reveals some of these mechanisms. Diabakate accused Mademba of kidnapping his two wives in 1897 while he was away from Sinsani conducting trade in Kenedugu. In his interrogation of Diabakate, the commandant of Segu pushed for clarification of the sequence of events; Diabakate revealed that he had left Sinsani for Kenedugu a year after Bojan

---

[56] Ibid.

[57] Brandy X. Lee, ed., *The Dangerous Case of Donald Trump: 27 Psychiatrists and Mental Health Experts Assess a President* (New York: St. Martin's Press, 2017).

[58] Psychiatrists also worry that those with strong paranoid delusions tend to take actions on their beliefs, which then puts individuals and communities at risk. Daniel Freeman and Jason Freeman, *Paranoia: A Twenty-first Century Fear* (Oxford: Oxford University Press, 2008), 17, 83; Wikipedia, "Paranoia," https://en.wikipedia.org/wiki/Paranoia.

left Segu, somewhere around early or mid 1894. Diabakate left his wives with 13,000 cowries (just over 10 francs) to cover their subsistence needs and assured the commandant of Segu that he instructed his fellow juula traders to look after whatever needs his wives might have. In his response to Diabakate's complaint, Mademba argued that Diabakate actually left Sinsani in 1893 and that without information on the whereabouts of their husband and without subsistence, the two women sought divorce in Mademba's court. Mademba apparently counseled the women to be patient but he could not "refuse them justice." Failure to provide subsistence "broke" the marriage contract. Mademba invited the local qadi to assess the wives' complaints. The qadi found that Diakabate had indeed abandoned his wives and ordered a three-month waiting period to provide Diakabate with the opportunity to return and provide for his wives. After the waiting period ended, Mademba declared them divorced and gave them permission to contract new marriages. At this point, Mademba apparently took them into his harem. I do not have any evidence from these women, so I cannot interrogate their motives. However, unattached women were socially and economically vulnerable and they may have welcomed the opportunity to join Mademba's household. In any case, the commandant of Segu dismissed the complaint as having no merit.[59] The Diakabate case was not isolated, however. Sometime in 1896, Mademba kidnapped *jeli* [Bamanakan: griot] Garan Kouyate's daughter Fatimata "against her will" and took her into his home. Kouyate, by the way, was one of Mademba's griots. One month later, he kidnapped Kouyate's wife, Kassoumou Kone, as well. Kouyate claimed that he resisted these actions. He eventually fled Sinsani for fear of being accused of conspiring against Mademba and being executed.[60] In an interview with Binke Baba Kuma and several Kuma notables, I asked them to explain Mademba's relationship with Kouyate. Kuma responded: "The *faama* took Kouyate's wife, his daughter, and the wife of his son. It was Garan who left to Dakar and returned with a letter from the Grand French [leaders ordering Mademba] to return his wife, daughter, and daughter-in-law."[61]

Under pressure from the Segu administrator, Mademba eventually responded to Kouyate's accusations. He did not deny taking Kouyate's wife and daughter, but argued that he was only applying "the laws and customs of the land," which, of course, he had himself defined. According to Mademba's interpretation, Kouyate, as the majority of the inhabitants of Sinsani, was under his "guardianship" and, as such, he has final dominion over them.

---

[59] Mademba, letter to cmdt. Segu, Sinsani, Sept. 18 [1897], ANM 1 E 220; Rap. pol., Segu, Sept. 1898, ANM 1 E 71.

[60] Attachment in Lt.-gov. Trentinian letter to cmdt. Segu, Kayes, Sept. 8, 1897, ANM 1 E 220.

[61] Interview with Binke Baba Kuma and Kuma elders, July 17, 1992, Sinsani.

Besides, he argued, Kouyate had two other wives, several other sons and daughters, and lots of slaves. If we permitted Kouyate to have his wish in returning his wife and daughter, Mademba argued to the commandant of Segu, everyone else will want the same prerogatives. If we permitted this, he added, then everyone in Sinsani and in the villages surrounding the town will be free to do what they want to do.[62] And then, Mademba added for good measure, we would have no longer any order in society.[63] Mademba here again conflated challenges to his control over his women with challenges to his control over his kingdom.

In July 1897, the village chief of Sinsani, Boua Cisse, and his brother Issa Cisse, fled to Segu seeking asylum. They stated to Captain Montguers, the commandant of Segu, that they feared for their lives at the hands of Mademba. This was a fairly dramatic reversal of fate, since Boua Cisse had been one of Mademba's most trusted advisors. Indeed, during Dubois's visit to Sinsani in 1896, Mademba had urged the reporter to meet with Boua Cisse to hear about the history of the town and its glorious past. The village chief, Dubois noted, was "a tall elder, wrinkled and white with age; all his energy was reflected in his eyes." Boua Cisse described how his once flourishing and wealthy city was destroyed by nearly three decades of Sinsani's heroic resistance against Futanke rule in Segu. Conditions were so dire that by the end

> hyena's stalked our houses and kidnapped our children ... Then the French came and crushed Segu and the Toucouleurs. With them joy has returned to us. Peace has reigned perfectly throughout the land ... We cultivate our fields without fear that the harvest will be stolen ... Merchants camp in the bush far from any security [but without fear]. Security is complete ... It was the whites who gave us all this. You ask if we are content with their presence and why do we rejoice in their presence? Do you now understand why the land was so easily submitted and completely tranquil.[64]

A year later, Boua Cisse was running for his life from the town he had helped rebuild.

On July 30, 1897, Mademba wrote to Captain Montguers about an incident "concerning a plot against me that I have resolved at Sansanding." Following Archinard's 1893 reorganization, Mademba was obliged to keep the commandant of Segu informed about administrative affairs and governance issues

---

[62] Mademba, letter to cmdt. Segu, Sinsani, Nov. 4, 1897, ANM 1 E 220.

[63] In November 1897, in response to a telegram from the lieutenant-governor, Mademba was ordered to put Kassoumou on a boat to Segu to rejoin her husband. "This woman," Mademba wrote, "cried continuously since I told her that she has to leave for Segu. She thinks that his is a punishment for having warned me of the assassination attempt on my life." Mademba, letter to cmdt. Segu, Sinsani, Nov. 13, 1897, ANM 1 E 220.

[64] Dubois, *Tombouctou la mystérieuse,* 92–94.

in Sinsani, but in this case he chose to inform the commandant after he had resolved the problem. The conspirators, Mademba wrote, were Boua Cisse, "whom I had named chief of Sansanding in 1891," his brother Issa Cisse, Kobile and Nadio, "two guards of my house," Mamadou Seykalou, "my domestic," his friend Tietemao, and also Bokar Diawando.

> I had complete confidence in these men, who had complete freedom to enter my house day and night, whom I treated very well and for whom I have always done my best, had a sudden change in attitude. One could easily detect these changes because when I gave them daily orders for their services, I was obliged to repeat them. When I asked Kobile, with whom I have the best relationship, why he did not do as I asked, he waited before responding without any other excuse that he "had lost his head."

Mademba continued that he "had conducted a secret inquiry into this plot."[65]

Mademba did not specify how he conducted this secret inquiry or what evidence he had. He was, nonetheless, convinced of the results.

> I discovered that the conspirators planned to spend a part of the night in my house with my wives. One of my wives, whom the conspirators trusted, told me to be on my guard. She overhead Kobile and his companions discuss how they planned on assassinating me during the night of Monday to Tuesday when I was asleep with my wife of choice. The conspirators told my informant to tell them when I was asleep.

Mademba's wife in this passage was Kassoumou Kone, whom he had kidnapped from Kouyate the year before.[66]

Several aspects of this passage are significant for our discussion. First, Mademba based his actions against the alleged conspirators on hearsay evidence from one of his many wives, who was selected by the conspirators in all likelihood because she was amenable to their plot. Hearsay evidence without corroboration is always tenuous. Second, and probably most revealing of Mademba's actions was the obvious conflation between alleged adultery (the conspirators planned on spending part of the night with Mademba's wives) and the alleged assassination plot (the conspirators planned to kill Mademba while he slept with his wife of choice for that night). No motivation is suggested for why the conspirators planned to kill Mademba. Mademba's fears about losing control over his women and fear over losing his status were powerful and conjoined obsessions. He had already laid out these fears in his coutumier of his kingdom.

"Armed with this information," Mademba went on, "I arrested the accused Monday morning and I held an immediate inquiry that established the facts

---

[65] Mademba, letter to cmdt. Segu, Sinsani, July 30, 1897, ANM 1 E 220.
[66] Mademba, letter to cmdt. Segu, Sinsani, Nov. 13, 1897, ANM 1 E 220.

almost exactly as stated. The court condemned Kobile, the principal guardian of my house, to death and the judgment was carried out in the presence of the whole town." It is not clear from Mademba's account, but it seems as if Kobile's trial, sentence, and execution occurred immediately. Mademba did not elaborate on what evidence he received that substantiated the alleged plot. It was probably unambiguous to Mademba that threats against his women and his person required immediate and harsh responses. Boua Cisse and Issa Cisse were fined and ordered to be deported to a French post to the south, near the contested areas where Samory and Babemba remained active. Mademba's court condemned Mamadou Seykolo, Bokar Diwandou, Tienteimalou, and Madio to two years in prison, but all four escaped Sinsani and were on the run either to Kayes in the west or to Baninko in the east. Mademba requested assistance from the commandant of Segu to help track down the escapees.[67] Mademba seemed to think that the problem in Sinsani was resolved. "Thank God," he wrote to the commandant of Segu on August 13, 1897, "calm has returned. The successor as village chief to Boua Cisse has been announced to the great satisfaction of the inhabitants of Sinsani and all have returned to their habitual occupations."[68]

Captain Montguers of Segu was deeply disturbed by Mademba's July 30 letter and the actions he described therein. Montguers was obviously aware of the wider debates circulating in the colony about corporal punishment and proportionality in sentencing. Montguers worried further about Mademba's obsessions that led to arbitrary punishments and the wider impact that these actions were having in Sinsani. Moreover, Mademba's exaction of Kobile was in direct violation of Archinard's 1893 prohibition of Mademba's authority to execute. Within days of receiving Mademba's letter, Montguers wrote to Trentinian of his concerns about Mademba's behavior. Montguers noted that he had officially received Mademba's letter and that he understood that an inquest was held by Mademba in Sinsani against the natives Mademba accused of having "intimate relations with his wives."[69] He learned that the inquest began when Mademba learned that members of his "entourage had spent part of the night in his house with his wives, which demonstrated a plot against his person." Montguers quickly pointed to the conflation between alleged adultery and alleged plot to kill Mademba. Montguers stated that "those who know Mademba understand his sensitivity, to say the least, regarding his female personnel and how publicly painful it would be if some violation of his conjugal domain actually occurred." Montguers went on to state that he had no evidence to prove or disprove Mademba's accusations, but he was very concerned about Mademba's version of the events and his judgments against

[67] Mademba, letter to cmdt. Segu, Sinsani, July 30, 1897, ANM 1 E 220.
[68] Mademba, letter to cmdt. Segu, Sinsani, Aug. 13, 1897, ANM 1 E 220.
[69] Capt. Montguers, letter to lt.-gouv., Segu, Aug. 6, 1897, ANM 1 E 219.

the defendants. Montguers noted that the six alleged conspirators received different sentences for the same alleged crime, some much harsher than others. Moreover, Montguers heard from some of the fleeing residents of Sinsani that Mademba had used torture to solicit confessions regarding the plot.

Fleeing Sinsani, Boua Cisse and Issa Cisse presented themselves to Montguers, stating that Mademba has accused them of adultery. "One of these [alleged conspirators]," Montguers argued, probably referring to Boua Cisse and echoing Dubois's description of him only a year ago, "was an old man whose advanced age has deprived him of the joys permitted in marriage" and thus likely innocent of the alleged adultery. "Innocent of the crime of treason against the person of the king that the French have given them, they have departed, worn down by the oft repeated inquests, by the corporal punishments too often repeated, and forced to suffer the same severe penalties as those currently extended in Sansanding." Despite his pronounced bias in favor of the refugees from Sinsani, Montguers reiterated that he could not ascertain the veracity of the claims on either side. He concluded, however, by noting that the situation regarding Mademba was "very delicate." He added, however, that he could not easily deny Mademba's formal request to telegraph the other districts in search of the escaped convicts.[70]

Lieutenant-governor Trentinian was not happy to receive Montguers' letter, but noted that the accusations contained in his letter unfortunately matched earlier accusations against Mademba and these deserved to be investigated. Trentinian thus ordered Montguers to go to Sinsani and to hold as "delicately as possible" a formal inquest into the alleged plot and Mademba's responses. Trentinian also gave his permission that Boua and Issa Cisse were to remain permanently in Segu until the conclusion of the Sinsani inquest and that their families in Sinsani were to be given free passage to join their elders in Segu.[71]

Mademba wrote to Montguers in September 1897, even before Trentinian's letter arrived in Segu, that Boua and Issa Cisse's sons had now fled Sinsani despite efforts by city notables to convince them to stay. They had, Mademba underscored, failed to make their submission to him. Mademba thought that their departure would be of no importance to Sinsani, but the slaves of the elder Boua and Issa Cisse, who had been abandoned by their owners, were approaching Mademba seeking their freedom. Mademba wrote that he was under obligations of tradition regarding master–slave relations that should masters fail to provide subsistence for their slaves, the relations were broken

---

[70] Ibid. Binke Baba Kuma and the Kuma elders told me that Mademba not only fined Boua and Issa Cisse so many cowries that they could not pay the fine but that he also cut down the trees outside of their house in Sinsani and then demolished the house itself; interview, July 17, 1992, Sinsani.

[71] Lt.-gouv. Trentinian, letter to cmdt. Segu, Kayes, Sept 8, 1897, ANM 1 E 220.

and slaves were to be freed.[72] Mademba's interpretation of these customary practices may have been shaped by his desire to punish the Cisse elders by liberating their slaves. Mademba asked Montguers for advice on this matter, but only if he thought otherwise.[73]

With his ear still to the ground and supported by spies who remained loyal to him, Mademba must have learned that Montguers was about to conduct a formal inquiry into the alleged conspiracy of July 1897. In October, he wrote to Montguers adding a new element to his case against Boua and Issa Cisse. Mademba was well aware of French concerns about "Muslim" conspiracies. In his October letter, Mademba accused the Cisse brothers of joining an unnamed marabout in preparations for a holy war against "us."[74] The disconnect between Dubois's version of Boua Cisse's pro-French sentiments and Mademba's allegation of Boua Cisse's involvement in an anti-French Muslim conspiracy could not be further apart.

Montguers arrived in Sinsani in mid October to begin his inquest into Mademba's accusations of the conspiracy against his life and into issues of equity regarding the punishments Mademba ordered following his own inquest into the conspiracy. Trentinian also had Montguers present a letter from him to Mademba. I do not know exactly what was in the letter, but from Montguers remarks I can assume that it authorized Montguers's inquest into the conspiracy, which was to take place in Mademba's presence. Trentinian also ordered that Kassoumou and her daughter be sent back to her husband, Garan Kouyate, now residing in Segu. Montguers began by taking depositions from the witnesses who had corroborated Mademba's version of the plot. Montguers did not have adequate competence in Bamanakan, so he relied on the translations offered by his "garçon," who spoke reasonable French as well as Bla. How adequate Montguers's interpreter was is not at all clear since he was not an authorized interpreter. The primary witness was Kassoumou Kone, Garan Kouyate's wife, whom Mademba has taken as his own wife and who had alerted Mademba of the plot. As a wife of a griot, which was an endogenous caste, Kassoumou was most likely also a griotte and thus conversant with the arts of praise singing.[75]

---

[72] There was significant latitude in the customary relationships between masters and slaves. Claude Meillassoux, "Esclavage à Gumbu," in *Esclavage en Afrique précoloniale*, ed. Claude Meillassoux (Paris: Maspero, 1975); Richard Roberts, "The End of Slavery in the French Soudan, 1905–1914," in *The End of Slavery in Africa*, eds. Suzanne Miers and Richard Roberts (Madison: University of Wisconsin Press, 1988): 282–307.

[73] Mademba, letter to cmdt. Segu, Sinsani, Sept. 6, 1897, ANM 1 E 220.

[74] Mademba, letter to cmdt. Segu, Sinsani, Oct. 5, 1897, ANM 1 E 220.

[75] David Conrad, ed. *A State of Intrigue: The Epic of Bamana Segu according to Tayiru Banbera* (Oxford: Oxford University Press for the British Academy, 1990); David Conrad and Barbara Hoffman, eds., *Status and Identity in West Africa: Nyamakalaw of Mande* (Bloomington: Indiana University Press, 1995); Tal Tamari, *Les castes de l'Afrique*

Kassoumou's deposition to Montguers's inquest was consistent with Mademba's version of the plot. Kassoumou explained that Kobile had confided in her about the planned conspiracy. Kassoumou explained that the conspirators confided in her because she pretended to support their plot. Kobile, it turned out, was Mademba's chief of the *sofa*, a role that made him one of Mademba's closest advisors and confidant. According to Kassoumou, the conspirators planned on killing Mademba and burying his body before alerting the commandant of Segu that Mademba was missing. Kobile also told Kassoumou that he was having intimate relations with Mademba's wives. Kassoumou admitted that she did not know the conspirators well and that she waited two days before telling Mademba about Kobile's alleged plot.

Alake Karaba, who succeeded Kobile as chief of the *sofa*, was the next witness. Karaba gave the same account as Kassoumou. Karaba had an interest in this conspiracy, if for no other reason than he replaced Kobile as chief of the *sofa* with all the respect and authority that position. Karaba did not explain in his testimony how he came to learn about the conspiracy. Two other *sofa*, Moriba Dembele and Kanuba Jara, provided the same accounts of the conspiracy as Kassoumou and Karaba. Montguers next deposed Mademba's cook, who had served Mademba for quite some time. The cook, however, testified that he "only poorly remembered" the events. He refused to swear to the veracity of the conspiracy, but he stated that he was very reluctant to "contradict" the *faama*. At some point, it was not clear when, Mademba accused his cook of trying to poison him. Nor was it clear that the cook was part of the original conspiracy or whether this was a new and separate conspiracy. Bokar, the final witness, stated that he did not know anything, but that he had heard other people talking about the conspiracy. With the formal inquest finished, Montguers expressed his immediate concern that all of the witnesses recited the names of the conspirators in exactly the same order. He worried that Mademba's presence at the inquest may have influenced the testimonies. Montguers also concluded that the "most delicate" part of the inquest – the conspiracy to kill Mademba – was not sufficiently proven.

In his report to the lieutenant-governor, which he did not complete until December 22, 1897, Montguers elaborated on several aspects of the inquest and of the alleged conspiracy. First, Montguers chided Mademba for not consulting with the commandant of Segu immediately upon learning of the alleged conspiracy. An impartial inquest should have taken place immediately. Now, three months after the alleged conspiracy and in the aftermath of Mademba's decision to punish the alleged conspirators, it was no longer possible to collect unbiased evidence of the alleged conspiracy. Second,

occidentale: Artisans et musiciens endogames (Nanterre: Société d'ethnologie, 1997); Thomas Hale, *Griots and Griottes: Masters of Words and Music* (Bloomington, Indiana University Press, 1998).

Montguers was concerned that regardless of the veracity of the alleged conspiracy, the punishments were not consistent. Why was Mademba's cook not
subject to the same punishment as Kobile? These differences in punishment
suggested some deeper contradictions in Mademba's handling of the affair.
Third, Montguers was bothered by the fact that Kassoumou's knowledge of the
conspiracy only emerged when Kobile confided in her. But why would Kobile
confide in Kassoumou, whom he did not know well? And why did Kassoumou
tell Mademba that the conspiracy involved not only Kobile but also Boua and
Issa Cisse and the others? Fourth, Montguers was not only concerned about
Kassoumou's motivation in telling Mademba about the alleged conspiracy but
he pointed out that Kassoumou was the only witness to testify to having heard
directly from one of the conspirators about the alleged plot. None of the
witnesses identified the sources of their information. Fifth, Montgeurs was
not convinced that Mademba or any of the other witnesses had provided
adequate evidence of a motive that the conspirators were pursuing. Sixth,
Montguers analyzed the assembled testimony regarding the two phases of
the alleged conspiracy. The first phase involved evidence of adultery being
committed with Mademba's wives. The second phase, that of the alleged
assassination plot, was supported by only one of all of the witnesses he
interrogated in Sinsani. Montguers accused Mademba of "revising his explanation" of the events in order to conform to the punishments that he had
ordered. The seventh point in Montgeurs's report returned to the testimony of
Mademba's cook. The cook, who spoke French and therefore could converse
directly with Montguers, formally retracted his admission of guilt in the
alleged plot to assassinate Mademba.

Montguers's December 1897 report was a damning indictment against
Mademba's abuses of power and his subsequent tinkering with witnesses to
produce a version of the events of July that Mademba believed justified his
actions to the French administration, especially when those accused of conspiring began to flee to Segu and elsewhere to escape Mademba's punishments.
The recitation of the alleged events in exactly the same order piqued
Montguers's interest. He went on to argue in the report that it seemed evident
to him that Mademba had "altered and dictated" the sequence of events to
support his theory of a conspiracy and that the witnesses recited these events
out of "fear or because they were bribed." Montguers faulted Mademba's legal
procedures, which he argued were designed to "force the admission of a crime
by innocents" and was, he stressed, a major miscarriage of justice. "No one in
Sansanding other than those natives interrogated," Montguers wrote, "could
swear that they heard about the plot directly from Kobile." The "general
sentiment" in Sinsani was that adultery with Mademba's wives may have
occurred, but that a "parallel" plot to assassinate him was fictitious.
Montguers concluded that the inquest in Sinsani found that "the facts presented by Monsieur Mademba were inexact" and that "there was no plot

against [the person of] Mademba, but only Mademba's exaggerated jealously over his women." Montguers concluded that "we should deplore these actions by Monsieur Mademba that he presents as necessary to maintain his prestige and authority."[76]

Between the inquest in Sinsani on October 17 and December 22, when Montguers finished his report, some further developments regarding Mademba and Kassoumou transpired. Of these events, I only have Montguers's report and two of Mademba's letters in November 1897. Montguers may not have discussed with Mademba his sense of the inquest's findings before he left Sinsani to return to Segu, but Mademba was worried about how the inquest had proceeded and he was angry about Trentinian's order that he return Kassoumou and her daughter to her husband. He would not let go of his conviction that he was "a victim of an assassination" plot and that he "awaits permission from the government" to punish the conspirators. Should he not receive such permission, he lamented, it would leave him in a "compromised and weakened position." Regarding Kassoumou, Mademba argued that "following the laws and customs of the Blacks, Garan could request the reintegration of Kassoumou," suggesting that Garan had by-passed the proper procedures by appealing directly to the commandant of Segu for redress. Mademba also suggested here that Kassoumou had run away from Garan and has sought protection with Mademba.[77] Mademba's request that he retain Kassoumou made its way up the ladder to Trentinian, who denied Mademba's request in a telegram directly to Mademba. In his December report, Montguers referred to this incident and argued that the departure of Kassoumou and her daughter will not appreciably weaken Mademba's authority or prestige.[78] Of course, authority and prestige are in the eyes of the beholder and, for Mademba, any weakening of his authority over his women was a direct challenge to his stature, which was exactly what the alleged conspiracy was all about. In his letter of November 13, 1897, Mademba wrote that Kassoumou "has not stopped crying since I told her of her move to Segu" and that she thought she has become "a victim of having helped me prevent the attempt to assassinate me." Mademba had grown weary of the administrative challenges to his authority. He wrote to Montguers that "I swear frankly, my captain, that I will be very content to see the final resolution of this affair [meaning both the Kassoumou affair and the conspiracy plot]

---

[76] Capt. Montguers, Note en réponse aux instructions dans lettre no. 25, Sept. 8, 1897, du lt.-gouv. du Soudan Français, Segu, Dec. 22, 1897, ANM 1 E 219.

[77] Mademba, letter to cmdt. Segu, Sinsani, Nov. 4, 1897, ANM 1 E 220.

[78] Capt. Montguers, Note en réponse aux instructions dans lettre no. 25, Segu, Dec. 22, 1897, ANM 1 E 219.

because after four months I am eager to occupy myself usefully with other things."[79]

Mademba could not have been more wrong about anticipating the final resolution of this affair. In fact, this affair was merely the beginning of an unwelcome and enhanced administrative scrutiny of Mademba. But first, Mademba had to bear the lieutenant-governor's reprimand that arrived in January 1898. Trentinian responded fairly quickly once he received Montguers report. "I am deeply unhappy and surprised by your inertia in opposing my orders and I do not see clearly the reasons for your opposition." Relying on Montguers's report, Trentinian stated that Mademba's alleged plot outlined in his July 30 letter "never existed. You have imagined all the pieces [of the plot] in order for you to take vengeance against the people of your entourage against whom you may have grievances of different sorts." Trentinian went on to question the veracity of Kassoumou's testimony. "This woman never witnessed anything. She says that the conspirators divulged their secrets to her." Trentinian was skeptical that conspirators would divulge such potentially dangerous secrets to someone they barely knew or trusted. Even more worrisome to Trentinian was the fact that even when Kobile "swore" to the plot, the only witnesses to this admission were "people under your command." Trentinian discounted the testimony of the other supporting witnesses because their testimony "was dictated by you [and repeated] out of fear." Moreover, Trentinian was concerned that all of the alleged conspirators had not received the same punishment, which suggested that even Mademba was not convinced that all were equally involved. Instead, Trentinian stated, "It was you, because of your burning red jealousy of your wives that you imagined this alleged plot in order to sentence Kobile and the others to punishments that were not justified by their complicity in adultery that they may have committed." Because the sentences imposed by Mademba on the alleged conspirators was totally disproportionate to the actual "crimes," Trentinian argued that "I am obliged to conform to the core principles from which neither you nor I must ever depart, I must revise the judgments you have rendered." With that, Trentinian freed all of the alleged conspirators and gave them formal permission to live outside of the États de Sansanding.[80]

If overturning Mademba's punishments was a blow to Mademba's authority and prestige, Trentinian pushed back even harder on Mademba's claim that he had acted as an African king.

> As justification for your barbarous procedures, you have invoked the example of other native *faama*s, Amadu, Babemba, etc. But you must remember, that when in recognition of the services you have rendered us,

---

[79] Mademba, letter to cmdt. Segu, Sinsani, Nov. 13, 1897, ANM 1 E 220.
[80] Lt.-gouv., letter to Mademba, Kayes, Jan. 13, 1898, ANM 1 E 220.

we created for you an exceptional situation and we have invested in you considerable power not for you to renew the exploits of old, but to create an administration based on justice and humanity.[81]

The disconnect between the role the French envisioned of their African collaborator who was presumably so deeply imbued with French culture, history, and civilization and his actions toward his subjects in Sinsani became a means for more intensive and invasive investigations into Mademba's administration. Trentinian's January 13, 1898, letter opened the door to these investigations, as we shall see in Chapter 7.

The year 1898 marked the watershed in the organizational history of the Soudan and the AOF. The military had achieved their goals of conquest: both Babemba, ruler of Kenedugu, and Samory were defeated. The military continued to face small-scale challenges, but there was little glory to be earned. The commercial house of Dèves and Chaumet wrote to the minister of Colonies in Paris that the capture of Samory marked the "beginning of a new era. The era of the sword has ended." Merchants, they argued, were now poised to "nationalize the fruits of conquest."[82] The minister of Colonies also understood the conquest of Samory and Babemba to signal the end of "military occupation, which should not continue indefinitely."[83] In a subsequent letter, the minister wrote to the governor-general that while the military officers will continue as administrators, "we must prepare for the inevitable transformation into a civilian administration." The minister also raised his concern regarding the most effective way to administer the immense territory of the Soudan.[84] The period between 1898 and 1899 actually marked the transition from military dominance to civilian rule. French West Africa was also wracked by scandal surrounding the Voulet–Chanoine affair and by ministerial decisions to reorganize the colony.

[81] Ibid.
[82] Dèves and Chaumet, letter to min. Col., np, nd, included in a file sent from the min. Col. to gouv.-gen., Paris, Jan. 31, 1900, ANM B 70.
[83] Min. Col., letter to gouv.-gen., Paris, Nov. 9, 1898, ANS-AOF 15 G 95.
[84] Min Col, letter to gouv-general, Paris, 9 Dec 1898, ANM B 165.

5

The Coming Storm, 1898–1899

Mademba and his États de Sansanding were but a small part of a much bigger storm that engulfed French West Africa between 1898 and 1899. This storm swirled intensely in metropolitan France, ignited in part by the Dreyfus affair and then spilled over into international diplomatic conflicts between Britain and France over East and West African boundary disputes. During the late 1890s, the Third Republic was wracked by political instability. Ministers of Colonies in Paris rarely lasted long in office, which made making policy, let alone implementing it, challenging. The French military's hold on the Soudan was weakened by successful conquest, stronger budgetary controls, and public controversies impugning the honor of the leading French Soudanese military heroes and the military more generally. With conquest virtually completed by 1898 and concerned about continuous budget over-runs, the Ministry of Colonies questioned the integrity of the Soudan as a colony. At the same time, the Ministry of Colonies was trying to suppress a major scandal involving two French officers sent on a mission to survey, claim, and demarcate the boundary between French and British possessions in West Africa. The Voulet–Chanoine mission, which grew in part out of these boundary disputes, took on a life of its own as news of horrific abuses further scandalized the military command, the colonial establishment, and the administration in the Soudan. This was the context in which Mademba and his kingdom were buffeted by increasingly strong cross-currents of policy, by individuals pursuing what they understood to be broader mandates about transforming the Soudan, and by those who sought to suppress more bad news out of the Soudan and about the military. Issues regarding the rule of law and administrative abuses of power pulled Mademba into unwanted scrutiny that pitted those with different French interests and African interests against each other.

The Investigation Intensifies

Lieutenant-governor Trentinian's reprimand of Mademba in January 1898 did not close the books on Mademba's responses to the alleged conspiracy against him nor did it damper the tensions in Sinsani. "A sort of panic has enveloped the populations of Sansanding" wrote Commandant Montguers in January 1898. "The inhabitants of Sansanding are fully aware of the *fama*'s conduct in this deplorable affair," and many residents were fleeing the town. The commandant interrogated the refugees upon their arrival in Segu. "All declared that they no longer wished to reside in Sansanding, where they live in fear of the *fama*." Montguers added that the refugees experienced a "heightened state of anxiety" and argued that the government should extend them hospitality given the situation in Sinsani.[1]

Most of these refugees were Mademba's *sofa* and his diverse collection of unfree people. Almost all of these were part of Mademba's huge entourage of several thousand that marched into Sinsani in 1891. Montguers referred to them as the "unfree of the crown." These "unfree" were not exactly slaves; Mademba had a pool of those as well. These unfree were rather prisoners of war, who were under constraints to live, support, and defend Mademba until the time when the French – or Mademba – would end their obligatory service. Archinard did not make clear in 1891 when he invested Mademba as *faama* of Sinsani whether Mademba's unfree were unfree indefinitely or whether there was a term for their service. In practice, these unfree were relatively free, but owed Mademba a certain amount of labor, service, and shares of the harvest each month or year. They did not, however, have freedom of movement. Montguers felt obliged to send back all refugees, but he worried that "it is impossible to verify their grievances in Sansanding" under the watchful presence of the *faama*. Moreover, were the French to return the refugees to Sinsani, they would likely be subject to the "resentments" of the *faama* and likely to flee again, but in the opposite direction of Segu. Montguers also worried that unless the exodus from Sinsani stopped, it would lead to a "fatal" depopulation of the town largely composed of these unfree residents of the crown. "It would not be in our interests to depopulate Sansanding, which might well be made into the headquarters of a new district in the future."[2] Montguers hinted that the better solution would be to dethrone Mademba rather than risk the depopulation of this important market town. On the other hand, since the refugees had reason to fear Mademba's retaliation, Montguers argued that the refugees should be permitted to remain in Segu. In so doing, Montguers also reinforced the refugees' sense that their grievances about Mademba had merit. This would contribute to the situation where this pool of refugees saw advantages to maintaining their stories about Mademba.

In his January 1898 letter to the commandant of Segu, Mademba complained about ongoing unauthorized departures. Mademba wrote that "all these people were part of the former captives of Amadu who were given to

---

[1] Rap. pol., Segu, Jan. 1898, ANM 1 E 71.
[2] Ibid.

me following the capture of Nioro. These people form the majority of the population of Sansanding. I therefore ask you to deny them refuge."[3] As "false rumors" spread that those who fled to Segu have been "declared free," more of Mademba's "unfree" fled Sinsani.[4] In April, Mademba signaled that the extended families of Boua and Issa Cisse, composed of 160 free and unfree people, left Sinsani with all their belongings to move to Segu to live with their elders, who had fled already in July 1897.[5] Not all refugees from Sinsani received a warm welcome in Segu. Foune Kouyate, daughter of *jeli* Garan Kouyate, whose complaints against Mademba contributed to the administration's original interest in Mademba's alleged abuses of power, ran away from her husband and fled to Segu. Montguers noted in his record book that he ordered Garan Kouyate to return his daughter to her husband, whom she "legitimately married" in Sinsani.[6]

Lieutenant-governor Trentinian weighed in on this issue in April 1898. He approved Montguers's decision to offer Sinsani's refugees "hospitality" in Segu if they could prove that their anxieties about remaining in Sinsani had merit. Trentinian admitted that this situation remained "delicate" despite his recent "reproach" of Mademba's behavior. He urged Montguers to collect additional evidence on the quality of Mademba's administration. Trentinian further invited Montguers to "very closely surveille the situation, collect evidence, and keep me informed of those items that are interesting regarding [Mademba's] administration."[7]

Mademba was keenly aware of the administration's increased scrutiny of his rule and especially his administration of justice. Thus, in August 1898, Mademba detailed to the lieutenant-governor the results of his investigation into a voluntary manslaughter case in Sinsani. Karamoko Coulibaly, an original resident of the town, killed one of his female slaves, Tieberesoro, in the course of punishing her for repeated absences from work in his fields. Coulibaly had punished Tieberesoro before, but this time it was with "unprecedented brutality." Mademba held an inquiry and collected depositions regarding the event. Mademba wrote directly to the lieutenant-governor, indicating that he had placed Coulibaly in prison and was awaiting the lieutenant-governor's decision as to Coulibaly's punishment.[8]

Mademba's new found caution may have come too late. By then he was already caught up in a major effort to redefine the colonial administration of French West Africa. From May to October 1898, the French military finally

---

[3] Mademba, letter to cmdt. Segu, Sinsani, Jan. 27, 1898, ANM 1 E 220.

[4] Mademba, letter to cmdt. Segu, Sinsani, Feb. 3, 1898, ANM 1 E 220.

[5] Mademba, letter to cmdt. Segu, Sinsani, Apr. 2, 1898, ANM 1 E 220.

[6] Renseignements pol., Segu, entry Sept. 23, 1898, register no. 2, ANM 1 E 113.

[7] Lt.-gouv. Trentinian, letter to cmdt. Segu, Kayes, Apr. 18, 1898, ANM 1 E 220.

[8] Mademba, letter to lt.-gouv., Sinsani, Aug. 10, 1898, ANM 2 M 34.

won its long-held goals of conquering Sikasso and capturing Samory, thus ending the major military threats to its goal of pacifying the Soudan. The minister of Colonies saw this as a new opportunity to tame yet again the military and impose its civilian model of colonial rule. Trentinian was on leave in France, where he was promoted to general. Despite Trentinian's original reluctance to return to the Soudan, the minister used the opportunity of Trentinian's reappointment as lieutenant-governor to lay out his agenda for a new colonial policy reflecting the changed circumstance in the Soudan. "*Fama* Babemba is dead and the power of Samory is destroyed as our old enemy has fallen into our hands. All this permits us to view as irrevocably conquered the final serious resistance of the native populations [of the Soudan]." Colonial Minister Guillain anticipated that the military would retain its core administrative roles for the time being, but "this military occupation will not be prolonged indefinitely. The military must prepare to yield to the inevitable transition to civilian administration." This transition from conquest must also yield to economic development. "The nearly completed pacification of the land will permit the natives to devote themselves to agricultural production with complete security. The future of the colony resides primarily in rubber and cotton, the principal wealth of the colony."[9] The minister added that Trentinian, of all the previous governors of the Soudan, "best understands the importance of economic development to the future of the colony." To this end, Trentinian organized several missions, including one by Émile Baillaud to survey the economic potential of the Soudan. We shall encounter Baillaud shortly, since he spent a few days with Mademba in Sinsani.

To accomplish these goals, the minister of Colonies ordered a series of administrative studies of l'Afrique Occidentale Française (AOF), and the French Soudan in particular. He wanted to strengthen the government-general and reign in the autonomy of the various constituent colonies. He thus ordered a formal inspection of the administration in the Soudan to be undertaken by the Service of the Inspector-General. The inspection of the Soudan was part of a larger inspection of the French empire authorized by new Minister of Colonies Decrais in August 1899. Not to be outdone or out maneuvered, Governor-general Chaudié had already in 1898 ordered an internal assessment of the Soudan as part of his own efforts to tame the military. At the same time, the Ministry of War seconded Captain Gustave Emmanuel Lambert of the Artillery branch of the Colonial Infantry as état major and commandant of Segu. Lambert's appointment to Segu represented a break in the hold that the infantry of the Marines had held over the administration of the Soudan. Lambert was not, therefore, as embedded in the

---

[9] Min. Col., letter to gouv.-gen., Paris, Nov. 9, 1898, ANS-AOF 15 G 92.

complex web of the bargains of collaboration that had sustained the colonial administration in the Soudan since Borgnis-Desbordes in 1880.

Political havoc in France surrounding the Dreyfus affair and the right's efforts to wrest power from the centrist republican governments led to the fraught context in which events in the Soudan seemed small and insignificant. But insignificance depends on perspective and on proximity to factors causing change. Certainly the antisemitism unleashed by the Dreyfus court martial had little direct bearing on the inhabitants of Sinsani and on the various efforts to reform the Soudanese colonial administration. But these events and political instability in France had a direct influence on the wider context in which decisions were made about how to deal with new evidence of Mademba's abuses of power and alleged crimes. This next section tracks back and forth between the events in France and those in the Soudan to provide a wider context for interpreting what happened in Sinsani in 1898–1899.

Wider Context

The court martial of Alfred Dreyfus in 1894 had little direct influence on French colonialism in West Africa or on the military who administered the Soudan. At least, not immediately.[10] Efforts to exonerate Dreyfus gained traction in 1896 with Lieutenant-colonel Georges Picquart's disclosure that the evidence used in the trial was forged and in 1898 with Émile Zola's famous attack on the evidence and the court martial itself fueled ongoing political tensions between right-wing, clerical, and antisemitic political interests and republican, anticlerical, and antimilitary parties. The 1890s were also marked by significant political realignments that fueled political instability as moderate republicans struggled to maintain power against the rise of those on the right and the left. The political collapse of the right-leaning government in 1898 ushered in increasing political instability in France.[11] These tensions manifested themselves in popular demonstrations, an abortive coup d'état in 1899, and increased political instability. Between May 1894 and June 1902, the French government fell no fewer than seven times, requiring the formation of new parliamentary alliances and majorities. This political instability translated directly into policy instabilities. During this period, the Ministry of Colonies had eight different ministers, some holding office for barely a month; the majority held office for less than nine months. While the ordinary business of

---

[10] James P. Daughton, "A Colonial Affair?: Dreyfus and the French Empire," *Historical Reflections/Réflexions historiques* 31 (3) 2005: 469–483.

[11] Roger Price, *A Concise History of France* (Cambridge: Cambridge University Press, third edition, 2014), 229–234. See also Madeleine Rebérioux, *La République radicale? 1898-1914* (Paris: Éditions du Seuil, 1975), 7–41.

government was largely carried out by bureaucrats, major policy decisions required ministerial management and direction.

The military wanted desperately to contain the Dreyfus affair and prevent further inquiries into its handling of the court martial. Military successes in West Africa were popular among both the military leadership and the French masses, but not with the Ministry of Colonies, which was concerned with budget overruns caused by military conquests.[12] Archinard had managed this brilliantly, at least until 1893, when the Ministry of Colonies recalled him from the field. Since his return to France, Archinard had been riding the wave of popular approval and was appointed the director of Defense in the Ministry of Colonies. He was promoted to general in 1896. Lieutenant-colonel Pierre Marie Gustave Humbert replaced Archinard as supreme military commander during 1891–1892. Humbert, however, was not as adept as Archinard in either military matters or handling the Ministry of Colonies and was quickly replaced. Humbert harbored deep resentment and blamed the governor of Senegal, the under-secretary for colonies, General Borgnis-Desbordes, and especially Archinard for his failures in the Soudan. Humbert's diatribes against the senior officers from the Soudan became more pronounced in 1896, when he started publishing articles and brochures stating his case. Humbert's diatribes fit the growing antimilitary sentiment in France that was exacerbated by the military's handling of the Dreyfus affair. By 1897, however, the rising tide of antimilitarism cost Archinard his position in Paris. He was posted to Indochina. General Desbordes also fell victim to this rising tide, and he too was posted to Indochina.[13]

The military leadership was also being challenged legally and politically on its handling of the Dreyfus case, its cover-up, and the trial against Émile Zola. By late 1898, the standing of the General Staff suffered. In September 1898, General Zurlinden was forced to resign as minister of War. He was replaced by General Charles Suplice Jules Chanoine, whose son was about to be caught up in a major scandal in the Soudan.[14] The reverberations of the Dreyfus affair went far and wide in French society, culture, and politics. It was also discussed in far-flung regions of the colonies. In 1899, Lieutenant Gaston Lautour discussed the Dreyfus affair with Mademba over dinner in Sinsani. Mademba was well informed about the events.[15]

---

[12] Chafer and Sackur, *Promoting the Colonial Idea.*

[13] Kanya-Forstner, *The Conquest of the Western Sudan,* 187–188, 236–237, 256–257; Cuttier, *Portrait du Colonialisme triomphant,* 520–522.

[14] Of the voluminous literature on Dreyfus, see Douglas Johnson, *France and the Dreyfus Affair* (London: Blandford, 1966); Jean-Denis Bredin, *L'Affaire* (Paris: Fayard, 1993); Eric Cahm, *The Dreyfus Affair in French Society and Politics* (London: Longman, 1996).

[15] Lieutenant Gaston Lautour, *Journal d'un Spahi au Soudan, 1897–1899* (Paris: Perin et Cie., 1909), 265.

As if instability in France were not enough, tensions between France and Britain rose significantly as the two imperial powers claimed the same territories in West Africa and along the Nile. The Scramble was about claiming territory preemptively. Most colonial claims on territory had only vague ideas about boundaries. France was interested in laying claim to the entire swarth of the Sahel – from Timbuktu through Djibouti on the Red Sea at the Gulf of Aden. In 1897, Major Jean-Baptiste Marchand set out from Brazzaville with 120 *tirailleurs* and a dozen French officers with the goal of reaching Fashoda on the White Nile and claiming all unclaimed territory along the way. In July 1898, Marchand arrived at Fashoda after a long fourteen months of grueling travel. Instead of meeting up with the Bonechamps expedition that had set out from Djibouti as planned, they confronted Herbert Kitchener, who had just defeated the forces of the Mahdi at Omdurman. Kitchener arrived at Fashoda in September, leading a large flotilla and a sprawling army. Kitchener and Marchand managed to diffuse a potentially volatile situation, in which Marchand's forces were vastly outnumbered, by agreeing to take no action until both parties heard back from their respective ministries. In the context of the Dreyfus affair and the French public's increasing antimilitarism, France stepped back from a possible war by agreeing to cede Fashoda and the upper Nile to the Anglo-Egyptian condominium in exchange for recognition of French claims along the Ubangi River.[16]

If the Fashoda incident ended amicably, the Voulet–Chanoine mission emerged as a major scandal that further threatened an already embattled French military command and contributed to the decision by the Ministry of Colonies to break-up the French Soudan. Captains Paul Voulet and Julien Chanoine both had significant Soudanese military experience and had been involved with the conquest of Wagadugu in 1896, but Voulet had somewhat more military experience than Chanoine.[17] According to Abd-el-Kader Mademba, Mademba's son and biographer, Voulet stopped at Sinsani in 1896, spent two days with Mademba, and recruited around a hundred volunteers from among the town's *sofa* for the march against Wagadugu.[18] Fresh from their success at Wagadugu in 1896, Voulet and Chanoine returned to a heroic welcome in France. Voulet was particularly adept at translating his military successes into promises of future heroic adventures in French West Africa.

[16] See Christopher Maurice Andrew and Alexander Sydney Kanya-Forstner, "Gabriel Hanotaux, the Colonial Party and the Fashoda Strategy," *The Journal of Imperial and Commonwealth History* 3 (1) 1974: 55–104; David Levering Lewis, *Race to Fashoda: European Colonialism and African Resistance in the Scramble for Africa* (New York: Weidenfeld and Nicolson, 1987).

[17] Kanya-Forstner, *The Conquest of the Western Sudan*, 241–243.

[18] Mademba, *Au Sénégal*, 100–101.

The two young captains managed to put together funding from the Ministry of Colonies and the War Ministry, as well as private sources from the colonial lobby in France to support a mission to the interior of French West Africa beyond the Mosse country that they had only recently conquered and onward into what was to become Chad in order to fortify French claims to these territories. Voulet and Chanoine proposed to further demarcate the vague boundaries between French and British spheres of influence of West Africa as they made their way to Chad, where they promised to end the reign of Rabih Zubair, one of the last remaining warrior states of the Sahel.[19] The Voulet–Chanoine mission was to meet up in Zinder with the Foureau–Lamy mission traveling across the Sahara before marching on Rabih Zubair. Given the growing antimilitarism surrounding the Dreyfus affair, the military and the colonial lobby were eager for more good news out of Africa. Julien Chanoine may have been acutely aware of these pressures since his father, the war minister, actively intervened in efforts to prevent a retrial of Alfred Dreyfus. However, due to political instability in France, General Chanoine was forced from the War Ministry in November 1898, after only two months in office. Captains Voulet and Chanoine probably felt significant pressure to succeed in their tasks and to meet up in time with the Foureau–Lamy mission.

Voulet and Chanoine received formal orders in May 1898 to return to West Africa and to prepare their mission to Zinder and beyond. Nor did it hurt the proposed Voulet–Chanoine mission that General Chanoine was named minister of War in Henri Bresson's government in September 1898. Voulet was ordered to recruit *tirailleurs* in Senegal once they landed in Saint Louis. They were to march to the Niger, where Voulet was to travel by river to Timbuktu and then onward to Say along the Niger. Voulet's task was to move the heavy military equipment by river. Chanoine was to head east from Segu into Mosse country, where he was to recruit regular and irregular troops as well as porters and to secure treaties before meeting up with Voulet in Say for the combined march to Zinder. The mission moved quickly from Saint Louis to Bamako, where the two groups separated on September 21, 1898. Voulet stopped by Sinsani en route to Timbuktu. He apparently confided to Mademba that he had nothing but praise for the previous services that the *sofa* had rendered. With Mademba's help, Voulet recruited numerous *sofa*, who eagerly volunteered to join Voulet's new mission. According to Abd-el-Kader Mademba, Voulet "imparted a sense of an energetic and brave officer, qualities that blacks always admire."[20] Chanoine also stopped at Sinsani on October 5, 1898, although I have no record of his visit. A few days before, during a brief halt at Segu, he learned that he had been promoted to captain. In that same letter,

[19] For background, see Dennis D. Cordell, *Dar al-Kuti and the Last Years of the Trans-Saharan Slave Trade* (Madison: University of Wisconsin Press, 1985).

[20] Mademba, *Au Sénégal*, 100–101.

Chanoine reported that while at Jenne, administrator Ponty, "who is one of our close friends, enthusiastically helped us recruiting and training two sections of Bambara soldiers."[21] Voulet arrived in Timbuktu on November 3, 1898, where he was welcomed by Lieutenant-Colonel Arsène Klobb, the commandant of the region. Voulet's contingent at this point consisted of 150 *tirailleurs*, a significant military force. Chanoine's contingent had some 350 regular and irregular troops under his command. Chanoine marched overland from Jenne and Bandiagara to Say through territory only partially conquered and still dangerous.[22] Together, this was a formidable army carrying heavy loads of weapons and baggage. When both contingents converged near Say along the Niger with plans to go overland to Zinder, they needed an even bigger army of porters.

Porters were supposed to be recruited voluntarily and be paid a nominal amount above the subsistence that they were provided. With the help of French district officers and African rulers, Chanoine recruited 800 porters. Eager to move their mission forward and under time pressure, both contingents entered a landscape scarred from its recent conquest and suffering severe drought. Food was scarce everywhere and people were hungry. Wells in Mosse country and further into the Sahel had dried up. Two years earlier, Lieutenant Hourst found villages in this region to have overflowing granaries and vibrant markets, where caravans from the Sahara exchanged their goods for those imported from the forest zone.[23] Finding adequate food for their army of troops, porters, and camp followers, which had blossomed into a moving community of nearly 1,700 people, proved much harder than either Voulet or Chanoine had anticipated. They encountered only desperately poor villages. With water increasingly scarce and food rapidly running out, pressures mounted on Voulet and Chanoine to squeeze whatever they could from these starving villages.

Faced with the reluctance of villagers to part with their dwindling supply of grain, the Voulet–Chanoine mission began to take whatever they wanted despite villagers' refusal to part with their stores. In late January 1899, the regular and irregular troops of the mission unleashed extraordinary violence in a land and time marked by violence. The soldiers sacked the village of Sansané Haousa on the right bank of the Niger River, burned the village, and took many women as slaves. Some of these slaves were redistributed to the irregular troops in the mission as part of the long-standing French military practice of rewarding their auxiliaries with shares of the booty. Traveling east,

---

[21] Julienne Chanoine, letter to director, Say, Dec. 24, 1898, ANOM Missions 49, reprinted in Isabelle Dion, *Vers le Lac Tchad: Expéditions françaises et résistances africaines, 1890–1900* (Milan: Collections Histoires d'outre-mer, 2014), 237.

[22] Émile Baillaud, *Sur les routes du Soudan* (Toulouse: Imprimerie Édouard Privat, 1902), 47.

[23] Hourst, *Sur le Niger et au Pays des Touaregs*, 239–240, 252–254, 261–266.

the mission encountered only villages suffering from draught and famine. Even more violence was unleashed by the mission. Not only were villages burnt but Voulet and Chanoine now conflated villagers' reluctance to share scare resources as acts of rebellion and let loose the fury of their troops. Men, women, and children were killed and many were hung from branches and left to rot. Rumors of the massacres, especially those at Sansané Haousa, appeared in the Parisian press in April 1899, leaked from correspondence sent back home by Lieutenant Péteau, who had disagreed strenuously with Chanoine's tactics and was disciplined by him for insubordination. Péteau left the mission in late January and made his way back to the Soudan.[24] As the Voulet–Chanoine mission moved eastward, temperatures rose, food supplies dwindled, water was scarce, and both troops and porters became ever more desperate. Smaller assaults led to bigger and bolder ones. The largest massacre occurred in early May 1899 in the town of Birni N'Konni, where many of the 8,000 inhabitants were killed or fled for their lives.

In response the reports in the French press, in April 1899, the minister of Colonies ordered Trentinian to send a mission to investigate the allegations of misconduct by the Voulet–Chanoine mission. Facing even more reports of abuses in the press, the minister telegrammed Trentinian that Voulet and Chanoine should be arrested for the alleged crimes. Trentinian ordered Lieutenant-Colonel Klobb to pursue Voulet and Chanoine and arrest them. Klobb set off from Timbuktu in late April 1899. Even as Voulet and Chanoine moved slowly eastward, Klobb was catching up. Klobb sent back cables describing the burned villages, the dried wells, and the bodies still hanging from trees. By July 10, Klobb was within reach of Voulet and Chanoine. He sent four of his *tirailleurs* to deliver a letter ordering Voulet and Chanoine's surrender. Voulet responded that he would not hand over his mission and that he would never surrender. On July 14, Voulet and some eighty *tirailleurs* ambushed Klobb and his small contingent and executed Klobb. Voulet and Chanoine became outlaws. Their mission disintegrated, with Voulet and Chanoine separating. Several of the surviving French officers in the original Voulet–Chanoine mission, probably seeking to rehabilitate their careers, took

---

[24] Cap. Chanoine, letter to Voulet, Chounga, Jan. 30, 1899, ANOM DAM 16, reprinted in reprinted in Dion, *Vers le Lac Tchad*, 246–248. See also Octave Meynier, *La Mission Jolland–Meynier* (Paris : Éditions de l'Empire français, 1947); Jacques-François Rolland, *Le Grand Capitaine* (Paris: Bernard Grasset, 1976); Jean-Claude Simoën, *Le Fils de rois: Le crépuscle sanglangt de l'aventure afriaine* (Paris: J.-C. Lattès, 1996); Colonel Jean François Arsène Klobb and Lieutenant Octave Meynier, *Á la recherche de Voulet: Sur les traces sanglantes de la mission Afrique central, 1898–1899*, ed. Chantal Ahounou (Paris: Cosmopole, 2001). See also Bertrand Taithe, *The Killer Trail: A Colonial Scandal in the Heart of Africa* (New York: Oxford University Press, 2009), which explores the mission in considerable depth. A copy of Meynier's book is located in his personal papers, SHD 1 KT 1001.

over and continued eastward to Zinder, but with a much reduced size.[25] Others straggled back to the Soudan.

News of Klobb's murder reached Say with the survivors of his mission in early August. From Say, the news spread quickly by telegraph. By the end of August, the French military command had ordered all units in the Niger and Chad region to be on alert for a possible violent confrontation with the remaining forces under Voulet and Chanoine's command. The minister of Colonies wrote to Governor-general Chaudié in October 1899 demanding to be kept informed of the progress of the formal inquiry into the "extremely serious gravity of the affair."[26] Panic among the French in the region persisted until proof of Voulet and Chanoine's deaths was confirmed in October 1899. Klobb was given a hero's burial. Far from bolstering the beleaguered French military command, the Voulet–Chanoine scandal further diminished the stature of the military and especially the military's standing in the Soudan.[27]

The Status of the French Soudan, 1898–1899

The Voulet–Chanoine affair accelerated the efforts by the antimilitary parties in the French government and in the AOF to tame free-wheeling French military in West Africa and in the process tighten control over the budget.[28] The appointment of Lieutenant-colonel Trentinian as lieutenant governor to replace Grodet in 1895 helped temporarily contain the annual budgetary hemorrhages, but even Trentinian was obliged to seek additional funds for military actions, especially those that sought retaliation for massacres of French military officers. This was evident in retaliations against the Tuareg around Timbuktu for the massacre of Bonnier's column, against Samory's forces for the killing of Lieutenant Braulot and his mission in 1897, and for Babemba's insulting expulsion of Captain Morisson's mission from Sikasso in February 1898. Even Governor-general Chaudié joined Trentinian in urging the minister of Colonies to authorize punitive expeditions.

With conquest now established, Chaudié reasserted the government-general's control over the budget and administration. As part of Chaudié's efforts, he commissioned Commandant Destenave to study the logic of the current administrative organization of the Soudan. Following his convalescence in

---

[25] Among this group was Lieutenant, later General, Joalland, *Le drame de Dankori: Mission Voulet–Chanoine; Mission Joalland–Meynier* (Paris: Argo, 1931).

[26] Min. Col., letter to gouv.-gen., Paris, Oct. 3, 1899, ANOM AOF I-6.

[27] The Voulet–Chanoine story is the subject of two recent books: the first a series of diaries by Colonel Jean François Arsène Klobb and Lieutenant Meynier, *A la recherche de Voulet*; and second, Taithe, *The Killer Trail*. This section draws heavily from Taithe's account.

[28] Colin Newbury, "The Formation of the Government General of French West Africa," *JAH* 1 (1) 1960: 111–128.

France, Trentinian resumed his governorship in November 1898, just in time
to enjoy the aftermath of the final military victories, the downward spiral of
the Voulet–Chanoine mission, and the rapid end of military hegemony in the
Soudan. In August 1899, the new minister of Colonies, Albert Decrais, ordered
a major administrative inspection of French West Africa, Indochina, and
French India, and in September 1899, he convened a commission in Paris to
evaluate a reorganization of the AOF and a reassessment of the status of the
Soudan within it.[29] Destenave's report on the viability of the Soudan as a
colony arrived in Chaudié's hands in November 1898. Destenave argued that
"the French Soudan, created by its circumstances, is currently a colony of
development, administered by the military, and without access to the sea. It
has, as we say, neither doors nor windows." The circumstances Destenave
referred to were the periodic military campaigns that were needed to protect
the territory already conquered by the French. As a consequence of its
circumstances, Destenave went on to argue, "The French Soudan is formed
of the juxtaposition of territories without connections between them, without
unity, without cohesion, composed of diverse races with their different languages, which due to the necessities of conquest remained joined to this
day."[30] Within the French Soudan, Destenave identified a complex patchwork
of different administrative units consisting of cercles (districts), regions each
containing three to four cercles, residences in which a French administrator
advised an African ruler, and one peculiar entity – the "États de Mademba."[31]

Destenave referenced the correspondence between the minister of Colonies
and the government-general regarding whether more centralization of authority would help contain budget excesses. Destanave argued against the minister's suggestion that increased centralization and budget controls worked in
tandem. He argued instead that with the end of conquest, centralization would
actually impede economic and administrative development. "The diversity of
the land and of the races, the tensions between political interests and political
needs, questions [about promoting] agriculture or commerce, complicate
decision making especially when only after one or two tours do governors
acquire sufficient knowledge and experience to carry such a burden."

---

[29] Kanya-Forstner, *The Conquest of the Western Sudan*, 250–255, 260. The Danel inspection, which forms a central part of Chapter 7, was part of this wider administrative
inquiry.

[30] Cmdt. Destenave, Projet d'organisation pol., administrative et défense de l'AOF, np, 1898,
ANS-AOF 18 G 2.

[31] The Soudan thus had seven cercles, six regions, which were vast expanses (region of the
Sahel based in Nioro; region of the south based in Siguiri; region of the north based in
Timbuktu; region of the northeast based in Macina; region of the east based in Dori; and
the Volta region to the southeast), each of which were subdivided into three or four
cercles, and two residences (Dinguiray and Kissi). And Mademba's state, which remained
in Destenave's report undefined.

Destenave concluded that the great distances across the AOF made centralization very difficult to implement and may actually be "prejudicial" to the interests of diverse regions of the AOF.[32] In the end, it was not clear what Destenave recommended in terms of a potential reorganization of the AOF and its constituent colonies.

Minister Decrais's commission in Paris met throughout September and October 1899. Chaudié, who participated in the commission, repurposed Destenave's 1898 report as part of his vision of a reorganized AOF in the aftermath of a successful era of conquest and pacification. Chaudié promoted further the importance of economic development and the crucial role of civilian governors in this process. Dismantling the military's hold over the Soudan would also result in major budgetary savings. Most significantly, Chaudié used Destenave's proposal that where pacification was not yet fully established the colony of the Soudan should be reduced to two huge military districts and the rest of the territory be divided among the coastal colonies of the AOF. Trentinian, recently reappointed as lieutenant-governor of the Soudan and serving as member of the committee, strenuously resisted these recommendations. Nonetheless, Chaudié prevailed, the commission recommended dismemberment of the Soudan. Trentinian promptly resigned as governor. On October 17, 1899, Minister of Colonies Decrais issued the decree reorganizing the AOF and dismantling the Soudan.[33] Colonel Audeod was named interim lieutenant-governor of whatever remained of the Soudan. This was the context in which Mademba found himself – swept up in a storm of profoundly changing politics of colonization and administration, where the very essence of his bargains of collaboration were questioned.

The Lambert Investigation, 1898–1899

Captain Lambert arrived in Kayes to report to the lieutenant-governor in November 1898 and arrived in Segu to replace Captain Montguers a few weeks later. This was Lambert's first administrative posting in West Africa, although he had begun his military career with five years in Algeria. Lambert was then posted to Indochina from 1885 to 1887, where he proved himself in several military expeditions. From 1887 until 1898, he spent tours in various metropolitan postings. In 1897, he was promoted to captain; the following year he was put "at the disposition of the Ministry of Colonies" and posted to the Soudan. He had little direct experience of Soudanese warfare, conquest, and administration and he did not seem to have significant ties with the French infantry soldiers of the Marines who dominated the ranks in the Soudan.

---

[32] Cmdt. Destenave, Projet d'organisation pol., administrative et défense de l'AOF, np, 1898, ANS-AOF 18 G 2.

[33] Kanya-Forstner, *The Conquest of the Western Sudan*, 260–262.

Lambert's relative unfamiliarity with the Soudan and its military experience may well have been exactly what the Ministry of Colonies wanted during this period of transition. Lambert was, however, eager to begin his new assignment.[34]

Lambert arrived in Segu just as the waves of refugees from Sinsani were pouring into the city. As he busied himself with settling into his new administrative role, he certainly perused the district's archives. Reading the archives of the district was an ordinary task of newly arrived administrators. He was therefore fully aware of his predecessor's inquiries into the alleged conspiracy against Mademba and the various accusations of kidnapping and malfeasance. And he was certainly aware of Trentinian's order authorizing hospitality to Sinsani refugees who could prove that their "anxieties" about remaining in Sinsani were well-founded.[35] Lambert, however, took his time to learn the job and get to know the local landscape. His first encounter with Mademba was most likely near the end of January 1899, when Mademba paid a visit to Lambert. Mademba arrived in Segu accompanied by "more than 200 people" with pomp and ceremony befitting the arrival of an African king. Lambert may not have been too impressed, since his entry in the district's log was very cursory.[36]

A few weeks before Mademba paid his official visit to Lambert in Segu, Émile Baillaud visited Mademba in Sinsani in mid January 1899. Baillaud was

---

[34] In his otherwise solid career, Lambert has one run-in with the senior command that occurred shortly after his tour in Segu. I doubt that this run-in influenced his pursuit of what was officially termed the "Affaire Mademba," but it is part of the wider context and provides some insight into the organization and ethos of the professional French military. Since 1891, Lambert had been seeing Mademoiselle Louise Honorine Euguène Panéro in Paris, where they were living "matrimonially." In an undated letter, which was filed sometime in 1903, Captain Lambert requested official permission to marry Mme. Panéro. Until the reforms of 1972, French soldiers were obliged to request permission form the minister to marry. Lambert addressed his request to the military governor based in Paris. General Faure Biguet, the military governor of Paris, rejected Lambert's request after investigating the moral standing of Mme. Panéro. In his letter to the minister of War, Faure Biguet noted that Lambert and Panéro had been living together since 1891, but what bothered the general more than anything was Mme. Panéro's vaguely defined "scandalous behavior" in the apartment that she rented that led to complaints by the other renters in the building. Moreover, Faure Biguet's inquiry into Mme. Panéro's finances revealed a stark disconnect between her stated income and her lifestyle. Nor could she name her father. All this, the general noted, "did not offer the projected union guarantees of respectability and the desirable proprieties." He therefore was obliged to deny Lambert the authorization he desired to marry Mme. Panéro. Lambert's personnel file does not contain evidence of an appeal or a subsequent request for marriage authorization. SHD Dossiers personnels (Gustave Emmanuel Lambert) GR 7 YF 72626.

[35] Lt.-gouv. Trentinian, letter to cmdt. Segu, Kayes, Jan. 10, 1899, ANM 1 E 220.

[36] Entry Feb. 22, 1899 [but really should be Jan. 22, 1899], Registre no. 2, Renseignements pol., Segu, ANM 1 E 113.

part of a larger mission organized by the Ministry of Colonies and Lieutenant-governor Trentinian to assess the future economic development of France's West African colonies and the Soudan in particular. Baillaud's specific mandate was to examine Soudan's economy and identify which areas of French commerce had significant market potential and which Soudanese commodities might interest metropolitan firms. Baillaud's mission also grew out of the Ministry of Colony and Chaudié's concern about the lack of inherent territorial and economic coherence in the Soudan. To this point, Baillaud argued that the colony of the French Soudan was indeed shaped by the exigencies of conquest and treaties and that the frontiers do not mark significant differences from their neighboring territories. But Baillaud made a case for the importance of what he termed the "land of the French Niger," where the river, its inhabitants, and its commodities provided the connections and the "logic" to this region. This grand river, Baillaud argued, "unifies" the total of the territory and the diverse races who live within it.[37] Baillaud was also struck by the immense possibilities of cotton, which grew in abundance along the Niger between Nyamina and Sinsani in particular.

Baillaud arrived in Sinsani by the river on January 18, 1899. Baillaud had been expecting a struggling village that had been "vigorously beaten" by the forces of Al Hajj Umar and the Futanke. While Sinsani was not quite as big and thriving as Nyamina, it was recovering its former glory and should have actually be called the "city of Sansanding" rather than being referred to as a village.[38] Most imposing was Mademba's palace. "For the first time in Africa, we have found ourselves in a large plaza in which the palace of the *fama* provides an imposing view. Before us was a wall measuring a dozen meters in height, pierced by a single door, and all etched with pinnacles at the top." Baillaud also noticed that in front of the walls of the palace were bales of cotton with their porters. Guarding the entrance to the palace was a crowd of idlers.[39] Baillaud's first impressions of Mademba's palace were important for the next stage of our story: the single door to the palace and the bales of cotton stacked along the walls.

Baillaud and his small troop mounted the stairs inside the palace door and entered a "vast room pierced with large windows," where they met a "man whose appearance was still young despite his age, who in a great blue coat upon which was pinned at shoulder height was the red ribbon on his medal. This small piece of fabric was worn by this man with a black face and a fine and distinguished carriage ... He introduced himself as *Fama* Mademba." After a polite exchange, Mademba offered them champagne, which was an "unexpected nectar," to refresh themselves. Baillaud quizzed Mademba on

[37] Baillaud, *Sur les routes du Soudan*, 2
[38] Ibid., 68, 84.
[39] Ibid., 84.

what he thought about the economic potential of the colony and how to develop it. Mademba responded that manpower was the key to unlocking the wealth of the land, but he noted that "we blacks are habituated to routines and rarely try anything new. But, within a short time, look at what we have accomplished here and see that we can reform the established habits" of labor. Baillaud responded that changing the routines of French peasants, who seemed even less malleable than Mademba's subjects, was a difficult task. With such changes in labor and with the new crops that Mademba was experimenting, Baillaud was convinced that banks of the Niger would become one of the richest places in the world.[40] Mademba added that he aspired to reproduce the successes he achieved in Sinsani elsewhere in the Soudan and thus "to complete the task that was given me, which is to contribute to rendering this land wealthy." Mademba pointed out that his five sons (he only counted some of his male children as such) have all been placed in French language schools. "If I could, I would send them all to school in France." Instead of aspiring to become employed in an office, Mademba wanted them to study "agriculture, others to study how care for livestock, and others how to manage people." Baillaud noted that "This is the speech of a sage ... We hope that he can realize his dreams."[41] Baillaud was impressed with Mademba's role as a modernizer, which dovetailed nicely with his mission to identify the economic potential of the Soudan. Mademba invited Baillaud and his fellow travelers to dine with him in the evening.

To help pass the time, one of Mademba's elderly servants accompanied Baillaud on a tour of the Sinsani. Baillaud described how weavers dominated all of the open spaces, how their small looms clanked continuously, and how the narrow bands of cotton were sewn together into the cloth and blankets that fueled the commerce of this region. One of Mademba's small children joined them and took Baillaud's hand as they strolled through the town. The boy wore a "bright white boubou and a red fez. The good people [of the town] saluted us amicably no doubt prompted by the presence of this child."[42] We cannot know for sure whether the amical welcome Baillaud described was prompted by the sight of the red fez-adorned child leading this tall European or whether the amical salute was part of the townspeople's performance in the presence of Mademba's guests.

At dinnertime, one of Mademba's griots went to fetch Baillaud. "With a voice of thunder, he sang a refrain in our honor and ended with a howl." A crowd of townspeople joined Baillaud and the griot en route to the palace. At the palace door, Baillaud's entry was halted by Mademba's large herd of cattle, goats, and horses as the herders returned the animals to the palace

[40] Ibid., 85.
[41] Ibid., 85–86.
[42] Ibid., 86.

stables. "We had a sense," Baillaud remarked, "that this was a patriarch's life ... Standing in front of the entry stairs were Mademba's wives, some of whom were very beautiful. With a child-like joy, they genuflected as their master passed and in their gracious smiles, there was something else besides submission." Baillaud did not elaborate on what he sensed lurked behind Mademba's wives' smiles. Throughout the entire meal, Mademba's wives and children marched in front of Baillaud and Mademba bringing dishes of food or cloth produced during the day or acquired in the market. As Baillaud returned to his boat after dinner, he was struck with the "grand harmony" he experienced in Sinsani and along the river.[43]

The harmony Baillaud experienced did not last long, at least in Sinsani. Sometime overnight between March 31 and April 1, 1899, Babo Diakite, a boy six or seven years old, went missing. Babo and his elder brother were staying with relatives in Sinsani while their mother, Coumba Diakite, was away for a few days. During their mother's absence, the Diakite boys worked repairing the walls of their relative's house. As the day wore on, both boys decided that they wanted to rest, but their "big brother," Bokary Kobile, pulled their ears in order to get them to resume their work. Babo went back to work, but his elder brother, Tiekoura, hid in the house of a neighbor (Gouro Tambouru). At evening time, Bokary Kobile went in search of the Diakite boys to fetch them for dinner. Bokary found Babo, but not Tiekoura. Bokary and Babo ate their evening meal in Mamay Djila's house. After dinner, Babo went out in search of his elder brother and disappeared. When Babo did not return, the next morning, Bokary Kobile went to Mademba to explain the disappearance. Mademba ordered his *sofa* to search the bush around Sinsani and alerted the town's inhabitants to Babo's disappearance. Alerted to her son's disappearance, Coumba Diakite rushed back to Sinsani, where she sought out Mademba. Coumba Diakite told Mademba that she had heard from Gouro Tambouru's wives that Gouro had told them that he had taken her son. Mademba ordered Gouro to his palace where he made him swear on the Qur'an in the presence of the almamy of Sinsani what he had done or seen. Gouro denied taking the child or even seeing him. Distraught, Coumba Diakite went to Segu to seek Captain Lambert's assistance.[44]

The sequence of events surrounding the disappearance of Babo Diakite was disputed and alternative interpretations swirled around Sinsani and Segu in the immediate aftermath of Babo's disappearance. Sinsani was a small corner of a much wider world being buffeted by uncertainties and fears. Within the context of the anxiety that residents of Sinsani were already experiencing, the version getting the most traction involved Babo entering Mademba's palace

---

[43] Ibid., 87.
[44] Pérignon, Rapport ... Sur les faites reprochés a M. Mademba, Segu, Mar. 15, 1900, ANS-AOF 15 G 176.

and never reappearing. Babo apparently was a regular visitor in the palace, where he went to play with Mademba's children and where he could always find a meal. A fuller inquiry into the origins of this rumor found that it seemed to have started with Gouro telling one of his wives that he had taken the child, but then gave the child to Kanouba, who in turn gave the child to Alate Karaba, who was Mademba's chief of the *sofa*. Karaba allegedly presented the child to Mademba for a ritual killing. This rumor focused on Mademba's decision to kidnap Babo and to behead him in order to turn his head into a magical grisgris.[45] This rumor gained some credibility through its details: Babo was beheaded in the palace's kitchen and his body stuffed into a cupboard. Just the year before, Mademba had been accused of kidnapping women and girls, so kidnapping a small boy seemed to fit this narrative. Moreover, rumors suggesting that Mademba engaged in witchcraft provided "proof" of Mademba's power.

Captain Lambert followed-up on Coumba Diakite's complaint about the disappearance of her son Babo by writing to Mademba, requesting that he conduct a formal inquiry into the boy's disappearance.[46] By this time, several weeks had elapsed. Mademba responded to Lambert with a lengthy but disjointed analysis of the events surrounding the disappearance of Babo Diakite, but with no clear solution to the boy's disappearance.[47] Mademba may have thought his letter would put an end to this issue. Instead, rumors of the boy's disappearance, alleged kidnapping, and alleged ritual murder took on a fierce life of its own, fueled by the continued flow of refugees from Sinsani and by another scandal involving Mademba.

Mademba was very proud that his experiments with cotton had borne such promising results during the harvest of 1889–1899. Baillaud had observed porters bringing cotton bales to Mademba's palace in January. By April 1899, Mademba wrote to Lambert that he had sent "all the cotton that was possible for me to collect" to Segu. When he calculated the total, Mademba sent over thirty tonnes of cotton to Segu for shipment to France.[48] This was an impressive amount of cotton that would provide the cotton brokers in Le Havre with the opportunity to assess the commercial potential of Soudanese cotton.

Much had changed between Baillaud's first visit to Sinsani in January 1899 and his return visit in June. Baillaud noted a subtle change in Mademba, who seemed "less solemn but even more patriarchal." Baillaud remained impressed with Mademba's plans for his sons to attend French professional schools, but he thought that Mademba's plans to send one of

---

[45] Coumba Diakite deposition in Pérignon, Rapport ... Sur les faites reprochés à M. Mademba, Segu, Mar. 15, 1900, ANS-AOF 15 G 176.

[46] Lambert, letter to Mademba, Segu, May 1, 1899, ANS-AOF 15 G 176.

[47] Mademba, letter to cmdt. Segu, Sinsani, May 18, 1899, ANM 1 E 220.

[48] Mademba, letter to cmdt. Segu, Sinsani, Apr. 8, 1899 and May 18, 1899, ANM 1 E 220.

his sons to the metropolitan "School of Political Sciences" so that he can become an ambassador reflected a delusion that Sinsani would eventually become independent. Baillaud wrote "I am afraid that the good man is deceived on the independence of Sansanding."[49] Baillaud was struck by Mademba's sense of his unconstrained power as an African king that bumped up against metropolitan efforts to tame the military by enhancing civilian rule and the rule of law in the colony.

Back in Segu, Lambert kept hearing from Sinsani's refugees' complaints about Mademba's behavior, including complaints about torture and the confiscation of cotton. Lambert also heard stories supporting the rumor that Mademba had ritually killed Babo Diakite. Cracks in the solid support Mademba had with most French military officers and with French travelers became evident over the summer of 1899. Lieutenant Gaston Lautour, officer of the Spahi (cavalry), was sent on an official mission to collect a prisoner held in Mademba's prison to return him to neighboring Sokolo, where Lautour was based. I have no archival record of Lautour's visit to Sinsani, but he included a remarkably revealing section of this visit in his published memoire. Lautour arrived in Sinsani with his troop of indigenous cavalry on July 28, 1899. As he marched closer to the Niger, Lautour remarked on the increasing fertility of the region, but he knew that he was entering Sinsani when he saw the "famous" walls of Mademba's palace. As had other visitors, Lautour noted that the "walls are decorated with pilasters, sculptures, and ornaments, but I saw only one opening, a small door through which a mounted horseman could barely enter."[50] Lautour dismounted and was ushered into the palace by one of Mademba's attendants. They walked through a spacious hall where merchants and travelers deposited their goods and then through three more small doors and passageways through storage rooms with heavy doors. Lautour mounted a staircase that opened up into another passageway where he saw a canon surrounded by five or six guards. Up another stairway, Lautour entered a huge gallery that took up the entire side of the palace, illuminated by the open bays visible from outside. "There, in the background was a platform and on the platform was a table overflowing with books and papers, and nearby a large gentleman wearing eyeglasses, reading. Here was a paunchy figure with an intelligent air and cunning eyes, sitting in a large, patched chair: this is Mademba, the *fama*." Mademba had decorated his study with "a print featuring five French generals, including Négrier and Dobbs, a portrait of the current tzar painted on a large cloth napkin, and two good paintings by Doctor Coup."[51] The print featuring the French generals made sense within the context of Mademba's bargains of collaboration with the French military

---

[49] Baillaud, *Sur les routes du Soudan*, 281–282.
[50] Lautour, *Journal d'un Spahi au Soudan*, 257.
[51] Ibid., 258–259.

and Mademba may have befriended Dr. Coup, but why display so prominently the image of the tzar? Did this reflect Mademba's sense of brotherhood with one of the few remaining powerful European autocrats?

After greeting each other, Lautour was directed to one of the two rooms in the palace for European visitors to rest while Mademba took his leave to view his rice fields. Lautour watched as Mademba prepared himself:

> I watched the *fama* as he shaved, put on his chéchia (red fez), his decorated boots, and his ample burnous (cloak). Shortly thereafter he descended and mounted his large chestnut colored horse, which was saddled, caparisoned, dressed up, and waited restlessly. Mademba was helped to mount, and then led by a griot playing a flute, chanting the glories of the king, the potentate snug on his noble beast, preceded by a guitarist and the flutist, announce to the wind that the high and mighty *fama* is leaving the palace to examine his fields. Along the way, other horsemen join the entourage, with horses prancing, follow their seigneur and master.[52]

Lautour was not as taken by Mademba's francophilia and his history of support for the French cause as were other Frenchmen in the Soudan. "Mademba is a Wolof," Lautour wrote in his memoires, "and as such he is antipathetic to the natives, who have imposed on them a despot from a rival nation." Lautour understood the long service Mademba had rendered the French leaders of conquest and understood that Mademba had been made *faama* in compensation for his services. But he noted, Mademba

> was at the cause of riots, fighting, and uprisings; becoming finally rich, he surrounds himself in his fortress with numerous slaves, livestock, weapons, and munitions. As a good Muslim, he hides his opulence from the public. He lives with his slaves, his wives, their children, who never leave the interior of the palace, and for whom the world is limited by the four walls that encircle their city.[53]

Lautour estimated that Mademba's herd of cattle consisted of at least 250 animals. With each worth 150–200 francs, the herd alone was worth 40,000 francs, which was a considerable fortune.[54] Lautour was struck by a prevailing sense of a "strange mystery, a silent power" that emanated from Mademba and from his palace. Lautour was also struck by Mademba's "extraordinary good fortune that made an employee of the postal service of Senegal into a king of the Niger." Lautour was intrigued by the two sides of Mademba's persona. On the one hand, there was

---

[52] Ibid., 260–261.
[53] Ibid., 263.
[54] Ibid., 269.

The bold character, the officer in the Legion of Honor, of whom all of his allies have a good impression, and who is, by all appearances, an honest administrator, who directs his lands, cares for his possessions, makes appointments and collects rents, exactly as an ordinary high bureaucrat. But, behind this is an unknown life, just as there is something behind those impenetrable walls, it is an occult life of the Wolof, a Muslim whose wealth is not merely in livestock and in his enormous lands, but in innumerable slaves and wives. Next to the administrator, there is the *fama*, who not only collects the required taxes, but who governs as a black king over a vast province of blacks of another race. He is an absolute potentate, more absolute than any of the seigneurs of feudal times because the blacks bend to a Muslim fatalism in a way that French people would never bend to the yoke of a Christian.[55]

With the "loud noise of fifes, drums, crincrins, cries" and galloping horses, Mademba returned from visiting his fields. After being offered an aperitif by Mademba, "a good Muslim nevertheless," Lautour joined Mademba for lunch. During lunch, Mademba regaled Lautour with stories of his visits to Paris. Mademba subscribed to newspapers and interested himself in politics, including the recent Dreyfus affair. They spoke of culture, religion, and the different ethnic groups of the Soudan. "In this gallery with its grand windows, one can recover a sense of the French influence."[56]

But only a bit of French influence.

As the grand seigneur, he maintains a crowd of parasites, who in exchange for his hospitality, glorify him as the magnanimous Richard. The *fama* gives them a speech and [as he listens to his audience he] thus keeps abreast of the events of the day ... A mass of children of all ages and both sexes enter from the private apartments. This is Mademba's family. His eldest sons are in school in Kayes and Saint Louis, while the girls cling to the mothers' boubous. The boys welcome me with a military salute and a "bonjour" in French ... Once finished eating, the parasites leave by taking deep bows, smiles, and salutes.

Only then, however, did the special meal appear, carried by a stream of women, each carrying calabashes of millet, aromatic sauces, rice, cooked meat, and a chicken dish. In addition, Mademba offered Lautour sardines and, to his surprise, tinned pork.[57] After dessert and coffee, Lautour lit his pipe and, in taking leave of Mademba, stopped in Mademba's library and took a novel for his siesta.

All of Mademba's European visitors enjoyed sumptuous meals in Mademba's palace. None questioned where the food came from. Having only

[55] Ibid., 264–265.
[56] Ibid., 265.
[57] Ibid., 267–268.

recently escaped from Sinsani, the former chief of the town, Fasiriki Kuma, told Captain Lambert in Segu in 1899 that "whenever a European passes through Sansanding, we [the residents] are obliged to furnish the *fama* chickens and eggs" and other foodstuff "without receiving anything."[58] In 1899, especially, such requisitions of food came at a time of increasing drought and food scarcity following an invasion of locusts that destroyed the millet harvest.

When Lautour went to check on his troops, he was surprised that Mademba had not seen fit to provide them with food. He confronted Mademba on his neglect, who only grudgingly agreed to provide Lautour's soldiers with food. This lack of generosity bothered Lautour, especially in light of Mademba's vast fortune. "After thirty years of service in the Postal Service and one military campaign in which everyone mentions his bravery, his retirement is lovely and his sinecure lucrative. Any Frenchman would welcome such a retirement." At dinner, Mademba was again charming. He confided to Lautour his parental ambitions for his sons: one has already graduated with his bachelor degree and the other, who was "even smarter," would be attending school in Grignon, France. Lautour offered Mademba salt in exchange for rations for his return to Sokolo, but Mademba bargained for more, arguing that millet was more expensive in Sinsani than in Sokolo.[59] Lautour left early the next morning with regret that he was leaving the Niger River. He did not mention whether he regretted leaving Mademba.

In early October 1899, Lambert responded to Lieutenant-governor Trentinian's request to assess a formal complaint the governor-general had received from Abdoul Drame about his mother, Mariam Aidara. Mariam Aidara had been one of Mamadou Lamine's wives, who upon the French suppression of Lamine's uprising in Senegal, had been distributed as war booty to Mademba. She fled Sinsani and had been given permission to reside in Segu. Lambert recorded Aidara's complaint. "I was often beaten, just as were all the *Fama*'s wives. With his own hands, I received almost daily ten to twenty lashes . . . Once, under the pretext that men had visited me at night, which was false and could not have happened, I received 300 lashes under his orders."[60]

Trentinian also ordered Lambert to send his agents to Sinsani and its outlining villages to get additional information on Mademba and his administration. Lambert responded that despite the difficulties of collecting

---

[58] Fasiriki Kuma quoted in letter, Lambert to Lt.-gouv. p.i., Segu, Nov. 24, 1899, ANS-AOF 15 G 176. See also the deposition by Zinarou Dembele, in Lt. Veil, adjoint au commandant de Segu, Rapport tournée fait à Sansanding, Nov. 24–27, 1899, ANS-AOF 15 G 176, who also described how the slaves of the *faama* requisitioned chickens, eggs, and milk that they brought to the *faama* when Europeans visited.

[59] Lautour, *Journal d'un Spahi au Soudan*, 270.

[60] Mariam Aidara, deposition, Segu, Oct. 2, 1899, ANS-AOF 15 G 176.

information, his agents succeeded in identifying several problematic issues. Villagers complained that the annual tax collection never seemed to end. Collecting taxes was irregular and the "*fama* always takes most of what is collected." Villagers also complained that following the most recent cotton harvest, they were "ordered" to bring all their cotton to Sinsani. They expected to receive millet and cowries in return. They complained that the "*fama* has received much money for the cotton" but they received nothing. Lambert asked why the villagers had not come to Segu to complain against Mademba. The villagers stated that Mademba refuses to authorize any departures for Segu except following "long interrogations" and has instituted "active surveillance" to prevent unauthorized departures for Segu. Lambert noted that "a *grand malaise* reigns in his lands."[61]

Lambert concluded that Mademba controls a territory with over eighty villages and receives considerable revenue from them. Yet, he pays only a nominal annual tax to the colony, which "is a serious loss" to the colony's budget. Lambert recommended that the French administration reappraise the annual tax from Mademba's territory, which had not changed since Archinard reorganized the region in 1893. But more significantly, Lambert raised the broader question of the status of Mademba's authority as *faama*, echoing the issue Destenave raised in his November 1898 report to the governor-general.[62] Perhaps, Lambert suggested, Mademba should be placed under the direct authority of the commandant of Segu. "In one word, M. Mademba would remain the nominal chief of Sansanding, but would operate under our control."[63]

Lambert's inquiries into Mademba's actions seemed to have unleashed the floodgates of complaints from residents of the États de Sansanding. Lambert received more detailed information on what would later be termed the *affaire coton*. "Natives," Lambert wrote

> have been deprived of all their cotton from the last harvest under the pretext that this was the governor's order ... Each village was obliged to furnish 2000 kilograms of cotton and those unable to provide this amount were subject to a fine of 40,000 to 200,000 cowries. The village of Siebugu, which has a population of 23 people of which ten are children, had to pay a tax of 1100 kilograms of millet, 240 kilograms of peanuts, and 1020 kilograms of cotton. They were also fined 248,000 cowries for failure to deliver sufficient cotton.

---

[61] Lambert, letter to lt.-gouv., Segu, Oct. 4, 1899, ANS-AOF 15 G 176.
[62] Cmdt. Destenave, Projet d'organisation politique, administrative et défense de l'AOF, n.p., 1898, ANS-AOF 18 G 2.
[63] Lambert, letter to lt.-gouv., Segu, Oct. 4, 1899, ANS-AOF 15 G 176.

Lambert also cited the chief of Goura village, who was also unable to provide the required cotton nor could he pay the fine imposed. The chief refused to leave his village for fear of being brought to Sinsani and "being killed there." To compound an already difficult situation, the left bank of the Niger suffered from a serious locust invasion that resulted in a steep loss of the millet harvest. Villagers were reduced to eating the leaves of the baobab trees.[64]

Stories surrounding the disappearance of Babo Diakite mushroomed during this period of general anxiety. Even Lambert was bothered by these stories. He wrote to the lieutenant-governor that "Among the numerous grievances I have received there is one that I do not believe and I am reluctant to send it on to you before we have sufficient proof. It involves the accusation of human sacrifice committed by M. Mademba." Nonetheless, Lambert went on that "certain natives have accused Mademba of having killed between twenty and thirty children to make grisgris in order to conjure spells." Lambert collected depositions testifying to these events as well. As a further aside, Lambert noted that Mademba had recently hosted in his palace a man who claimed to be from Mecca but whom Lambert believed was "an emissary from a Moroccan cult." This man had come from Timbuktu and after his stay of between one and two weeks with Mademba, was returning to Timbuktu. Mademba apparently gave this man some cowries, a woman, and a horse. Lambert also stated that Mademba regularly received marabouts from the Sahel and from Bamako and also gave and received presents.[65] Lambert did not elaborate on these observations. He did not have to, since the senior French administration was keenly aware of their shared fear of Muslims and the potential for radical Muslim movements.

The compounding evidence of alleged abuses of power and crimes of various sorts came at an inopportune moment for Mademba. The edifice that the French military had constructed during the two decades between 1880 when Borgnis-Desbordes began his Soudanese campaigns through the Voulet–Chanoine affair in 1899 began to crumble. Mademba had forged his bargains of collaboration within the structures of power that kept the military in command of the Soudan. General Trentinian, who replaced civilian Governor Grodet in 1895, managed to keep the military's grip on the Soudan intact for another half decade before he resigned in the face of increased pressure to dismember the Soudan and curtail the military's control. The storm that wracked the administrative structures of the Soudan pulled Mademba deep into it. As Trentinian left office and as the Soudan was dismembered, Governor-general Chaudié appointed William Ponty to act as his delegate administering what remained of the colony, now called Haut

---

[64] Lambert, letter to lt.-gouv., Segu, Oct. 31, 1899, ANS-AOF 15 G 176.
[65] Ibid.

Sénégal et Moyen Niger. Acting with utmost caution in this time of uncertainty, chaos, and enhanced scrutiny over colonial affairs in the aftermath of the Voulet–Chanoine affair, Lieutenant-governor Colonel Audeoud, who was serving as interim governor, ordered Mademba to Kayes on November 24, 1899 for obligatory residence as the investigation into his alleged malfeasance and crimes deepened.

6

Rule of Law and the Bargains of Collaboration
Mademba on Trial, 1899–1900

The real reason is that the *Fama* is *Fama* by the French and he can do whatever he wants.[1]

The *Fama* commands like the French, but in addition, he rules like Black kings with all their requirements and their whims.[2]

At this moment of increasing anxieties shared by French colonial military officers and Africans living in Sinansi, and when drought and locusts threatened basic survival, Mademba found himself under house arrest in Kayes, the capital of the colony. Mademba was not pleased to leave Sinsani under a cloud of cascading allegations, but when ordered to do so, he obeyed. Mademba arrived in Kayes at the moment of significant transition in colonial administration. General Trentinian had resigned in October 1899 when the Ministerial Commission on the Status of the l'Afrique Occidentale Française (AOF) in Paris concluded that the colony of the Soudan should be reorganized and parts divided among neighboring colonies of the federation, leaving a rump entity called Haut Sénégal and Moyen Niger. Colonel Audeoud was named interim lieutenant-governor, serving until a new civilian candidate could be appointed. On December 28, 1899, the governor-general appointed William Ponty, a civilian with considerable Soudanese experience in which he shared conquest with many of the French officers who had created the French Soudan, the delegate of the Governor General for Haut Sénégal and Moyen Niger. While serving as Archinard's personal secretary, Ponty and Mademba shared the march and battle for Amadu's capital at Nioro over New Year's day 1890–1891.[3] Both were part of Archinard's inner circle of advisors and Ponty obviously appreciated the roles Mademba played in Archinard's military campaigns and conquest of the French Soudan.

---

[1] This quote refers to the execution of Kaoule in Sinsani in 1897. Third deposition, Alate Karaba, Segu, Jan. 3, 1900, ANS-AOF 15 G 176.

[2] Almamy of Sinsani, quoted in Danel, Service du *Fama* du Sansanding, Kayes, Jan. 11, 1900, ANS-AOF 15 G 176.

[3] Sy, "Capitaine Mamadou Racine Sy," p. 35.

Mademba thus settled into house arrest in Kayes (although he lived at least part of the time in Médine, a village on the Senegal River just outside of Kayes and the site of the French fort where a major battle against Al Hajj Umar was fought in 1857). In March 1900, Mademba wrote to Governor-general Chaudié stating that he remained "ignorant" of why he was obliged to remain in Kayes and demanding to know the reasons for his incarceration. Even though he claimed to be ignorant of the causes for his incarceration in Kayes, he nonetheless demanded that he be permitted to clear his name before "French justice."[4] News had obviously reached Mademba that Inspector-general Henri Danel, who was leading the inspection of the administration of the Soudan and who had investigated allegations of Mademba's abuses of power, had in early January 1900 written to Governor-general Chaudié requesting that the dossier of Mademba's abuses be forwarded to the attorney-general of the AOF for prosecution.[5] Mademba's request to stand before a French judge made its way to the minister of Colonies, who responded that "in no case should Mademba be permitted to bring this [case] before French courts."[6] In the end, Mademba was not permitted to stand before a French court nor was he ever subject to a trial in any formal sense. Instead, Mademba was subject to a set of overlapping investigations that raised critical issues regarding the rule of law, colonial administration, and the bargains of collaboration in French West Africa after two decades of French colonial rule and experimentation.

This chapter investigates the investigations. Between October 1899 and mid October 1900, when Mademba returned to his kingdom, we have three nested investigations. Each investigation was progressively narrower than the previous one. The first was the intensification of Captain Lambert's investigation into Mademba's alleged crimes and abuses of power that he had already started in the spring of 1899. Lambert and his adjoint, Lieutenant Veil, conducted investigations in both Segu and Sinsani from October 1899 through mid January 1900 and collected dozens of formal depositions. The second investigation was conducted by Inspector-general Henri Danel as part of a wider inspection of the colonial administration of the French Soudan. The minister of Colonies authorized this inspection in August 1899 and Danel conducted work in the Soudan between November 1899 and March 1900, when he died suddenly from a severe case of dysentery just outside of Kayes. Danel's untimely death ended the pressure his continued presence could have

---

[4] Mademba, letter to gouv.-gen., Médine, Mar. 5, 1900, ANS-AOF 15 G 176. I shall interrogate this letter more fully later.

[5] Inspector-gen. Danel, letter to min. Col., Kayes, Mar. 2, 1900, ANOM Direction du Contrôle 894. Danel here referred to a telegram that he had sent the governor-general on Jan. 12, 1900, regarding his just completed investigation of Mademba.

[6] Min. Col., confidential letter to gouv.-gen., Paris, Mar. 24, 1900, ANS-AOF 15 G 176.

put on the colonial administration to address Mademba's status and his alleged abuses of power. The third investigation was conducted by Captain Pérignon, a career soldier of the infantry of the Marines, whom Ponty had appointed to replace Lambert as commandant of Segu at the end of January 1900. Pérignon was an old Soudanese hand.[7] Ponty charged Pérignon with investigating the allegations against Mademba as well as Lambert's investigation itself. Between February and March 1900, Pérignon investigated Lambert's investigation with the goal of assessing the credibility of his witnesses and their testimonies.

Lambert conducted the widest investigation into a full range of Mademba's alleged crimes and abuses of power. Sinsani's inhabitants accused Mademba of ritual murder, rape, kidnapping, excessive beatings, murder, extortion, and falsely claiming that French authorities had authorized supplemental requisitions of cotton. Lambert collected depositions regarding these allegations, which formed a central part of the growing archive on Mademba. Danel's investigation focused on the quality of Mademba's administrative service and whether Mademba had abused his authority. Thus, while Danel was aware of the range of crimes attested to through the depositions that Lambert was collecting and invoked these acts in his report, his formal investigation was limited to the inspection of administrative service. Danel thus examined what was called in the archives the *affaire coton* in which residents of Mademba's territories claimed that Mademba had demanded a fixed amount of cotton from each village as a form of supplemental tax, which he in turn then sold to the French administration. Pérignon's investigation focused on the case of Babo Diakite, the boy who disappeared in Sinsani overnight between March 31 and April 1, 1899, and was alleged to have been ritually murdered by Mademba, and the *affaire coton*. By the time Pérignon investigated Mademba, the accusations of rape, murder, kidnapping, excessive beatings, and the accumulated evidence to these crimes had been excluded.

This chapter investigates how these investigations eventually led Ponty to recommend to Governor-general Chaudié that Mademba be released from house arrest and be returned to his kingdom. Chaudié in turn made this recommendation to Minister of Colonies Albert Decrais. Upon reviewing not only the recommendation but also a significant part of the archives regarding Mademba that included Danel's report, copies of Lambert's reports from October through November 1899, and Veil's report from Sinsani, in May 1900 Minister Decrais was disinclined to accept Chaudié's recommendation.[8] Decrais's hesitancy reflected his concern that Mademba's release from house

---

[7] While completing his tour at Segu, Pérignon wrote a small book on the history and ethnography of the Middle Niger region, *Haut-Sénégal et Moyen-Niger: Kita et Ségou*.

[8] Copies of Lambert's and Veil's reports were filed together with Danel's investigation into Mademba in Danel Inspection, ANOM Direction du Contrôle 903.

arrest would undermine France's commitment to the rule of law and the prestige of French civilization in Africa. In September 1900, Decrais relented and Ponty finally granted Mademba the freedom to return to his kingdom. Ponty also left Mademba's kingdom intact, although he created a new position of "resident" of Sinsani to be filled by a European employee of the Native Affairs Department. What did Ponty's release of Mademba and Decrais's hesitancy signify about the rule of law and the bargains of collaboration in the new civilian-dominated republican-inspired colonialism in French West Africa?

The core of this chapter is drawn from a thick file held at the National Archives of Senegal. The original paper trail was assembled by Captain Lambert in Segu in late January 1900, which he called the "Dossier Mademba." Lambert's dossier found its way to the government general of West Africa and included the three overlapping investigations and their related correspondence. The file stops abruptly in late 1900 when Mademba returned to Sinsani and then picks up again with correspondence surrounding his death in 1918.[9]

The Intensification of Lambert's Investigation

Since his arrival in Segu in mid November 1898 to begin his new post as commandant de cercle, Captain Lambert was eager to get to work. Since Trentinian's rebuke of Mademba in 1897, Mademba renewed his commitments to provide the commandant of Segu with monthly reports on the situation in his kingdom. Mademba's monthly reports were prosaic at best and usually formulaic. All tended to begin with "I have the honor of reporting to you that the political situation in my *États* is very calm during the month of . . . just finished. The most perfect tranquility reigns in all my villages."[10] It could be that Mademba had mastered the bureaucratic art of not reporting anything of consequence. Mademba's sense of the "most perfect tranquility" was not, however, shared by all of the inhabitants of his kingdom.

Mademba did not inform Lambert of the disappearance of Babo Diakite during the night between March 31 and April 1, 1899. Mademba did not write about this event until May 18, after he had conducted a search and his own inquiry. His report also followed Babo Diakite's mother's formal complaint about the disappearance of her son to Lambert in Segu. Mademba knew that Lambert would likely be making further inquiries as well. In some of his

---

[9] Lambert's "Dossier Mademba" details the investigation up to Jan. 21, 1900. "Affaire Mademba" is the title of the larger file that includes the three investigations, related correspondence, and correspondence relating to Mademba's death in 1918, ANS-AOF 15 G 176.

[10] See for example, Mademba, letter to cmdt. Segu, Sinsani, Apr. 8, 1899, ANM 1 E 220.

monthly reports, Mademba offered information relating to his various agricultural experiments. In April, Mademba wrote that "all the cotton that I have been able to furnish this year has been sent to Segu."[11] Mademba was obviously proud of this cotton harvest and Baillaud had already noticed the sizeable quantities of cotton being collected in Mademba's palace during this January 1899 visit.

As Lambert settled into his post in Segu, he also began to surround himself with a group of African intermediaries who helped him with his regular administrative duties. Precisely because few French district officers took the time to learn local languages and immerse themselves in the cultures and politics of local communities, they were obliged to depend on Africans that they thought were loyal to them. Lambert actually claimed by January 1900 to have attained a "fair" ability in Bambara, knew well all of the chiefs of the district, and was knowledgeable about Islam, he nonetheless relied on African intermediaries.[12] In particular, Lambert relied on Tierno Hamedin, who was the qadi of Segu and who was "influential among the natives and feared by them." Hamedin translated Arabic and spoke French better than most inhabitants. Hamedin in turn had a network of other intermediaries, including Boi Ba, who served as his principle agent. Lambert thus built a pool of loyal intermediaries, whom he referred to as his "agents" and who provided him with intelligence.[13] As we know all too well, African intermediaries could simultaneously serve their European patrons and their own interests.

In August 1899, Lambert responded to an inquiry from the interim lieutenant-governor relating to local tax revenue. Budgetary discipline was a central theme in the metropolitan debates surrounding the AOF and lieutentant-governors were pressed to raise revenue wherever they could. In his reply, Lambert considered that the annual tax of 3,000 francs Mademba was obliged to pay for his kingdom "light," especially in comparison to the taxes paid by villages reporting to Segu. If Mademba's subjects were to pay the same tax rate as Segu villagers did, then the revenue from Sinsani would be ten times as large.[14]

As Lambert dug deeper into his investigation of Mademba, the issue of cotton and taxes became entangled in ways that blurred the lines between Mademba's role as an agricultural innovator and his political authority in

[11] Mademba, letters to cmdt. Segu, Sinsani, Apr. 8 and June 7, 1899, ANM 1 E 220. See also Roberts, *Two Worlds of Cotton* for a fuller story of Soudanese cotton and colonial development.

[12] Lambert, letter to gouv.-gen., Segu, Jan. 20, 1900, ANS-AOF 15 G 176.

[13] Pérignon, Rap. Pol. du cercle, first quarter 1900, Segu, ANM 1 E 71; Pérignon, entry Mar. 15, 1900, Renseignements pol, Segu, ANM 1 E 113.

[14] Lambert, letter to Chef de bataillon, Cmdt. de la région du Niger, Segu, Aug. 29, 1899, ANM 1 D 102.

Sinsani responsible for tax collection. Over the course of March and April 1899, Mademba sent to Segu over thirty tons of cotton in order for the colonial government to ship this supply to France to assess its suitability for the French textile industry, which was increasingly worried about sustainable sources of raw material to feed its looms. Mademba, who had not yet been paid for the cotton, sent his agent, Jeli Bambo, to Segu with the written receipts Mademba had gotten from the shipment of cotton. "I ask you to give to Jeli Bambo, the bearer of this letter, the value [of the cotton] by deducting the sum of three thousand francs which represents the amount of my annual tax to the local service."[15] In effect, Mademba paid his annual tax that year out of the proceeds of the sale of his cotton. Mademba did not make clear what he planned to do with the surplus revenue from the sale of the cotton, but we can assume, given his subjects' complaints about the *affaire coton*, that he kept it for himself.

While the tax rate and the *affaire coton* raised questions regarding the special status that Mademba enjoyed as *faama* of Sinsani, a letter written by Abdoul Drame on August 17, 1899, to the governor-general began to shake the edifices of Mademba's kingdom in ways that no one anticipated. Drame's letter was thus the third leg – the other two were the disappearance of Babo Diakite and the *affaire coton* – of the intensification of Lambert's investigation into Mademba's administration of his États de Sansanding. There is a sweet irony here, since Abdoul Drame was an African employee of the Post and Telegraph Department based in Saint Louis and his letter may have started a cascading flow of official complaints against the king who began his career as an African employee of the Post and Telegraph Department.

About a year before he sent this letter to the governor-general, Drame visited Sinsani in the hopes of seeing his mother and his sisters. His mother, Mariam Aidara, had been a wife of Mamadou Lamine. When the French suppressed Lamine's rebellion in December 1887 and executed him, they rewarded their African soldiers and auxiliaries with captured booty, including women. Mademba, who participated in the campaign against Mamadou Lamine, received Mariam Aidara and her two daughters. Her son, Abdoul Drame, was probably sent to either the school of hostages in Saint Louis or in Kayes, which became the training ground for many African employees of the colonial state. Sometime in 1898, during his visit to Sinsani, Abdoul Drame was shocked to see the condition of his mother and one sister, who were "imprisoned" in Mademba's palace and subject to severe beatings. Drame implored Mademba to release his family. Mademba replied that the "land was in revolt, all his people are emigrating, and if he released [Drame's mother], this would add to the add threats he faced." Mademba urged Drame to be patient, with the promise that he would eventually release his

---

[15] Mademba, letter to cmdt. de Cercle, Sinsani, May 22, 1899, ANS-AFO 15 G 176.

mother. After he returned to his post in Saint Louis, Drame wrote twice to Mademba about releasing his mother. Mademba did not reply.[16]

In his letter to Governor-general Chaudié, Drame presented himself as an honorable supplicant. He referred to the governor-general as "our father and our master," twice invoked French justice, and profusely apologized for having to bring to his attention "the actions at once arbitrary and tyrannical of Monsieur Mademba, *fama* of Sansanding . . . Having become *fama*, he began treating everyone as slaves, subjecting the four to five hundred women imprisoned in his palace to horrors and monstrous acts daily." Mademba also "attacked my sisters, who were with my mother in the *tata* [Bamanakan: fort, in this case, palace] and whom he absolutely wanted to make his wives, which was not only barbarous, but is considered immoral even in the Soudan." Mademba also confiscated all of his mother's goods. Drame further described "the poor women in the *tata* are subject to incredibly [bad] treatment. [Mademba] administers on them two and even three hundred lashes of a rawhide whip by his men." But such whippings pale in comparison to "his absolutely unheard of meanness and barbarity by dragging the poor women through the crowd without any clothes, not even a shred of cloth to cover their nudity" before being whipped. "This is not something that we do." Drame's information, he stated, came not only from his mother but also from the "people of the village."[17]

Drame ended his letter with the logical conclusion that we will hear often repeated in the official investigations and in the discussions about how the colonial administration should respond to Mademba's alleged acts. "If in compensation for the services [he rendered to France] he was placed at the head of a land, this was not done in order to permit his capricious behavior and his torture of everyone. This was not the sole fault of the French government, which everyone knows [acts with] goodness and equity."[18] Drame's accusations of Mademba's abuses of power raised serious concerns at a time of scandal and political uncertainty. Moreover, Drame's accusations that Mademba acted as he did under the authority of France raised fundamental questions about colonialism and the rule of law. When the governor-general did not respond, Drame wrote again on December 1, 1899 asking for clarification on the situation of his mother.[19] However, Governor-general Chaudié had acted rather quickly on Drame's original letter by asking Lieutenant-

---

[16] Abdoul Drame, letter to gouv.-gen., Saint Louis, Aug. 17, 1899, ANS-AOF 15 G 176. See also Miriam Aidara, deposition, Segu, Oct. 2, 1899, ANS-AOF 15 G 176.

[17] Abdoul Drame, letter to gouv.-gen., Saint Louis, Aug. 17, 1899, ANS-AOF 15 G 176.

[18] Ibid.

[19] Abdoul Drame, letter to gouv.-gen., Saint Louis, Dec. 1, 1899, ANS-AOF 15 G 176.

governor Audeoud to investigate the situation regarding Mariam Aidara. Audeoud passed the task to Lambert in Segu.[20]

Lambert quickly set to work. Mariam Aidara was now living in Segu with one daughter, which made a "long interrogation" possible. Lambert provided a translation of Aidara's statement.

> Previously, before the visit of my son to Sansanding, I was often beaten as were all the *fama*'s wives. By his own hand, I received almost daily 10–20 lashes. Just before the arrival of my son and under pretext that men had come to me, which was false and which was impossible, by his order I received 300 lashes by Kanouba Jara, who is always charged with this task. After the departure of my son, I was beaten even more harshly. Around two months ago, after having received another letter from my son, the *Fama* called me and my little girl to him and in front of his men, he chased me from his house ... He kept my little girl, who was 13 years old and is named Issa, who was given to me by Baya Ba, wife of al hajj Bouguni [after the 1893 rebellion]. Around 14 months ago, he [Mademba] took my little girl by force and made her his wife.[21]

In her statement, Mariam Aidara accused Mademba of domestic violence and of rape of a child. At the time of her rape, Issa would have been only eleven years old. Islam permits sexual relations with a child wife as soon as she enters puberty. Domestic violence in late nineteenth–century Soudan was probably quite common, but the regularity and intensity of the beatings Aidara received far exceeded what might be considered the norm.[22]

Attending the interview with Lambert was Madina Drame, Aidara's daughter, who also gave a statement. "Around four years ago, the *Fama* called me and ordered me to lie with him. I refused, so he ordered that I receive 100 lashes and then took me by force ... Despite his promises of presents, I did not wish to remain his wife, but I was forced to because he threatened my mother with a thousand lashes if I rejected him." Madina Drame then added "If all the women imprisoned in the *tata* were to come here, they would all tell you how unhappy there are." Madina Drame and Mariam Aidara both stated that "the *Fama* considers all the inhabitants of his territory as his slaves and whenever a women, married or not, appeals to him, he brings her into his *tata*

---

[20] Lambert, letter to lt.-gouv., p.i., Segu, Oct. 4, 1899 and Lambert, letter to gouv.-gen., Segu, Jan. 20, 1900, ANS-AOF 15 G 176.

[21] Lambert, letter to lt.-gouv. p.i., Segu, Oct. 4, 1899, ANS-AOF 15 G 176.

[22] For context, see Emily Burrill and Richard Roberts, "Domestic Violence, Colonial Courts, and the End of Slavery in the French Soudan, 1905–1912," in *Domestic Violence and the Law in Africa: Historical and Contemporary Perspectives*, eds. Emily Burrill, Richard Roberts, and Elizabeth Thornberry (Athens: University of Ohio Press, 2010), 33–53. On sexual relations with girls as debated by Islamic law in colonial Zanzibar, see Elke E. Stockreiter, "Islamic and Colonial Discourses on Gender Relations and Female Status in Zanzibar, 1900–1950s," in *Domestic Violence and the Law in Africa*, 118–132.

and she can no longer leave."[23] Drame and Aidara thus provided the first view into the inner workings of Mademba's palace since Captain Montguers's investigation of Mademba's alleged conspiracy against him in 1897, which had revealed his obsessive worry about his control over his wives.

In his report to the lieutenant-governor, Lambert explained how difficult it was to get candid information on Mademba and his administration. Mademba, who was keenly aware of the power of information, tried to control what information flowed out of Sinsani and into the hands of the French administration by first holding a lengthy interrogation with anyone wishing to leave Sinsani. His control was far from solid and Lambert managed to find additional sources of information from former residents of Sinsani who were now living in Segu and from villages in and surrounding Mademba's territories. All reported that villages within Mademba's territories wanted to pay their tax directly to Segu and be administered by Segu because within his territories, the collection of the tax "never ends and at any moment they are required to bring more to Sansanding." Villagers also complained that during the last cotton harvest, they were obliged to bring all of their cotton to Sansanding and those villages that did not have enough cotton had to buy additional cotton to fulfill their obligations. "They received nothing for their cotton and everyone knows that the *Fama* received lots of money from the cotton."[24]

Among those providing information was Jeli Bala, who stated that about two years before, he began long-distance trading. During his absence, he discovered that Mademba had thrown his wife, Yakare, in prison and had punished her first with 120 lashes and then with another 80 lashes under the pretext that she had led Mademba's wives to Jeli Bala's house. "This is impossible. The *Fama* lives in a double walled *tata* in which the interior apartments have only one entrance, which is guarded day and night. My wife remains in the *Fama*'s palace." At the beginning of September 1899, Garan Kouyate's daughter, Fini Kouyate, and her husband sought to leave Sinsani and join him in Segu. Mademba's *sofa* arrested them and brought them to Mademba. Fini Kouyate remained imprisoned in Mademba's *tata*. Garan added a list of seven additional wives of Sinsani's residents taken by Mademba, including those of Boua and Issa Cisse. Lambert admitted that he could not verify Kouyate's claims, but was nonetheless "certain that the detained women were in Mademba's house ... A grand discomfort reigns throughout [Mademba's] territory ... Not a year goes by in which there have not been daily complaints against the *Fama*."

Lambert concluded that the only certain solution to the disturbing conditions in Sinsani was to "depose Mademba, which will bring a rapid end to the

---

[23] Lambert, letter to lt.-gouv. p.i., Segu, Oct. 4, 1899, ANS-AOF 15 G 176.
[24] Ibid.

abuses of authority and bring satisfaction to his subjects." Lambert recognized that this was unlikely, so he quickly proposed that Mademba be placed directly under the authority of the commandant of Segu. "In a word, Monsieur Mademba would remain the nominal chief of Sansanding, but would operate under our direct authority."[25] Lambert argued that Mademba's position as *faama* might have been at one time justified as a reward for loyal service to the French, but his subsequent behavior and abuses of power under the authority of the French and the French Republic demanded a revision of that authority. Lambert next dug deeper into the *affaire coton*, which was to become a major issue in the subsequent investigations.

"Nearly every day," Lambert wrote to the lieutenant-governor in October 1899, "I received complaints from the natives of Sansanding regarding the abuses committed by the chief of that territory. These complaints have recently stopped following measures taken by the *Fama* of Sansanding." Lambert was convinced that Mademba wanted to prevent "me from learning about his misdeeds and from gaining information on how he obtained cotton this year. He said that he is the absolute master in his territory and that all property belongs to him. He also said that those who want to go to Segu are those who speak in the language of anarchy." Although Lambert worried that he could no longer continue his investigation because "no native is permitted to come to Segu and my agents no longer want to go to Sansanding because they are afraid of Mademba," he was confident of the results of his preliminary investigations.

"Natives complain above all of having all their cotton from the last harvest taken from them by the *Fama* under the pretext that this was ordered by the Governor. M. Mademba claimed that the cotton was a supplementary tax imposed by the French and that he received no compensation." Mademba ordered each village regardless of size to deliver 2,000 kilograms of cotton and those villages unable to do so were subject to fines ranging from 200,000 to 400,000 cowries. The tiny village of Diebougou, composed of twenty-three people, of whom ten were children, was obliged to deliver 1,100 kilograms of millet, 240 kilograms of groundnuts, and 1,020 kilograms of cotton. Because Diebougou's supply of cotton was short of the required amount, it was fined 248,000 cowries. Balidiougou, the chief of Maraupena, was forced to pawn his wife, his son, and his father in order to raise the fine Mademba imposed for not meeting his quota. Because he could neither meet his quota nor raise the cowries to pay the fine, the chief of Goura locked himself in his home and has not left because he feared being taken to Sinsani and executed. Mademba's demands for cotton as well as millet arrived at the same time as villagers were facing famine. "The large part of the millet harvest has been lost to locusts and

25 Ibid.

the inhabitants have been reduced to eating leaves. They believe that the *Fama* stole their cotton, which was their last resource."[26]

While Lambert felt confident about Mademba's role in the cotton tax, he felt less certain that "he had sufficient evidence," despite many complaints regarding allegations that Mademba engaged in human sacrifice. Even though Lambert stated that he did not "want to bring this issue" to the lieutenant-governor's attention, he did so anyway. At the core of these allegations was the disappearance of Babo Diakite. "Certain natives accuse [Mademba] of having killed between 25 and 30 children since his arrival in Sansanding in order to make them into grisgris ... Since the last attempt [Babo Diakite], all the children are kept in the courtyards and never leave. Last year at this time, a *fama*'s men killed a young female slave in the village of Valentiguila." Ten months before, the granddaughter of Bafing Jara disappeared. "Numerous witnesses saw the *fama* assisted by Sangaule, Jeli Bamba, and Massary Taraore took the body in a canoe during the night. They said that M. Mademba conveyed the child to the other side of the river, where they cut up the child, threw some parts into the river and kept the head." Lambert attributed this story to Issago Hiero, a "secret agent" of the *faama* in Segu and supported by several Somono. "The most recent human sacrifice was committed during the night of 31 March and that victim was the young child, Baba, son of Coumba Diakite."

To provide substance to his conclusion, Lambert included the deposition of Mahlalo Jara, one of Mademba's *hommes de confiance*. Issago Hiero confirmed Jara's deposition. In his deposition, Jara stated that Gauro Tamboura admitted to him that he was the one who "took the child to Mademba and it was he who cut off the child's head ... Cherif Fadoulay recited a verse from the Qur'an. The head remained in the *Fama*'s house and the body was wrapped in a red cloth." Around ten days later, Jara was again in Mademba's palace, when he overhead a conversation between Mademba and Tamboura. Mademba told Tamboura that people were accusing him of kidnapping the child, so Mademba planned to put Tamboura in prison for a few days, then interrogate him, and release him. Jara heard that Mademba promised Tamboura 110 francs plus the release of his wives. Lambert also cited other witnesses who claimed that Mademba alone kidnapped the child. Moriba recounted how he had entered Mademba's *tata* on the night of the disappearance and saw Bamba, Laminy, and Gauro standing around something wrapped in red cloth. Moriba was thrown in prison and whipped. He reported that Laminy told him that Mademba was afraid that he, Moriba, had seen something and that he would talk to the commandant de cercle. Moriba added that Laminy had also

---

[26] Lambert, Lambert to lt-gouv., Rap. au Sujet des faits proches au *fama* Mademba, Segu, Oct. 31, 1899, ANS-AOF 15 G 176.

said that if "he said nothing, he has nothing further to fear." Lambert stated that Coumba Diakite had now formally accused Mademba of having killed her child. Based on the evidence he collected, Lambert wrote to the lieutenant-governor that he "was absolutely convinced of Mademba's guilt and I have proof."[27]

Based on the evidence that Lambert had provided in his October 4, 1899 report on Abdoul Drame's letter to the governor-general, in which he found evidence to support Drame's claims about Mademba's misconduct, Lieutenant-governor Audeoud followed the standard bureaucratic method of passing the problem up the ladder. Audeoud's letter was carefully crafted to say very little. But he did lay out what would become a major defense of the actions that the colonial government would take in the Mademba affair. Audeoud wrote that based on Lambert's report, "it seems certain that the complaints by Abdoul Drame are not without merit and that Mademba has committed numerous abuses of authority in the exercise of his functions as *fama* of Sansanding." Audeoud succinctly put Mademba's status in context: Mademba was an officer in the Legion of Honor and the "high office" he now holds was confided to him by Colonel Archinard in 1891 as compensation for the "numerous services" Mademba had rendered to France "without end." Audeoud paraphrased Archinard's instructions that "Mademba was engaged 'to govern his provinces as Blacks prefer to be governed, but with a spirit of justice, humanity, and disinterest that places the good of the people before the personal interests of he who governs.'" In a brilliant sleight of hand in which he drew on his resentment of Paris's decision earlier that month to dismember the Soudan, Audeoud stated that given the recent "actual state of affairs," "the États de Sansanding now belong to the colony of Senegal." Audeoud signed off placing the decision on how to proceed with Mademba squarely in the hands of the governor-general.[28]

Given the evidence collected by Lambert and the scrutiny the administration of the Soudan was receiving, especially with the pending arrival of Inspector-general Danel, Governor-general Chaudié could do no less than order an official inquiry into the allegations of Mademba's abuses of authority and his role in the alleged ritual murder of Babo Diakite. Because no impartial investigation could be conducted in Sinsani while Mademba was present, Lieutenant-governor Audeoud ordered Mademba to Kayes in order to investigate Mademba's role in the alleged "atrocious cruelty" of the young boy's murder.[29] By November 20, Mademba wrote to Lambert in Segu that he was set to depart for Kayes in three days. As befitted an African king, Mademba

---

[27] Lambert, Lambert to lt-gouv., Rap. au Sujet des faits proches au *fama* Mademba, Segu, Oct. 31, 1899, ANS-AOF 15 G 176.

[28] Lt.-gouv. p.i., letter to gouv.-gen., Kayes, Nov. 28, 1899, ANS-AOF 15 G 176.

[29] Ponty, letter to Pérignon, cmdt. Segu, Kayes, Sept. 26, 1900, ANM 1 E 220.

dispatched a number of his horses in advance and was planned to meet up with them in Koulikoro for the overland trip to Kayes and departed with a "numerous entourage." Mademba also informed Lambert that he had put his nephew, Mamadou N'Diaye, as his representative in charge of his kingdom during his absence to be assisted by a council of notables appointed from chiefs of villages in his territories.[30]

As Mademba passed through Segu en route to Kayes, Lambert wasted no time in pursuing his investigation among Sinsani residents in Segu. Fadoulay Aidara, who was ill the day that Babo Diakite disappeared, stated that "everyone accuses the *Fama* of having killed Babo and since then, no one lets their children leave the village." Aidara added that he "could be persuaded that the *Fama* killed the child because he is a bad man and he has done much that is bad." Although he had no direct evidence of Mademba's guilt, Aidara's statement to Lambert indicates two important aspects of the widely shared rumor: first, that Mademba was a bad person who did bad things so therefore it was conceivable that he could have killed Babo Diakite; and second, everyone accepts that Mademba killed the child. As Luise White reminds us, rumors may not be evidence that is admissible in a court but they gain traction because they help explain current predicaments and the inexplicable.[31] In this sense, the rumor that Mademba ritually murdered Babo Diakite was part of the local discourse of power and powerlessness and helped explain Mademba's seemingly enormous coercive power and "proof" of his outsider status.

Lambert also interviewed Fasiriki Kuma, a former chief of Sinsani who was now in Segu having also fled Sinsani. Kuma told Lambert that "Everything that we have, the *Fama* takes, and each time a European passes through Sansanding, we all must provide the *Fama* with chickens and eggs. His men come to collect kilograms of millet and we have never received anything for the cotton we provided." Kuma continued that "all the people say that Gauro took the child and brought him to the *Fama*. He has not been seen since. I won't say anymore because I am afraid of the *Fama*." Lambert concluded his letter by stating that three of Mademba's men, who were traveling with him, attempted to suppress any interrogations Lambert's agents were having with Sinsani residents in Segu.[32]

After Mademba's departure, Lambert dispatched his second in command, Lieutenant Veil, to Sinsani to interrogate residents there. Veil left Segu the same day that Mademba left Sinsani. Tierno Hamedin, Lambert's chief intermediary, accompanied Veil on this investigative mission to Sinsani. Although

---

[30] Mademba, letter to Lambert, Sinsani, Nov. 20, 1899, ANM 1 E 220; Lambert, letter to lt.-gouv. p.i., Segu, Nov. 24, 1899, ANS-AOF 15 G 176.

[31] Luise White, *Speaking of Vampires: Rumor and History in Central Africa* (Berkeley: University of California Press, 2000).

[32] Lambert, letter to lt.-gouv. p.i., Segu, Nov. 24, 1899, ANS-AOF 15 G 176.

Mamadou N'Diaye invited Veil to stay with him in Mademba's *tata*, Lambert had instructed Veil to find quarters elsewhere in order to have as much autonomy as possible in conducting his interviews. Veil managed to find an empty house not far from the central plaza directly across from Mademba's palace. Almost immediately, N'Diaye sought to impede Veil's investigation. N'Diaye warned the villagers that anyone who spoke to Veil "will have their dog's mouth broken." Worried that N'Diaye's threat imperiled his ability to collect evidence, Veil had his interpreter tell the villagers that he will personally hold N'Diaye responsible for any acts of brutality committed against anyone who spoke to him. According to Veil, N'Diaye was a "large and handsome man of thirty years" who can speak, read, and write French. N'Diaye, who was Mademba's nephew, grew up in Saint Louis, where he attended the School of Arts et Métiers and was trained as a carpenter. N'Diaye was "very energetic," but he was "universally detested because of his brutality. He insults and beats everyone."[33] Veil then ordered N'Diaye to fetch the witnesses that Lambert had identified. Most of them were no longer in Sinsani. Several were accompanying Mademba to Kayes; Mademba had sent others on missions outside of his territories. Some of those who remained in Sinsani were willing to be interviewed, but not all. Those who refused to be interviewed were sent to Segu. The former chief of the Somono, whom Mademba had replaced, came to Veil on his own and stated that "he has much to tell to the commandant of Segu." Veil authorized his departure to Segu.[34]

Despite N'Diaye's efforts to dissuade Sinsani's residents from talking to Veil, "all day and well into the night, a parade of people waited outside my house to talk to me about the disappearance of the child or the *fama*'s administration." Boli Sangaule, a Maraka elder, told Veil "that since the disappearance of that child, no child has been allowed out without a big person." Sangaule also discussed the *affaire coton* in which each village was required to provide twenty large baskets of cotton – "enormous baskets" – as a special tax demanded by the French. "No one was compensated ... The porters [who carried the cotton] were furnished and fed by the inhabitants. The *fama* kept the entire salary." By salary, we can assume Sangaule meant the proceeds from the sale of the cotton. Kisma Mangane, a marabout resident in Sinsani, stated that "everyone is afraid of the *fama*. He kills people and fines them one million cowries ... He only frequents those who make grisgris. He takes as his wife the mother, the daughter, and the sister; this is something that even the Bambara do not do."

---

[33] Lt. Veil, "Rap. du Lt Veil, adjoint au commandant de cercle de Segou au sujet d'une tournée fait à Sansanding le 24 au 27 Novembre," Segu, Nov. 27, 1899, ANS-AOF 15 G 176.
[34] Ibid.

Veil interviewed Coumba Diakite. Coumba Diakite's first husband, Kobile Diakite and the father of Babo, had been executed by Mademba as punishment for his alleged involvement the 1897 conspiracy. Coumba was now married to Mamary Djiba, one of Mademba's *hommes de confiance*. Coumba Diakite then quoted Yahia Dembele, who in turn quoted Gauro Tamboura that "It was I who took the child. I gave him to Bamba, who gave the child to Kanouba Jara, who gave the child to Alate Karaba, who then gave the child to the *fama*." Diakite told Veil that she took Tamboura to Mademba and told him about the testimony. Mademba turned to Tamboura and interrogated him, but he said nothing. Mademba then said that if Tamboura "again spoke of this incident, bad things will happen to him." Present at that meeting with Mademba was also Mamadou N'Diaye, Alate Karaba, Kanouba Jara, and the almamy. Mademba told the group that "if anyone again speaks of this incident, he will tear out their mouth." Diakite added that once she returned to her house, Lela Dembele, Kanouba Jara's wife, warned her that if she discussed this again, she would have "her mouth torn out." Veil interviewed Lela Dembele, who said that she knew nothing. Given Lambert's instructions, Veil then ordered Coumba Diakite and Lela Dembele to Segu for further interrogations there. Veil also interviewed Yahia Dembele, who confirmed the narrative that Coumba Diakite had told.

Altogether Veil kept busy in Sinsani. He quoted directly interviews with twenty informants and he conducted additional interviews in the villages of Madina and Valentiguila. Mea Demba, who was a griotte and the mother-in-law of Garan Kouyate, who played a role in the 1897 investigation, recounted that Mademba took both Kouyate's wife and her other daughter, Marietou Demba, at the same time. When she complained to Mademba, he threw her in prison for fifteen days and put her daughter in irons for six months. Since Mea Demba was very old and she wanted to be reunited with her daughter and son-in-law now living in Segu, Veil authorized her departure. Veil also followed-up on Demba's accusation that Marietou Demba still remained inside Mademba's *tata* and asked Mamadou N'Diaye to release her. N'Diaye responded that he did not know this woman and that she may be one of Mademba's wives. Veil did not pursue the case of Marietou Demba because "he did not want to assist in the departure of [this woman] from the *fama*'s house during his absence."

Sega Demba, a slave of Fatima Ba, one of Mademba's wives, who regularly served Mademba food and drink, came to Veil late at night for fear of being seen and therefore punished. She admitted to seeing Babo Diakite in Mademba's house three days after he disappeared together with Gauro Tamboura, Alete Karaba, and Mademba. After that, she never saw the child again. She also requested permission to leave Sinsani for Segu, but Veil did not authorize her departure most likely because she admitted to being a slave of one of Mademba's wives. Siga Sidibe, one of the guards stationed outside of the only door to Mademba's palace, declared during his daytime visit to Veil that he knew nothing, although he admitted that Yaro Fadio told him that he had seen the child enter Alate Karaba's house. Sidibe, however, was not finished telling his story. He returned at night to Veil's house and told him that he "saw the child enter [Mademba's palace] with Alate Karaba, Gauro, Bamba, and Kanouba. The child did not leave. No one can leave [the palace] without me seeing them." Sidibe feared that someone had seen him coming to talk to Veil and asked for Veil's protection. Veil authorized Sidibe's departure for Segu.

In a quite telling interview, Fasiriki Cisse, one of the remaining Cisse elders of Sinsani, said that he and three other major household heads of Sinsani wanted to leave for Segu. He alone had an outlying agricultural village with 267 people who belonged to him. Cisse was obviously referring to a slave village. Together, the four Cisse household heads controlled "about half of the population of Sinsani." Cisse complained that whenever a European passes through Sinsani, "the *fama*'s slaves come searching for millet, chickens, eggs, and milk. We are never compensated for this. Even today, Mamadou N'Diaye requisitioned a chicken and four eggs." Veil put in parentheses that he never received anything from N'Diaye. Cisse concluded that "No one can enter Sinsani without fearing [for their lives]. The village is deserted. No one has security, neither of goods nor of their persons." Delegations representing the Somono and the griots came to Veil with their grievances, "which are all the same: abuses and kidnapping of women and slaves by Mademba's men."

Veil also heard more about the cotton requisition. The brother of the old and blind chief of Madina village explained that Mademba imposed a surtax of twenty baskets on cotton on the village. Because the village could supply only three baskets, Mademba fined them 240,000 cowries. And because the blind chief did not visit Mademba in Sinsani, he fined the chief an additional 10,000 cowries. The brother of the village chief of Valentiguila told Veil that his village did indeed provide twenty baskets of cotton, for which they did not get paid. He also stated that Mademba not only took three slaves from the village chief but had confiscated the village fields and redistributed them to his own people.

Veil did not hear only complaints. The almamy of Sinsani, one of Mademba's most loyal subjects, insisted that his visit was "purely personal and spontaneous" and that "everything is well, everything is perfect" in Sinsani. When Veil pushed him about the "noise" of the inhabitants' complaints and fears, the almamy stated that the rumors "do not have any foundation and the child is simply missing and will soon be returned." The almamy was referring to the disappearance of Babo Diakite, which had occurred eight months previously. Veil was not convinced by the almamy's efforts to provide an alternative narrative of the situation in Sinsani. Based on the evidence that he collected in Sinsani, Veil concluded that "Under the shelter of our power, the *Fama* reigns here with terror; it is under our name that he abuses his authority; it is by invoking our intervention that he maintains his authority." "I fear," Veil continued, "for our reputation that our flag will not much longer cover[-up] these facts."[35]

While Veil was in Sinsani, Lambert kept busy in Segu collecting addition testimonies. During Mademba's passage through Segu, Lambert asked him to order Laminy, Mamary Djiba, Gauro, and Moriba to Segu. Mademba agreed to write to his nephew to order their appearance, except for Gauro, the key witness to Babo Diakite's disappearance. Mademba had sent Gauro on a hunting expedition to the east to collect egret feathers. Lambert found this excuse too convenient and wrote that "if these people have really departed Sinsani, this would be for me evidence of Mademba's bad intentions and his guilt." Lambert managed to interview Alate Karaba, Kanouba Jara, and Mamary Taroare, among several others. What was striking in Lambert's interviews with Mademba's *hommes de confiance* was their statements condemning Mademba. Kanouba Jara testified that "he was in charge of administering whippings. I often received orders to beat [Mademba's] women, sometimes 300 lashes." Kanouba added that "we are all captives of the French, who gave us to the *Fama*. Were we able to be attached to Segu, we would be much happier." Jara's wife, who attended the interview, stated that the brother of her husband, who was also likely a *sofa*, told her the day after Babo Diakite disappeared that he had seen Gauro take the child during the night and enter Mademba's palace. Alate Karaba, Mademba's chief of the *sofa*, explained that when the child was not found, a few days later, Mademba ordered Karaba to convene a meeting of Sinsani's inhabitants in order to combat a spreading rumor about Mademba's role in the disappearance. Mademba wanted to put a stop to what he called "a language of anarchy." Mamary Taroare stated that the "*Fama* takes everything that we have." The chief of Nyamina, who happened to be in Segu visiting family, told Lambert that "Mademba is a very bad man, who has done many bad things in Sansanding."

Among the most damning testimony regarding Mademba's treatment of women that Lambert collected came from Mariam Babi.

> I was taken prisoner by the *Fama* after he killed my father around six or seven years ago together with my mother, my sisters, all my father's wives, and all our captives. The *Fama* also took all our gold jewelry of which we had a lot, all our belongings, and our large herd of cattle. Imprisoned in the *Fama*'s palace, I was raped several years ago before I was even a woman. Last month, the *Fama* gave me as a female slave to the village chief of Sansanding. I would much rather return to my mother than remain a slave.

[35] Ibid.

My sister Lalia was also raped [by the *Fama*] when she was very little. About a month ago, she was given as a present to become the female slave of the son of Abderahman of Bamako. My mother would very much like her returned to her. There are a lot of wives and female slaves in the *Fama's tata*. If someone were to give them their liberty, they would be very happy and would return to their families. Very few would want to return to the *Fama* because he is an evil man.

Nianausu Taraore, the chief of the Somono of Sinsani, told Lambert that everyday his fishermen are obliged to provide Mademba with ten fresh fish and dried fish. Taraore concluded his testimony by stating that "The *Fama* inspires a great fear because he is sustained by the French."[36]

Lambert's Depositions

Since he was first ordered by Lieutenant-governor Audeoud to investigate Abdoul Drame's accusations against Mademba, Lambert had been conducting formal interrogations in Segu. Lambert had been summarizing these testimonies in his reports and letters to Audeoud. The interrogations were formal affairs and Lambert produced a written deposition for each one. We can image how Lambert collected them by examining the deposition itself. Extrapolating from the deposition, the witness was likely called into the commandant's office in Segu, where the witness would be seated opposite the commandant – Lambert was present at all of the interrogations – and usually two or three other Europeans. The European officers would be dressed in uniforms. I do not know if the Segu office had European civilian employees in 1899 or 1900, but it is possible since civilian employees of the Native Affairs Division were posted to Sinsani on a regular basis starting in 1900. By late October 1899, Lambert began collecting the refugees' depositions together with Segu's qadi, Tierno Hamedin, who served as translator and who transcribed the interrogation in Arabic. Apparently, Hamedin presented himself as the "qadi of the province" and claimed that he had been qadi to Amadu Tall in Segu. Hamedin further claimed that Archinard had named him qadi of Segu. Hamedin managed to gain Lambert's confidence, as he had many of the previous commandants of Segu. He was "very intelligent" and exerted "unlimited influence over the blacks" in the district.[37] Hamedin was apparently eager to collect derogatory material on Mademba.

An Arabic version of the deposition was always paired with the French version. Lambert and the other Europeans present signed each deposition,

---

[36] Lambert, letter to lt.-gouv., Segu, Nov. 28, 1899, ANS-AOF 15 G 176.
[37] Pérignon, letter to Ponty, Segu, Apr. 7, 1900; Ponty, letter to gouv.-gen., Kayes, May 10, 1900, ANS-AOF 15 G 176.

thus rendering them legally witnessed documents. Between October 2, 1899 and January 15, 1900, Lambert presided over thirty-five formal interrogations of witnesses. At least two copies of each deposition were made.[38] These depositions thus became part of the "Dossier Mademba" and were thus available to those conducting the two other investigations and to the senior administrators – including the minister of Colonies – who participated in the decision regarding what to do with Mademba.

Around half of the witnesses were women and the other half men. Most harbored grievances against Mademba. Some were probably willing to give testimony even in front of what was undoubtedly an imposing and intimidating setting. Others were probably reluctant and their testimonies were brief at best. Table 6.1 captures the distribution of testimony by gender of the witnesses.

The witnesses' experiences with Mademba were clearly gendered. Almost all of the women Lambert interviewed accused Mademba of violence against them, including regular beating, excessive lashings, rape, and forceful confinement that sometimes included prison. At least one out of every three female informants accused Mademba of raping them; others couched similar complaints in terms of their being forced to marry Mademba. Discussing rape in front of male interrogators is never easy, which indicates only how deep their anger and resentment of Mademba went. It could very well be that the numbers of lashes women recounted were not actual lashes but merely proxies for many. Regardless of the actual number of rapes or lashes, the scale of violence inflicted by Mademba against women was astounding. Some women complained that Mademba confiscated their wealth, especially jewelry but also livestock. Some of Lambert's male informants supported the women's claims of violence. Several complained that Mademba took whatever young girls he wanted and that he had hundreds of wives.

The men complained mostly about Mademba's abuses of power in the requisition of cotton, the imposition of excessive fines, the execution of Kaoule in 1897 during Mademba's imagined conspiracy of men to invade his inner harem, and arbitrarily being thrown in prison. Many men reported being fearful of Mademba's vindictiveness. Crossing Mademba often resulted in beatings and imprisonment, if not execution. On the other hand, Mademba rewarded loyal service, especially through the gifts of women.

More male informants than female ones discussed Babo Diakite's disappearance. Many of his female informants were confined to the palace, so they might not have been witnesses to the allegations of Mademba's ritual murder of the young Diakite. It could also be that Lambert, under orders from

---

[38] I first read copies of these depositions in Bamako, where they are filed in "Dossier des diverses affaires, Sansanding, 1899," Segu, ANM 1 E 220. They also appear in "Affaire Mademba," ANS-AOF 15 G 176.

Table 6.1 Depositions collected by Captain Lambert, October 1899–January 1900

Gender	Accusations	Accusations	Accusations	Accusations	Accusations	Accusations
F	300 lashes	Raped	Beat her	Confined unwillingly		
F	100 lashes	Raped	Beat her	Confined unwillingly		
F	1000 lashes	Raped	Confined unwillingly			
F	Babo Diakite					
F	100 lashes	Kidnapped	Beat her	Confined unwillingly	Took all of her jewelry	Thrown in prison
F	100 lashes	Took all of her goods	Beat her			
F	Frequently beaten	Beat her	Thrown in prison			
F	200 lashes	Beat her				
F	Beat her for refusing to marry him	Also beat her mother and sisters	Mother thrown in prison			
F	400 lashes	Beat her	Thrown in prison			
F	Tore up certificate of freedom	Given as slave to another				
F	Beat her	Thrown in prison				
F	1000 lashes	Regular beatings	Throw in prison			
F	100 lashes	Raped				
F	Took all of her jewelry	Raped	Beat her	Raped sister as well		
M	Cotton requisition	Afraid				
M	Babo Diakite	Forced to be silent				
M	Babo Diakite	Forced to lie				
M	Cotton requisition					

Table 6.1 (*cont.*)

Gender	Accusations	Accusations	Accusations	Accusations	Accusations	Accusations
M	Cotton requisition	Heavy fines				
M	Cotton requisitions	All kinds of requisitions				
M	Cotton requisition	Heavy fines				
M	Cotton requisition					
M	Cotton requisition	Heavy fines	Taking young girls			
M	Babo Diakite					
M	Babo Diakite					
M	Babo Diakite					
M	Babo Diakite	Taking young girls	200 wives			
M	Babo Diakite					
M	Babo Diakite					
M	Kaoule's execution	1897 conspiracy				
M	Kaoule's execution	1897 conspiracy				
M	1897 conspiracy	Fearful	Beat him	Thrown in prison		
M	Takes everything					
M	Kaoule's execution					

(Source: ANS-AOF 15 G 176)

Lieutenant-colonel Audeoud to investigate the Diakite disappearance, asked those questions more directly to his male informants. In any case, the corpus of formal depositions Lambert collected provided a rich archive of the range of crimes and abuses Sinsani's townspeople accused Mademba of having committed.

Inspector-general Danel's Investigation

Henri Danel had considerable colonial experience before Minister of Colonies Decrais ordered a formal administrative inspection of the Soudan in August 1899. Although Decrais was only recently appointed as minister of Colonies, he inherited serious questions about the administrative coherence of parts of the empire. Danel's mission was therefore part of a wider investigation into the organization and administrative performance of the French colonies of IndoChina, India, and the Soudan.[39] The ministry's efforts in West Africa also involved the commission to assess the viability of the colony of the Soudan itself, which held its deliberations during September and October 1899 in Paris.

Because the Ministry of Colonies was carved out of the Ministry of the Navy, it was not unusual for officials in the Ministry of Colonies to have had naval experience. Henri Eloi Danel was born in 1850 and entered military service in 1867. By 1872, he was promoted to sublieutenant and in 1880 promoted to lieutenant. I do not know much about his military service, but he was obviously well regarded by his superiors because he was awarded the rank of Chevalier in the Legion of Honor in 1880. In 1885, he joined the Inspection-General Service of the Ministry of the Navy and was posted to Saigon. Members of the Inspection-General were highly regarded and formed a pool of senior administrators in the colonies. Chaudié had been Inspector-general in the Ministry of the Navy before being named governor-general. Likewise, Danel served as interim lieutenant-governor of Indochina for several months in 1889 before returning to the Inspection-General. Danel was then appointed as governor of Reunion in 1893 and governor of Guyana in 1895. Danel did not remain long in the senior ranks of the colonial administration. In 1898, Danel returned to the Inspection-General service of the Ministry of Colonies with the rank of Inspector-General.[40]

---

[39] Chef, Direction du Contrôle, l'Inspecteur Général des Colonies, Note pour la Première direction, Paris, Aug. 8, 1899, ANOM Soudan XIX-1. Decrais saw himself as a reformer and initiated this inspection within weeks of being appointed minister of Colonies.

[40] For background on the Inspection-General, see Marcel Marion, *Dictionnaire des Institutions de la France aux XVIIè et XVIIIè siècles* (Paris: Auguste Picard, 1923); Frederick F. Ridely and Jean Blondel, *Public Administration in France* (London: Routledge and Kegan Paul, 1969); Glineur, *Histoire des Institutions administratives Xè–XIXè siècle.*

Danel was highly regarded within the Inspection-General service. Already in 1887 he received praise from his superiors that was leavened with some concerns about his enthusiasm.

> M. Danel is a precious collaborator ... After only two and a half years in the Inspection, he is on top of all administrative and financial issues, for which he has a very special competence. Very engaged with his new career, he deploys a zeal, which without exaggerating, can benefit from a mild moderation in certain circumstances. I consider him an enthusiastic functionary and one to whom we can always confer the most complex missions.[41]

This was the one critical note in his otherwise exemplary personnel file. Danel received his orders to lead the inspection of the Soudan on August 13, 1899 and arrived in the Soudan in mid November, around the same time as Mademba was settling in to his obligatory residence in Kayes. In assigning Danel to the investigation in the Soudan, the minister of Colonies had no idea just how complex this mission was to become.[42]

As far as I can tell, this was Danel's first visit to the Soudan. He worked quickly. Between his arrival in Kayes in mid November 1899 and when he filed his investigations around the middle of January 1900, Danel conducted at least thirteen investigations into administrative personnel. Danel conducted two investigations in Bamako, four in Kati, two in Timbuktu, and one each in Segu, Jenne, Koulikoro, and Sinsani. Traveling between them involved considerable time. Many of Danel's reports were cursory, especially if he did not find anything worrisome in his investigations. His report on Captain Lambert was relatively short and full of praise. Danel remarked first on how successful Lambert was in collecting the annual tax. "Despite the losses to agricultural by the locusts, some villages have managed to pay twice the level of their annual tax assessment." Danel placed the success of the tax collection squarely on Lambert's "intelligent zeal." "This happy result," Danel wrote, "is due to the firm and benevolent rule of the commanding officer, Captain Lambert of the Infantry, who in only one year administering Segu has demonstrated strong purpose in all branches of his service."[43]

The Ministry of Colonies had a formal template for the official investigative reports. The actual physical structure of the report is worth exploring. Danel used official, printed report folios, each page roughly twice as large as a standard A2 sheet of paper. The most striking and the most useful aspect of

---

[41] Chef de Service central de l'Inspection, Bulletin individual de notes, Paris, Dec. 10, 1887, ANOM Dossiers personnels (Danel) 3540.

[42] L'Inspecteur général des Colonies, ANOM Direction du Contrôle 894.

[43] Inspecteur-gen. des colonies Danel, Service du commandant de cercle – Segou, Jan. 15, 1900, n.p. [probably Kayes], ANOM Soudan XIX-1.

these official report forms was that each large folio sheet was attached to another yielding five vertical columns: two on one side and three on the other. Each vertical column provided space for different parties in the investigation to respond. The first column on the left side was the widest and was dedicated to the "Verified Facts and Observations by the Inspector [filled in the rank] of the Colonies." The second column on the left side was allocated to "Explanations and Observations by the Head of the Service being Verified [i.e. investigated]." In smaller print, the head of the Service was to indicate what orders and instructions were given in order to redress the irregularities identified. On the right-hand side of the folio, the first column on the left was dedicated to "New Observations of the Inspector [fill in the rank]" in response to what the head of the Service had to say. The middle column was for the "Observations of the Inspector General of Colonies," especially if the inspector who conducted the original investigation was junior. And finally, the last column was "Follow-Up on the Investigation by the Competent Administration or Service." What makes this particular format so potentially useful is that it provides space in the same document for a conversation among different branches of the same administrative unit, and in this case, the colonial administration.

To return briefly to Danel's report on Lambert, Danel had indicated that he was pleased to observe that Lambert had succeeded in putting more French currency into circulation and had plans to further increase the volume of French currency circulating in the district. In the column "Explanations and Observations by the Head of the Service being Verified," Governor-general Chaudié wrote that "Those are excellent results and one would be wrong not to recognize this."[44] Chaudié had nothing further to say about Lambert and did not date his response, although he must have written his comments well after Danel submitted his report and thus after Lambert had been relieved of his post as commandant de cercle of Segu. The investigation into Mademba's administrative service, however, was very different, as was Chaudié's response.

Danel actually visited Sinsani to assess Mademba's administration firsthand, but Mademba was already in Kayes and Danel did not see Mademba in situ.[45] Danel collected most of his evidence in Segu, where he examined the emerging archive of Mademba's administrative service and drew on Lambert's investigation.[46] Danel's report on Mademba was relatively short, but went to the heart of the status of Mademba's kingdom in a changing colonial

---

[44] Ibid.

[45] Danel, letter to Procureur-gen., Koulikoro, Jan. 21, 1900, ANS-AOF 15 G 176.

[46] There is a slight discrepancy regarding the date that Danel completed his report on Mademba. The cover sheet indicated Jan. 11, 1900, while the date in the column where Danel wrote his report and signed it was Jan. 14, 1900.

administration.[47] On the cover page of his report, Danel wrote in *"Fama"* in the space allotted for the description of the service being investigated. Despite the promise that the agent being investigated had the option to respond to the report, I have no indication whether Mademba was given the chance to review and respond to Danel's report. Given his March 5, 1900, letter to the governor-general in which he claims to be ignorant of why he was forced to remain in obligatory residence, Mademba never indicated that he was conversant with Danel's report. It could be that because Mademba held an anomalous category of service – that of a *faama* – he was not subject to the same rights that other functionaries had.

Although Danel's report recognized the range of crimes Mademba was alleged to have committed, the report focused on two core aspects: the administrative status of *faama* and his alleged abuse of power in regard to the requisition of cotton as a supplemental tax. Danel set his report into the context of Archinard's 1891 investiture of Mademba as *faama* of Sinsani.

> When in 1891 the territory of Sansanding was established and placed under the authority of Mademba, the commandant supérieur of the Soudan in a letter of investiture (this was the official title of the document that I attach here), dated 7 March, he addressed the new *Fama* thusly: "You have accepted in regard to me and by extension in regard to France the engagement to govern these provinces as the Blacks prefer to be governed, but with the spirit of justice, humanity, and disinterest that place the well-being of the people you govern above your personal satisfactions."

Rhetorically, Danel set up the opening of his report in such a way as to alert the reader to the context and potential tensions of Archinard's appointment of Mademba as *faama*. The next paragraph develops this theme.

> At that moment, Mademba, because of his services, may have warranted the consideration and the eloquent appreciation bestowed on him by the commandant supérieur. However, there was certainly an imprudence in permitting a modest employee of the Post and Telegraph [service], to which he was qualified, the possibility of founding a royal dynasty under the shelter of the pavilion of the Republic of France.

For an inspector of the colonial administration, who was charged with evaluating the quality of the functionaries in the pursuit of their jobs, Danel found

---

[47] I have two versions of Danel's report: one is the original, seven-pages long, it is located in the ANOM Direction du Contrôle 903; the second, which is a copy, is four-pages long and is located in ANS-AOF 15 G 176. These are handwritten copies, so differences in penmanship can account for the difference in length. The original includes a short comment by Ponty, which is absent in the copy. Danel, Service du *Fama* de Sansanding, Segu, Jan. 14, 1900, ANS-AOF 15 G 176 and ANOM Direction du Contrôle 903.

Archinard's efforts to promote a version of indirect rule incongruous and imprudent. In particular, Danel was disturbed by both the elevation of a modest employee of the Post and Telegraph Department into a king, but also the creation of a royal dynasty within the republican tradition of France. These were both significant policy issues, but Danel next drew on crude racism to explain why Mademba slipped away from the standards Archinard had set. "For those who know the Blacks, it would be very likely that once in possession of a power given under the conditions of the letter of investiture of 7 March, Mademba would forget his promises and violate his instructions. This is what occurred."

Danel also described what he saw as insubordination, which in his order of things trumped the evidence of criminal acts.

> Mademba was scarcely troubled with a few [critical] remarks [from senior administrators], of which he has taken no account. Nor did he execute certain formal orders, several times reiterated; strengthened by his sense of his impunity, he gave free rein to his passions. Today, his subjects accuse him of all kinds of crimes: thefts, kidnapping, imprisonment, rape, murder, nothing lacks in this collection. The administration is aware of numerous complaints and it is up to the administration to deal with these issues.[48]

Instead of pursuing the allegations of crimes, which Lambert had documented, Danel stuck closely to the mandate of his assignment: to investigate the administrative service of Mademba. "This inspection," Danel wrote, "will only examine financial issues. And the fact, established by witnesses consulted in Sansanding and in Segu that in regard to the sale of cotton, is sufficient to justify in the eyes of this inspection the revocation of the functions of the *Fama* of Sansanding, without prejudice in regard to the other acts of which he may be the author." Later in the report, Danel stated that "we have intentionally neglected all that did not directly relate to taxes, which included accusations of crimes." In this statement, Danel was careful to explain that the narrowing of his investigation into the *affaire coton* should not be used by the senior administration to avoid fuller investigation into those alleged acts.

Danel then developed his case for why the *affaire coton* justified the ending of Mademba's tenure as *faama*. "It was the village chiefs, Mademba's trusted men, who came to complain that they could not satisfy the demands of the master who overwhelmed them with taxes and fines." Danel then cited evidence of the excessive nature of Mademba's requisitions. What is striking about this evidence is that Danel reproduced it word for word as it appeared in two of Lambert's

---

[48] This list of alleged crimes was the only statement underlined in the copy of Danel's report in the Ministry of Colonies files.

reports to Lieutenant-governor Audeoud.[49] Based on his review of Lambert's service, Danel was impressed with his zeal and his careful, methodical administration. Danel's confidence in using Lambert's evidence stemmed from the fact that there were so many corroborating witness, "who could be multiplied infinitively." Regarding the nature of the evidence, Danel argued that it was challenging to corroborate witness testimony with other, especially written, evidence because Mademba did not provide receipts for the requisitions of millet, groundnuts, and other commodities with the exception of cotton. "In contrast, it is easy to verify their [the witnesses'] assertion in regard to cotton. By examining the administrative books in Segu, one can establish that the *Fama* received 6127 francs for cotton he provided to the administration." After villagers who had provided Mademba with the required cotton learned from villages in neighboring districts that they were not required to provide cotton, and that Mademba had been paid but they had received nothing, a "general discontent developed." Quoting Fasiriki Kuma, "Mademba betrayed the French and stole from us." Danel's description of Fasiriki Kuma also appeared in almost identical form in Lambert's November report.

At this stage in his report, Danel summarized his findings and ironically reversed Archinard's 1891 instructions to Mademba.

> The *Fama* considers the territory of Sansanding to be his personal property and all the inhabitants as his slaves. Despite his degree of civilization, despite his encounters with Europeans, it is his Negro spirit that has taken over; if he commands like the French, he has according to his subjects, all the excesses of Black kings. Naturally, he pretends to act only on the orders or with the approval of the French.

Danel raised the issue of how Mademba's malfeasance and the alleged criminal acts might tarnish the prestige of the French and to their stated commitments of civilization.

> In the eyes of the population who have seen that we put [Mademba] as the head of the land and they know that we are well informed [about his acts], we must bear the responsibility for his odious acts, which are so clearly contrary to our national spirit and commitments to justice and humanity ... Indeed the only solution that will work is the revocation of Mademba from his functions as *Fama* as well as those as controller of Post and Telegraph Service, from which he has been seconded. Moreover, against all rules, he still receives an annual salary from the local budget of 6960 francs.

---

[49] See Lambert to lt.-gouv., Rap. au Sujet des faits proches au *fama* Mademba, Segu, Oct. 31, 1899, and Lambert, letter to lt.-gouv. p.i., Segu, Nov. 24, 1899, ANS-AOF 15 G 176.

Danel returned again to the anomalous nature of Mademba's administrative service. He was at once *faama* – king – of a territory under some form of French authority in which he is supposed to act within the obligation to conform to French civilization and French values of justice and humanity. He has obviously failed to live up to this standard. But Danel went further to suggest that even as Mademba acted as *faama*, he remained a titular French functionary who received an annual salary even if he was for the moment seconded to another administrative service. As a French functionary, he was bound to perform his role in accordance with French administrative procedure regarding that service. Was there, however, a category of "king" in the French colonial administration? And if not, was Mademba still bound by the broad rules regulating his role as a member of the Post and Telegraph Department?

In his concluding recommendation, Danel argued that the status of the États de Sansanding and Mademba's role as *faama* should be ended.

> Therefore, the constitution of the territory of Sansanding, which was established by the letter of 7 March 1891, has no longer any reason to exist. The moment has arrived when without inconvenience, the territory could be attached to the Segu cercle without the need to augment its administrative personnel and without crushing the annual tax of its enlarged population. In fact, attaching the territory would generate at least an additional one thousand francs to the local budget.

Should attaching Sinsani to Segu not appeal to the senior administration, Danel proposed another solution: make Sinsani and its territories a separate cercle, but put a European functionary at its head. But these were simple solutions to the more complex and salient issue regarding Mademba's status as *faama* and what rules governed his administration.

Governor-general Chaudié wasted no time responding to Danel's investigation into Mademba's service. Chaudié was in Kayes, probably overseeing the transition between Lieutenant-governor Audeoud and William Ponty, the new delegate of the governor-general for the Soudan, who had only been appointed on December 31, 1899, and had barely had time to settle into his new job when Danel submitted his report. Chaudié was conversant with the complaints and allegations of Mademba's actions, since he had received some of those complaints directly and because Captain Lambert's reports of October and November 1899 had likely been forwarded to him by Audeoud. Chaudié's response, which he signed on February 1, 1900, provided the seeds for the administration's defense of Mademba that were fleshed out in part by Captain Pérignon's investigation in February and March 1900.

> The Mademba affair, about which I know directly from a political report by the commandant of Segu, is at once more delicate and more serious than it would appear in the eyes of M. Inspector-general, head of the

mission, who naturally focused on the brutal acts that emerged in the course of his investigations into the financial affairs that he has established.

If we were in a colony constituted according to ordinary forms, nothing would be simpler than to repress the maladministering functionary by alerting the Attorney-general conforming to the Code of Criminal Instruction as stated in the 1868 circular to Inspectors and to let justice take its course.

But is Mademba really a functionary if he exercise the power and authority devolved to him as *fama* of Sansanding?[50]

Chaudié made four crucial interventions in these first three sentences of his response to Danel's report on Mademba. First, he stressed that the "brutal acts" Mademba was alleged to have committed were not within the direct purview of Danel's investigation into the financial affairs of the territory of Sinsani, but those alleged acts had influenced Danel's assessment of Mademba's financial service. Second, was Mademba actually an ordinary functionary bound by the ordinary rules of administrative service when he was appointed as *faama*? What rules governing his administrative service should therefore prevail? Third, in invoking the 1868 circular regarding the obligations of inspectors to report criminal wrongdoing to the attorney-general, Chaudié was asserting his deep knowledge of the role of the inspectorate and therefore undermining Danel's authority. And fourth, Chaudié asked rhetorically whether ordinary rules of administrative service prevailed in a colony like the Soudan that was not constituted by ordinary structures of government. All of this contributed to the "delicate" nature of the case against Mademba.

Chaudié's response to his own question about whether or not Mademba was a functionary and therefore subject to established rules governing the actions of administrators was a categorical "No." Chaudié argued that the rules that should govern Mademba's administrative service must stem from Archinard's March 7, 1891 letter of investiture. Archinard was at the time supreme military commander of the Soudan, which was effectively the military equivalent of governor. "By recognizing our suzerainty, the *fama* gained the rights to all fees and taxes and nowhere does it state that these fees and taxes are not to be determined by the *Fama* himself. He has the right to maintain and support an army, etc ... etc." Chaudié strategically left out the line Danel had quoted from Archinard's letter that Mademba was "to govern his provinces as the

---

[50] Gouv.-gen. Chaudié, Suite Donnée à la Vérification par l'Administration ou par la Division compétente, Kayes, Feb. 1, 1900, in Danel, Service du Fama de Sansanding, Segu, Jan. 14, 1900, ANS-AOF 15 G 176. Also in Danel, Service du Fama de Sansanding, Segu, Jan. 14, 1900, ANOM Direction du Contrôle 903.

Blacks prefer to be governed, but with a spirit of justice, humanity, and disinterest that places the good of the people before the person interests of he who governs." This phrase profoundly limits the scope of the line Chaudié quoted. The bigger problem in invoking Archinard's 1891 letter of investiture was that it was so vague and therefore did not adequately define the conditions of acceptable and unacceptable administrative behavior. In any case, neither Danel nor Chaudié investigated the significance of Archinard's 1893 revision of Mademba's mandate and authority following the 1892–1893 rebellion.

The next aspect of Chaudié's defense of Mademba was to invoke the long history of his services to French conquest and to France, "which were recognized from the beginning and for a long time thereafter such that in 1896, on the recommendation of Colonel Trentinian and approved by me, he received the high honor of becoming an Officer of the Legion of Honor at a solemn ceremony in Kati presided by me before an audience of officers, administrators, and numerous natives." This was an *ad hominem* argument that effectively argued a man so well respected and honored by the French could not be the perpetrator of the "brutal acts" Danel accused him of.

Chaudié then turned the problem of Mademba on its head by suggesting that all of the noise about Mademba actually stemmed not from Mademba but from Captain Lambert. Referring to the period in which Mademba was so highly regarded and respected, Chaudié wrote that

> This was the situation regarding Mademba until quite recently, when Captain Lambert of the Infantry Line was placed at the head of the Segu district . . .
>
> It is to be concerned that this officer, who has never before served in the Soudan, could not evaluate acts whose seriousness were exaggerated by intermediaries fatally jealous of the situation of high prestige enjoyed by the *Fama*. Moreover, the officers and commandants of districts neighboring Sansanding, who have long experience in the Soudan and who cannot be doubted, have information that is completely contradictory to that collected by Captain Lambert.

To defend Mademba, Chaudié cast dispersions on Lambert. These dispersions stemmed from Lambert's lack of Soudanese experience, which somehow helped to explain his naïve acceptance of Africans' testimonies regarding Mademba's brutal acts. The key phrase here is "fatally jealous intermediaries," who were jealous of Mademba's high standing among French colonial administrators and soldiers. Lambert was easily duped by these "fatally jealous intermediaries." In contrast, those officers and administrators with long Soudanese experience were able to see through these machinations of "fatally jealous intermediaries" and therefore could identify truth more clearly. Chaudié's neglect to cite Captain Montguers's investigation of Mademba's responses to the alleged conspiracy to invade his harem in 1897 and Colonel

Trentinian's forceful rebuke of Mademba's actions in that case is surprising. Lambert's reports and collection of evidence of Mademba's crimes were consonant with what Montguers's had discovered two years before.

Chaudié went on to trivialize the complaints that Lambert had collected and that Danel had incorporated into his report.

> It is certainly not in my interests to establish that Mademba did not commit reprehensible acts, but it is important to take into consideration the circumstances of the population and the context and therefore not to provide too compliant an ear to the grievances of a village chief who is obliged to provide a chicken and eggs to European travelers. How different is this situation in Sansanding from those who live along the *route de ravitaillement*?

Chaudié acknowledged that the *affaire coton* was a problem. As mandated by the inspection form, the senior administrator had to propose how to deal with the issues raised in the report. Chaudié stated that he was prepared to deal appropriately with the situation by requiring that Mademba reimburse the inhabitants – or directly to the administration – the sum he received for the sale of the cotton. Chaudié also proposed that he will assign an assistant to the commandant of Segu to take up permanent residence in Sinsani to oversee directly Mademba's administration of his territories. In addition, Chaudié stated that he would require Mademba to remain another three months in Kayes under obligatory residence. During this period and away from Mademba's direct involvement, Chaudié promised to examine more fully the contradictory evidence regarding the Mademba's alleged acts and crimes. Chaudié concluded that "At that time, I will make a decision regarding the appropriate level of repression without losing perspective on all the previous services Mademba has rendered to us. My decision will be informed by taking into consideration the political order, which will militate either for or against the maintenance of Mademba in the États de Sansanding."

Danel was not satisfied with merely submitting his report on Mademba to the governor-general. Nor was Danel pleased with how cavalier Chaudié was in his response to his investigation. Chaudié had tried to dissuade Danel from forwarding his investigation to the attorney-general. After some back and forth between the two, Chaudié finally conceded to Danel that he "should do what you think you must do."[51] As his superior had already identified in 1887, Danel had "a zeal, which without exaggerating, can benefit from a mild moderation in certain circumstances."[52]

---

[51] Copies of telegrams dated Jan. 19–24, 1900, included in Inspecteur-gen. Danel, letter to min. Col, Kayes, Mar. 2, 1900, ANOM Direction du Contrôle 894.

[52] Chef de Service central de l'Inspection, Bulletin individuel de notes, Paris, Dec. 10, 1887, ANOM Dossiers personnels (Danel) 3540.

Danel was clearly concerned about the evidence he collected regarding Mademba's malfeasance because on January 21, 1900, just a week after he completed his report and even before he learned of Chaudié's response, Danel wrote to the attorney-general of the AOF in Saint Louis, placing the Mademba affair squarely in his hands. "Based on information I collected in Sansanding and corroborated in Segu, his subjects accuse Mademba of various other crimes, he is accused of taking from his villages cotton in addition to the ordinary taxes by claiming that the French had ordered this supplemental tax, which he then sold to the local service for 6127 francs, which he kept for himself." Danel admitted that he did not fully understand "Mademba's peculiar and personal situation," which the attorney-general could easily discover in Saint Louis, he was nonetheless obligated by article 29 of the Code of Criminal Procedure and by the January 18, 1888 regulations governing the Inspection Service of the Ministry of Colonies to bring this situation to the attorney-general's attention.[53] Article 29 of the Code of Criminal Procedure (which was underscored in the Ministry of Colonies' Decree 27 of January 18, 1888 regarding the service of the Inspection in the Colonies) obligated any public servant who, in the performance of his duties becomes aware of any crime or offense (including corruption), must immediately inform a prosecutor of the state and transmit to him all of the information, reports, and acts relating to this crime or offense.[54] Thus, in the performance of his functions and adhering to the rule of law, Danel felt obliged to send this note regarding Mademba's alleged crimes to the attorney-general.

Chaudié was livid. He sent a telegram to Danel that the attorney-general had informed him that Danel had submitted a formal complaint regarding Mademba. "You submitted this complaint even before you could have known what kind of response I would make in regard to your investigation."[55] Danel fired back his response.

> I maintain the reasons outlined in my letter to the attorney-general. It is my consideration that the law should engage all the information that we have provided and to assess whether Mademba is a functionary since he receives a budgeted salary and above all if as a French citizen, he falls

---

[53] Danel, letter to Procureur-gen., Koulikoro, Jan. 21, 1900, ANS-AOF 15 G 176. In his note, Danel cited page 72 of the *Bulletin Officiel* regarding the regulations governing inspectors of the Ministry of Colonies.

[54] Decree 27, "Instructions sur le service de l'Inspection aux Colonies," January 18, 1888, *Bulletin Officiel de l'Administration des Colonies*, Vol. 2, 1888, 72–75. On article 29, see *Code d'Instruction Criminelle de 1808 (Texte intégral de la version en vigueur en 1929)*, http://ledroitcriminel.fr/la_legislation_criminelle/anciens_textes/code_instruction_crimi nelle_1929/code_1808_1.htm.

[55] Gouv.-gen. telegram to inspector-gen., Saint Louis, Feb. 27, 1900, ANS-AOF 15 G 176.

under the jurisdiction of the law regarding the much more serious [crimes] of which M. Governor is certainly aware.[56]

Danel was raising the stakes of his investigation into Mademba by invoking not only Mademba's putative status as a functionary, who receives a formal salary, but about the rule of law more generally.

The attorney-general refused to accept Danel's submission and pursue a prosecution into Mademba's alleged abuses of power and crimes. In a telegram to Danel, Chaudié stated that "I am of a completely different opinion that you are concerning the Mademba affair. I agree fully with the decision of the attorney-general that pursuing the complaints against Mademba will not be susceptible to a useful outcome."[57] However, had the attorney-general accepted Danel's request to pursue the investigations and prosecution into Mademba, it is not clear which jurisdiction would have been the most appropriate one precisely because Mademba had conducted these alleged abuses and crimes in his official capacity as an "agent" of the French administration and thus subject to the jurisdiction of *le droit administrative*. If the administrator's actions amount to a *faute personnelle* rather than an administrative act, then the public officer is considered personally liable and the case proceeds in civil courts.[58] Had the attorney-general agreed to pursue the case against Mademba, he would have in all likelihood brought the case before the nascent civil courts in French West Africa. This is exactly what minister of Colonies did not want to happen. Given Danel's tendency to zealously pursue his findings, had he not died suddenly in March 1900, we can assume that Danel would not have easily let go of his concerns regarding Mademba.

I am at a loss to explain Chaudié's defense of Mademba. I am not sure whether Chaudié had any kind of relationship or even sustained contact with Mademba where the loyalty from the bargains of collaboration could gain traction. Moreover, Mademba's bargains were primarily with the French military with whom Chaudié had sparred for years. The only known event where they had contact was in Kati in December 1896, when Chaudié personally pinned the officer of the Legion of Honor on Mademba in a very public ceremony.[59] The rank of officer in the Legion of Honor was awarded to those who held the rank of chevalier for at least eight years and continued to serve

---

[56] Inspector-gen., telegram to gouv.-gen., Kayes, Feb. 27, 1900, ANS-AOF 15 G 176.

[57] Gouv.-gen. Chaudié telegram to Danel, Mar. 2, 1900, Saint Louis, included in Inspecteur-gen. Danel, letter to min. Col, Kayes, Mar. 2, 1900, ANOM Direction du Contrôle 894.

[58] Fairgrieve and Lichere, "The Liability of Public Authorities in France," 166.

[59] I have not verified exactly what this award was. Chaudié was in Kati December 23–25, 1896, when this ceremony took place. *JOAOF*, Jan. 2, 1897, #64, 6. Chaudié admitted giving Mademba this award in his Jan. 14, 1900, letter, Gouv.-gen. Chaudié, Suite Donnée à la Vérification par l'Administration ou par la Division compétente, Kayes, Feb. 1, 1900, in Danel, Service du *Fama* de Sansanding, Segu, Jan. 14, 1900, ANS-AOF 15 G 176. There

with "eminent merit." Mademba arrived for the ceremony in Kati on horse-
back accompanied by 500 of his "bravest" *sofa.*[60] Could Chaudié's defense of
Mademba have stemmed from the fear that should the case against Mademba
proceed, then his own stature would be tarnished by his role in awarding
Mademba that impressive medal for his contribution to France's mission? In
any case, Chaudié planted the framework for Mademba's defense, but now
needed evidence to support it. Chaudié pursued two sources: assessments of
Mademba from commandants of neighboring districts, and a more formal
inquiry from Captain Pérignon, who replaced Lambert as commandant of
Segu. Chaudié only received an assessment from the district of Gumbu in
addition to Pérignon's reports from Segu.

Captain Chenaro of the Infantry of the Marines served as commandant of
Gumbu. He happened to be in Saint Louis in early March 1900 when the
governor-general asked him to provide an assessment of his views on
Mademba and his administration. Relying on his memory, Chenaro drafted
a response the same day. Chenaro described that relations between Gumbu
and Mademba's territories as not being very active, consisting mostly of the
annual transhumance of the herders from the Sahel, who crossed Gumbu into
the well-watered plains along the Niger River. "I have never received any
complaints regarding the administration of the territory of Sansanding and
I have never heard even the slightest rumor of malcontentment regarding
Mademba's administration." Chenaro also reported that Lieutenant Giraud,
commandant of neighboring Sokolo, had never reported problems with
Mademba and that during a long tournée in Mademba's territories, he had
only "the very best impressions."

Chenaro also responded to the governor-general's request for his personal
opinion of "the disgrace" confronting Mademba. "I believe that no rigorous
measure full of justice and aware of the general situation can be taken against
this old, proven, useful, and powerful servant only following a deep and
scrupulous inquiry conducted by an 'experienced colonial' investigating evidence that results from independence of judgment, wisdom, and proven
administration and above all, by devotion to the general cause." Chenaro
juxtaposed this "experienced colonial" to "an accidental debutant," obviously
disparaging Lambert if not also Danel.[61]

Chenaro provided little direct evidence on the issues regarding Mademba's
malfeasance and his alleged crimes, but his argument went a long way to
supporting what Chaudié had already laid out in his defense of Mademba and

---

appears, however, to be no record of this award in the Musée de la Légion d'honneur et
des ordres de chevalerie, personal communication, Christine Minjollet, Oct. 24, 2018.

[60] Mademba, *Au Sénégal*, 98–99.

[61] Capt. Chenaro, letter to gouv.-gen., Saint Louis, Mar. 2, 1900, ANS-AOF 15 G 176.

his criticism of Lambert's investigation and Danel's report.[62] Chenaro's report also indicates the closing of the guard around Mademba by invoking how only those with long Soudanese experience could ever hope to understand the complexities and self-interests of Africans' complaints. And this brings us to Captain Pérignon's investigation. It is not clear who terminated Lambert's tenure as commandant of Segu, but his termination arrived late in January 1900 and Pérignon took over on February 1.

The Pérignon Investigation

In replacing Lambert with Captain Aristide Auguste Baptiste Francois Pérignon, Chaudié and Ponty found a loyal solider of the Infantry of the Marines with significant Soudanese experience. Pérignon had served in the Soudan since at least 1895, when he commanded the 4th regiment of the *Tirailleurs Sénégalaise*, and served as commandant de cercle of Kita before taking up his position at Segu. During his tenure in Segu, he drafted a study, "Généralités sur les regions du Haut Sénégal et du Moyen Niger" in 1900 that was published the following year in Paris.[63] In his draft study, completed sometime in November or early December 1900, Pérignon lavished praise on Mademba. "In 1891, Sansanding became a state whose administration was confided upon M. Mademba, whose zeal and qualities had long been appreciated by the supreme military commander. Mademba was formerly the controller of telegraph services. He was originally from Podor (Senegal). *Fama* Mademba is currently (in 1900 still) in his position and he has won the sympathy of all officers who have known him."[64] Although written near the end of his tenure at Segu, Pérignon held a strongly positive opinion of Mademba, as did many French officers with long Soudanese experience.

Pérignon took over the administration of Segu on February 1, 1900, even though Lambert had requested that he stay on and despite Danel's very positive assessment of his service. In one of his final reports from Segu, Lambert reiterated his position that Mademba should not return to Sinsani. "It would be idle to return to this case, which has been the object of numerous reports and letters. However, the honor of our name demands that the *Fama* not return. If he does, we fear that there will be a general exodus [from his

---

[62] Ponty, Rap. Pol., Haut-Sénégal Moyen-Niger, Jan. 1900 [Kayes, Feb. 17, 1900], ANS-AOF M 115. Thanks to Wallace Teska for locating this report.

[63] Pérignon, Généralités sur les regions du Haut Sénégal et du Moyen Niger, Segu, 1900, ANS-AOF 1 G 248; it was published as *Haut-Sénégal et Moyen-Niger: Kita et Ségou*.

[64] Ibid. Pérignon was replaced as commandant of Segu on Dec. 10, 1900, by M. Graffe, trainee administrator, entry Dec. 10, 1900, Renseignements politiques, Segu, ANM 1 E 113.

territory] if not worse."[65] Sometime in January 1900, Lambert went to Sinsani, where he threw open the single door of Mademba's palace and streams of women fled. In one of his first quarterly political reports, Pérignon described the situation in Sinsani:

> The situation in the district is good with the exception of Sansanding . . . When *Fama* Mademba left, everyone did as he pleased and no one listened to his representative. Anarchy had begun. It became complete when the Captain, my predecessor, went to Sansanding and opened the *tata*. This action gave to the malcontents of this state the authorization to do whatever they wished. This authorization led many people and entire families to emigrate. Mademba's representative, Mamadou N'Diaye, had his authority annulled and disorder was at its height. This was the context in which I was called to become Commandant de cercle.[66]

What was the meaning of the term "anarchy" for daily life in Sinsani? In a barely coherent letter dated February 3 and addressed to Monsieur Uncle, Mamadou N'Diaye described how Lambert came to Sinsani sometime in January 1900 and publicly announced that Mademba was no longer *faama*, that he was in prison in Kayes, and that he will never return to Sinsani. Lambert stated "I am now the white *fama* and the black *fama* is no longer the master. That is finished." N'Diaye wrote that "we no longer command anything, that *Fama* Mademba no longer commands. [Instead N'Diaye quoted Lambert] 'It is only me, *Fama* Lambert, who commands.'" N'Diaye then described how Lambert ordered all of Mademba's slaves and domestics out of the *tata* and redistributed them among people he identified by name. "All of your captives have been distributed in Segu by Captain Lambert." N'Diaye also described how Lambert distributed Mademba's cattle. As far as he could, N'Diaye provided accounting of who got what goods from Mademba's palace.[67] Pérignon reported that the situation in Sinsani in early February had grown so confusing that even Mademba's loyalists including Kanouba and the almamy were preparing to divide Mademba's possessions, claiming that Lambert had authorized them to do so.[68] In mid February, Pérignon set off for Sinsani in order to "prepare for Mademba's return" and to install Bouriquet, who was an employee of the Native Affairs Department, to serve as resident following Chaudié's orders. Bouriquet was to oversee tax collection, the administration of Sinsani, and to reconcile disputes that arose from these areas. Pérignon was convinced that his visit and Bouriquet's residency had started to calm the situation in Sinsani. Nonetheless, Pérignon wrote that

[65] Lambert, Rap. Pol., Segu, Jan. 1900, ANM 1 E 71.
[66] Pérignon, Rap. pol. du cercle pendant 1ère semestre, Segu, 1900, ANM 1 E 71.
[67] Mamadou N'Diaye, letter to Mademba, Sinsani, Feb. 3, 1900, ANS-AOF 15 G 176.
[68] Pérignon, entry Feb. 4, 1900, Renseignements pol., Segu, ANM 1 E 113.

"every day I receive complaints from slaves of Mademba or from slaves given by him to the *sofa*. I resolve these complaints as best as I can as I await the return of the *Fama* to adjudicate the more doubtful cases. Little by little, the inhabitants who fled Sinsani have started to return. The situation in Sinsani is calm."[69]

During his visit to Sinsani in mid February, Pérignon conducted the first of two inquiries. This one was quite informal. At a town palaver, Pérignon sought to reassure Sinsani's inhabitants and to promote calm. He listened to grievances and agreed to remove Mademba's officials who were little esteemed. He pushed back on the townspeople's resentment of Mamadou N'Diaye, requesting that they obey him as they would obey the *faama*. Pérignon told the townspeople to anticipate the return of Mademba, but offered them no concrete timetable.

On March 9, 1900, the governor-general ordered Pérignon to return to Sinsani and to conduct a formal inquiry into the disappearance of Babo Diakite and the *affaire coton*. The range of crimes and malfeasance that Mademba was accused of was now narrowed to just two. Why was the evidence of Mademba's brutal treatment of women, kidnappings, and rape neglected in favor of the Babo Diakite case and the supplemental cotton requisition? Both the Babo Diakite case, which was linked to accusations of Mademba's participation with ritual murder, and the *affaire coton* were about abuse of power. But Lambert had collected dozens of formal depositions testifying to a range of crimes that Danel had taken sufficiently serious to alert the attorney-general of the AOF to Mademba's alleged culpability.

Pérignon spent five days in Sinsani. During his stay in Sinsani, he conducted nineteen formal interviews. All of the interviews took place in public before all of the chiefs of the cantons and villages of the États de Sansanding. All of the witnesses who came before Pérignon and the assembled chiefs swore on the Qur'an, "which (so I was told) was an important formality not done for the previous testimonies and which among the Black, who are a very superstitious people, is of significant importance." By suggesting that Lambert did not also require his witnesses to swear on the Qur'an, Pérignon raised questions about the validity of the depositions Lambert collected. We should also remember that Pérignon was collecting testimony about the disappearance of Babo Diakite almost a year after he had disappeared. Pérignon did not identify who the assembled chiefs were nor how many attended. Pérignon filed his report on March 15.[70] Pérignon did not identify

---

[69] Pérignon, entry Feb. 21–28, 1900, Renseignements pol, Segu, ANM 1 E 113. See also Pérignon, Rap pol du cercle pendant 1ère semestre, Segu, 1900, ANM 1 E 71.
[70] Pérignon, entry Mar. 15, 1900, Renseignements pol., Segu, ANM 1 E 113.

who translated for him, but the depositions he collected appeared in French in his report. Pérignon's report reflected a serious engagement with the issues of Babo Diakite's disappearance and the *affaire coton*. He addressed these issues separately. The largest part of his report was dedicated to the disappearance of Babo Diakite and all of the interviews he conducted focused on this case. Pérignon's strategy in producing this report may have been to accept the evidence regarding Mademba's abuse of power in regard to the *affaire coton* but to undermine the accusations of ritual murder and in the process to cast aspersions on the veracity of Africans' testimony in general.

Pérignon began his report by recapitulating the narrative of Babo Diakite's disappearance, by attending carefully to the timeline of his disappearance, and by interrogating Gauro Tamboura's testimonies. "Mademba is accused of kidnapping the child with the intention of making grisgris. According to some depositions collected earlier, the child was seen entering the *tata* accompanied by one person, but according to others, he was seen entering the *tata* accompanied by many people. This was around sun set or six thirty . . . Others say it was eight thirty." Pérignon then quoted Kanouba, who testified that he saw the child leave the *tata* at nightfall, which allowed Pérignon to conclude that it was impossible for Mademba to have killed the child that night. Pérignon next turned to Gauro Tamboura, who during Mademba's initial inquiry had in the days immediately after Babo's disappearance sworn on the Qur'an in front of Mademba and the almamy that he had not taken the child. Sometime later, Gauro reversed his testimony and admitted to having taken the child only to reverse his testimony yet again. Pérignon was disposed to question Gauro's veracity and stability. Based on this cursory assessment of the evidence, Pérignon concluded that Mademba's role in the ritual murder of Babo Diakite was fictitious.

> It is very probable that these depositions, which are contradictory, and these stories of grisgris that no one has ever seen, are due to the ambition of several blacks who would like to obtain a better situation and who profited from the kidnapping of a child for an unknown goal created all the pieces of the story that is the object of this report.[71]

Pérignon here invoked the key trop of fatally jealous rivals inventing rumors and influencing naïve Europeans to besmirch Mademba that Chaudié had originally used in his response to Danel.

Pérignon noted that Babo Diakite "was very frequently in the *tata*, where he ate with the *Fama*'s children." Thus, witnesses who saw Babo enter the *tata* did not witness anything extraordinary and could easily have confused previous visits with the one in question. Pursuing the contradictions within the testimonies regarding Babo Diakite's entry and departure from the *tata* on the

---

[71] Pérignon, Rapport . . . Sur les faites reprochés à M. Mademba, Segu, Mar. 15, 1900, ANS-AOF 15 G 176.

night he disappeared as well as the contradictory nature of Gauro's testimony, which formed the foundation of the rumor regarding the ritual murder, Pérignon concluded that "no material proof was produced and all the testimonies were based on hearsay recounted by people who do not like the *fama*. Thus, the accusation of the kidnapping and murder of the child against M. Mademba can no longer be retained."

The witnesses Pérignon recorded in Sinsani provided uneven and often contradictory versions of the disappearance of Babo Diakite. Some supported the version that Gouro stole the child. Others reported seeing Babo three days after the alleged disappearance in Mademba's *tata*. Sega Demba, one of Mademba's female slaves, swore that she saw Babo in Mademba's *tata* three days later. Kanouba Jara, Mademba's chief of the *sofa*, swore that "the child left the *tata* with the *Fama* just after nightfall." Siga Sidibe, one of the *sofa* guards at the *tata*'s door, stated that he saw "the child enter the *tata* with Alate Karaba, Gauro, Bamba, and Kanouba, but that could have been two days before the child's disappearance." Another guard of the door, Makan Kourouma, stated that he did not see anything, but added that "I have been threatened with prison if I say anything." Pérignon could have explored Kourouma's statement further, but he did not. On the nineteen witnesses brought before the commandant and the chiefs, ten swore that they saw nothing. Perhaps they did not see anything or perhaps they shared Kourouma's fear that if they did say anything then they would be punished.

Pérignon saved Gauro Tamboura's testimony for last.

> [He] stated that he swore that he had taken Babo and given him to the *Fama* because everyone said that he did it, that God wanted him to die and that is why he said it was he. He also stated that the Qur'an does not prevent lying, and in these conditions, he does not consider his sworn testimony truthful, but that he has nothing to fear so he will tell me the truth. He swore that he did not take the child. When one is fearful, when one throws you in prison, when one attacks you, it is better to say what they want to hear.

Despite this somewhat garbled testimony, Gauro stated that while he was innocent of kidnapping Babo, he admitted to being afraid of being beaten and thrown into prison. Pérignon did not pursue Gauro's lead on this issue. Instead, he concluded that Gauro's testimony – whether he kidnapped Babo or not – was a product of "mental problems and under the influence of superstitions."[72]

In a nineteen-page report, Pérignon devoted only two pages to the *affaire coton*, yet it was this act that Danel privileged as evidence of Mademba's malfeasance. Pérignon played on the ambiguities surrounding Mademba's role in the *affaire coton* by highlighting the vagueness of the rules governing

---

[72] Ibid.

Mademba's administration and the lack of evidence regarding Mademba's intention to abuse power. Pérignon admitted that Mademba did deliver a large quantity of cotton to the colonial government of the Soudan and that "the cotton had not yet been paid for." Pérignon cited without reference a statement attributed to the lieutenant-governor ordering all commandants de cercle to provide cotton to the administration in order to assess its qualities for the metropolitan textile industry. Thus, when Mademba stated that he was collecting the cotton on orders from the French government, he was not misrepresenting them. Citing Mamadou N'Diaye, at the time of the cotton harvest, the majority of the villages in Mademba's territory had not yet completed their annual tax payments. Thus, Mademba held in reserve payment from the government for the cotton until the villages completed their tax obligations. Pérignon omitted that had Mademba returned to the villages the proceeds he received from the sale of their cotton, they would have easily been able to pay off their taxes. Moreover, Pérignon noted that much of the population of Sinsani was composed of Mademba's *sofa*. "These *sofa* owe him a certain amount of labor each month and a portion of the cotton came from this source." And finally, Pérignon reminded the governor-general that in his letter of investiture, Mademba was given the right to collect from his subjects "all that he considered necessary."

Based on the evidence he collected and the ways in which he structured his arguments, Pérignon concluded that even though "there would be many advantages to us to manage the territory ourselves," the claim that Mademba kidnapped a child for a ritual murder is not substantiated and therefore cannot justify the revocation of Mademba. "The *Fama* will now have close to him a European and although he is not completely loved as a result of a campaign by several jealous blacks, his authority will not be reduced upon his return." Pérignon added that the chiefs of Mademba's territories all stated that they were prepared to "obey and execute his orders" as soon as he was allowed to return. The chiefs, however, reminded Pérignon that the famine in the region was severe and that if they could not provide the full complement of millet required, it was not because of ill-will, but because there was so little food in their villages.

Pérignon could probably not resist resolving one final issue regarding Mademba's alleged abuse of his wives and female slaves.

> The majority of the *Fama*'s wives have returned to the *tata* (the door remains open day and night and all are free to come and go as they please). Only the wives and female slaves who left when the door was opened by the commandant de cercle [Lambert] and who have not returned are those who were captured during the campaigns of Nioro and Segu.[73]

---

73 Ibid.

The Acquittal of Mademba

Once in receipt of Pérignon's report, Ponty wasted little time pondering how to resolve the Mademba affair. On March 31, 1900, Ponty wrote to the governor-general that Pérignon's report clearly indicated that there was "no proof as to the culpability of the *fama* in regard to the disappearance of the young Babo Diakite." Ponty reprised the contradictory testimonies, pointing to the influence of "echoes of the rumor" regarding Mademba's role in the disappearance and pointed to Gauro Tamboura's retraction of his confession. Ponty concluded

> In the absence of absolute proof and in regard to certain considerations that militate in favor of Mademba's innocence, it is necessary to see in the accusations leveled against him the machinations cleverly woven by enemies of the *Fama*. Encircled by jealous blacks who coveted the chieftaincy of Sansanding, M. the commandant of the cercle of Segu was fatally circumvented [in his investigations]; that is what the second investigation has just proven.[74]

I am not convinced that Pérignon provided Ponty with sufficient proof to support the claim that jealous Africans misguided Lambert and that they were the cause of the accusations against Mademba. However, identifying fatally jealous Africans as the source of the accusations against Mademba had become the administration's solution to the political problem of what to do about Mademba.

In regard to the cotton question, Ponty wrote that "it is understood that Mademba will reimburse the price" to the villagers. Moreover, according to the rights accorded Mademba by his letter of investiture, "it is not for us to say that he committed a theft when he was merely exercising his rights to collect a portion of his subjects [harvests] that they had not fulfilled." Ponty then recommended that the governor-general release Mademba from "residence in Kayes" so that he can return to his territories as soon as possible.

Ponty further narrowed the case against Mademba. Dropped from Ponty's report were testimonies Pérignon had collected regarding the inhabitants' fear of retribution, which was evidence itself of Mademba's abuse of power. In terms of the *affaire coton*, Pérignon has spun the evidence of Mademba's requisition of cotton in terms of Mademba's implementation of the lieutenant-governor's orders – thus identifying the source for Mademba's claim that the French had ordered this extra requisition – and argued that Mademba's failure to compensate the peasant producers had to do in part with their failure to pay taxes and due to his *sofa*'s obligations to share their harvest with him. In so doing, Ponty also invoked Archinard's 1891 letter of investiture as the source

---

[74] Ponty, letter to gouv.-gen., Kayes, Mar. 31, 1900, ANS-AOF 15 G 176.

of Mademba's rights. That this letter was vague on what exactly were those rights and what rules governed Mademba's exercise of those rights was not an issue that Ponty seemed willing to engage.

Ponty still had to deal with what to do with the evidence that Lambert had collected and Danel had used in his report. To be sure, African intermediaries could exert significant influence on gullible French colonial officials. This was the single most powerful explanation Chaudié and Ponty had to discount the accumulated evidence that Lambert and Danel had assembled against Mademba. Further proof that there was a conspiracy by rivals fatally jealous of Mademba emerged from Pérignon's additional investigations.

Ponty was certainly pleased to report to the governor-general in May 1900 that Pérignon had proven that Tierno Hamedin "played a most active role" in the denunciations of Mademba and "was the real instigator of the accusation" regarding his role in the disappearance of Babo Diakite.[75] Ponty based his conclusion on Pérignon's report of April 7, 1900, parts of which also appeared in Pérignon's first quarterly report of 1900. Upon his return to Segu from his March investigation in Sinsani, Pérignon pursued his inquiries about Mademba and Lambert. "In the course of my inquiries," he wrote, "it appeared that the cause of the situation was the jealousy of natives and especially the qadi of Segu, who was a personal enemy of the *Fama* and who hoped to succeed him as chief of the canton." How convenient was Pérignon's identification that the cause of Mademba's troubles was "intermediaries fatally jealous of the situation of high prestige enjoyed by the *Fama*," exactly as Governor-general Chaudié had laid out in his response to Danel on February 1, 1900. On the other hand, perhaps it was true that Tierno Hamedin had influenced Lambert and his investigation. Pérignon explained further a "very delicate inquiry" yielded information that "this same qadi was a force in the circle where he constituted an authority that rivaled that of the commandant and that he used for the worst purposes. Moreover, this same person enjoyed the devotion of the native staff and was informed of events in the cercle even before the Commandant."[76]

According to Pérignon, Tierno Hamedin was qadi of Segu under Amadu and Colonel Archinard permitted him to remain in that position following French conquest in 1890. "A very intelligent and very clever man, he always succeeded in obtaining the nearly absolute confidence of the commandants de cercle who served in Segu, most particularly my predecessor, which he used and abused." Highly regarded as a "grand Muslim ... Tierno exerted unlimited influence even to the point of inspiring fear. Everyone knew that the commandant was chief, but some had to fear that it was really Tierno." Upon

[75] Ponty, letter to gouv.-gen., Kayes, May 10, 1900, ANS-AOF 15 G 176.
[76] Pérignon, Rap. pol du cercle pendant 1ère semestre, Segu, 1900, ANM 1 E 71.

assuming the role as commandant of Segu, Pérignon fired the cercle's guards and political agents, none of whom spoke French and most of whom were Hamedin's "creatures." Pérignon replaced them with employees who spoke French and could render him "serious services," including one secret agent he sent to surveil Hamedin. Pérignon's secret agent came to him with evidence that in pursuing his role as qadi, he was abusing his authority and misapplying Muslim law in order to amass a "pretty fortune." In another case, reported by a European agent of the Native Affairs Department of Segu, Hamedin convinced a village chief to give him cattle to pay his taxes only to turn around and sell them to the local administration. In regard to Hamedin's role as qadi, Pérignon argued that Hamedin "renders judgments that benefit the richest the most." At the end of this report and without citing any conclusive evidence, Pérignon stated "In concluding, I want to state that Hamedin, a personal enemy of M. Mademba, was the principal promoter of the denunciations brought against him." Pérignon removed Hamedin and sent him with an escort to Kayes for an official investigation into undefined crimes. Pérignon also sacked Boi Ba, one of Hamedin's "principle agents" and sent him to Touba.[77]

Ponty was particularly pleased to see Tierno Hamedin in trouble because he had a personal history with Hamedin. From personal knowledge, Ponty told the governor-general that Hamedin never served as qadi of Segu under Amadu and Archinard never appointed him as qadi. Instead, after the fall of Segu in 1890, Hamedin sought "asylum" among the Somono, where he continued his intrigues against the French. "We should have executed him," Ponty bluntly stated. Archinard eventually pardoned Hamedin, who was nonetheless put under house arrest in Nioro. He eventually made his way back to Segu, where he ingratiated himself with the commandants "by deceiving the vigilance of the authorities." Ponty was therefore not surprised that Pérignon should identify him as the fatally jealous promoter of false information about Mademba.[78]

While still under house arrest, Mademba wrote to the governor-general on March 5, 1900, after he received an update from his nephew, Mamadou N'Diaye, about the deteriorating situation in Sinsani. In his letter, Mademba shifted tones from respectful solicitation to bristling anger. Mademba also framed elements of his defense against the rumors of his crimes that invoked both his status as a civilized agent of French civilization, but also reiterating the trop that jealous rivals were the cause of these completely false rumors.

> I have the honor to report to you that since your departure from Kayes,
> I remain ignorant of the reasons that prevent me from returning to

---

[77] Ibid.
[78] Ponty, letter to gouv.-gen., Kayes, May 10, 1900, ANS-AOF 15 G 57.

Sansanding and I await patiently your decision in my regard. Nonetheless, I protest the constraint to leave because in the street I hear rumors that I will no longer be permitted to return to Sansanding, that I have been removed [from my position] because of bad treatment inflicted on my wives, and for having killed a child in order to make grisgris. These accusations pain me because they are not permitted even among the most barbarous black people.

I am innocent, My Governor, of these monstrous acts. I respectfully request that you authorize me to go before the [French] courts and before the [French] leaders who have made me who I am and whom I have served.

I have certainly been denounced by a jealous person, who wants to hurt me. If I were found guilty before [French] justice, I will submit to its judgment. My conscience makes me very hopeful about my cause. That is why I am eager to find out who my accusers are in order to prepare for my defense in front of French courts of the land.[79]

Mademba also notified the governor-general that he received updates every day from natives arriving from Sinsani regarding the status of his household and his belongings. Mademba blamed Lambert for "illegally stealing" his goods and distributing them among Africans who have disloyal to him. "All the slaves and servants of my wives have been distributed in Segu. Captain Lambert gave eighteen to Tierno Hamedin, a Tukulor marabout, who is [Lambert's] principal agent who threatens the commandant's punishment against any native who manifests even the most minor sympathy towards me, saying that the French no longer recognize me as chief of the land." Mademba accused Lambert of arresting Alate Karaba and Kanouba, who were Mademba's trusted *sofa*, and bringing them to Segu, where he threatened them with death unless they testified to Mademba's crimes and misdeeds. Mademba further accused Lambert of seeking out Aminata Traore and her daughter, taking the daughter as his wife, and giving Traore eighteen of Mademba's family slaves. Mademba provided accounting of at least sixty of his household's slaves who were distributed to named individuals who apparently testified against him. Mademba described Fatimata Diali, "one of my wives, who was given to me at the fall of Segu and who was with me in Kayes in 1890 and has never left me since. Until, that is, the day when Captain Lambert told her, and all the others, that she was free and they she never had to see me again." Mademba concluded his letter with a request to the governor-general that the he order the restitution of all his household goods and members that

---

[79] Mademba, letter to gouv.-gen., Médine, Mar. 5, 1900, ANS-AOF 15 G 176.

had been taken by Lambert and reiterated his request to be permitted to bring his case before French courts.[80]

Governor-general Chaudié appears to have accepted Ponty's recommendation based largely on Pérignon's reports that the evidence against Mademba contained in Lambert's and Danel's reports was problematic at best and likely the product of jealous individuals seeding rumors with the intention of harming Mademba. Chaudié in turn forwarded the recent dossier of the inquiries into the "credibility" of the accusations against Mademba – as proposed by Pérignon and Ponty – and his recommendation for the release of Mademba from compulsory residence and his return to his position as *faama* of Sinsani to Minister of Colonies Decrais with the added recommendation that a permanent European resident be assigned to Sinsani. Decrais also had access to Danel's report on Mademba, which included fourteen depositions collected by Lambert. In Chaudié's letter to the minister, the case against Mademba had been limited to the alleged murder of the child and the abuse of power associated with the "abusive levy" of cotton.

Decrais responded to Chaudié's assessment that while it was "still possible to preserve Mademba's title as *fama* of Sansanding" by having next to him a European resident "with real authority," "these measures seem too indulgent" and urged the governor-general to "postpone implementing them" until a definitive inquiry regarding these two issues is completed.[81] Decrais, however, did not accept the narrowing of the case against Mademba to these two issues.

> In addition to these two complaints, the inquiry must also investigate into the *fama*'s general attitude and procedures that if proven are difficult to leave without sanction. Taken as a whole, the dossier that you have transmitted to me together with that of Inspector-general Danel makes this [larger issue] unfortunately very clear. I have received notably from M. Danel the texts of 14 depositions that Captain Lambert, commandant de cercle of Segu, recorded and which, whatever their significance for the two principal accusations, attest to excess of all sorts and violence by the *fama* as well as the hatred that is the result. [Mademba's] way of proceeding resembles, according to general sentiment recorded by Captain Lambert, that of "Babemba and Amadu" in governing exclusively "in one's personal interest." We need to consider the impact of continuing his tenure on our reputation for justice and loyalty.

Minister Decrais's response was clearly a slap in the faces of Chaudié and Ponty, who had sought to undermine Lambert's and Danel's credibilities. Instead of disregarding the testimonies Lambert collected, Decrais actually took them seriously and demanded that the follow-up inquiry into Mademba

---

[80] Ibid.

[81] Min. Col. Decrais, letter to gouv.-gen., Paris, May 18, 1900, ANS-AOF 15 G 176.

examine not only the Babo Diakite case and the *affaire coton* but also the whole range of abuses of which Mademba was accused. Indeed, Decrais considered that these issues be even more central to the Mademba case than the two issues pursued by Chaudié and Ponty. Decrais worried that "it was in the disconnection between the many appreciations forwarded regarding Mademba" and these alleged abuses that "the conduct of the *fama* will not be judged fully."

Decrais again urged the governor-general not to pursue these further inquiries "in the ordinary courts" but in terms of how a rational person would make sense of the "inconsistent evidence" and the "events poorly established." Decrais nonetheless raised the question whether the accusations against Mademba, proven or not, had undermined Mademba's ability to govern effectively.

> I ask myself whether, following above all these incidents, Mademba should continue to be invested with an authority that in regard to the population was merited but also contested. I therefore urge you to examine whether it would be preferable to simply depose Mademba, to name another [native] to assume that authority, or to suppress all indigenous authority in Sansanding in favor of a European resident there.[82]

In a postscript to this letter, Decrais gave back to Chaudié sufficient latitude to reach whatever decision regarding Mademba he thought best and promised that he would support it. But he noted that reading the dossier had left him with a "painful impression." He urged that whatever decision the governor-general would take should be well received by the population. The minister's letter is actually the last document relating to the 1899–1900 "Affaire Mademba" in the Dakar archives dossier dedicated to this inquiry. Ponty did not release Mademba from obligatory residence until September 26, 1900, nearly four months after this exchange with Decrais.

In the meantime, in obligatory residence, Mademba continued to worry about his household and his wives and blamed Lambert for his troubles. During his absence from Sinsani, "that officer violated my home and in the central courtyard of my house he declared before my wives who were assembled there that I am nothing and that all my wives are free to leave. He gave them all safe conduct passes to Segu and they profited from this situation to leave." In his letter to Ponty, he described where they had gone and asked for his help in ordering the respective commandants de cercle to return his wives to him in Kayes.[83]

Mademba also worried about his children. I do not know how many children he had given his huge harem, but he had a special affinity for several of his sons. Mademba had impressed Baillaud in 1898 about the plans he had for his sons

[82] Ibid.
[83] Mademba, letter to Ponty, Kayes, May 10, 1900, ANM 1 E 220.

and how eagerly he promoted their education. He continued to do so while in Kayes. He wrote to Ponty explaining that his son Gustave, who was fifteen at the time, held a colonial scholarship at a lycée in Saint Louis. Mademba requested that Ponty propose to the General Council that Gustave be permitted to use his scholarship to attend the École d'agriculture de Grignon, one of France's *grands écoles*, located just outside of Paris. Ponty forwarded Mademba's request to the governor-general and added his strong support.

> For all the services M. Mademba rendered to us during the time of conquest should make us sympathetic to his request to support his son's studies at the agricultural school in Grignon. Moreover, at this moment when the issue of development of our colonies is at the forefront, it is in our great interest to promote as far as possible the agricultural training of our natives.[84]

Mademba's investment in Gustave's education was also an investment in his identity as a modernizer, which was to become much more important following the end of his obligatory residence in Kayes.

Meanwhile, the situation in Sinsani deteriorated further. In March and April, Pérignon had maintained that conditions in Sinsani were improving, the level of "anarchy" considerably reduced due to the presence of Resident Bouriquet. In March, conditions were "perfectly calm."[85] By April, Pérignon was getting worried again. Although he claimed that conditions remained perfectly tranquil, he noted that there was little administrative order. "As soon as possible, we must have the *fama* return or we must administer the territory ourselves because no one obeys the *fama*'s representative."[86] In May, Pérignon had to remind the chiefs of Mademba's territories that they were behind on the annual tax.[87] Resident Bouriquet probably did not last long in his post in Sinsani and a few months later, Louis Coviaux, also a civilian employee of the Native Affairs Department, replaced him.

Coviaux bluntly stated in mid June that the situation in Sinsani was not satisfactory. "Most recently," he wrote to Pérignon, "upon receiving telegrams indicating that the *Fama* would shortly return, the non-free belonging to the *Fama* began to leave Sansanding." Coviaux responded assertively to stop the exodus of what was likely Mademba's *sofa*: he declared that any leader of groups leaving would be hung from trees. He also ordered village chiefs to stop the fugitives and return them to Sinsani. The *sofa*, in turn, argued that Captain

---

[84] Mademba, letter to Ponty, Kayes, Aug. 9, 1900, ANS-AOF 15 G 98; Ponty, letter to gouv.-gen., Kayes, Aug. 11, 1900, ANS-AOF 15 G 98. A draft of Ponty's letter regarding Gustave is located draft letter, Ponty to gouv.-gen., n.p. [Kayes], n.d. [1900], ANM B 77.

[85] Rap. Pol., Segu, Feb. and Mar. 1900, ANM 1 E 71.

[86] Rap. Pol., Segu, Apr. 1900, ANM 1 E 71.

[87] Entry May 22, 1900., registre no. 2, Renseignements pol, Segu, ANM 1 E 113.

Lambert had declared them free. Coviaux had to disabuse them of this notion. Nor did Coviaux's troubles with the *sofa* end with their attempted exodus. When he called a meeting of the *sofa* to exert them to begin planting, which they had not yet done, only a tiny handful appeared. Even the chief of the *sofa* failed to attend, claiming that he was sick. Coviaux could not count on assistance from Mamadou N'Diaye, who "no one obeys" and who had also not started planting on Mademba's vast fields.

In general, Coviaux wrote that "if the spirit of the population is not quite in open rebellion, it is not much better. This situation should not be tolerated by us." Coviaux proposed two explanations for this situation: the first was the result of Lambert's "proclamation of liberty" and the second was the liminal and provisional nature of the administration in Sinsani, by which Coviaux echoed Pérignon's argument that either Mademba should be returned or the French should assume direct administration of Sinsani. Coviaux quoted Sinsani's residents as arguing that "since the *Fama* has not yet returned, it is because he will not return." Thus, in the absence of effective authority, only anarchy reigned in Sinsani.[88]

Over the summer, conditions in Sinsani had further deteriorated. Pérignon went to Sinsani to investigate increasing complaints against Mamadou N'Diaye and by mid August, Coviaux had thrown N'Diaye in prison. "It had become urgent," he wrote to Pérignon, "to suppress this insolent man who profits from his authority to steal slaves as well as free people, who loots houses while armed, and who is in revolt against our authority."[89] The senior administration could no longer postpone dealing with the deteriorating situation in Sinsani. Thus, on September 26, 1900, Ponty finally ordered Mademba released from house arrest and returned him to Sinsani and to his "kingdom."

> After more than eight months absence from Sansanding for reasons I do not have to reiterate here, you will today regain the seat of your State. This is the evident proof that the government, following a thorough inquiry into the accusations against you have recognized the falseness of them and as in the past we confirm our confidence in you and to which you never ceased to be entitled.
>
> In order to avoid a return to similar incidents, always painful even if you were not responsible, I am pleased to inform you that the Governor-general has decided to appoint a functionary who will reside near you in Sansanding and you will benefit from his authority for the wellbeing of the land under your administration ... Far from diminishing your

---

[88] Coviaux, letter to cmdt. Segu, Sinsani, June 14, 1900, ANM 1 E 71.

[89] Coviaux, letter to cmdt. Segu, Sinsani, Aug. 20, 1900, ANM 2 D 102. Pérignon merely stated that N'Diaye was imprisoned for abuses, entry Aug. 1900, registre no. 2, Renseignements pol., Segu, ANM 1 E 113.

powers, the resident will help prevent those jealous individuals who try to weaken you with their disloyalty and their wild theories.

I hope, M. Mademba, that this painful moment will disappear forever. I am confident above all with the future of the region conferred to you, that you will not listen to the voice of personal resentment, but instead work together with the new resident to serve most ardently the interests of the wider community and not your own interests. It will thus be shown to France that she was not mistaken in making you her representative in one part of the banks of the Niger.

In conclusion, I want to recall the Commandant Supérieur's letter to you of 7 March 1891 above all "to administer your subjects as the blacks prefer to be governed but with the spirit of justice, humanity, and disinterest that places the happiness of the people above the personal satisfaction of those who govern." I wish you a good health and much success because I know that you have the heart to prove to those who have only recently served in the colony and who do not know your long and loyal service [that they were wrong to doubt you].[90]

This is a remarkable letter, in which Ponty argued that the bargains of collaboration – the long and loyal service – trump the deep concerns about elevating personal interests – abuses of power – over the public good. Even though Ponty referred to the serious inquiry that revealed the falseness of the many and varied accusations against him, he felt compelled to warn Mademba that he needed to change his behavior in order to prove wrong those French officials – like Lambert, Danel, and Minister Decrais – who raised serious legal and ethical questions about Mademba's administration, his commitment to French civilization, and his treatment of his subjects and his wives. Ponty thus drew tight onto the old guard of Soudanese officers who had both experienced Mademba's loyalty and who understood the challenging contingencies of administering a colony like the Soudan. Ponty and Chaudié's arguments also stressed that the Soudan was no ordinary colony and therefore the normal rules and regulations did not yet operate, which therefore served to explain away the occasional irregularity and abuse of power. Ponty's letter was in essence a challenge to the ideas and practice of the rule of law, which paradoxically was at the forefront of Ponty's efforts to reform colonial administration.

Mademba probably would have wanted pomp and ceremony for his return to Sinsani, but he and his entourage arrived too late in the evening in mid October 1900 and only the inhabitants of the banks of the river greeted him.[91]

---

[90] Ponty, letter to Mademba, n.p. [Kayes], Sept. 26, 1900, ANM 1 E 220. Ponty's letter also appears in Mademba, *Au Sénégal*, 104–106.

[91] Abd-el-Kader Mademba argues that Mademba departed Kayes on November 2, 1900, but archival records from Sinsani and Segu give mid October dates. Mademba, *Au Sénégal*, 104.

In a very cryptic description, Coviaux described that "nothing but friendly, the reception lacked enthusiasm, but this cannot be used as a measure of the sentiments towards the *Fama*." Over the next few days, however, men, women, and chiefs from Sinsani and the surrounding villages paid their respects to their "old chief." At a meeting that Mademba convoked, all of the chiefs attended. Mademba opened the meeting by paying homage to France and then exhorted the chiefs to make more effort enlarging their fields and increasing their herds. "After feeding your families and paying your taxes, you should all sell your extra produce to Segu," Mademba lectured. That was how to develop the economy of the region. Mademba then opened the meeting to complaints. "Many spoke," reported Coviaux. "Some said that since the opening of the *tata*, last January, many household heads, fearing disorder, have left for neighboring districts. But now, with the return of the *Fama*, they will certainly return." Many complained about Mamadou N'Diaye. "Without exception, all spoke of their joy in seeing the *Fama* and all swore their obedience and devotion to him and to France."[92] Mademba had a lot of rebuilding to do, not only his household and his authority, but his reputation and his persona.

This would be a fitting place to end this chapter, but I still need to explore several significant aspects of the case against *Faama* Mademba and the meanings of his acquittal. These include the nature of evidence collected from Africans, the role of rumor in Africans' testimonies, the competing rules of law, and the bargains of collaboration. Africanist historians have long engaged in a robust discussion of the nature of African testimonies and the historicity of oral histories. We have become keenly aware of how easy it is to influence the interview processes, although not always in obvious ways. African informants have a high degree of agency in their responses. We are reminded of Amadou Hampaté Bâ's seminal engagement with oral traditions in which he notes the power of public scrutiny to recount history according to accepted narratives, but that Africans were not above "hoodwinking" colonial administrators (and presumably Western scholars).[93] How does this apply to the testimonies collected by Lambert, Veil, and Pérignon? As Inspector-general, Danel was willing to accept the legitimacy of the depositions Lambert collected, in part because they were formal and witnessed. However, we do not know about the validity of the translations for any of the testimonies collected. Almost all French colonial officials relied on African translators, some of whom had personal interests in the testimonies being collected. This was the

---

[92] Coviaux, letter to cmdt. Segu, Sinsani, Oct. 14, 1900, ANM 1 E 219. See also entry month of October 1900, no date specific, registre no. 2, Renseignements pol., Segu, ANM 1 E 113.

[93] Amadou Hampaté Bâ, "The Living Tradition," in *General History of Africa: Methodology and Prehistory*, ed. Jacqueline Ki-Zerbo (London: Heinemann, 1981), 166–203.

argument put forward by Chaudié, Ponty, and Pérignon regarding Lambert's collection of depositions, but I think their arguments were focused less on the distortions in translation and more on the influence of "fatally jealous intermediaries" in shaping accusations against Mademba. Their criticism focused on Tierno Hamedin, which they used to discredit the accusations regarding Mademba's alleged role in the murder of Babo Diakite.

The disappearance of Babo Diakite was unusual in a town like Sinsani, where small children roamed freely for much of the day, often joining friends and kin for meals. What made Diakite's disappearance especially unusual was that it coincided with growing uneasiness in Sinsani. This growing uneasiness had much to do with Mademba's behavior toward women and toward his subjects. Mademba demanded loyalty and punished easily. Mademba also extracted wealth from his subjects, including supplemental requisitions of food and cotton. Mademba grew his wealth and extended his harem as many of his subjects increasingly felt less secure with their families' subsistence, and even its members. Exacerbating this situation was the famine of 1898–1899 that further eroded Sinsani's inhabitants sense of security. In this context, it is not hard to imagine how a rumor that Mademba was engaged in ritual murder and the production of grisgris to enhance his power and his wealth gained traction. Did those who recounted the story of Mademba's role in the ritual murder of Babo Diakite necessarily believe in the truthfulness of the story or did the story help explain their unease and resentments?

Less easy to explain is how the range of crimes and abuses of power attributed to Mademba and recounted in the thirty-five depositions collected by Lambert and Veil were neglected in the subsequent investigations. Danel certainly played a role in the narrowing of the case against Mademba by focusing primarily on the *affaire coton* and only generally on the wider abuses of power associated with his administration. To be fair, Danel's mandate was to evaluate Mademba's administrative service and, in this purview, the cotton requisitions justifiably loomed large, precisely because Sinsani's inhabitants complained that Mademba invoked French government orders to justify the requisition of the cotton. Danel also raised concerns about how Mademba's brutal behavior under the authority of the French colonial state undermined the principles of good governance and public interest over personal gain. Danel gave the testimonies Lambert collected sufficient credence to forward some of them to the minister of Colonies. Chaudié's response to Danel's report of Mademba further narrowed the scope of the case and provided the elements for a more fulsome rebuttal that needed evidence to support it. Pérignon's investigation provided Chaudié and Ponty with the necessary elements to make that rebuttal work, but in the process, Pérignon limited his investigation to the alleged ritual murder of Babo Diakite, for which he found no compelling evidence, and about the *affaire coton*. In terms of the *affaire coton*, Pérignon argued that the colonial government actually did order increased purchases of cotton and therefore Mademba's requisition could be interpreted as fitting within that broad request. Pérignon also discovered the fatally jealous intermediary in the form of Tierno Hamedin, who neatly fit the case of someone with personal grievances against Mademba who was prepared to seed rumors and denunciations. Paradoxically, Ponty alluded to the allegations of brutal and self-interested behavior even as he dismissed the false accusations of major crimes and abuses of power.

But why drop the case against Mademba of brutality and abuse of power in his treatment of women and his subjects? Part of the answer lies in the narrowing scope of the inquiries, some of that justified by the mandate of Danel's investigation. On the other hand, Minister Decrais was deeply bothered by the collection of Lambert's depositions that Danel included in his report to the ministry. On the other hand, the loyalty that lay at the heart of the bargains of collaboration probably led to the behavior contained in the depositions as being from fatally jealous intermediaries querulously spreading false rumors about Mademba. These complaints could therefore be dismissed as being shaped by those interested in besmirching Mademba's reputation.

What do these nested investigations tell us about the competing rules of law in *fin de siècle* French Soudan? It clearly tells us that context matters, especially in the wake of the Voulet–Chanoine scandal and the 1899 reorganization of the colony of the French Soudan in which the rule of military law privileging authority and obedience was being supplanted by efforts to promote a civilian rule of law. That moment, however, had clearly not yet arrived. These nested investigations also underscore the persistent power of the bargains of collaboration over the interests of African subjects in Sinsani.

7

"An Unexpected and Precious Collaborator"
Mademba's Redemption, 1900–1906

Mademba was no doubt relieved to return to Sinsani and eager to regain the reins of his household and kingdom following his house arrest in Kayes for the past eleven months. Mademba had clearly survived his most challenging test yet. However, the world he returned to along the banks of the Niger River was no longer the same. The tempests that had blown through the Soudan for the past two years showed no sign of diminishing. The political order that the military had built was weakened and the new civilian order had barely had time to take shape.

But new tempests were building and these would further test Mademba and his world, even as he set about rebuilding his authority. In 1903, Governor-general Ernest Roume decreed a new colonial legal system that placed the rule of law and legal transparency at the heart of judicial actions; the new legal system also prohibited the new native courts from taking into consideration the legal status of litigants, thus preventing the courts from hearing cases relating directly to slavery and to the master–slave relationship. And in 1905, following the slave exodus that started in Banamba earlier that year, the governor-general finally decreed the prohibition on new enslavement. Together, these changes to the legal underpinnings of slavery and chiefly authority transformed the relationship Mademba had with his subjects, especially with his *sofa*, the nominally unfree prisoners of war that formed the core of Mademba's workforce in Sinsani.

In the midst of these tempests, Mademba temporarily regained traction on his authority and his reputation through his promotion of cotton production. By 1906, cotton led to Mademba's redemption and gave him the opportunity to remake his history yet again. This is where Mademba fashioned his final years as *faama* and his legacy. Mademba was already forty-eight when he returned to Sinsani in 1900.

Chastised and Surveilled: The Resident of Sansanding

Already in May 1900, five months before he was released from house arrest, Governor-general Chaudié with the advice of Lieutentant-governor William Ponty proposed to the minister of Colonies that to ensure that Mademba would not again stray from his assigned role, a European "with real authority" would be stationed in Sinsani.[1] What role did Chaudié and Ponty envision for this European resident "with real authority"? On the eve of Mademba's release, Ponty defined the attributions of the Resident of Sinsani in a series of two dispatches on September 26, 1900, in which he stated that the object of the Resident was the "discrete control" of the administration of the "native sovereign."[2] The most proximate model for the role of the Resident discretely controlling the administration of a native sovereign was Archinard's appointment of Captain Underberg as Resident of the newly reestablished kingdom of Segu in 1891. At the "big palabre" on April 11, 1890, Archinard stated that the "French have not come to Segu to take the land and to govern themselves, but with the intention to return to the Bambara what the Toucouleur have stolen from them." Archinard added some caveats that obligated the new *faama* to keep the Resident informed of all administrative decisions and to share a portion of tax revenue.[3]

Archinard's first experiment in indirect rule did not turn out well. I have no record to suggest that Archinard changed his understanding of the Resident's role when he appointed Bojan to replace Mari Jara on May 29, 1890, the day Underberg executed Mari Jara. I can only assume that Archinard's model of the Resident's role was what Chaudié and Ponty had in mind when they proposed this model of "discrete control" but without such coercive control.

But there were significant differences between the men who filled this role in Segu in 1890 and in Sinsani in 1900. In Segu, Underberg was captain of the artillery in the Marines, a man with considerable military and leadership experience. In contrast, Louis Coviaux was an employee of the l'Afrique Occidentale Française (AOF) Native Affairs Department. In the administrative hierarchy of French West Africa, below the governor-general and lieutenant-governor were the commandants of the cercles. During the formative years of conquest and colonization, almost all of these commandants were drawn from the officer corps of the military. Most held at least the rank of lieutenant if not captain. Based on the September 22, 1887, decree, these administrators stood at the head of the cercles and were responsible for all of the civil and financial services of the district.[4] They reported directly to the lieutenant-governor. To assist these district administrators were a variety of clerks or deputies appointed from the Native Affairs Department. In some districts, special

---

[1] Min. Col. Decrais, letter to gouv.-gen., Paris, May 18, 1900, ANS-AOF 15 G 176. Chaudié and Ponty had already agreed to this solution in January 1900.

[2] Cmdt. Segu to Gouv. H.-S.-N., Sujet de la Résidence de Sansanding, Segu, May 18, 1908, ANM 2 D 102. Ponty's dispatches are #493 and #494, Sept. 26, 1900.

[3] See Chapter 3.

[4] See Saliou M'Baye, *Histoire des institutions coloniales françaises en Afrique de l'Ouest: 1816-1960* (Dakar: Imprimerie St. Paul, 1991).

deputies were assigned to financial roles or to other specialized tasks. Another clerk from the Native Affairs Department might be charged with maintaining all of the correspondence.[5] And below these Native Affairs employees were the "hordes" of Africans serving as a vast army of intermediaries. Some districts were better populated with French officials than others. Those in outlying districts, far the Saint Louis or Dakar or even the colonies' capitals, often had far fewer European employees.

According to Raymond Buell's classic survey from the 1920s, French administrators were either classified as administrators of colonies or agents of the civil service. By the time Buell was writing, the civilianization of the colonial administration had taken hold and many of the administrators of the first category were no longer French military officers. In 1913, two-thirds of administrators held bachelor's degrees; many were graduates of the École Coloniale in Paris.[6] They were the products of competitive admissions and three years of instruction under the early guidance of scholar-administrators such as Maurice Delafosse. These administrators were appointed by the governor-general. Those recruited in the second category ideally had lycée training and entered the civil service via a competitive exam. Buell noted that those in the civil service ranks had lower qualifications and smaller salaries than those appointed as administrators. "Upon receiving an appointment, such an agent is usually assigned as an assistant to an administrator or to a bureau in the secretariat where his work is largely clerical. To a visitor, it appears that many of these agents perform work which in British colonies is performed by native clerks." Advancement for agents in the civil service ranks was possible and some could be promoted to administrator after passing an examination and spending a year at the École Coloniale in Paris.[7] The hierarchy of colonial administrators was clearly marked and the Resident of Sinsani appointed from the Native Affairs Department could not expect to be housed in a palace, as Captain Underberg was in Segu. The degree of authority that the new Resident in Sinsani may have expected to wield and the respect he actually received were also quite different.

In the months before the new Resident arrived, Captain Pérignon, the commandant of Segu, described the situation in Sinsani as "perfect tranquility." The new Resident, Louis Coviaux, arrived in Sinsani in late May or early

---

[5] Alexandre Camille Sabatié, *Le Sénégal: Sa conquête et son organisation (1364–1925)* (Saint Louis: Imprimerie du Gouvernement, 1925), 355–356.

[6] Armelle Enders, "L'École Nationale de la France d'Outre-Mer et la formation des administrateurs coloniaux," *Revue d'histoire moderne et contemporaine* 40 (2) 1993: 272–288; Emmanuelle Sibeud, *Une science impériale pour l'Afrique? La construction des savoirs Africanistes en France, 1878–1930* (Paris: Ecole des hautes études en sciences sociales, 2002), 110.

[7] Raymond Leslie Buell, *The Native Problem in Africa* (original New York: Macmillan, 1928; reprinted London: Frank Cass, 1965), vol. 1, 983–984.

June 1900 together with rumors about Mademba's imminent return. Fearing the return of Mademba, Coviaux wrote, "the non-free belonging to the *Fama* decided collectively to leave Sinsani." Coviaux seemed pleased to have stopped the exodus of the *sofa,* but getting them back to work on Mademba's fields remained a problem. The *sofa* continued to invoke Captain Lambert's original statement to the women incarcerated in Mademba's palace that they were now free and then extending this declaration to them as well. Coviaux worried that delaying planting would risk the next harvest, especially during a time when famine threatened the region, so he ordered the *sofa* to gather together despite being warned by Mamadou N'Diaye and Balla, Coviaux's own guard and interpreter, that the chief of the *sofa* no longer had authority over his followers. Only a third of the *sofa* attended Coviaux's meeting. Coviaux reported that he listened to their grievances, but then ordered them to begin work on Mademba's fields the next morning. Only eight *sofa* out of one hundred and fifty who attended the meeting went to the work the next morning. Before the day was over, even these eight stopped working.[8]

These acts were a clear affront to Coviaux's authority. He decided to punish the "more troublesome" *sofa* and to select a new chief for them. After examining the group who responded to his orders, Coviaux selected the "most intelligent and the strongest" of this pool. With the help of this new chief, Coviaux again summoned the *sofa* and this time half attended. Again the *sofa* collectively refused to work and threatened to go directly to the commandant of Segu in order to pay their tax directly and thus, presumably, to be freed from their obligations to Mademba. Coviaux concluded that the threatened exodus of the *sofa* and their refusal to work on Mademba's fields were part of the same problem and yielded a "general situation that is not satisfactory."

Being a Resident was clearly an assignment that he wanted, but Coviaux was frustrated with his obvious lack of authority. "You have sent me here," he wrote to Captain Pérignon in Segu, "to ensure the surveillance [of the region]. I have not delayed in attempting to become part of the administration and to intervene in all the questions, even those that are absolutely private." Coviaux added that "you have always made clear to the leaders and notables [of Sinsani] of their responsibilities to the government and therefore to the *Fama*, who is the government's representative in Sansanding. You have also promised them that a white would reside in their city. They appeared to have understood you clearly, but they seemed to forget their promises as soon as you left their city." Coviaux complained that despite Pérignon's intervention, Sinsani's inhabitants continued to refuse to pay taxes, believing that the tax rate would be lower if someone other than Mademba was in power. Coviaux concluded that if the situation in Sinsani was "not yet one of open rebellion, it

[8] Coviaux, letter to cmdt. Segu, Sinsani, June 14, 1900, ANM 1 D 102.

was not much less." He linked the situation to the persistent belief that since "the *Fama* has not yet returned, it is because he will not return." Coviaux argued that the government should not tolerate this situation of near rebellion and argued that he as Resident should be given "greater authority to execute orders that circumstances may require me to execute."[9]

Coviaux probably expected that simply being a white official would empower him and bestow on him the authority that he wanted. The inhabitants of Sinsani and especially the *sofa* had a different sense. Coviaux was also frustrated by Mamadou N'Diaye, Mademba's nephew and his chosen representative. "No one," Coviaux wrote, "obeys him, no one pays their taxes to him, and [the *sofa*] refuse his orders to work the fields." Moreover, N'Diaye wasted little time in "abusing the situation that we gave him. No one is willing to complain because they believe that the white man is in collusion with him. Mamadou allowed the population to believe this [lie]." The problem was that N'Diaye was "not devoted to our cause." Following up on Pérignon's instructions to engage in a discrete inquiry into N'Diaye's actions, Coviaux discovered that N'Diaye preyed upon crimes committed by residents of Sinsani for his own gain. For example, a *sofa* named Lamine kidnapped a woman and her child from Nyamina and then sold the girl to another Sinsani villager. Learning of these dealings, Mamadou N'Diaye confiscated the woman and the girl, gave the woman to another *sofa*, who was his friend, kept the girl for himself, and seized the 80,000 cowries Lamine had received for the girl. In another case, Sinsani resident Nakry "found" a slave in the bush. Nakry took the slave to Sibila town, where he sold him. N'Diaye punished Nakry by demanding that he remit the 65,000 cowries he received from the sale and fined the buyer of the slave in Sibila 85,000 cowries for contravening the prohibition on selling slaves. N'Diaye thus pocketed 230,000 cowries from these two crimes.[10] Fearing the deteriorating situation, Commandant Pérignon took another trip to Sinsani in late July to investigate N'Diaye's alleged improprieties.[11]

By the end of July, Coviaux managed "little by little" to establish his authority, to begin to collect the tax, and to exhort the *sofa* to work Mademba's fields. In August 1900, Coviaux reported that he had arrested Mamadou N'Diaye. "In the interests of the *Fama*, of our population, and especially of the prestige of our flag, it has become imperative to suppress the activities of this insolent man who has taken advantage of his authority to steal captives, to enslave free people, to engage in armed robbery, and who is fully in

---

[9] Ibid.

[10] Coviaux to cmdt Segu, "Des Affaires de Mamadou, représentant du *Fama*," Sinsani, July 26, 1900, ANM 1 D 102.

[11] Entry, July 26, 1900, register no. 2, Renseignements pol., Segu, ANM 1 E 113.

revolt against our authority."[12] Mamadou N'Diaye did not submit willingly to his arrest. Around August 18, Coviaux ordered N'Diaye to come to his house. N'Diaye refused. Coviaux then dispatched his newly appointed chief of the *sofa* armed with a sword and four additional *sofa* to renew his order that N'Diaye surrender to him. N'Diaye not only refused again but he armed himself with a revolver and threatened Coviaux's men. Coviaux organized a larger contingent of his men and marched to N'Diaye's house, where they subdued and imprisoned him. By the end of August, Pérignon described these events to Ponty, arguing that Mamadou N'Diaye was a threat to the French authority and that his crimes and acts of pillage required harsh punishment.[13]

With N'Diaye out of the way, Coviaux had a clearer path to assert his authority. However, he had barely six weeks to bask in his new found authority before Mademba returned from house arrest in Kayes. After nearly eleven months in house arrest, Ponty released Mademba without fanfare and with little warning. Indeed, the news of Mademba's release arrived in Sinsani at nearly the same time as Mademba did. Far from being a triumphant return, Coviaux noted that the reception of Mademba's arrival back in Sinsani on October 14, 1900, "lacked enthusiasm." Over the next several days, however, men, women, and the notables from surrounding villages came in uninterrupted streams to pay their respects. In a speech, Mademba exhorted his audience to expand their fields, plant new crops, and rebuild their herds of livestock. This was the way to increase their wealth.[14]

Long a champion of Mademba, Pérignon was pleased with his return. Pérignon wrote that "with the arrival of the *fama*, the question of [the future of] Sansanding has been closed."[15] Even as well disposed toward Mademba as he was, Pérignon had acknowledged already in February 1900 that Mademba "is not loved" by the residents of Sinsani.[16] Pérignon expected that with Mademba back in Sinsani, order would return. Indeed, within six weeks or so of Mademba's return, Pérignon rushed to finish his book-length "Haut-Sénégal et Moyen-Niger: Kita et Ségou" and ended his term as commandant. I do not have a record of Pérignon's decision to end his term as commandant after only ten months. This was a much shorter tenure than normal for commandants, especially since there were no pressing military needs at that

[12] Coviaux to cmdt. Segu, "Des Affaires de Mamadou, représentant du *Fama*," Sinsani, July 26, 1900, ANM 1 D 102; Coviaux, letter to cmdt. Segu, Sinsani, Aug. 20, 1900, ANM 1 D 102; Entry, Aug. 1900 [n.d. specified], register no. 2, Renseignements pol., Segu, ANM 1 E 113.

[13] Coviaux, letter to cmdt. Segu, Sinsani, Aug. 20, 1900, ANM 1 D 102; Captain Pérignon, Sujet Mamadou N'Diaye, letter to lt.-gouv., Segu, Aug. 31, 1900, ANM 1 D 102.

[14] Coviaux to cmdt. Segu, Au sujet de l'impression produite par le retour du *Fama*, Sinsani, Oct. 14, 1900, ANM 1 E 219.

[15] Pérignon, Rap. pol., Segu, third quarter 1900, ANM 1 E 71.

[16] Pérignon, Rap. pol. du mois, Feb. 1900, Segu, ANM 1 E 71.

time. Pérignon's short tenure suggests that he was sent to his position in Segu to reestablish order and to provide Chaudié and Ponty with the "evidence" to have the case against Mademba dismissed. Once Mademba safely returned to Sinsani, Pérignon probably felt that he had accomplished his tasks and left. He had, indeed, reestablished order, refurbished Mademba's honor, and rewarded loyalty forged through the bargains of collaboration.

By December 1900, civilian administrator Graffe replaced Pérignon as commandant of Segu. Graffe was, however, only a "trainee" administrator and was replaced by administrator Dupont early the following year.[17] In his first political report, Graffe described the worsening famine and contrasted this with the "most perfect tranquility" in Sinsani. "On its side, Sansanding has seen the return of its chief, Mademba, and has become completely tranquil. The village chiefs have all paid homage to the *Fama* and in testimony to their feelings, they each brought him presents."[18] As the Resident of Sansanding, Coviaux must have been deeply ambivalent about Mademba's return. On the one hand, his assigned task was to "discretely" direct the administration of the États de Sansanding as the power behind the throne. He should have been pleased to have Mademba return so that he could take on that role. Yet, Mademba's return in mid October cut Coviaux's efforts short. One of the puzzles in the archives is Coviaux's relative silence after his October report on Mademba's return. After the flurry of correspondence over the summer and into the fall 1900, few of Coviaux's letters and reports have survived. In one exception, Coviaux posted a fairly extensive report on Mademba's application of Ponty's policy of prohibiting the movement of slaves, which reiterated principles already decreed by Governor Louis Grodet in 1895.[19] Coviaux described how a small slave caravan consisting of four traders and twelve slaves passed through Mademba's kingdom, generously distributing kola to village chiefs to encourage them not to report the caravan. One "more sincerely inclined" chief arrested the caravan and brought the group to Mademba, who immediately fined the caravan chief 50 francs and seized the slaves. Mademba issued the slaves certificates of liberty but did not immediately free them. Instead, Mademba placed the freed men and women with "honorable" household heads as temporary "domestics," which was to last until the end of the next harvest season. The freed men and women received subsistence in exchange for four days of labor on the household head's fields per week and three days free to work for themselves. Once a month, the freed people were obliged to visit the *faama* in order for him to assess their treatment. At the end of the harvest, the freedmen and women would be freed

---

[17] Traoré, *La saga de la ville historique de Ségou*, 153.

[18] Cmdt. Graffe, Rap. gen. sur la pol., second [sic] quarter 1900, Segu, Dec. 31, 1900, ANM 1 E 71.

[19] Klein, *Slavery and French Colonial Rule in French West Africa*, 127–128.

to go wherever they wished or to settle in Sinsani. Freed boys would remain with their new guardians until they reached twenty years of age and girls until their reached marriageable age. Only the *faama* could agree to the marriage and the bridewealth would belong to the bride.[20] In October 1901, Mademba reported that he had intercepted two canoes transporting seven traders and twenty-seven slaves from Bandiagara to Nyamina. In addition to liberating the slaves, Mademba also confiscated from the traders 53 francs and 175,800 cowries, which he was dispatching to the Segu district treasury.[21] In acting as he did, Mademba made a clear statement that he was fully reformed and acting with complete transparency in all colonial requirements.

At some point in mid 1901, Coviaux was either posted elsewhere or went on an extended leave. He was replaced as Resident by L. Chaulin, also an agent of the Native Affairs Department. Chaulin was especially preoccupied with collecting the new tax assessed on Mademba's state. During the first half of 1901, Ponty authorized a higher tax for the États de Sansanding. Mademba informed the commandant of Segu that he was "entirely in agreement with the modifications to the financial administration of his kingdom."[22] Chaulin took very seriously the "census" required in making this new assessment and set out to evaluate the value of the tax collected thus far. Inhabitants of Mademba's *États* paid their tax in a variety of forms: cowries, millet, groundnuts, and sheep. Using a conversion rate of 10 centimes per kilogram of millet, 5 centimes per kilogram of groundnuts, 5 francs per sheep, and around 800 cowries per franc, Chaulin arrived at 22,222 francs in taxes paid. In his discussions with Mademba, the *faama* assured Chaulin that they could fairly easily raise another 10,000 francs of revenue, yielding at least three times the value of tax to the Segu budget than before the new assessment.[23] Mademba now more than ever willing to show his commitments to the well-being of the colony, telegraphed the new administrator in Segu that his *États* could optimistically pay 50,000 francs in taxes for 1902. Mademba anticipated a bumper harvest. Chaulin, however, died suddenly in early October before he could complete his census. It is unclear what Chaulin died of, but the Segu administrator wrote that "sanitary measures are being taken as a result."[24]

---

[20] Coviaux, Rapport mensuel, Apr. 5, 1901, Sinsani, ANM 1 E 71. See also Duke Bryant, "Changing Childhood."

[21] Mademba, letter to cmdt. Segu, Boukabougou, Oct. 28, 1901, Collection Timothée Saye (probably ANM 1 E 71 or 1 E 219).

[22] Mademba, letter to cmdt. Segu, Sinsani, Sept. 11, 1901, Collection Timothée Saye (probably ANM 1 E 71 or 1 E 219).

[23] Adjoint Chaulin, letter to cmdt. Segu, Sinsani, Sept. 11, 1901, Collection Timothée Saye (probably ANM 1 E 219). According to Chaulin, Sinsani had collected 2,436,100 cowries, 102,224 kilograms of millet, 28,400 kilograms of groundnuts, and 316 sheep.

[24] Rap. pol., Segu, Sept. and Oct. 1901, ANM 1 E 71.

Mademba's enthusiasm to prove his worth to the colonial state and significantly raise the taxes that his subjects had to pay had its own consequences. Since 1891, inhabitants of Mademba's kingdom had used migration to neighboring districts as a means of escaping Mademba's harsh rule. The flight of inhabitants increased dramatically during the period when rumors of Mademba's return to Sinsani preceded his eventual release from house arrest in Kayes. There were, however, two streams to this movement: the first was those protesting increased taxes, especially when neighboring districts applied much lower rates; and second was the *sofa*, those unfree prisoners of war given to Mademba in 1891without clear limits on their service. At times, these two streams were indistinguishable. At other times, their complaints clearly differentiated their motivations for leaving Mademba's kingdom. Both streams deepened after 1900. We will address the *sofa* situation in the next section because it is bound up with the larger policies of changing the legal system and ending slavery, but here we will briefly describe the tax evasion movement.

Migration has long been part of the tool kit of survival in Africa. Given the generally high land to labor ratio, especially in the Sahel and grasslands of West Africa, moving to new lands has been a regular feature of social and community life. Part of these movements was related to farming practices, because soils were quickly depleted and farmers needed fresh plots to till as they let their old fields rest for several years. Rotating fields in this manner was a rational response to declining yields. But these rational agronomic practices were easily conjoined to political motivations. And political motivations of all sorts have long figured into Africans' decisions to migrate to other more promising regions. The Segu administrator described abandoned fields in many villages throughout Mademba's kingdom.[25] Already in 1901, the administrator instructed the Sansanding resident to "formally oppose" the tendency among "many natives" to leave Sinsani for Segu.[26] During the tax collection season in 1905, a third of the population in some villages hid to avoid being enumerated. Mademba tried to stop this movement.[27] In July 1906, the Segu administrator reported that a situation had emerged among several villages where the village chiefs have "pressured the population of this region to emigrate to neighboring villages in the districts of Sokolo, Nampala, and Siraoma to escape the [heavy] tax" in Mademba's kingdom.[28] By 1906, the administration's policy was that individuals and groups were free to emigrate as long as they paid their taxes before leaving.[29] Old grievances, new taxes, and farming practices all contributed to decisions to migrate.

---

[25] Rap. pol., Segu, Feb. 1905, ANM 1E 71.
[26] Rap. pol., Segu, June 1901, ANM 1 E 71.
[27] Rap. pol., Segu, Apr. 1905 and Rap. pol., Sinsani, Apr. 1905, ANM 1 E 71.
[28] Rap. pol., Segu, July 1906, ANM 1 E 71.
[29] Mademba, letter to administrator Sokolo, Sinsani, July 13, 1906, ANM 1 D 102.

Chaulin's unexpected death so early in his tenure as Resident also set back the colonial state's apparatus of surveillance. In the interim, the Segu administrator had to add Sinsani to his already large portfolio of tasks. It is not clear when a new Resident was assigned to Sinsani, although the archival record suggests that Louis Coviaux returned to that position. In May 1904, Coviaux was reassigned and left Sinsani after serving as resident on and off for nearly four years.[30] We learn in a letter to Lieutenant-governor Ponty that Mademba had the responsibility to provide the Resident with a dwelling and to furnish it. Mademba, however, may have begrudged the Resident the kind of furniture he himself enjoyed in his palace because Coviaux requested that the chairs in the Resident's home be returned to him because they were his own property.[31] As a form of passive resistance to the presence of the European Resident in Sinsani, Mademba may well have tried to make the Resident's life as unpleasant as possible without appearing to oppose him directly. In July 1904, Fernand Daniel arrived in Sinsani as the new Resident.[32]

Daniel was eager to begin his new job. He requested from the Segu administrator "detailed instructions" concerning the tasks his new role in Sinsani required.[33] What is surprising is that Daniel seems to have accepted his appointment as Resident of Sinsani without first having received information about that role. In responding to Daniel's request, the Segu administrator forwarded Daniel copies of Ponty's 1900 letters originally sent to Coviaux. "This correspondence," the Segu administrator wrote, "indicates that the *Fama* alone exercises direct authority in the États de Sansanding. The functions of the Resident consist above all in supporting this authority and in discretely controlling the fashion in which it is exercised. From this point of view, the instructions of September 1900 have not changed at all."[34] The Segu administrator added that the one new area of the Resident's authority was over the census and tax collection. Daniel reported in November that he had just completed a census tour of Mademba's kingdom. He was pleased that Somono villagers were willing to provide tax revenue that was even higher than the previous year.[35]

Daniel's request for clarification of his role coincided with a broader effort of reform of the colonial administration in French West Africa. Just as

---

[30] Despite the sometimes challenging relationship between Mademba and Coviaux, the two kept in contact after Coviaux left Sinsani in May 1904.

[31] Administrator adjoint Segu, comment on letter from Coviaux to administrator Segu, Jan. 4, 1904, Sinsani, ANM 1 D 102; Administrator adjoint Segu, letter to Ponty, Segu, May 6, 1904, ANM 1 D 102.

[32] Rap. pol., Segu, July 1904, ANM 1 E 71.

[33] Ibid.

[34] Administrator Segu, letter to Résident Sinsani, Segu, July 29, 1904, ANM 1 D 102, referring to Ponty's letters #493 and #494.

[35] Daniel, Rap. pol., Sinsani, Nov. 1904, ANM 1 E 71.

Coviaux had experienced, these agents grappled with limitations to their authority and prestige even as they represented French colonial authority. What exactly were the responsibilities of such agents and what were the limits on their authority and independence of action? Sometime between 1903 and 1905, around the time when Daniel was set to take up his posting as Resident of Sinsani, the secretary-general of the Political Affairs Department in Saint Louis wrote to the governor-general that the current system of district administration was generally insufficient to manage often huge territories and diverse concentrations of different ethnic groups in most cercles in the federation. When the district administrator left on tours to various parts of his district, he left behind at the district headquarters a skeleton crew barely able to handle normal administrative business. Instead of regularly going out on tours, the district administrator "generally sends an agent to be Resident in outlying areas." The secretary-general went on to argue that

> These agents, sent to the interior of cercles to replace the administrator, rarely possess the same experience or exercise the same authority [as the administrator] necessary to resolve disputes or initiate policy. Moreover, the natives are very aware of differences in rank and realize that only the commanding officer has high prestige. This situation does not inspire trust [in the Resident agent] and natives often appeal directly to the administrator. It follows from this state of affairs that there is an unfortunate delay in resolving the incessant relations with the indigenous population ... [Moreover], desiring to do well, but also suffering from their isolation, [these Resident agents] sometimes consider themselves to be leaders of their administrative units in which they all too frequently have a tendency to experiment with personal administration, which goes against our general policy. They have often made inappropriate interventions in indigenous life [yielding] abuses whose repetition could only have regrettable influences on the development of good administration in the country.

The secretary-general was concerned not only with the tendency of these agents to develop personal rule but such experiences of "independent habits" make these agents less successful in subsequent postings which, "they consider below their former positions as heads of posts." "In conclusion," he added, "Residents are obstacles to the uniformity of administrative procedures and to the unity of political views that are essential to the development of a cercle."[36] The secretary-general was here describing what Delavignette would later refer to as "real rulers of empire."[37]

---

[36] Sec.-gen., Affaires pol., letter to gouv.-gen., Saint Louis, n.d. [probably after 1903, but before 1905], ANS-AOF 18 G 4.

[37] Delavignette, *Freedom and Authority in French West Africa.*

Among the Resident's many tasks was to facilitate celebrations, especially those enhancing the prestige of France and its colonial endeavors. The January 1905 visit to Sinsani by Lieutenant-governor Ponty and a team of colonial inspectors provided Daniel with such an opportunity. Mademba was always a fan of such celebrations and regularly spent the Bastille Day festivities with the Segu administrator. "The head of the colony arrived in Sansanding on January 30 to enthusiastic welcome by the population and by a certain number of village chiefs. The homes of the *Fama* and the Resident as well as the streets and the open spaces were coquettishly decorated with the tri-colored flags and *arcs de triomphe*." Daniel used the lieutenant-governor's visit to argue that the "natives [of Sinsani] have long accepted French colonial rule. Their respectful attitude to the governor is the best proof of that fact."[38] Daniel remained at this post until late in 1906. A new Resident arrived in February 1907. This new Resident left few reports in the archives except to signal another visit of the governor-general together with the lieutentant-governor in late February 1908. This illustrious entourage received the "warmest and most respectful welcome" from the *faama*, the resident, the now present European trader, and Sinsani's inhabitants.[39] In contrast to the celebrations welcoming the senior French administrators, stood Mademba's more boisterous celebration of Ramadan in October that year. "Proceeded by his usual escort of griots and servants carrying the national flag as well as drums, the *Fama* Mademba leads the way to the central market place where his son, Cheikh, leads the ceremony."[40]

Not all functionaries shared the same engagement with their work. Some were content to do as little as necessary, while others wanted to do the best that they could in support of the larger mission of their agency. In 1908, a new Resident, M. Bonnel, was appointed to Sinsani. He probably shared with Coviaux, the first Resident, a concern about his assignment and most significantly about his authority. In his letter to the lieutenant-governor, the Segu administrator raised two issues relating directly to the consequences of Ponty's 1900 instructions to "discretely control the administration of the native sovereign," namely Mademba. The Resident's task was complicated by the need to surveil and if necessary intervene ever so discretely as to leave the authority of the *faama* as intact as possible. Intervening thus meant to do so in such a manner that no one knew. "This results," Segu administrator Bornèque argued, "in a situation where the prestige of this functionary in the eyes of the natives and Europeans has been denuded and which effectively allows them to ignore the existence of the Resident." The second blow to the Resident's prestige and status was the derelict condition of the physical

---

[38] Daniel, Rap. Pol., Sinsani, Jan. 1905, ANM 1 E 71.
[39] Résident Sinsani, Rap. pol., Sinsani, Feb. 1908, ANM 1 E 71.
[40] Résident Sinsani, Rap. pol., Sinsani, Oct. 1908, ANM 1 E 71.

residence of the Resident. Bornèque did not suggest outright that Mademba had "ill will" toward the Resident and was thus consciously trying to undermine his authority. Instead, he suggested that Mademba no longer had the same "vigor and authority" as he used to have.[41]

Did the effort to reform the colonial administration result in any significant change in the Sinsani Resident's prestige and authority? Here the Segu annual report of 1917 provides some clues.

> If we have the right to assess the *Fama*'s politics, we are in fact seriously ill-informed about what happens in the region of Sansanding. From time to time, noise regarding very different events emerges that is very difficult to verify. Following the events of 1900, Governor Ponty re-established Mademba at Sansanding but also gave the order that an agent of the Native Affairs Department take on the role to "discretely control the native administration by assuring that the natives do not recognize his surveillance and interventions." This situation, as M. Ponty recognized, was very delicate. The Resident risked taking on a role [of increased surveillance and interventions] or [he risked] becoming useless. In considering this situation that had become no longer useful and had become damaging to the prestige of the European who held that position, the Administration in 1911 decided to suppress the Residence of Sansanding. Since then, the Segu administrator conducts a variety of regular courtesy visits and to serve as an intermediary between the governor and M. Mademba.[42]

Mademba was able to outlast and outmaneuver the colonial administration's effort to tame his rule through the appointment of a relatively low-level agent of the Native Affairs Department. In part, he was able to do so because in reaffirming his positions as king, Ponty enshrined inherent contradictions in the role of the European Resident. And without an astute European Resident, few in the colonial administration knew exactly what was going on inside Mademba's kingdom. Noise did occasionally get out. But most often, whatever news emerged from Sinsani resonated with the broader politics of the colonial administration. We turn next to assessing the linked roles of the new legal system of 1903 and the end of slavery, which effected Sinsani primarily through the actions of the *sofa*, the prisoners of war given to Mademba as part of their punishment.

---

[41] Administrator Segu, letter to lt.-gouv., Segu, May 18, 1908, ANM 1 D 102; see also Administrator Segu, letter to Resident Sinsani, Segu, May 16, 1908, ANM 1 D 102. Mademba actually suggested to Resident Bonnel that he should move temporarily into the new school being built in Sinsani until his residence was repaired. Mademba, letter to Resident, Sinsani, May 15, 1908, ANM 1 D 102.

[42] Rap. Pol. annuel, Segu, 1917, Jan. 15, 1918, ANM 1 E 72.

Twin Challenges to Mademba's Authority: The End of Slavery and Legal Reform

The investigation into Mademba's alleged crimes and abuses of power and his obligatory house arrest in Kayes from November 1899 into October 1900 coincided with a sea change in colonial rule in French West Africa. The military's hold over the region was progressively weakened in favor of increased civilian and bureaucratic rule. In that fitful and uneven process of change, which occurred over a decade at least, the guiding principles included regularity, the rule of law, and budgetary control. By its very nature, the civilian rule of law required regularity or at least the appearance of regularity. But regularity as a form of administration also bit deeply into the autonomy that the military rulers of the colony had long prized. Budgetary control was also a form of regularity in which the ordinary and recurrent expenses could be anticipated and exceptional costs better understood and evaluated. Military conquest stood in marked distinction, since the exceptional need for funding for immediate challenges of conquest and the unexpected costs to protect what had been conquered had become the norm, but without establishing clear limits. Regularity and the rule of law were thus designed to tame the military and to facilitate a transition to civilian rule now that the pressures of conquest and pacification had diminished. Regularity and the rule of law were also supposed to constrain and socialize civilian administrators. Mademba understood well these pressures; he also understood how to keep appearances of regularity even while he maintained space for his own power and authority.

The end of slavery and legal reform were deeply interwoven. In particular, the 1903 decree establishing the new colonial legal system prohibited the new courts from recognizing the legal category of the slave. This prohibition effectively undercut masters' abilities to use the colonial state to help them control their slaves. In December 1905, the governor-general decreed the prohibition on alienating a person's freedom, thus effectively ending new enslavement. However, neither the 1903 legal reform nor the 1905 decree ended slavery per se. Taken together, however, these two acts ended the colonial state's recognition of slavery and thus created conditions in which slaves could leave their masters without fear that the state's agents would return them to their masters. Slavery, of course, did not end when the state ceased to recognize its legality. Some slaves left their masters; others remained with them; and still others used this opportunity to renegotiate the conditions of their continued relationships. Vulnerable people, especially women and children, were still enslaved, still transported from where they were captured to where their services were in demand, and still lived in servile conditions.[43]

---

[43] See Benjamin Lawrance and Richard Roberts (eds.), *Trafficking in Slavery's Wake: Law and the Experience of Women and Children* (Athens: Ohio University Press, 2012).

Many of these same conditions prevailed in Mademba's kingdom after his return from house arrest.

Among Captain Pérignon's first tasks upon taking up the commandant of Segu was to squash the "anarchy" that had been reigning in Sinsani since Captain Lambert had opened the gates to Mademba's palace in January 1900 and declared that the women held therein were free. According to Pérignon's own accounts, Lambert also declared all those in Sinsani who were unfree that they were now free as well. How Lambert's alleged liberation effected Mademba's *sofa* is not clear. Part of the problem resides in the ambiguity of the unfreedom that the *sofa* experienced. As you will recall, upon the conquest of Segu in 1890 and Nioro in 1891, Archinard captured large numbers of warriors who fought with Amadu. These captured warriors were effectively prisoners of war. Imprisoning this many enemy combatants was impossible within the existing capacities of the colonial state. Nor was this part of the wider traditions regarding the disposition of captured warriors in the Soudan. In the precolonial period of the eighteenth and nineteenth centuries, captured warriors would likely be enslaved. Some would be sold into the regional slave trade and some would be incorporated into the ranks of the slave warriors of the victorious army. Archinard likely adapted this latter track.

> After Amadu's escape from Nioro, all the slave soldiers came to me requesting a new master. Almost all of these were Bambara, who had gotten rewards from serving Amadu. I have given these prisoners to Mademba, just as I gave the prisoners of Segu to Bojan. Here is a good army of some 2,000 professional warriors, who in the hands of an able leader, can further our goals in the region and especially help to rid the land of dangerous looters.[44]

Archinard ordered the warriors and their families captured in Nioro to follow Mademba back to Nyamina. In addition to the 2,000 soldiers, their families, their slaves, Somono who had been resettled in Nioro, and other original inhabitants of the Niger River region also received permission to accompany Mademba.[45]

After Archinard enthroned Mademba as *faama* of Sinsani on March 7, 1891, Mademba led his entourage of captured warriors, their wives and families, as well as the Somono and various griots toward their new home in Sinsani. Once settled in Sinsani, the *sofa* owed Mademba military service and they worked on his fields five days a week. In addition, they were also obliged to give Mademba a third of the harvests from their own fields, which they

---

[44] Archinard quoted in Méniaud, *Pionniers*, II, 77, 82.
[45] Méniaud, *Pionniers*, II, 79. to Mademba's own statement to Parisian newspapers in 1906, the number of *sofa* was actually 400–500.

worked during their free time.[46] This was fairly onerous labor service and was actually on the more rigorous end of the customary labor obligations of ordinary slaves. The labor regime of slaves in Maraka commercial centers such as Banamba had become more rigorous during the 1890s in response to the growing demand for grain in Bamako. Newly arrived slaves in centers like Banamba worked all the time for their masters, but they also received all of their subsistence from their masters. The labor regime for slaves elsewhere in the Middle Niger region ranged from four or five mornings of labor for their masters with afternoons and two or three full days free to work for themselves.[47]

It was no surprise that the *sofa* were worried about Mademba's impending return. Coviaux wrote in June 1900 that following Lambert's "declaration of liberty," the *sofa* "no longer obey Mamadou N'Diaye," Mademba's representative. The *sofa* also disobeyed Coviaux when he ordered them to resume work on Mademba's fields.[48] Eventually, Coviaux managed to coax them back to work. And then Mademba returned. When Mademba returned in mid October 1900, it was far too late for him to oversee the planting of his fields. In June 1901, right at the core of the planting and weeding seasons, Coviaux signaled the "tendency by many natives to leave the États de Sansanding to settle in the district of Segu." The Segu administrator in turn ordered Coviaux to "formally oppose the departure of natives in obligatory residence in Sansanding." He also ordered Mademba to interrogate those inhabitants not under obligatory residence who wished to leave to determine whether their decisions were valid.[49] The Segu administrator here distinguished the *sofa* from the free residents of Sinsani and ordered the *sofa* to remain in Mademba's service.

The *sofa* were not pleased with the order to remain in Sinsani and in April 1902 they resumed their efforts to leave Sinsani. Understanding the symbolic role of paying their tax to the colonial state, the *sofa* offered to acquit their responsibilities directly to the Segu administrator and thus be "free" of their responsibilities to Mademba. As the Segu administrator described,

> The former *sofa* of Amadu Seku, who were given in 1890 to the *Fama* of
> Sansanding and who have always worked for him, have come [to Segu] to

---

[46] Cmdt. Segu, letter to Resident Sinsani, Segu, July 29, 1904, ANM 2 D 102. This letter addresses the changes to the labor regime of the *sofa*, which was reduced from this standard to three mornings a week, plus no obligation to share the harvest.

[47] Richard Roberts and Martin A. Klein, "The Banamba Slave Exodus of 1905 and the Decline of Slavery in the Western Sudan," *JAH* 21 (3) 1980: 375–394; Richard Roberts, "Slavery, the End of Slavery, and the Intensification of Work in the French Soudan, 1883–1912," *African Economic History* 49 (1) 2021: 47–72.

[48] Coviaux, letter to cmdt. Segu, Sansanding, June 14, 1900, ANM 1 D 102.

[49] Rap. pol., Segu, June 1901, ANM 1 E 71.

request their complete freedom and that of their families under the pretext of paying their personal tax. This request seems to be justified and I will take up the issue with the *Fama* during my next visit to Sansanding.[50]

At that next meeting with Mademba, the Segu administrator warned Mademba that in the not too distant future, "all the *sofa* will have complete freedom." In the meantime, however, they agreed to reduce the *sofa*'s labor requirements to three mornings a week with the remainder of the week free to work for themselves. This revision of labor requirements brought the *sofa* more in line with "the customs and practices of the land" and with the eventual goal of reducing even further these demands. The administrator reported that the *sofa* were favorably disposed to this resolution.[51] The *sofa* did not, however, remain satisfied for long. In January 1903, Ponty responded to the Segu administrator's efforts to halt the most recent exodus of *sofa* from Sinsani. "I urge you," he wrote, "to use all means to avoid a total exodus of the inhabitants [of Sinsani]." Ponty also tried to reformulate the bases of the tension between Mademba and his *sofa*. "Captain Lambert was soundly mistaken [when he offered the inhabitants of Sinsani their liberty]. That action was contrary to the historical foundation of our colonial expansion in this land. In effect, Colonel Archinard settled [the *sofa*] in this land in order to assure its repopulation and to distance this group from Kaarta." For Ponty, the tensions between Mademba and the *sofa* were not about the conditions of their servitude but about repopulating this part of the Middle Niger, fostering economic growth, and minimizing the threat of rebellion.[52]

Despite Ponty's effort to reframe the *sofa* problem, French policy in regard to the *sofa* and more generally in regard to slaves had begun to take shape: French efforts were designed above all to maintain order, to assure the respect of the French colonial state as well as its representatives, to maintain the productive capacity of the economy, and at the same time to recognize the legitimate right of the unfree to claim more of their "freedom." Thus, in their efforts to reduce potential crises, the French sought to return to customary levels of labor obligations that had often been transgressed by masters since colonial conquest ushered in stimulus to the regional economies and masters sought to benefit by squeezing more labor from their slaves and dependents. In 1904, the Segu administrator captured these policy considerations when he stated that in regard to the Mademba's *sofa*, "[o]ur efforts have tended to satisfy their demands while at the same time and in the political interests [of the colony] to maintain them under the authority of the *Fama*." Satisfying

---

[50] Rap. pol., Segu, Apr. 1902, ANM 1 E 71.
[51] Rap. Pol., Segu, May 1902, ANM 1 E 71.
[52] Ponty, letter to Segu administrator, Kayes, Jan. 29, 1903, ANM B 150.

their demands, however, meant reducing even further their labor requirements. "This year," the administrator wrote, "the *Fama* also agreed to abandon
his claim on one-third of the *sofa*'s harvests from their fields."[53] In July 1904,
the Segu administrator described the beginning of the end of slavery in his
district. Some "individuals in the service of others," which was an oblique
reference to slaves, have requested that they "no longer be required to cultivate
for others. These requests are always reconciled. The masters exhibit only
weak opposition to the emancipation of their servants."[54] The ease with which
these masters responded to slaves' request to be freed was certainly not how all
masters in the region responded to slaves' initiative to end slavery.[55]

Lambert's January 1900 declaration of liberty continued to play a central
part in the efforts by the *sofa* to secure their freedom and that of their families.
Mamadou Doumba Koita and Fouseinou Kone apparently took advantage of
Lambert's declaration and fled Sinsani. "This is to say that in 1900, M. the
commandant of Segu gave the order and said that all who wish to leave to go
back to their homelands must pay tax. Wishing to return to our homelands,
we paid our tax in Segu." However, they left behind their families in Sinsani.
They had since asked Mademba to send their families to them and promised
to pay their taxes. Mademba apparently responded that they should return to
Sinsani to make their request. They declined, fearing what might happen to
them if they returned to Sinsani. Thus, in 1904, Koita and Kone wrote to
Ponty beseeching him as "our father and our mother" to assist them in their
efforts to reunite their families back in their homelands.[56] I have no record of
Ponty's response. In July 1904, sixty-five *sofa* collectively left for Segu to claim
their freedom.[57] By the time these *sofa* had left Sinsani, Resident Daniel had
started work on his latest census. By August 1904, he had completed his
survey, which he then separated between the population of Sinsani itself and
the population of the États de Sansanding.

Daniel identified only 671 *sofa*. This was only a third of the approximately
2,000 *sofa* that Archinard had given to Mademba in 1891. This suggests that
by 1904 roughly two-thirds of Mademba's original contingent of *sofa* had
already left Sinsani. I have no way of ascertaining how accurate Daniel's
1904 census was – or whether the original 2,000 number was accurate – nor
how serious an inquiry he conducted in the rural hinterland of Sinsani. His
census only included one town, Tosma, which had a population of 453, but we
know that Madamba's kingdom had several large villages because Lambert in

[53] Segu administrator, letter to new Resident Sinsani, Segu, July 29, 1904, ANM 2 D 102.
[54] Rap. pol., Segu, July 1904, ANM 1 E 71.
[55] See Klein, *Slavery and French Colonial Rule in French West Africa.*
[56] Mamadou Douba Koita and Fouseinou Kone, letter to lt.-gouv., n.p., n.d. [but 1904],
ANM 1 D 102.
[57] Rap. pol., Segu, July 1904, ANM 1 E 71.

Table 7.1. *Population of the États de Sansanding, 1904*

Sinsani town	
Maraka	709
Former *tirailleurs*	113
Freed *sofa*	671
Griots	31
Ironworkers	13
Leatherworkers	10
Total	1,547
États de Sansanding	
Total Muslim population	6,816
Total traditionalists population	14,380
Total	21,196[1]

[1] Denombrement de la population des États de Sansanding, Sinsani, Aug. 1904, ANM 5 D 43.

1899 had collected data on Mademba's requisition of cotton and the overall tax from several villages he identified by name. Even using Daniel's population estimates, the remaining *sofa* constituted nearly 44 percent of the total population of Sinsani town itself and roughly 3 percent of the total population of Mademba's kingdom. Since we can assume that the *sofa* were at least nominally Muslim – they were after all warriors of Amadu – they then constituted nearly 10 percent of the Muslim population of the kingdom. More significantly, the sixty-five *sofa* who left collectively in July 1904 thus constituted around 10 percent of the *sofa* who remained under Mademba's control. Daniel's census also neglects to identify the Somono and Bozo residents, who had previously constituted a sizeable portion of Sinsani's population. Since at least 1899, Mademba's kingdom had witnessed a steady leakage of inhabitants. And this leakage continued. In January 1905, the Sokolo administrator wrote to Daniel that he has received "many" requests from migrants from Mademba's kingdom to reside in Sokolo district. The Sokolo administrator rejected these requests and threatened to expel them if they did not voluntarily return.[58] By planting season 1906, the migration from several prominent villages in the northern portion of Mademba's kingdom had become a "revolt." Instead of chasing these refugees back into Mademba's kingdom, tax collection agents from Sinsani and Sokolo decided to collect the

[58] Administrator Sokolo, letter to Resident Sinsani, Sokolo, Jan. 12, 1905, ANM 1 D 102.

Sansanding tax rates from these migrants, but to let them remain. However, Sokolo officials arrested the four leaders of this revolt, sent them to Sinsani, where they were tried before the provincial court and sentenced to one year in prison, which they served in Segu.[59]

By spring 1905, the *sofa*'s quest for liberation was overshadowed by the wider exodus of slaves that expanded outward from Banamba in increasing circles over the next seven years. The end of slavery involved far more than the struggles and negotiations among former masters and former slaves. The end of slavery contributed to the linked transformations in the society and economy of the region. Beginning first in the region of Banamba in the spring of 1905 and spreading outward in time and space, slaves from Segu began to leave their masters in 1907 and slaves from the Sahelian districts of Sokolo and Gumbu began to leave by early spring 1908. The end of slavery contributed to new challenges to authority and power and to stresses within households. After initial confusion, hesitation, and efforts to prevent the slaves from leaving, French policy on the slaves' exodus – and on slavery itself – became clear. In December 1905, Governor-general Ernest Roume formally decreed an end to practices leading to the alienation of a person's liberty, effectively prohibiting new enslavement, and outlawed yet again the slave trade.[60]

I have described the events in Banamba 1905 elsewhere. In March 1905, well before the beginning of the planting season, large numbers of slaves began to leave their masters. Fearing the loss not only of their slaves, but also of the labor needed for their fields, by the middle of May Maraka masters armed themselves and confronted the departing slaves, many of whom had also armed themselves. The Bamako administrator ordered chiefs of neighboring villages to halt the exodus and return the slaves to Banamba, but slaves kept leaving. Acting lieutenant-governor Fawtier together with a detachment of armed tirailleurs raced to Banamba to end the crisis. Fawtier talked to both slaves and masters and reached a reconciliation in which slaves agreed to return to their fields and masters agreed to reduce the labor requirements of their slaves. By April 1906, the slaves of Banamba resumed their exodus. This time, the French did nothing to stop it. In essence, the French were no longer willing to lend the support of the colonial state to the maintenance of slavery.[61]

Slaves were quick to understand the implications of these twin decrees: slaves were the ones who pushed the limits of the colonial state's willingness to

[59] Rap. pol., Segu, July 1906, ANM 1 E 71.
[60] Sec.-gen. Merlin, Instructions aux Administrateurs de la Sénégambie-Niger sur l'application du Decret du Nov. 10, 1903, portant reorganization du Service de la Justice, Gorée, Oct. 1904, ANM 2 M 459.
[61] See especially, Roberts and Klein, "The Banamba Slave Exodus"; Roberts, "The End of Slavery in the French Soudan."

support the rights of slaves over those of their masters. In spring 1907, the slave exodus spread to the districts of Bamako, Segu, Kayes, Kita, Bafoulabe, Sikasso, and Bouguni. Between April and June 1907, the Segu administrator counted 5,331 slaves out of an estimated slave population of 25,000 who had requested formal permission to leave the district.[62] Ponty also clarified the official French position: any slave who paid their taxes was now free to go wherever they wished.[63] This was how Mademba's *sofa* had acted already in 1904. Most slaves left during the period from the end of the harvest to the beginning of the new planting season, from roughly December through early June. Slaves probably wanted to reap whatever benefits they could from their harvests or to leave early enough to start farming somewhere else. In contrast, leaving during the agricultural season put slaves at the greatest risk for survival.

The exodus of slaves from neighboring Segu and Sokolo districts in 1907 did not go unnoticed in Sinsani. Unfortunately, the archive is silent on the volume and velocity of slave departures from Sinsani. I have one surviving letter from May 1908 that hints at the "many former slaves who have changed their residence" and had in the process requested formal permission to leave. Slaves probably sought to leave quickly. "The [slave] household heads take their wives and children [with them in order to avoid] their former masters' pretexts to force the latter to remain with them." This somewhat oblique statement suggests that former slaves and former masters fought over the rights of former slave families to accompany their male household head. The Segu administrator qualified the policy: "adult children are free to remain or to follow their parents. Young children will always remain with their mothers. If marriage [between the former slaves] was not conducted according to custom, then the woman and her children will follow the mother." The Segu adminis-trator knew that disputes regarding the status of slave households and the status of its members would arise so he placed this burden of resolving these disputes in Mademba's hands. "It is up to the *Fama* to resolve [these disputes] between former masters and former slaves without our involvement."[64]

By September 1908, the end of slavery in Sinsani and Segu had likely run its course. No doubt, there were on-going efforts by some freed slaves to negotiate new relationships with their masters; others requested to leave and then either returned to their homelands or resettled elsewhere.[65] There is a hint in the archives that a free wage labor market had not yet emerged, making the recruitment of workers a challenge. In September 1908, a French merchant

---

[62] Rap. pol., Segu, June 1907, ANM 1 E 72.
[63] Ponty, letter to administrator Segu, Kayes, Apr. 18, 1907, ANM 1 E 177; see also Gouv.-gen., letter to min. Col., Dakar, June 22, 1908, ANOM Soudan I-11.
[64] Administrator Segu, letter to Resident Sinsani, Segu, May 4, 1908, ANM 1 E 219.
[65] Compare with Gumbu, Roberts, *Litigants and Households*, chapter 4.

wishing to travel by canoe to Mopti requested the Sinsani Resident's assistance in securing workers for his voyage. The Sinsani Resident then asked Mademba to assist in this matter. Mademba responded that unfortunately, "no man was willing to work for M. Mercier in order to travel to Mopti . . . Only free people remain [in Sinsani] and we cannot force them [to work]."[66] Mademba's remark that only "free people remain" hints that by this time the end of slavery had not only led to the decline in the pool of coercible slaves but also Mademba's pool of coercible *sofa*.

The end of slavery and the subsequent decline in coercible labor coincided with legal reform. Whereas the end of slavery was initiated by slaves and ultimately forced the French colonial administration to put into practice its rhetoric about its commitment to free labor, legal reform was part of the colonial administration's effort to enhance the authority of the government-general by reigning in the wide latitude district commandants and administrators had over punishments. The principles of the 1903 reform of the French West African legal system were regularity, transparency, and proportionality. Military administrators had a relatively benign view of corporal punishment since many probably linked such punishments with the maintenance of their authority. In contrast, the senior civilian administrators from the time of Governor Louis Grodet in 1894 were staunchly opposed to corporal punishment, which they understood to be "unworthy of our civilization."[67] Without a robust system of prisons, eliminating corporal punishment from the tool kit of district administrators circumscribed their ability to discipline and thus challenged their authority.[68] But the problem remained. Almost as soon as he took over the leadership of the Soudan, Lieutenant-governor Ponty railed against the inconsistencies and general lack of proportionality in punishments. In reviewing district administrators' periodic reports on punishments that they administered, Ponty admonished them to the need to administer punishments that fit the crime or misdemeanor offense. For example, Ponty chastised the Segu administrator for sentencing both a criminal accused of attempted kidnapping with the intention of selling a person and a person accused of showing disrespect to a military officer to fifteen days in prison. These punishments were not proportional.[69]

In 1902, Governor-general Roume charged a commission with assessing the existing irregularities of the legal system in French West Africa and with proposing changes. By mid 1903, the commission had concluded its task

---

[66] Mademba, letter to Resident Sinsani, Sinsani, Sept. 2, 1908, ANM 1 D 102.

[67] Gouv. Grodet, letter to cmdt. sup., Région Est (Bamako), Kayes, Jan. 26, 1894, ANM 2 M 59.

[68] Florence Bernault, ed. *Enfermement, prison et châtiments en Afrique: Du 19e siècle à nos jours* (Paris: Karthala, 1999).

[69] Ponty, letter to administrator Segu, May 2, 1901, Kayes, ANS-AOF 15 G 60.

and proposed ninety-six articles that were debated and passed by the General Council in Senegal before going up the ladder to the minister of Colonies, who in turn reviewed the proposed legislation before sending it up to the National Assembly. In presenting the legislation, Minister of Colonies Gaston Doumergue argued that the time has come for France to "unite under one system and under one common law, taking into consideration the rights of our nationals, the needs of the indigenous populations, and the higher interests of our policies, those systems of laws previously separate and independent."[70] On November 10, 1903, the National Assembly voted to enact the legislation into law. The new legislation effectively created not one but two parallel system of courts – one for French citizens, naturalized Frenchmen, and other European nationals and the other for the various indigenous populations – that was conjoined at the top through a system of appeals that could go up to the highest appeals court – the *Chambre d'homologation* – that was charged not only with appeals but with validating contested judgments. For our purposes, the new legal system created a series of new native courts that included the village tribunal (chaired by the village chief), the provincial tribunal (chaired by the provincial or canton chief), and the district court (chaired by the French colonial administrator). Village tribunals were designed to facilitate the reconciliation of the disputants and no written records were required. At the provincial level, misdemeanors and minor crimes were adjudicated together with civil and commercial disputes. Records of the cases and judgments were required. Once the tribunal issued its judgment, the disputants were asked if they wanted to appeal the judgment. If they decided to do so – and only a tiny handful of appeals were actually processed – then the case record would go up the ladder to the district tribunal. The district tribunal, also required to maintain written records, heard not only appeals but also more serious criminal cases. The requirement that written records of cases be maintained at the provincial and district tribunals also helped the lieutentant-governors and the magistrates at the *Chambre d'homologation* scrutinize the records for legal inconsistencies, disproportional punishments, and questions regarding the application of customs. Written records and periodic surveillance were built into the legal reform in order to assure the rule of law, transparency, and the application of the "higher interests of our policies." The implementation of the new legal system and the establishment of the new native courts took another fourteen months or more, but many new courts were up and running by mid 1905, just in time to serve as new institutions

[70] Min. Col., Rapport au Président de la République, suivi de décret portant reórganisation du service de la justice dans les colonies relevant du gouvernement-général de l'Afrique occidentale," *Journal official de la République française*, Nov. 24, 1903.

dealing with potential disputes that emerged from the end of slavery and the wider transformations in Soudanese society and economy.[71]

Mademba, as king of the États de Sansanding, had been caught up in the broader efforts by civilian administrators to bring greater regularity and transparency to the administration of French West Africa and the Soudan in particular. Mademba certainly had time to contemplate these changes as he sat under house arrest in Médine and Kayes for nearly eleven months. Even after his release from house arrest and his return to Sinsani in October 1900, Mademba remained keenly aware of the increased surveillance and scrutiny of his administration. He understood that increased surveillance meant that his authority was now further constrained. Mademba also felt a deep and enduring obligation to his French patrons for their efforts on his behalf, both in the past and at present. Especially after his brush with these forces of change, Mademba probably realized anew that his continued hold on power rested on the sustained support of his patrons. In a letter to Archinard in December 1905, in which he discusses his experimentation with various American strains of cotton, Mademba wrote that "even though I do not often write [to you], do not conclude that I have forgotten the reason you chose me to administer this little portion of this vast land that you conquered for France." Mademba continued "At no point have I ever forgotten all the good advice you gave me concerning the efforts I should make to develop economically the province placed under my orders. I have worked constantly to merit your continued confidence [in me]."[72]

The imposition of the legal reform of the justice certainly did not arrive in Sinsani without Mademba knowing quite a bit about it. Mademba kept current on politics in Dakar and Paris. The 1903 legal reform legislation probably gave Mademba pause as he confronted what it meant to have new transparency regarding his dispensation of justice. The new mandate regarding the rule of law bumped up against Mademba's sense of himself as king and thus the final arbiter of justice and of life and death, which he had described in his 1897 report on customs. If you recall, Mademba had been given a relatively free hand in disciplining the residents of his state and had regularly thrown individuals he found guilty of crimes and even minor affronts to his authority into a local prison in Sinsani. In that prison, inmates suffered beatings and deprivation of food and water. Mademba also regularly employed his authority to enact capital punishment following often cursory trials. The new legal system with its focus on regularity, transparency, proportionality, and the prohibition on corporal punishment cut deeply into Mademba's hitherto

---

[71] For more detail on the French West African colonial legal reform of 1903 and the "troublespots" that emerged from changes that coincided with the end of slavery and legal reform, see Roberts, *Litigants and Households*.

[72] Mademba, letter to Archinard, Sinsani, Dec. 7, 1905, SHD 1 K 109.

autonomous application of justice. Under the 1903 legislation, Mademba became the president of the Tribunal de Province of Sansanding and was obliged to hold public sessions and to keep written registers of the cases – divided between civil disputes and criminal cases – brought before the tribunal. Gone was Mademba's authority to take a criminal's or rebel's life. Only the lieutenant-governors and the governor-general held this power and only after the case had been assessed by the *Chambre d'homologation*. Because Mademba had to submit the court registers regularly to the administrator in Segu, gone, too, was Mademba's authority to punish some individuals more strenuously than others.[73]

The provincial tribunal of Sinsani was up and running by September 1905. The activity of this court was slow. The docket for civil and commercial disputes heard a total of one dispute from September through December 1905. Make Kanouba was in court on September 11, 1905, because his wife, Fatimata Kone, refused to move with him to his new house in Sinsani. Kone in turn requested a divorce, which the court granted.[74] In contrast, the docket for misdemeanor and correctional cases heard nine cases during this same period. The cases ranged from beatings to theft to "sequestering" a person against their will. Mademba ordered the defendants to prison ranging from eight days to three months. None of the defendants appealed.[75] With the establishment of the new legal system, Segu-based Native Affairs employee Charles Correnson described how the provincial tribunal had become

> the court of major importance. With its jurisdiction over minor offenses and civil and commercial matters of all kinds, the tribunal sees native life in all its variations. It is truly an indigenous court. The only administrative intervention occurs when the humanitarian principles of our civilization are disregarded. At all other times, the parties freely defend their grievances according to their habits. This court is the best school of customs and the people.[76]

The Sinsani tribunal, however, did not fully live up to Correnson's potential because like so many other provincial tribunals in the Soudan during these formative years, most of the judges serving on the tribunals were Muslim when

---

[73] Cmdt. Segu, letter to Resident Sinsani, Segu, Mar. 17, 1905, ANM 2 D 105.

[74] État de jugements rendus en matière civile et commerciale, Tribunal de province, Sinsani, fourth quarter 1905, ANM 2 M 92. Already in 1903, before the new legal system was introduced, Coviaux had written that "thefts as well as beatings and wounds are the principle offenses that bring natives before the courts."

[75] État de jugements rendus en matière correctionelle, Tribunal de province, Sinsani, fourth quarter 1905; also État de jugements rendus en matière correctionelle, Tribunal de province, Sinsani, Sept. and Nov. 1905, ANM 2 M 92.

[76] Charles Correnson, De l'orientation de la justice et des moeurs chez les populations de la région de Segu, Segu, Sept. 5, 1907, ANM 1 D 55-3.

the majority of the population remained traditionalists. Colonial administrators favored Muslims as judges in part because of their literate training and their regular application of the Maliki legal school.[77] However, the 1903 legal reform mandated that judges represent the population in the district and thus apply custom.[78]

After this burst of activity at the Sinsani provincial tribunal in the last quarter of 1905, I have no further record of its judgments. There are a few references to specific cases in the correspondence between Segu and Sinsani, but aside from the five registers of the Sinsani tribunal from September through to December 1905, no additional court registers seem to exist. According to the 1903 legislation, quarterly registers of each provincial tribunal according to fixed formula separating civil and commercial disputes from misdemeanor and minor criminal cases must be maintained and regularly submitted to the district headquarters.[79] How then can we explain these missing court registers? It could simply be that they are lost. On the other hand, there is a hint in the archives that instead of holding formal court appearances, Mademba preferred to reconcile disputes in private. "The tribunal of Sansanding does not render any judgments. The *Fama* instead reconciles all who present themselves to him."[80] Especially after his near demise in 1899–1900, Mademba scrupulously abided by administrative rules, always maintaining a correct and disciplined attitude, but he did very little to enforce these rules if they seemed to diminish his authority. We saw this behavior with the various Native Affairs employees who were posted to Sinsani as Residents. In the case of administering justice, although Mademba presided over the provincial tribunal of Sinsani, he sat next to other judges and he was obliged to record cases and file them with the Segu administrator. Mademba may have construed these formalities regarding transparency of judgments, public hearings, and the rule of law as undermining his authority as *faama*. On the other hand, if he could render justice – or reconcile disputants – in private in his palace, these actions would bolster his authority. How he handled criminal cases, especially those that imposed prison sentences, I do not know because the registers have not survived or were never kept. To further complicate matters, there was an incident in 1911 that I will examine more fully in the

---

[77] See Richard Roberts, "Custom and Muslim Family Law in Native Courts of the French Soudan, 1905–1912," in *Muslim Family Law in Sub-Saharan Africa: Colonial Legacies and Post-colonial Challenges*, eds. Shamil Jeppie, Ebrahim Moosa, and Richard Roberts (Amsterdam: Amsterdam University Press, 2010), 85–108.

[78] Admin Segu, letter to Resident Sinsani, Segu, May 7 and Aug. 18, 1905, ANM 2 M 34. The August letter indicated that the *Chambre d'homologation* annulled the verdict of the Sinsani tribunal because it did not adequately represent the religious and ethnic mix of Mademba's kingdom.

[79] See Roberts, *Litigants and Households,* chapter 3.

[80] Rapport sur la justice indigène, Segu, fourth quarter 1909, ANM 2 M 92.

next chapter. This incident involves an attack on Mademba's son, Ben Daoud Mademba, who was serving as secretary of the provincial tribunal. This incident indicates that the Sinsani tribunal was indeed meeting, although how regularly I do not know. In contrast to his slow-walking of legal changes, Mademba found in cotton a means to refurbish his image.

The King Remade: Cotton as King

Cotton brought down Mademba in 1899 and cotton was his resurrection as king. When Colonel Trentinian became lieutenant-governor of the Soudan in 1895, he understood the pressures to fulfill the agenda of conquest, but he also understood the pressure from Paris to tame the military and to give the new colony of the Soudan a mission that resonated with the needs of the metropole. Conquest of West Africa coincided with increasing competition from European as well as American and Asian cotton textile producers and threatened continued access to raw materials for French textile industries.[81] During the course of conquest, several European traders and planters had become interested in the cotton of the Soudan. By 1896, samples of local cotton were in the hands of cotton brokers of Le Havre.[82] In 1897, Trentinian decided to assist this effort by buying a large quantity of cotton with the intention of sending it to France. In 1898, Trentinian ordered local administrators – including Mademba – to buy large quantities of cotton and he sponsored several scientific and commercial missions to survey the economic potentialities of the new colony, which included an industrial spinner from Le Havre, Étienne Fossat.[83] Trentinian was especially interested in promoting long-staple cotton varieties, especially American ones.[84] Fossat was the son of a major cotton merchant in Le Havre and therefore familiar with the business of cotton and textile production. Fossat arrived in Kayes in December 1898 and set out to acquire samples of local cotton in every district along the Niger River, which was presumed to be the premier cotton zone. Fossat managed to collect samples from Kita, Bamako, Segu, Sinsani, Jenne, and

---

[81] For a fuller discussion, see Roberts, *Two Worlds of Cotton*; Sven Beckert, *Empire of Cotton: A New History of Global Capitalism* (New York: Alfred A. Knopf, 2014).

[82] Rapport commercial, agricole et industriel sur le Soudan Français, 1898, ANOM Soudan XIII-13; P. Georges Mias, letter to cmdt. sup., Kayes, Apr. 6, 1893, ANOM Soudan XIII-1a.

[83] Trentinian, letter to cmdts. du cercles de Kayes, Kati, Bamako, Segu, Sumpi, Goundam, Jenne, San, Bandiagara, and the *Fama* de Sansanding, Kayes, Dec. 21, 1898, ANM B 77; Henri Lecomte, *Le Coton: Monographie culture et histoire économique* (Paris: Carré et Naud, 1900), 424–425.

[84] Yves Henry, *Le coton dans l'Afrique occidentale française* (Paris: Agustin Challamel, 1906), 149–150.

Mopti. "Across the vast territory from Kayes to Timbuktu," Fossat wrote in his final report, "nearly all villages have vast fields of cotton that serve as the primary material for the numerous native weavers in every village." But it was only in Sinsani, where "in Mademba's storehouse that I was able to find 20,000 kilograms of raw cotton, which I bought because of its good quality." "It is certain," Fossat concluded, "that the future of our colony Soudan will depend on agricultural production, not the least of which will be cotton." This cotton, Fossat added, will help France lessen its "heavy dependency" on American sources of cotton.[85] Altogether, Fossat acquired around 120 tons of cotton that he sent back to Kayes, where it was ginned and packed. Because Fossat did not arrive back in Kayes before the rains started and because the ginning and packing was inexpertly done, much of the cotton that eventually arrived in France was spoilt.[86]

Fossat's report of his mission and the industrialists' initial assessment of Soudanese cotton sent to France was lukewarm, but still encouraging. Trentinian was now convinced that cotton was the way of linking the new colony to France economically. But the key was to find varieties of cotton more suited to French industrialists' needs and to improve the ginning and baling processes. Reducing freight costs of moving cotton from the Middle Niger to Saint Louis or Dakar had also become a critical factor in making Soudanese cotton competitive with other imported cotton in France. The Kayes to Bamako railway was making slow but steady progress and would arrive in Bamako in 1904, promising a significant reduction in freight costs. However, political crises in France in 1899 led to the decision to restructure the Soudan, which in turn led Trentinian to resign as governor.

In the meantime, French metropolitan interest in Soudanese cotton continued. In March 1901, delegates from metropolitan regional cotton syndicates formed the Industrie Cotonnière Française under the leadership of Albert Esnault-Pelterie. Esnault was a leading textile industrialist whose factories in Amiens had over 1,000 looms.[87] He vigorously pursued a colonial raw materials policy and by November 1902 the manufacturers' association had formed a branch designed to encourage cotton production in the colonies. At its November 1902 meeting, Esnault reported to the executive committee of the Syndicat Général de l'Industrie Cotonnière Française that he had held productive interviews with important "personalities" associated with his colonial cotton initiative. Among these personalities were General Trentinian, Lieutenant-governor William Ponty, Governor-general Ernest Roume, and

[85] E. Fossat, "Le Coton du Soudan," report of the mission sent to min. col., Le Havre, May 28, 1900, ANOM Soudan III-4.

[86] Henry, *Le coton dans l'Afrique occidentale française*, 150–154.

[87] James Torrance, "A Glimpse of the Textile Mills at Amiens," *Textile World Record* 26 (Oct. 1903–Nov. 1904): 595.

"Le *Fama* Mademba of Sansanding."[88] The Association Cotonnière Coloniale (ACC) came formally into existence in 1903. "Following the example of Russia in Turkistan, England in Egypt and the Indies, and Germany in Togo, these men want to encourage cotton production in Africa, notably in the Soudan," lauded the *Dépêche Coloniale* in 1903.[89] "It is in the valley of the Niger," wrote Captain Lenfant to a Le Havre merchant and vice president of the ACC in 1903, "that you will create la France cotonnière."[90]

The ACC was established as a semiautonomous colonial arm of the French textile manufacturers' syndicate, whose tasks were to promote cotton production for export to France by assisting in seed distribution, agronomic outreach, and in erecting ginning and pressing stations. Ginneries served the dual purpose of preparing cotton for use and of separating out the seed. The seed was then culled to eliminate poor-quality cotton and to provide a reservoir for the next planting season.

In October 1903, shortly after the establishment of the ACC, Governor-general Roume firmly committed his administration to promoting peasant-produced cotton in French West Africa during a speech at an ACC banquet.

> If you will allow me this counsel, you should direct your attention first to establishing a system of purchases, which will permit the black cultivator, during the first few years at least, to be assured the disposal of all his harvest. It is the price and the price alone that will give [the African peasant] confidence and which will let him devote himself to this culture out of which he will be assured of a profit.[91]

American cotton, however, dominated both the French and the world markets. Metropolitan spinners would only be interested in Soudanese cotton if the quality and the price were right.

In the 1904–1905 cotton season, the first in which the ACC participated in the Soudan, it distributed some 20,000 kilograms of imported cotton seed, mostly Sea Island and other American long staples, to village chiefs in designated cotton regions. "Each village," remarked Ponty in his annual report that year, "has its fields of cotton." He anticipated that cultivators "will bring their next harvests to the ginning stations, [just] as our peasants bring their wheat to the mill."[92] The French continued to think in extravagant terms: they saw the

---

[88] *Bull. ACC* 1903–1904: 14.

[89] "La culture du coton," *Dépêche Coloniale*, Jan. 7, 1903. See also Christopher Maurice Andrews, Peter Grupp, and Alexander Sydney Kanya-Forstner, "Le mouvement colonial français et ses principales personalités, 1890–1914," *Revue française d'histoire d'Outre-Mer* 42 (4) 1975: 640–673.

[90] Lenfant, letter to Charles Marande, Paris, Feb. 5, 1903, quoted in J. Brenier, "La culture du coton dans les colonies Françaises," *Bull. ACC* 2 1903: annex.

[91] Roume, "Discourse de M. Roume," *Bull. ACC* 2 Oct. 12: 1903.

[92] William Ponty, Note sur la Colonie du Haut-Sénégal-Niger, Paris, June 25, 1905, ANOM Soudan I-2 bis.

future bringing 400,000 hectares under American cotton without special projects and with the existing population. At the very least, the agronomist Vuillet expected to have an annual yield of 60,000 metric tons.[93]

In its efforts during these formative years, the ACC's participation in *la politique cotonnière* ran more or less parallel with the colonial state's. The ACC targeted the Middle Niger valley as the preliminary center for its activities. It erected a ginnery at Segu in 1904, although it did not commence operations until 1905 and it was not running at full capacity until 1906. In 1905, the Segu ginnery produced 2,000 kilograms of cotton fiber. The ACC also directed its energies to selecting new varieties of cotton seeds. In a generally enthusiastic letter to Governor-general Roume in 1904 Esnault-Pelterie, president of the ACC, noted that initial reports of Africans' responses to the new seeds and metropolitan interest in cotton were positive.[94]

As an avid consumer of colonial and metropolitan news, Mademba was certainly aware of the growing interest in promoting Soudanese cotton. Mademba's interest in cotton predated these latest initiatives. He was a keen ally of Trentinian's efforts to search for a new economic future for the Soudan. Already in 1897, Mademba solicited from Trentinian's office long-staple American cotton seed, probably Sea Island and other Georgia varieties, which he sowed during the rainy season that year. Mademba wrote to the Segu commandant in September 1897 that the Georgia cotton that he had sown at the same time as indigenous cotton was already bearing flowers and was therefore well ahead of the indigenous varieties.[95] Mademba cotton trials fit a wider pattern of his experimentation with different crops of potential value to the metropole. In addition to cotton, Mademba planted wheat and "European" tobacco as well as varieties of fruit trees and vegetables. By January 1898, Mademba reported that his experiments with Georgia cotton and European tobacco "left nothing to be desired," but his efforts to grow wheat had failed miserably.[96] He also experimented with livestock, all of which impressed Baillaud during his visit to Sinsani in 1898. As we saw in Chapter 7, Mademba's enthusiasm for cotton led in part to the investigations over his abuses of power.

Mademba returned to his kingdom too late in 1900 to direct the planting season. I have no good records on what Mademba planted in the 1901–1902 or 1902–1903 seasons. This was the time when he was negotiating with his *sofa* about their work regime. But he clearly experimented with different varieties of American and Egyptian cotton. The 1903–1904 season, however, provided a

---

[93] Vuillet, Régions cotonnières du Soudan, n.p., Aug. 18, 1904, ANM 1 R 79.

[94] Esnault-Pelterie, President ACC, letter to Gouv.-gen. Roume, Paris, Apr. 2, 1904, ANM 1 R 79.

[95] Mademba, letter to cmdt. Segu, Sept. 1, 1897, Sinsani, ANM 1 E 220.

[96] Mademba, letter to cmdt. Segu, Jan. 1, 1898, Sinsani, ANM 1 E 220.

new opportunity for Mademba to demonstrate his commitment to building the economic future of the Soudan. This was the first season in which the ACC was active and it promoted especially the cultivation of nine different American cottons. In each of 206 villages, the ACC provided the village chief with a single variety in order to insure that the cotton plants did not easily hybridize, as well as instructions on planting and weeding. The ACC also provided nominal payment to the village chief for his efforts. The 1904 harvest was very promising, with abundant yields.[97] In the 1904–1905 season, the ACC gave Mademba a sizeable share of its imported American cotton seed.[98] The Segu administrator remarked that "Mademba's sole preoccupation is currently the cultivation of exotic cotton to which he devotes all his efforts."[99] Mademba planted sixty-seven hectares in Mississippi cotton and one hectare each of King, Peterking, and Excelsior varieties. Mademba did not have one large plantation; instead, he spread his Mississippi cotton among the villages of Sinsani, Thain, Sibila, Madina, Gomakoro, and Nierela. Throughout the Soudan, the rains failed after September 1904, just as the cotton plants were germinating. This was an exceptionally dry year and the cotton crop suffered. Mademba's planting of mostly Mississippi and Excelsior varieties proved to be early geminating and therefore somewhat more resilient to the drought. With the assistance of the ACC and the colony's department of agriculture, Mademba squeezed four tons of cotton from his field. His 1905 harvest was ginned and packed in Sinsani and sent to Le Havre through the auspices of the ACC.[100]

Lieutenant-governor Ponty, who together with Governor-general Chaudié had taken a risk in releasing Mademba from house arrest and return him to his kingdom in Sinsani, rewarded Mademba for his commitment to cotton by nominating him for the rank of officer in the Order of Agricultural Merit in 1904.[101] After his fall from grace, Mademba was clearly thrilled with this new honor, which he proudly included along with his other medals on his cape. In October 1904, he wrote to his patron Archinard congratulating Archinard on his appointment as commander of the colonial army and then transitioning to his news. "The month of October has been for me a month of celebration. This month I have rejoiced in the high and well-deserved distinction you received and for the medal of agricultural merit that I received upon the nomination by Wm Ponty, the first governor of Haut-Sénégal-Niger." Later in his letter to Archinard, Mademba noted that the good news in October helped to dispel his

---

[97] Henry, *Le coton dans l'Afrique occidentale française*, 173–175, 183–184.
[98] *Bull. ACC* 1905: 22.
[99] Rap. pol., Segu, July 1904, ANM 1 E 71.
[100] Henry, *Le coton dans l'Afrique occidentale française*, 188–190; *Bull. ACC* 1905: 23.
[101] Anonymous, "*Fama* de Sansanding, Distinctions honorifiques," *Bulletin Administratif du Gouvernement général de l'Afrique occidentale française*, Sept. 1904, 645.

grief in September, when his son, Gustave, who had been a "brilliant" student during his first year of his baccalaureate at the lycée in Algiers, had returned to Saint Louis ill and then died. News of his son's death "did not discourage me from sending three of my other sons to Lycée in Toulouse."[102]

Mademba also buried his grief over his son's death by intensifying his efforts to promote his cotton crop. At the April 1905 meeting of the ACC, just as Mademba's cotton was being prepared for shipment to Le Havre, Ponty declared that "the time as arrived the enter into the stage of industrial [cotton] production. The experiments conducted by the colonial administration and by the Association Cotonnière Coloniale have demonstrated that the natives are ready to develop their cotton crop and they have adopted the new seeds furnished to them." Ponty envisioned that in a few years the Soudan would "feed important quantities of cotton to our French factories."[103] During that April meeting, Esnault also drew attention to reports that despite the drought, Mademba had harvested four tons of "excellent cotton."

J. Vuillet, the director of the Agricultural Service in Haut-Sénégal-Niger, oversaw the planting and harvesting of Mademba's cotton during the 1904–1905 season using only indigenous techniques and tools. The only difference in this year's cotton crop was the care taken to keep the Mississippi and Excelsior fields separate from local varieties of cotton. Once harvested, the cotton was ginned by women using time-consuming local techniques.

Vuillet convinced the ACC to bring a cotton press to Sinsani (see Figure 7.1), so that the pressing and baling of the ginned cotton could be done according to metropolitan standards. Ponty charged Vuillet with accompanying Mademba's cotton to Le Havre, where it arrived in a physical condition "analogous to American cottons to which it will be compared" in forty-kilogram bales.

Once Mademba's cotton arrived in Le Havre (see Figure 7.2), it was taken by the spinning house of David and Maigret in Epinal (Vosges) for assessment. A sample of Mademba's cotton was also sent to Manchester for assessment. Upon opening the bales, David and Maigret found the cotton to be of a "rare property," largely free of leaves and dust, although some of the bales contained cotton with too much seed. After careful industrial testing, which included both spinning and weaving, David and Maigret concluded that Mademba's cotton was "middling fair" and yielded strong yarn and cloth that was very soft and very white. They stated "without doubt Sansanding cotton can advantageously replace superior American cotton that are preferred in the best

[102] Mademba, letter to Archinard, Sinsani, Oct. 30, 1904, SHD Papiers Réquin (Mademba letters to Archinard) 1 K 109; Mademba, Au Sénégal, 109.
[103] "Revue des colonies," Bull. ACC 7 June 1905: 5–6.

PRESSAGE DU COTON DU FAMA MADEMBA

Figure 7.1 Cotton press preparing Mademba's cotton, 1905.
(Source: *Bull. ACC* 1905, with permission from the Bibliothèque Nationale de France)

LES COTONS DU FAMA MADEMBA AU HAVRE
(Photographie prise par M. A. Hémet dans les Docks du canal de Tancarville.)

Figure 7.2 Mademba's cotton bales at Le Havre, 1905.
(Source: *Bull. ACC* 1905, "Les balles de coton '*Fama* Sansanding' au port du Havre," with permission from the Bibliothèque Nationale de France)

spinning factories of Vosges."[104] The report from Hanmer and Company in Manchester was equally enthusiastic. "This cotton is the most perfect class that I have ever seen. It is clean and even brighter than 'Fair' American grade cotton so that we would classify this cotton higher than that of the United States. It will easily compete with American cotton as long as one can produce important quantities."[105] These initial responses to Mademba's commitment to Soudan's cotton future marked the beginning of Mademba's redemption.

Mademba redoubled his cotton production during the 1905–1906 season. Yves Henry described Mademba's cotton as "no longer experiments, but veritable production on a grand scale combined with a practical spirit that one cannot praise enough." M. Estève, an agent of the ACC charged with

---

[104] "Rapport de MM. David et Maigret sur le cotton de Sansanding à la filature et au tissage," *Bull. ACC* 1905: 55–60. See also "Notes sure l'exposition de Liège," *Questions Diplomatiques et Coloniales*, ninth year (201) July 1, 1905: 547–548, fn 3.
[105] "Revue des Colonies," *Bull ACC*, 1905: 11.

overseeing the cotton experiments in Nyamina and Sinsani, described the "enormous effort by the inhabitants of this region and the constant surveillance by *Fama* Mademba" that contributed to the very promising cotton crop that year.[106] Given the success of Mississippi varieties the year before, in 1905, Mademba planted 214 hectares of Mississippi cotton in fourteen villages in his *États*. The largest fields were sixty hectares in Sinsani and eighteen hectares each in Gomakoro, Thain, and Sibila. Mademba also planted just under thirty-nine hectares in Excelsior varieties, but in smaller fields. Sinsani's Excelsior field was 1 hectare and the largest field was 2.6 hectares in Kayo village.[107] Mademba was obviously pleased with his continued progress in promoting cotton and the attention he was getting. In December 1905, Mademba wrote to Archinard wishing him a happy new year and described his efforts to "develop economically the province that you placed under my orders," and thus to live up to the confidence Archinard placed in his abilities. Mademba described how his effort to promote rubber had failed due to the lack of rain, but he basked in the success of his cotton experiments. "Last year," Mademba wrote,

> I experimented with Mississippi cotton with very strong success. After having ginned the cotton in Sansanding, I sent it to Le Havre, where it was judged to be among the very best American cotton varieties. This year I will plant around 250 hectares in cotton, partially in Mississippi and in Excelsior. These two varieties have are already growing very well. It will shortly be ready to harvest.

Mademba noted that he was pleased to be an "auxiliary" to Lieutenant-governor Ponty's effort to develop the colony and especially in regard to exotic cotton varieties. Mademba also stated that the "natives are unanimous that American cotton provides a superior yield to aboriginal cottons."[108]

Buoyed by the positive responses he received, Mademba pushed his subjects to increase their cotton production during the 1905–1906 season. Mademba reported to the ACC that the number of villages producing American varieties of cotton doubled and that he expected to yield six tons of cotton by the end of the harvest. Mademba anticipated that the harvest would double again by the end of the 1906–1907. The era of industrial-level output of cotton from the Soudan was clearly within reach. Esnault, the president of the ACC, noted with some irony in his address of November 6, 1906 that if the amount of cotton export from the Soudan seems somewhat limited, "it is because the women,

---

[106] Yves Henry, "Campagne cotonnière de 1905, n.p., n.d., ANS 1 R 102; "Nouvelles des colonies," *Bull. ACC* 3 Apr. 1906: 329.

[107] Ibid. Estève included a hectare count in his report to the ACC, but it was less precise than Henry's assessment, "Nouvelles des colonies," *Bull. ACC* 3 Apr. 1906: 331.

[108] Mademba, letter to Archinard, Sinsani, Dec. 7, 1905, SHD Papiers Réquin (Mademba letters to Archinard) 1 K 109.

who gin the cotton by hand, are so impressed with the quality of these new cottons that they keep most of the crop for their own use before allowing the rest to be exported to France."[109] The regional handicraft textile industry along the Niger River remained robust and absorbed a large part of the cotton harvest.[110]

Mademba's fortunes – especially his political ones – seemed ascendant. The reception of Mademba's cotton in France vindicated Ponty's faith in the bargains of collaboration that had tied Mademba so closely to his French patrons. Mademba was delivering not only new-found political stability to Sinsani, but proof that the Soudan was well on its way to become a useful colony for French industrialists in need of raw materials. Roume and Ponty visited Mademba in July 1906 during their tour of the colony. During their relatively quick visit, they took time to visit Mademba's cotton fields.[111] The high point of Mademba's redemption, however, came during his trip to France in fall 1906, where he participated in the colonial exposition in Marseille, in his visits to Le Havre's cotton market and to French textile mills, and in his participation at the banquet of the ACC in Paris. In July 1906, all the chiefs of his villages came to Sinsani "to salute the *fama* on the occasion of his voyage." At the beginning of August, Mademba left Sinsani for Marseille.[112]

Mademba arrived in Marseille in early September 1906 to participate in the cotton section of the Colonial Congress, which focused on scientific and economic potential of France's colonies for metropolitan developments. The Colonial Congress was part of the larger Colonial Exposition of Marseille. Esnault-Pelterie presided over the sessions dedicated to cotton. The merchants, industrialists, planters, and government officials attending the cotton sessions agreed that promoting the production of colonial cotton "is an absolute necessity for the future prosperity of the entire cotton textile industry."[113] During the discussion following Yves Henry's lengthy report on cotton in French West Africa, Mademba responded to Esnault's observation that the cotton yield during the 1905–1906 season was "feeble" by noting that the climatic conditions that year were "exceptionally unfavorable." Mademba added that the natives fully appreciated the qualities of the American cotton varieties distributed by the ACC. Part of the reason that cotton exports from the Soudan remained so slender was because "the women buy all this cotton

---

[109] "Discourse de M. Esnault-Pelterie," *Bull. ACC* 1906: 424; on Mademba's 1905–1907 cotton seasons, see *Bull. ACC* 1906: 375, 424.

[110] Roberts, *Two Worlds of Cotton.*

[111] Rap. pol., Segu, July 1906, ANM 1 E 72.

[112] Rap. pol., Segu July and Aug. 1906, ANM 1 E 72.

[113] Allocutions prononcées par M. Esnault-Pelterie, Président, à l'ouverture des travaux de la section, Quatrième Division, Agriculture: Deuxième Section: Le Coton, *Compte Rendu des Travaux du Congrès Colonial de Marseille, Exposition colonial de Marseille, 1906* (Paris: Augustin Challamel, 1908), vol. 4, 253.

from the market for their own uses. But now that American cotton is no longer so rare, the harvests will increase." Mademba cautioned that despite increased cotton production, the high costs of transport remained a barrier to the bright future of colonial cotton. Ensault seconded Mademba's remarks and the members voted unanimously to urge the colonial authorities to work as quickly as possible to enhancing the means of transport in "our colonies."[114] It was clear from his participation in the discussions regarding colonial cotton that Mademba was being taken seriously as an emerging leader in promoting Soudanese cotton exports and as the local expert.

Consistent with his new celebrity, Mademba traveled from Marseille to Le Havre, where he met with Monsieurs Fossat, father and son, who gave him a tour of the port's famous cotton bourse, where cotton was sorted and classi-fied, both essential steps toward setting a price. From Le Havre, Mademba went to Rouen, where C. Berger took Mademba on a tour of his two spinning factories – La Ruche and L'Abeille. Mademba followed "with intense interest the transformation" of raw cotton into yarn and asked numerous questions about each machine in the process. Berger passed Mademba off to his Rouen colleagues, Lemarchand Frères and Keittinger, who showed Mademba around their textile factories. Mademba was "extremely taken by all the industrial activities and declared himself amazed by the importance of the capital invested in the cotton textile industry." At Amiens, Mademba toured Esnault's weaving factories as well as those of Barbet-Massin and Company.[115] Mademba was invited to participate in the ACC's Board of Directors' meeting in Paris on October 4, 1906. The ACC was concerned with improving yields and the directors asked Mademba about the potential for increasing Soudanese cotton yields using plows. Mademba responded that plows were still scarce in the Soudan, but the real challenge to increasing production was to provide African farmers with sufficient American cotton seed to allow them to increase their fields – it was argued that, once these farmers experienced the results of the American cotton, they would "continu-ously increase their fields."[116]

Mademba was an honored guest at the ACC's 1906 banquet, which was a lavish affair held at Palais d'Orsay to honor Governor-general Ernest Roume and his efforts to promote cotton development in French West Africa. The minister of Colonies, Milliès-Lacroix, attended as well as senior officials from the president's office and the Ministries of Commerce and Industry, the president of the Paris Chamber of Commerce, three current lieutenant-governors (including Ponty), several former ministers, and leaders of industry.

---

[114] Discussion, Quatrième Division, Agriculture: Deuxième Section: Le Coton," *Compte Rendu des Travaux du Congrès Colonial de Marseille*, 273–274.
[115] "Nouvelles des Colonies," *Bull. ACC* 1906: 372–373.
[116] Ibid., 375.

Esnault opened the ceremonies by praising Roume and the government-general for working "hand in hand" with the ACC in a shared mission to promote the production of cotton in France's colonies. Esnault also acknowledged the roles played by Lieutenant-governor Ponty and the several agronomists whose work in the Soudan had been so promising. Esnault next turned to Mademba, seated prominently at the banquet.

> *Fama* Mademba, chief of the États de Sansanding, an intelligent man who is devoted to France, is no less enthusiastic [about the future of Soudanese cotton]. Guided by Governor Ponty, he has fully understood the bright future of cotton production in the Soudan. In taking into his hands the production of cotton in his land, he has brought to us a precious competition [to the American cotton crop]. It is, therefore, a pleasure to see him today at this table. It is he who wanted to come [to France] to sell his first harvest of some considerable importance and to learn more about what he can do to develop this source of wealth.[117]

Before raising a toast to Governor-general Roume, Esnault reiterated that the promotion of colonial cotton was a joint enterprise of the public and private sectors and a project worthy of the attention of the government of France.

Roume, in his turn, underscored his commitment to this vision of a joint enterprise to promote colonial cotton production. One of the core missions, Roume told his audience, of colonial administration was "to make available the resources of the colony under his control to the service of the mother country." From his perspective, the most important task was to encourage African peasants to produce the crop on their own fields. "Our natives are by their nature cultivators, who quickly understand the value of new crops, and who are willing to adapt their cultivation to the new methods ... We can make significant progress by persuasion, by instruction, and by the examples of our experimental farms." Roume then turned to Mademba, who was an example of the success of this approach. "Without him, our excellent auxiliary, *Fama* Mademba, whom M. Esnault-Pelterie has lauded for his intelligence and his spirit of initiative, we would never have delivered his cotton harvest to the market of Le Havre."[118] Roume ended his speech by toasting the mission of the ACC.

Between the ACC's Board of Directors' meeting at the beginning of October and the ACC banquet at the beginning of November, Mademba spent several weeks in Paris. Mademba had been to Paris before, but this was his first visit as a celebrity. Two of Mademba's sons, both of whom were studying in the lycée in Algiers, and his "extremely tall" nephew accompanied him.[119] A Parisian

---

[117] "Discourse de M. Esnault-Pelterie," *Bull. ACC* Nov. 6, 1906: 438–424.
[118] "Discourse de M. Roume," *Bull. ACC* Nov. 6, 1906: 447–452.
[119] "Un loyal serviteur de France," *Le Petit Journal*, Sept. 22, 1906.

newspaper captured Mademba's importance to this task: "The Colonial Cotton Association, whose rivals from England and Germany recognize how more successful it has become than they are, have found in Mademba an unexpected and precious collaborator."[120] Mademba used his time not only to bask in the attention he received as the modernizer of cotton cultivation in the Soudan and thus as a potential savior of France from its dependence on cotton from the American market but to remake his image and to promote a particular version of his history. Remaking his image and remaking his past were part of the same process – the bricolage (the subject of the next chapter).

Mademba returned to Sinsani in time to oversee the 1906–1907 cotton harvest. Although the rains in 1906–1907 were abundant, they fell sporadically, and the cotton plants in the Segu area were deprived of water just at the crucial point of the plants' maturation. Scientific studies at the colony's experimental fields were beginning to yield data that indicated that American cottons were very sensitive to the reliability of the rains, the fertility of the soil, and excessively vulnerable to local insects.[121] Perhaps Mademba's redemption through cotton was as fleeting as the rains.

---

[120] "Le roi Mademba et l'avenir du Soudan," *Les Temps*, Oct. 26, 1906. A very similar report with the same misspelling of Sansanding appeared under the title "Un roi cultivateur: l'avenir du Soudan et le culture du coton," in *La Lanterne*, Oct. 26, 1906.

[121] Rapport sur l'emploie des subventions accordées par le Département à l'ACC, n.d. [1909], ANM 1 R 118.

Remaking Mademba, 1906–1931

Mademba's visit to France and particularly the month he spent in Paris was pivotal to his effort to remake his image and burnish his status. Mademba certainly basked in the prominence his cotton had received by the ACC, at the Marseilles Congress of September 1906, and by his visits to the textile heartland of France, where he witnessed the great industrial transformations of raw cotton into textiles. Cotton was a part of his efforts to rebrand himself, but his effort also involved strategic efforts to reconfigure the narrative of his rise to position of king of Sansanding. During his visits to Marseille and Paris, Mademba took time to meet with journalists, who then promoted his revitalized narrative. Between the end of September and the end of October 1906, Mademba's story appeared in at least six French newspapers and weekly journals. Some, such as *Le Figaro*, reported on Mademba's visits to Rouen and on the quality of his cotton.[1] Others, including *Le Petit Journal*, *Le Petit Parisien*, and *Les Temps* ran headlines such as "A Loyal Servant of France: The *'Fama'* Mademba at the *Petit Journal*," "A Visit by the King Mademba: A True Friend of France," and "The King Mademba and the Future of the Soudan."[2] *Le Petit Journal* and *Le Petit Parisien* did not merely report on Mademba's visit but provided a vehicle to promote Mademba's revised narrative. The Parisian journal *L'Illustration* published a photograph of Mademba in Paris accompanied by a nephew and an interpreter (see Figure 8.1).[3] Above the caption, "An African King in Paris," this photograph shows Mademba in the sartorial dress of a solid bourgeois and stood in sharp contrast to the exotic attire of other royalty from French colonies. *Le Temps* captures this juxtaposition of colonial royalty.

> There is at present in Paris a king, who is very dark, but this is much less noticeable than Sisowath or even formerly Dinah Salifou.[4] It is true that he does not wear a red burnous with gold fringes, and neither red leather

[1] *Le Figaro*, Sept. 28, 1906.
[2] *Le Petit Journal*, Sept. 22, 1906; *Le Petit Parisien*, Oct. 27, 1906; *Les Temps*, Oct. 26, 1906.
[3] *L'Illustration*, Nov. 10, 1906.
[4] This refers to visits to France by Sisowath Monivong, who in 1904 became king of Cambodia, which was a protectorate and part of French Indochina, and to Mohammad

Un roi africain à Paris : le fama Mademba (appuyé sur une canne),
son neveu et son interprète.

Figure 8.1   Mademba in Paris, 1906.
(Source: *L'Illustration*, Nov. 10, 1906, with permission from *L'Illustration*)

boots, nor a hat like a little pagoda. Instead, he is dressed like you and me
except that he wears the Legion of Honor rosette on the label his frock
coat. And yet he is *fama*, that is, king of Sousouding (sic) on the Niger.
But he much prefers that we call him "sir," like a simple white ... It
should be added that Mademba, former employee of the telegraph service
at Saint Louis, and Toucouleur by race, not only speaks the purest French,

Dinah Salifou Camara, who was king of the Nalu in the Riviers du Sud region of Guinea
and participated in the Exposition of Paris in 1889.

but thinks like a Frenchman, and, which is even more rare, he has the same moral conceptions.[5]

The very ordinariness of Mademba's Parisian attire was part of the new persona that he wished to present. "He much prefers," wrote Les Temps, "to be called 'monsieur' just as a simple white person." "Mademba is simplicity itself," described Le Petit Parisien. He portrayed himself as a man who disdained the complex protocol of royal visits. "He is not escorted by chamberlains or the marshal of the court . . . This king opens the door himself with a simplicity that is completely democratic." According to these stories, this self-styled democratic king was actually an ordinary man, selected by the French for lofty purposes. Le Petit Parisien began its article on Mademba by noting "some interesting things," among which was that Mademba "was an employee of the Telegraph service who became King."[6] Les Temps explained that Archinard had already had his eyes on this "little employee" before he made Mademba king. A similar description appeared in Le Petit Journal. "It is difficult to remember that this simple chief, an employee in Saint Louis, with a solid education, who once walked the Paris boulevards in 1883 and who the Parisians now regard as a grand black sovereign."[7]

Mademba's transformation from a lowly but loyal employee of the colonial Post and Telegraph Department into a king fits a powerful and enduring trope: it has a strong resonance with the European fairy tale of the Frog Prince. While Mademba was certainly not an ugly frog and Archinard not a spoiled princess, the emphasis on the ability to see a prince underneath a lowly exterior and the nurturing of loyalty (or love) helped the transformation of the frog into a prince is clearly alluded to in these brief references to Mademba's rise to position of king. The author of the article in the L'Illustration went further than his fellow journalists by planting the idea that Archinard had not merely rendered Mademba's transformation from a colonial employee into a king but that he had "returned [to Mademba] the throne of his forebears."[8] L'Illustration statement that Archinard was merely returning Mademba to his rightful position suggests that Archinard was righting a past wrong and helped disarm the deep paradox of how an agent of Republican France could create a king in its colonial empire.

These articles about Mademba's 1906 visit to France also employed the transformation trope in another way. Mademba was no longer merely the subject of transformation, but the agent of transformations. The first was

---

[5] "Le roi Mademba et l'avenir du Soudan," Les Temps, Oct. 26, 1906. A very similar report with the same misspelling of Sansanding appeared under the title "Un roi cultivateur: l'avenir du Soudan et le culture du coton," in La Lanterne, Oct. 26, 1906.

[6] Le Petit Parisien, Oct. 27, 1906.

[7] Le Petit Journal, Sept. 22, 1906.

[8] L'Illustration, Nov. 10, 1906.

the transformation of Sinsani, "which our adversary Ahmadou totally burned and pillaged during his passage," turning that "once flourishing city into a desert." "Now," wrote *Le Petit Parisien*, "prosperity has returned to the banks of the Niger that were previously devastated."[9] The second transformation was linked to this one and fit the biblical trope of transforming of swords into plowshares.[10] Upon enthroning Mademba, Archinard gave Mademba "five hundred prisoners of war, true bandits, who were not worth the rope to hang them with ... Once made king ... by persuasion Mademba inspired in these rebels a taste for productive work and actually, these former bandits have become good heads of enormous households and good workers who find their incomes in the production of cotton."[11] The author of the *L'Illustration* article echoed this double transformation orchestrated by Mademba. "Without doubt, Sansanding does not compare to the kingdoms of Asiatic sovereigns, but we only need to know that Mademba deserves credit for transforming a population of brigands – the former bands of Samory and Amadou – into intelligent farmers who are devoted to France. For that, Mademba deserves all our appreciation."[12] With only slight variations, the *Les Temps* article reproduced this narrative.

The authors of these articles knew that they had a good story: here was a black king, transformed from an employee of the colonial Post and Telegraph Department into a loyal and devoted sovereign to the French colonial cause, but one who was modest, who spoke a "pure French," and who was capable of transforming a desert into a flourishing region and in transforming hardened bandits into productive farmers and hardworking fathers. Cotton was the reason Mademba was in France and cotton was certainly part of the story about Mademba and his multiple transformations.

Les Temps made cotton central to its article on Mademba. "Once the Association Cotonnière Coloniale began to introduce the production of cotton along the banks of the Niger, Mademba understood immediately the importance of this task." As soon as Governor-general Roume decided against permitting European concessions to lead the campaign for cotton production, "Mademba became the principle agent in the task of persuasion [of African farmers to plant American and Egyptian cotton varieties] and he succeeded beyond our hopes." In the interview with *Les Temps*, Mademba "expressed enthusiasm regarding the results he obtained ... This is a man of affairs who

---

[9] *Le Petit Parisien*, Oct. 27, 1906.

[10] Isaiah 2:4: "They shall beat their swords into plowshares, and their spears into pruning hooks. Nation shall not lift up sword against nation. Neither shall they learn war anymore."

[11] *Le Petit Parisien*, Oct. 27, 1906.

[12] *L'Illustration*, Nov. 10. 1906.

has an intelligence that is clearly superior."[13] *Le Petit Journal* lauded Mademba "who came to France to discuss one of the most important colonial questions: that of the production of cotton in the French Soudan."[14] More importantly, the article argued, the success of Mademba's cotton augers well for the future, "when Soudanese cotton will partially feed French markets and thus render our industry less tributary to foreign importers."[15]

French journalists were clearly taken by Mademba. And Mademba did not hesitate to use the French journalists to promote his own narrative. I know that Mademba had a very pleasant interview with M. Dutey-Harispe of *Le Petit Journal*, since the journalist was identified in the article. Mademba also gave an extensive interview to *Le Petit Parisien*. *Le Petit Parisien* noted that the "history of the ascension to the throne of this sovereign is still poorly known, but it is worth being told." "In a French that was irreproachable," Mademba used this opportunity to lay out the foundations of a hagiography that his son would later embellish.[16] *Le Petit Parisien* quoted Mademba directly as he narrated his story.

> Raised by General Faidherbe in Saint Louis du Sénégal, I was among the first negroes sent to the French School founded by that officer. That institution had the name "School of the Sons of Chiefs and Hostages" and only enrolled the children of those who had made their submission and who were given as a guarantee of their loyalty to the metropole in order for their children to be educated *à la française*. General Faidherbe personally occupied himself with me. He enhanced not only my instruction, but also my education. When I reached the age of adulthood, I entered the post and telegraph service. I constructed telegraph lines with a rifle in my hand. During the revolt of 1880–81, I received the medal of Chevalier of the Legion of Honor. When General Gallieni became governor of the military in the Soudan, I received the title of diplomatic agent and I took command of the auxiliary cavalry during the expedition against the marabout Mahmadou Lamine.

Mademba's story as recounted in *Le Petit Parisien* jumps next to Archinard's repression of Amadou and Mademba's enthornment. Mademba's roles during the decade-long conquest of the Soudan were not elaborated. Some of this missing story between Faidherbe and Archinard appeared in the *Le Petit Journal* article, which in turn did not narrate Mademba's earlier life.

> Mademba was in 1880 employed in the telegraph service in Saint Louis (Senegal). He was taken by General Borgnis-Desbordes to construct the

---

[13] *Les Temps,* Oct. 26, 1906.
[14] *Le Petit Journal,* Sept. 22, 1906. *Le Figaro,* Sept. 28, 1906, used the exact same sentence in its article on Mademba's cotton
[15] *Le Petit Journal,* Sept. 22, 1906.
[16] *Le Petit Parisien,* Oct. 27, 1906. See also Mademba, *Au Sénégal,* 9.

telegraph line and to organize the telegraph service in the Soudan. This was during difficult times, at the beginning of conquest ... Mademba served as chief of partisans, and whose energy, cold-bloodedness, and intelligence became precious to our cause. He displayed all these qualities in 1881 and 1883, when he was in charge of construction, with a rifle in his hand, the telegraph line from Kita to Bamako. In 1885, through tact and skill, he constructed the telegraph lines through Fouta, land of the inveterate Toucouleur [enemy]. Later, General Gallieni, at the time colonel, made Mademba a diplomatic agent. But it was especially from 1890–1893, during the fiery campaigns of Colonel Archinard, today general, that Mademba was given leadership over several thousand Africans [auxiliary troops]. He was wounded at Ouossebougou and he only escaped death by a most lucky break.[17]

In these two interviews in September and October 1906, Mademba planted elements of the narrative of his life that he wanted to present: he was chosen by several different French generals (Faidherbe, Borgnis-Desbordes, Gallieni, and Archinard) for special assignments, many of which were dangerous, but all were challenging; he constructed the telegraph lines with a rifle in his hand, signifying that he was both technically and militarily proficient; he had the ability to lead teams of construction workers as well as African auxiliary soldiers; he was above all loyal to the French cause and was recognized for that through his several Legion of Honor medals; and shared the battlefield with the heroic French military leaders and was wounded on the battlefield. To have shared blood on the battlefield with fellow French officers was a powerful statement of loyalty, which demanded reciprocity.[18] Both of these articles also promoted Mademba's cotton and his role as an agricultural modernizer.

Mademba left France on November 12, 1906. His two-month visit to France was clearly the apogee of his French-facing rehabilitation. And he used his visit well, promoting a particular narrative about his history that continued to resonate, even as he failed to deliver on the promises of a glorious cotton future and a modern, enlightened colonial administration.

Declining Yields and Renewed Controversies

Echoes of the 1899 investigations in Mademba's alleged abuses of power and forced marriages in his household again threatened Mademba's newfound redemption. This new concern began in May 1906, even before Mademba departed for France, but the investigation into these new allegations occurred during Mademba's absence. On May 25, 1906, Sougoule Doucoure wrote to the director of the Native Affairs Department in Dakar that following the

---

[17] *Le Petit Journal*, Sept. 22, 1906.
[18] Mann, *Native Sons*, for his discussion of the "blood debt."

capture of Nioro in 1891, Archinard gave his mother, Cira Doucoure, his younger brother, Diadie, and himself to "*fama* Mademba Sèye of Sansanding." "My mother," Doucoure wrote to the director, "was a princess in Nioro. Mademba forced her to marry him." Doucoure then described the harsh treatment that he and his brother received at the hands of Mademba. When Doucoure first tried to leave Sinsani, Mademba threw him in prison for over a month, during which time he "nearly died of hunger and thirst." "We are not his slaves," Doucoure wrote, yet his mother and younger brother remain against their will in Mademba's palace. "Today," Doucoure argued, "my brother, myself, and my mother wish to go to Nioro in order to escape the poor treatment we receive from *Fama* Mademba."[19] Doucoure's letter was forwarded to Kayes, where Lieutenant-governor Ponty responded quickly because the Doucoure case raised many of the same issues that Abdoul Drame had raised in 1898 that started the 1899–1900 investigations into Mademba's actions in Sinsani. Ponty ordered the Segu administrator to investigate Doucoure's complaint, but cautioned "I know that I do not have to insist that you employ all possible tact and discretion in pursuing this investigation because it raises issues in regard to the personality of the *Fama* and to all the eminent services he has rendered to the French cause."[20] The Segu administrator in turn ordered the Sinsani Resident to investigate this issue.

The Sinsani Resident questioned Doucoure's younger brother, Diadie Doucoure, whom he described as very clean and properly dressed. Diadie told the Resident that "he likes being with the *Fama*, who treats him like a son and there is [therefore] no reason to leave." Diadie also explained that during his spare time, he cultivated a small garden and sold the produce in the Sinsani market for his own benefit. The Sinsani Resident did not question what Diadie may have meant by "spare time," but that term may refer to the free time given to slaves to work for themselves. As to his mother, Cira Doucoure, the Sinsani Resident noted that since she was a "wife of the *fama*, she was not permitted to leave the *tata*." This is also a potentially revealing statement. Did Diadie mean that because his mother was a proper Muslim wife, she was living in purdah or that Mademba did not permit any of his wives to leave? In addition, Diadie told the Sinsani Resident that his brother had a "lively discussion" with Mademba before he left three years before. Diadie concluded that he considers himself a "free man," that he was never incarcerated either in Mademba's *tata* or in prison as his brother alleged, and that he wishes to stay with the *faama* because he is well treated.[21]

---

[19] Sougoule Doucoure, letter to director, Native Affairs Department, Dakar, May 25, 1906, ANM 1 E 219. A similar letter was also sent to the gouv.-gen., see lt.-gouv., letter to admin. Segu, Kayes, Aug. 4, 1906, ANM 1 E 219.

[20] Ibid.

[21] Résident Sinsani, letter to admin. Segu, Sinsani, Aug. 28, 1906, ANM 1 E 219.

Commandant de la Bretsche forwarded the Sinsani Resident's assessment of Dourcoure's accusation to the lieutenant-governor. The lieutenant-governor argued that the Resident's interview with Diadie Doucoure did not constitute an "adequate refutation" of the Doucoure's allegations because he did not interview Cire Doucoure, and ordered him to conduct a "complementary inquiry."[22] De la Bretsche conducted a "long and confidential interrogation" with Diadie Doucoure in Sinsani. De la Bretsche also seems to have interviewed Cire Doucoure, who together with her two infant sons, was "seized" by Amadou after he killed her first husband. Archinard, in turn, gave Cire Doucoure and her two sons to Mademba after his conquest of Nioro. Cire Doucoure became one of Mademba's wives. Cire Doucoure, whom de la Bretsche described as "old and impotent," never sought to leave "furtively" Mademba's household.[23] This negative statement did not, however, constitute positive evidence of Cire Doucoure's desire to remain with Mademba.

Based on this ambiguous evidence, Ponty upon returning from leave wrote to the governor-general that Sougoule Doucoure's allegation this his brother and his mother were being held in "captivity" in Mademba's palace had no merit. Ponty concluded that Diadie Doucoure was some sort of "intimate factotum" of Mademba who "is absolutely free and the administrator of Segou is convinced that he would not stay with *Fama* for a minute against his will." Ponty thus considered this matter closed and almost certainly breathed a sigh of relief that this incident did not morph into another full-scale inquiry into Mademba's behavior toward the members of his household.[24]

The Doucoure threat passed through Sinsani before Mademba returned from his triumphant trip to France. Mademba had ridden his experiments with cotton up a prestige escalator and used his new prominence to recast his story for the French public. Before he left France, he had declared that cotton would be Soudan's bright future and contribute to France's industrial strength by reducing France's dependence upon imported American-grown cotton. Mademba arrived back in Sinsani too late to oversee his cotton production, but he still managed to squeeze out enough cotton to keep his promises alive. Over the following years, however, recurring droughts, the end of slavery, and persistent demand from the local handicraft textile sector eroded the glorious future that Mademba had promised both French advocates of colonial cotton and African cultivators.

---

[22] Lt.-gouv., p.i., letter to cmdt. Segu, Kayes, Sept. 16, 1906, ANM 1 E 219.

[23] Lt.-gouv., draft letter to gouv.-gen., n.p., n.d. [but probably Oct. or Nov. 1906], ANM 2 M 34.

[24] Ibid.

Notwithstanding his late return, Mademba managed to send sixty-seven bales of cotton to France. The ACC's ginning station was up and running in Segu, which facilitated Mademba's exports.[25] The ACC began to spread its risk by establishing ginning stations in other areas of the colony. From Kayes, where cotton production was spreading quickly, the ACC exported 191 bales of cotton and Mademba, also extending his reach, purchased cotton in Koutiala region and sent fourteen bales to France for assessment.[26] The ACC continued to have high hopes for Mademba's cotton and Esnault-Pelterie anticipated that Mademba would be able to deliver five tons of cotton to Le Havre. However, Esnault raised concerns about the persistent irregularity of Soudanese cotton quality.[27] The ACC began increasingly to turn its attention to Koutiala, which it viewed as a region "particularly rich in cotton" and not subject to the periodic droughts and inundations that devastated the cotton fields around Segu. ACC agent, M. Level, who was based in Segu, now "constantly goes to Koutiala."[28] The rains were especially good during the 1909–1910 season and Mademba managed to export 2,500 kilograms of cotton from his fields to France. Mademba's share of the total Soudan cotton exports that year was a mere 7 percent. The ACC noted that Mademba remained "one our principle collaborators at the present time." At the same time, however, the ACC seemed to be cooling its enthusiasm for Soudanese cotton. Charles-Michele Côte, the secretary-general of the ACC, noted at the annual meeting that despite the harvest that year being good, "in the Soudan, we have had lots of disappointments."[29] The 1910–1911 cotton harvest was good and total exports to France from the Soudan reached forty-three tons, but Mademba's share of these exports dropped to 2 percent.[30] Mademba, who was so prominent in ACC reports during the early phase of cotton colonialism, appeared less frequently in the ACC's discussions after 1908. For the 1911–1912 cotton season, the Soudan exported sixty tons and none of the exports were attributed to Mademba.[31] The regional handicraft textile industry remained vibrant and

---

[25] "Nouvelles des Colonies," Séance de Sept. 27, 1907, Comité de Direction, *Bull. ACC* 1907: 198.

[26] "Nouvelles des Colonies," Séance de Nov. 6 and Dec. 18, 1907, Comité de Direction, *Bull. ACC* 1907: 241, 261–262.

[27] Allocution de M. Esnault.-Pelterie, Assemble Générale, Mar. 17, 1908, *Bull. ACC* 1908: 326–327.

[28] "Nouvelles des Colonies," Assemblée Générale, Mar. 11, 1909, *Bull. ACC* 1908: 348–349.

[29] Rapport de M. Charles-Michele Cotes, Assemblée Générale, Mar. 16, 1910, *Bull. ACC* 1910–1911: 533–534, 547.

[30] Rapport de M. Charles-Michele Cotes, Assemblée Générale, Mar. 15, 1911, *Bull. ACC* 1910–1911: 853.

[31] Rapport de M. Charles-Michele Cotes, Assemblée Générale, Mar. 12, 1912, *Bull. ACC* 1912: 293.

TRIAGE DU COTON DU FAMA MADEMBA

Figure 8.2   Women sorting Mademba's cotton, 1905.
(Source: *Bull. ACC* 1905, with permission from the Bibliothèque Nationale de France)

thus local spinners and weavers bid up the price of cotton, which undercut the incentives of cotton producers to sell to the export market (see Figure 8.2).[32]

The ACC did not give up on the Soudan. At a banquet in 1912 for Governor-general William Ponty, who had long been an advocate for Soudanese cotton and for the mission of the ACC, Esnault-Pelterie made a strong case for the need to persist in its joint efforts to promote cotton production in French West Africa.

> In this Soudan, where the experience of cotton growing did not yield the results you expected, where we have experienced some temporary disappointments, I am convinced that with persistent and energetic efforts, we will soon see fields of cotton extending from Podor, on the shores of Senegal River, to Kita and beyond on the vast plains of Niger. We are convinced that

[32] For more detail, see Roberts, *Two Worlds of Cotton.*

this land, since the day it became French, which gave us so much satisfaction from so many points of view, will not disappoint all our hopes.[33]

A serious drought in 1913–1914 damaged the cotton crop in the Segu region, further delaying the grand hopes of the cotton future.[34] Mademba, however, seems to have hedged his bets on the crops that would propel the region's prosperity. By 1908, Mademba was again experimenting with rice and tobacco.[35]

Mademba's shift away from cotton may also have been a response to the changes in his labor force. One of the unintended consequences of Mademba's lauded transformation of his prisoners of war (the horde of brigands) into productive farmers was that these farmers wanted to work for themselves and for their "numerous families," rather than for Mademba. In the previous chapter, I explored the *sofa*'s efforts to escape Mademba's command and to protest the level of obligatory labor that they owed him. The end of slavery, beginning around 1905, further pressured Mademba and the colonial administration to liberate the *sofa* as well as the slaves. By 1908, the exodus of slaves peaked in the Segu and Sinsani region. Increasingly the *sofa* demanded that they should pay taxes on their own accord, thus effectively signifying their status as free peasants. In February 1908, the *sofa* who remained in Sinsani reached a deal to take effect in 1909 that made them responsible for their own taxes, at triple the current rate, as recognition of their new status as independent farmers.[36] Nothing in the archives, however, declared the *sofa* formally free, but the responsibility to pay taxes testified to their new status. The *sofa*'s new freedom not to work for Mademba coincided with the downward trend in Mademba's cotton production. Cotton production required significant labor inputs and Mademba could no longer count on access to large pools of unpaid coerced labor.[37] As Mademba's *sofa* increasingly shifted their labor to support their own households, Mademba was forced to rethink his abilities to continue to deliver on the promises of a bright cotton future. To further complicate Mademba's situation and his abilities to orchestrate his kingdom's economic development, his health deteriorated significantly in November 1910, when

---

[33] Discourse de M. Esnault.-Pelterie, au banquet offert par l'Association Cotonnière Coloniale à William Ponty, Gouverneur Général de l'Afrique Occidentale Française, Feb. 8, 1912, *Bull. ACC* 1912: 322–323.

[34] Communication de M. Level, Agent d'ACC, Assemblée Générale, Mar. 26, 1914, *Bull. ACC* 1912: 585; Rapport de M. Henri Doron, sec.-gen., Assemblée Générale, Mar. 18, 1912, *Bull. ACC* 1912: 14.

[35] Résident Sinsani, Rap. pol., Sinsani, Feb. 1908, ANM 1 E 72.

[36] Résident Sinsani, letter to cmdt. Segu, Sinsani, Feb. 10, 1908, ANM 1 D 102; Cmdt. Segu, letter to Résident Sinsani, Segu, Feb. 24, 1908, ANM 1 D 102.

[37] See also Mademba, letter to M. Bonnel, Sinsani, Sept. 2, 1908, ANM 1 D 102, in which Mademba regrets that he can no longer provide requested labor for M. Bonnel's commercial expedition to Mopti since all of the slaves had become free people.

the commandant of Segu reported that Mademba was "gravelly ill." By December, Mademba was no longer in "danger," but he remained easily fatigued.[38] Mademba did recover, but with some diminished capacity. He next confronted an emerging crisis regarding increasing Muslim militancy in Sinsani.

Unruly Muslims

Following French conquest, Muslims along the Middle Niger valley engaged in rebuilding their communities and participating in the expansion of commerce. The new colonial legal system, decreed in 1903 but implemented in 1905, led to a rearticulation of Muslim identity and a mobilization of Muslims against the proposed reforms. The decree did not recognize the legal status of qadi courts, although qadis were to serve as judges on the new native courts and to adjudicate African disputes and applying African customs. In effect, these reforms made Islamic law merely one of a variety of African customs. Qadis thus served as judges on the new courts often side by side with animist judges.[39] Muslims in the Segu region were deeply opposed to these new courts, where they would likely have their disputes adjudicated by a mixed panel of judges. The Segu administrator wrote in 1905 that Muslims believed themselves "to be superior" to animists and "wanted their cases to be judged by their peers."[40] In 1906, the Segu administrator rotated the Muslim judges in an effort to reduce the "antagonism among judges of different statuses [i.e., customs]" and in order to find more capable judges. Commandant de la Bretesche replaced Omar Ba, who served as both the Muslim assessor and the Arabic translator for the provincial court, because he lacked "independence" by adjudicating a case in which he had an interest, and because he provided a "dangerously specious translation of a legal text." Antagonisms between judges representing different customs persisted well into 1912.[41]

These tensions over who had the authority to judge disputes between Muslims may also have helped to strengthen Muslim identity by more clearly defining the boundaries between believers and nonbelievers and pushing

---

[38] Rap. pol., Segu, Dec. 1910, ANM 1 E 72.

[39] See Roberts, "Custom and Muslim Family Law in Native Courts of the French Soudan."

[40] Rap. sur le fonctionnement des tribunaux indigènes, second quarter 1905, Segu, ANM 2 M 92. See also Rebecca Shereikis, "From Law to Custom: The Shifting Legal Status of Muslim *Originaires* in Kayes and Médine, 1903–13," *JAH* 42 (2) 2001: 261–283 for a discussion of how Muslims responded to a 1912 decree further minimizing their legal status.

[41] Cmdt. de la Bretesche, letter to gouv., Segu, Dec. 6, 1906, ANM 2 M 34; Rap. sur le fonctionnement des tribunaux indigènes, Segu, first quarter 1906, ANM 2 M 92; Rap. sur le fonctionnement des tribunaux indigènes, second quarter 1906, Segu, ANM 2 M 92; Rap. judiciare, 3ème trimestre 1910, Sokolo, ANM 2 D 94.

believers to deepen their knowledge of Islam and Islamic law. In an insightful report written in 1907, Charles Correnson noted that many Muslims in the Segu region who claimed Muslim status thought that they were "absolutely independent from custom" remained nonetheless "ignorant of the rules regarding Islamic law." He pointed to disputes over of inheritance and oath-taking as examples where Muslim practices remained largely dependent upon Bambara or Mande custom. Correnson attributed this synchronism to the mid nineteenth–century conquest and rule by the Umarians, who imposed Islam on their subjects. After the French conquest, "many of these recent converts kept their status as Muslims, but actually only in name." Correnson added that these Muslims' engagement with Islam remained superficial despite the recent increase in Islamic proselytism by marabouts.[42]

By 1909, increased Muslim proselytization began to roil Mademba's kingdom. Mademba had become disturbed by noise emanating from Bozo villages about a marabout from Nioro who was proselytizing primarily among young Bozo men. Under the leadership of this unnamed Nioro marabout, Bozo villages had become sharply divided into two "hostile" camps: on one side were the Bozo elders who remained animists and on the other were the newly converted young Bozo Muslims. Mademba set out on a tour of these Bozo villages in April 1909 accompanied by another marabout, Ibrahima Kamara also called Ibrahima Haidara. In each village, Mademba heard the same complaints from the Bozo elders. "They all complained of arrogance with which their sons are treating them by calling them infidels. These young people now claim to be Muslims and they no longer obey their elders. They also have renounced the paternity of their fathers by taking on Muslim names." Ibrahima Haidara, Mademba's marabout, preached that this behavior by young Bozo Muslims to their parents was "completely foreign," as Islam had always promoted respect for one's fathers and mothers even if they are "idolaters." Mademba went on to explain to the young Bozo Muslims about the dangers of their new found enthusiasm for Islam, that it may be a passing phase, and he counseled them to reconcile with their elders. Mademba ended his report by stating how successful his reconciliation was: "I left everyone happy from this affair. The new Muslims are back at work for their households. As for the marabout, I ordered him to return to Nioro and never again to come to these Bozo villages." Mademba added that "the [French colonial] government has liberated consciousness, but will not tolerate fanaticism on the part of any religious sect." Just to ensure future tranquility, Mademba prohibited the construction of any new mosques unless village leaders and household heads requested new mosques directly.[43] Mademba's strategy was

---

[42] Charles Corresnon, De l'orientation de la justice et des moeurs chez les populations de la région de Segu, Segu, Sept. 5, 1907, ANM 1 D 55-3.

[43] Mademba, letter to admin. Segu, Sinsani, Apr. 23, 1909, ANM 1 B 150.

to bolster the authority of household heads. But it was exactly this generational tension that had found expression through conversion to Islam.

As Correnson had argued in 1907, these new native courts were works in progress. Even though these new courts were to apply "age-old" custom, subtle changes in the nature of the law and legal practice in these new courts were being applied. Correnson had already noted that the African magistrates had to be instructed about France's humanistic principles. "The new judges," wrote the commandant of Segu, "make commendable efforts to assimilate our way of dealing with matters of justice. Except for a few understandable mistakes, we are succeeding little by little in making judgments according to fairness and according to the gravity of the fault." The new African judges were also obliged to adapt to the profound changes to the criminal law. In his report on the status of African customs, the Segu administrator noted that "in the area of criminal law, we have profoundly modified the rules of custom in order to conform to the essential principles of our penal code. The suppression of corporal punishment has obliged us to construct a new type of punishment that will substitute for previously imposed punishments."[44] He was referring to prisons. Despite these gradual changes, the provincial court in Sinsani rendered no judgments since Mademba preferred to reconcile personally all those who brought their disputes before him.[45] Mademba continued to see the native court as his domain over which he sat in his seemingly benevolent role reconciling disputants as long as they conformed to his sense of patriarchal authority as he had expressed it in his apparent reconciliation in the Bozo villages.

In late 1910, Mademba fell gravely ill. He was fifty-eight years old and although he was out of danger by December that year, he remained "very weak."[46] His son, Ben Daoud Mademba Sèye, who resided in Sinsani, took on some of Mademba's administrative tasks, including serving as secretary and court clerk. In May 1911, Governor-general Ponty decreed a formal end to using Arabic in rendering judgments in native courts and in all other formal correspondence. Thereafter, all legal judgments and all minutes taken during court cases were to be taken exclusively in French. Ponty singled out Muslim law, arguing that "despite its special cadre [of experts], it cannot remain outside of the general evolution of our entire West African possessions ... and must harmonize with current necessities and new needs."[47] In so doing, however, Ponty further eroded the standing of Muslim jurists working within the colonial legal system, including those at the province native courts.

[44] Rap. sur les coutumes et institutions juridiques, Segu, 1909, ANM 1 D 206.
[45] Rap. sur la justice indigène, second quarter 1909, Segu, ANM 2 M 92.
[46] Rap. pol., Segu, Dec. 1910, ANM 1 E 72.
[47] Gouv.-gen. Ponty, letter to gouv. Haut-Sénégal-Niger, Dakar, Sept. 18, 1911, ANM 2 M 1. See also Lydon, "Obtaining Freedom at the Muslims' Tribunal."

Although in principle Ponty was committed to the free expression of religion, he drew on long-standing French concerns about militant and pacific Islamic traditions and increasingly sought to surveil and regulate those groups that the French considered militant. Between 1909 and 1911, Ponty issued a series of circulars that grew out of his broader *politique des races* (native policy) in which he sought to curtail the political authority of Muslims by urging his lieutenant-governors to avoid placing Muslims as chiefs over non-Muslim communities, by increasing the surveillance of itinerant Muslim teachers and preachers, and by limiting Muslim judges in native courts in predominantly animist districts.[48]

French conquest and its linked sets of transformations contributed to an era of social, economic, and cultural change. The end of slavery was a crucial component to these processes of change, which led to the exodus of former slaves and the establishment of new communities.[49] Among the new communities being created were "emancipatory" ones associated with Muslim teachers.[50] Nioro, the former capital of the Umarian empire, emerged as a particularly fecund site for the development of these new communities in the decades after the end of slavery. Already in 1906, a leading Tijaniyya cleric, Shaykh Sidi Muhammad al-Akhdar, was arrested for having "incited" Muslims in Banamba among other towns in the Soudan. Before his arrest, Skaykh Sidi Muhammad appointed Shaykh Ahmad Hamallah as his successor in Nioro. Hamallah's teaching encouraged the making of new communities in which established social hierarchies were often undermined, including the relations of masters and slaves, elders and cadets, and men and women.[51]

This wider context might help explain why Mademba turned against Ibrahima Haidara in the summer of 1911. In 1909, Mademba had traveled together with Ibrahima Haidara to help quell the generational tensions in Bozo villages associated with recent Islamic conversion. Sometime between 1909 and 1911, Ibrahima Haidara and his family moved to Nioro. By June 1911, Ibrahima Haidara was back in Sinsani and had surrounded himself with a considerable number of disciples. Without quite explaining why, on June 15, 1911, Mademba arrested Ibrahima Haidara and sixty-five of his disciples and sent them to Segu for house arrest. The commandant of Segu suggested in his

---

[48] Harrison, *France and Islam in West Africa*, 49–56; Benjamin F. Soares, *Islam and the Prayer Economy: History and Authority in a Malian Town* (Ann Arbor: University of Michigan Press, 2005), 55, 73.

[49] Roberts, "The End of Slavery in the French Soudan"; Roberts, *Litigants and Households*.

[50] See especially Cheikh Anta Babou, *Fighting the Greater Jihad: Amadou Bamba and the Founding of the Muridiyya of Senegal, 1853–1913* (Athens: Ohio University Press, 2007) and Sean Hanretta, *Islam and Social Change in French West Africa: History of an Emancipatory Community* (New York: Cambridge University Press, 2009).

[51] Ibid., 62–71; Soares, *Islam and the Prayer Economy*, 63–64, 78–80. The Umarian imprint remained powerful in Nioro as well, Robinson, *Paths of Accommodation*, 155–156.

monthly report that officials from Nioro had requested this action in order to prevent this group from "fomenting new troubles."[52]

Islamic proselytization and the expansion of mosques and Qur'anic schools in Sinsani coincided with these wider transformations of social life and contributed to the heightened tensions there. This was the context in which Mademba's son Ben Daoud started offering French primary education in Mademba's palace. Ben Daoud had attended the White Fathers' school in Segu and then the Lycée of Algiers. He was now back in Sinsani, where besides offering classes, he served as the secretary of Sinsani's provincial court. On December 29, 1911, Moctar Diallo, a marabout and "professor of Arabic," who was born in Segu but living in Sinsani, went to the Sinsani provincial court to file a complaint against Bambo Kone, one of Mademba's griots. According to Diallo, Bambo Kone's son, Fana Kone, stabbed Diallo's ten-year-old nephew, Hamadou Ba, with a knife. Hamadou Ba's injury was not serious, but Diallo was understandably furious and went to Mademba to complain about this act to tell him that it was his intention to pursue a case against Bambo Kone at the court because he was responsible for the acts of his son. Mademba told Diallo to seek out his son, Ben Daoud, the secretary of the native court, in order to file a formal grievance. The native court was actually located inside Mademba's palace in a space that doubled as a school, where Ben Daoud taught classes.[53] Diallo then found Ben Daoud and told him about the incident. Ben Daoud took down Diallo's complaint and asked that he return to the tribunal that evening. Ben Daoud called in Bambo Kone, who gave his testimony that evening. Moctar Diallo and Bambo Kone were both together in the tribunal/school room in Mademba's palace when Ben Daoud summed up the complaint to both parties and then asked them to leave, presumably until the next meeting of the tribunal. Bambo Kone left the tribunal. Diallo obviously misunderstood Ben Daoud's remand of the case to the provincial court. He thus assumed that the case had been heard and that Bambo Kone had not been punished. Diallo was furious. He pulled out his knife and stabbed Ben Daoud twice. Before Ben Daoud collapsed, he hit Diallo in the nose. Everyone fled the room. Samba Dia, who was the court's interpreter, returned and helped Ben Daoud hide elsewhere in the palace. Diallo returned shortly thereafter armed with two rifles. Several men, probably Mademba's attendants, tackled Diallo, disarmed him, and delivered him to Mademba's *sofa*.[54] Luckily for Ben Daoud, Captain Lepoivre,

---

[52] Rap. pol., Segu, July, Aug., and Sept. 1911, ANM 1 E 72.

[53] Procès-verbal, interrogation de Sine Sow, second witness, Sinsani, Jan. 4, 1912, 1911, ANM 2 M 34. This incident made its way up the ladder to the government.-general, telegram lt.-gouv. HSN to gouv.-gen., Bamako, Jan. 22, 1912, and letter procureur-gen. to director Affaires pol., Dakar, Jan. 25, 1912, ANS-AOF M 90. Many thanks to Wallace Teska for locating these files.

[54] Procès-verbal, interrogation de Samba Dia, third witness, Sinsani, Jan. 4, 1912, ANM 2 M 34. Dia served as interpreter at the Sinsani tribunal. Also, Procès-verbal, interrogation de Sine Sow, second witness. Three witnesses – Dia, Kone, and Sow reported that it was

head of the public works division, was in transit in Sinsani at this time and provided first aid. Later that same evening Ben Daoud was transported to Segu, where Dr. Moreus tended to his wounds, which "were very deep, but were not life threatening."[55] On the day of the attack, Mademba wrote to the commandant of Segu informing him that "his son, Ben Daoud, secretary of the provincial tribunal, in the course of his exercising his functions was the victim of an attempted murder by a marabout of Sansanding, named Moctar Diallo ... Moctar Diallo is in preventive custody in prison."[56] Shortly thereafter, Moctar Diallo was transported to Segu, where he was tried before the tribunal de cercle. At his interrogation five days later, Diallo stated that "I did not know what I was doing, but I was inspired by God."[57] "The assailant," wrote the commandant of Segu, "is a Muslim fanatic, who declared that he was inspired by Allah. He was condemned by the tribunal de cercle to three years in prison." The commandant also noted that Ben Daoud was now nearly completely recovered from his wounds.[58]

In January 1913, Ben Daoud was appointed headmaster of the new village school of Sinsani, formally called the Écoles du Fleuve. At the time, Ben Daoud was nineteen years old. He was Mademba's fifth son and he had attended the Lycée of Toulouse from 1904 to 1905 and the Lycée of Algiers from 1905–1911, where he studied Greek, Latin, Arabic, French, history and geography, mathematics, and design. Ben Daoud graduated the Lycée of Algiers with a certificate d'études secondaires, which was equivalent to the "masters" who graduated from the École Normale de Saint Louis. In September 1913, the new school in Sinsani opened with forty pupils, half from Sinsani and half from neighboring villages. In January 1914, Ben Daoud was transferred to Bamako, which was clearly a promotion.[59]

Mademba, who was suffering from another bout of illness in the summer of 1913, wrote to the commandant of Segu that he would try to attend, as he always did, Bastille Day celebrations in Segu, but his health remained quite "precarious."[60] The archival record for Sinsani and from Mademba probably reflected his loss of vigor, since it became very thin after this date. In October 1913, the commandant of Segu noted that the required register of court cases

two men who tackled Diallo upon his return; the commandant of Segu reported that it was women who disarmed Diallo.

55 Procès-verbal, interrogation de Ben Daoud Sy, Segu, Dec. 31, 1911, ANM 2 M 34.
56 Mademba, letter to cmdt. Segu, Sinsani, Dec. 29, 1911, ANM 2 M 34.
57 Procès-verbal, interrogation de Moctar Diallo, Sinsani, Jan. 4, 1912, ANM 2 M 34.
58 Rap. pol., Segu, Jan. 1912, ANM 1 E 72.
59 Inspecteur de l'enseignement, Bulletin d'Inspection, Notes sur les Écoles de village de Sarafere, de Sofara et de Sansanding, Sinsani, Jan. 16, 1913, ANM 1 G 177; Monod, Inspecteur de l'enseignement, Bulletin d'Inspection, École de Sansanding, Sinsani, Mar. 20, 1914, ANM 1 G 177.
60 Mademba, letter to cmdt. Segu, Sinsani, July 7, 1913, ANM B 150.

was not being maintained for the Sinsani provincial court.[61] In July 1914, World War I broke out. The war had significant implications for Mademba as several of his sons were recruited.[62]

Mademba's End and the Rewriting of Mademba

With the outbreak of the war in 1914, Mademba's health deteriorated. "*Fama* Mademba Sy has repeatedly given us serious concerns about his health. Even though he has retained his lucid spirit, he has little strength to engage effectively with his administrative functions of his state, which have been taken over by his two sons Ben Daoud and Madiouma Sy."[63] The recruitment of many French administrators for the war in France and efforts to recruit Africans for the colonial army increased tensions throughout the colony. During the early phase of the war, some Africans responded positively to the calls for recruitment and for contributions to the war effort to protect "the mother country." In some households, former slaves used recruitment as an opportunity to renegotiate their status within the household as they volunteered to join the army in place of the masters' sons.[64] But as the war dragged on, tensions over recruitment increased. The 1915–1916 recruitment was the largest yet and it came fast upon the devastating famine of 1914–1915. The Segu administrator noted that recruitment targets were not being met in part because household heads were increasingly reluctant to let their sons be recruited lest their ability to produce subsistence be undermined. "We have to resign ourselves to the inevitability that a certain number of sons remain in their households," he argued.[65] Pressure to meet recruitment goals led to increased intervention by the colonial administration, which in turn stimulated a wave of recruitment rebellions through French West Africa. The first serious recruitment rebellion broke out in Beledugu in October 1915 and spread quickly to Banamba, Nioro, and Gumbu. The largest occurred in Upper Volta in November and December 1915. From there, the recruitment rebellion spread westward into the recently created San district in the Baninko region east of Segu.[66] In March 1916, more than a thousand armed men attacked French military recruiters.[67]

---

[61] Rap. pol., Segu, Oct. 1913, ANM 1 E 72.

[62] See Echenberg, *Colonial Conscripts;* Marc Michel, *Les Africains et la Grande Guerre: L'appel à l'Afrique (1914–1918)* (Paris: Karthala, 2003); Mann, *Native Sons.*

[63] Rap. pol. annuel, Segu, 1918, ANM 1 E 72.

[64] Roberts, "The End of Slavery in the French Soudan"; Klein, *Slavery and Colonial Rule in French West Africa*, 205–222.

[65] Rap. Pol., Segu, n.d. [but June 1917], ANM 1 E 72.

[66] Mahir Saul and Patrick Royer, *West African Challenge to Empire: Culture and History in the Volta-Bani Anticolonial War* (Athens: Ohio University Press, 2001), 104; Michel, *Les Africains et la Grande Guerre*, 55–61.

[67] Rap. pol., Segu, Mar. 1916, ANM 1 E 72.

Mademba's own household did not hesitate to heed France's call. Eight of Mademba's nine sons enlisted in the colonial army. The three eldest – Racine, Abd-el-Kader, and Cheikh – joined the earliest. They were followed by Madiouma, Abidine, and Ben Daoud, who had enlisted but were rejected, probably due to their failure to pass the physical evaluation.[68] Still in the military in 1919 were Racine, Abdoul Karim, and Lamine as well as Abd-el-Kader. Abd-el-Kader was a decorated soldier, having been wounded in action, and had risen to become a lieutenant in the Colonial Infantry. Abd-el-Kader would eventually be promoted to captain and commander of a brigade, the highest rank available to Africans.[69] Based in Dakar, Racine was a lieutenant charged with the provisioning of African troops. Lamine was a sergeant. Mademba's son Cheikh, an underlieutenant in the Colonial Infantry, died in battle on August 22, 1918, defending the metropole.[70] Abderramane, Mademba's youngest son of these nine, was probably still too young to be recruited.[71]

On July 25, 1918, Mademba succumbed to his chronic ailments and old age in Sinsani.[72] He was sixty-six years old. Lieutenant-governor Brunet advised the governor-general of Mademba's death and asked him to alert Abd-el-Kader Mademba to his father's passing, to express his condolences, and to ask if Abd-el-Kader had any particular views on how to organize Mademba's funeral. Although not the eldest, Abd-el-Kader had become the most promin-ent of Mademba's sons. Not only had he become one of the very few African officers in the Colonial Infantry serving in France, he was decorated for bravery. According to Marc Michel, Abd-el-Kader was a protégé of General Mangin, the architect of the "black force" to support metropolitan France's interests. Abd-el-Kader was also one of four African officers who participated in Blaise Diagne's famous 1918 recruitment drive, demonstrating to potential African recruits just how far up the military hierarchy African soldiers could rise.[73] As the elected representative of the Four Communes in France's National Assembly, Diagne skillfully negotiated France's need for additional African troops by being named Commissaire of Recruitment, with a rank and

---

[68]   Racine Mademba, letter to lt.-gouv., Kouluba, Oct. 18, 1918, ANM 2 D 87.

[69]   Echenberg, *Colonial Conscripts*, 38–42.

[70]   Chef du Cabinet Militaire, telegram to gouv.-gen., Paris, Oct. 26, 1918, ANS-AOF 15 G 176. See the article in *Le Figaro*, Aug. 13, 1918. Cheihk was still alive during this final battle of the war.

[71]   Liste des enfants du *Fama* Mademba, in Abd-el-Kader Mademba, letter to gouv.-gen., Paris, May 2, 1919, ANS-AOF 15 G 176; family tree included in Décès du *Fama* Mademba, 1918–1919, ANM 2 D 87.

[72]   Lt.-gouv., telegram to gouv.-gen., Kouluba, July 27, 1918, ANS-AOF 15 G 176; Mademba suffered from kidney failure and rheumatism, Rap. pol. annuel, Segu, 1918, ANM 1 E 72.

[73]   Abd-el-Kader Mademba, letter to gouv.-gen., Paris, May 2, 1919, ANS-AOF 15 G 176; Michel, *Les Africains et la Grande Guerre*, 68–69.

accompanying pomp and ceremony equivalent to a governor-general. Diagne's recruitment mission in 1918 yielded the highest number of African recruits since the outbreak of war.[74] Abd-el-Kader's participation in Diagne's recruitment drive added to his prestige and linked him to another powerful patron.

Abd-el-Kader and Racine were in Dakar when news of Mademba's death arrived. Governor-general Angoulvant wrote back to Brunet that he was saddened by Mademba's death and that Mademba remained "a most wonderful example to his compatriots of loyalty and pure devotion to France." The governor-general asked that Brunet pass his condolences to Mademba's family in Sinsani and that Brunet should consult with Mademba's family about the colonial government's participation in Mademba's funeral.[75] The minister of Colonies specifically requested that the governor-general express his condolences to Abd-el-Kader, whom he referred to as "Lieutenant Indigène Mademba," and not to forget to recognize the significant services Mademba rendered during the pacification of the Soudan and his active role in promoting the economic development of the colony.[76]

Even as the funeral was being planned, Mademba was "secretly buried according to custom" on the morning of July 27.[77] Lieutentant-governor Brunet probably meant according to Islamic practice, which requires burial as soon as possible within twenty-four hours. The Native Affairs deputy administrator, M. Dionisi, who raced to Sinsani to serve as representative of the Segu administrator, reported that the burial took place amidst a "calm population" and without incident.[78] The funeral – as opposed to the burial – was therefore to be a more formal affair, with the pomp and ceremony befitting a loyal servant of France, an officer in the Legion of Honor, and a king. Since Mademba was also a king, his death immediately opened up a struggle over the status of Mademba's kingdom and the potential problems associated with succession to that high office. Even as Mademba's health was failing, the issue of succession was already raised by the Segu administrator in January 1918. "The question of the future of the États de Sansanding is necessarily postponed during the life of *Fama* Mademba. Whenever the succession is open," the Segu administrator wrote, "it is certain that the decision will be difficult and will require careful and firm action on the part of the commanding officer."[79] Part of the problem was that no matter the high regard the French had for Mademba and his administration, "we [the colonial government] remain very poorly informed about what occurs in the region of

[74] Johnson, *The Emergence of Black Politics in Senegal*; Echenberg, *Colonial Conscripts*.
[75] Gouv.-gen. telegram to lt.-gouv., Dakar, July 27, 1918, ANS-AOF 17 G 18.
[76] Min. Col., telegram to gouv.-gen., Paris, July 31, 1918, ANS-AOF 15 G 176.
[77] Lt.-gouv., telegram to gouv.-gen., Kouluba, July 27, 1918, ANS-AOF 15 G 176.
[78] Segu administrator, telegram to lt.-gouv., July 29, 1918, Segu, ANM 2 D 87.
[79] Rap. sur l'organisation du Cercle de Segu, Segu, Jan. 16, 1918, ANM 1 E 72.

Sansanding."[80] As plans for the official funeral were underway, so too was a swirling set of intrigues regarding the succession to the *faama*-ship, the distribution of Mademba's estate, and the provision of subsistence for Mademba's widows, orphans, and surviving servants. The lack of clarity on these questions brought forth a host of claimants for shares of Mademba's estate and created opportunities for those with long-standing grievances against Mademba to seek their revenge.

As Abd-el-Kader and Racine made their way from Dakar to Sinsani to help plan the funeral and to organize Mademba's estate, Lieutenant-governor Brunet was thinking about the administrative problems that Mademba's death initiated. Brunet proposed that the colony provide a pension for Mademba's widows and underage children, just as the French administration had done when Aguibu, the *faama* of Bandiagara, died in 1907.[81] The thornier issue was the status of Mademba's kingdom. Just a week after Mademba's death, Brunet sent a telegram to Governor-general Angoulvant marked "extreme confidential" in which he proposed a transitional solution. "The death of *Fama* Sansanding opens the question of what those who established this charge [the kingdom of Sansanding] had in mind regarding the succession. They never considered it more than a personal reward that was to disappear with the beneficiary." Yet in 1893, Archinard more or less promised dynastic succession of Mademba.[82] Brunet here seemed to foreclose the idea of succession to the *faama*-ship. On the other hand, he considered that there may be value in maintaining "the enclave that constitutes the États de Sansanding" because of its long-term commitment to the economic development of the colony. Brunet then floated the idea that Lieutenant Abd-el-Kader be seconded from active duty to serve as the Resident of Sansanding according to established administrative regulations governing the position. Brunet further argued that Abd-el-Kader's military training and proven devotion to France "offer us the best guarantees that we will not encounter other pretenders to the political succession of the *Fama*."[83] The minister of Colonies signaled his "interest" in examining whether Mademba should be "replaced as *Fama* of Sansanding with equal authority" by a member of his family or by another candidate. The minister framed this particular succession as part of a solution to the broader problem of the general lack of confidence the French had in their African chiefs, and avoiding direct French administration.[84]

---

[80] Rap. pol. annuel, Segu, 1918, ANM 1 E 72.

[81] Lt.-gouv., telegram to gouv.-gen., Kouluba, Aug. 3, 1918, ANS-AOF 15 G 176. For more detail on Aguibu, see Saint-Martin, "Un fils d'El Hadj Omar."

[82] See Chapter 4.

[83] Lt.-gouv., telegram to gouv.-gen., Kouluba, Aug. 3, 1918, ANS-AOF 15 G 176.

[84] Min. col., telegram to gouv.-gen., [Paris], Aug. 7, 1918, ANS-AOF 15 G 176. Copies of the minister's and Brunet's telegrams were also sent to the "Commissaire République" who was Blaise Diagne.

Governor-general Angoulvant put a forceful and unambiguous stop to these proposals. Angoulvant wrote that he "believes that we must seize this opportunity to make clear that we will not tolerate the creation of heredity fiefs in any form. Designating a son of Mademba to succeed him is contrary to the fundamental principles of our native policy and the policy of suppressing all large kingdoms." Angoulvant further ordered Brunet to take necessary measures that will make Sansanding into a "normal administrative regime and under the rule of native chiefs judiciously chosen from within the principal indigenous families."[85] Brunet backed down and wrote back that he was "completely in agreement" to the suppression of the États de Sansanding and prevention of the establishment of any hereditary fiefdom. He persisted, however, in pushing the idea of establishing a Residence in Sinsani that would report to Segu as an administrative solution to the problem of overseeing such vast districts.[86] Shortly after this flurry of communication, Brunet departed to officiate at Mademba's funeral in Sinsani.

Mademba's official state funeral was held on August 17, 1918, amid the requisite pomp and ceremony. Racine and Abd-el-Kader had arrived a few days earlier. In their capacities as lieutenants in the colonial army, they led the honor guard composed of the company of *tirailleurs* based in Segu, who were under the command of Captain Lanransan. The Segu administrator, the deputy administrator, who was serving as Resident of Sinsani, and various other military and administrative leaders were in attendance as Lieutenant-governor Brunet gave the eulogy. Brunet's eulogy followed the hagiographic outline of Mademba's rise to prominence among the military heroes of French conquest. Brunet admitted that he had heard much of this from Mademba directly when he first met Mademba in Sinsani in May 1918. At that time, Brunet was traveling with Blaise Diagne during his recruitment mission. No doubt, Abd-el-Kader was along on this mission, since he was part of Diagne's entourage.

> On that hot evening in May, when we were vaguely aware of the presence of the river, the *Fama* recalled in a deep voice the events in which he took part that were part of the moving adventures of conquest and the early organization [of the colony], that history that now took on a new vitality because it came from one of the authors and witnesses of this heroic period. Because here was a collaborator and a companion in arms of the great soldiers of the Soudanese period: Borgnis-Desbordes, Gallieni, Humbert, Bonnier, Combes, Archinard. [Mademba] had shared the exhaustion and the risks of the columns that carried our prestige and our colors from the escales of the Senegal to the banks of the Niger and established French domination on the ruins of the empires of Mamadou Lamine, Amadou, and Samory.

[85] Gouv.-gen., telegram to min. Col. and lt.-gouv., n.p., Aug. 12, 1918, ANS-AOF 15 G 176.
[86] Lt.-gouv., telegram to gouv.-gen., Kouluba, Aug. 12, 1918, ANS-AOF 15 G 176.

Brunet continued by noting that Mademba was a "pioneer" in making French conquest possible by laying the telegraph lines so necessary to the military effort. He then traced Mademba's rise into the inner circles of the French military leadership, moving seamlessly from telegraph technician to political agent to military leader of African auxiliaries. "On multiple occasions, Mademba demonstrated [to the French military leaders] his utility through his leadership, his knowledge of African languages and of African mentalities, and the certainty of his information." Of course, Brunet did not fail to mention that at the battle of Ouossebougou on April 26, 1890, Mademba was "gravely wounded by a shot to his chest" as he commanded a troop of African auxiliaries. Brunet cited more of Mademba's exploits and Archinard's reward to Mademba of the "title of *Fama* over the newly created États de Sansanding" and Archinard's letter of investiture that charged Mademba with "administering his subjects following their customs, but with a spirit of justice, humanity, and disinterest in order to improve the well-being of the people below you and not the self-interests of those who govern." Brunet acknowledged the 1896 award to Mademba of the rank of officer in the Legion of Honor, but glossed over the troubles surrounding Mademba during the siege of Sinsani from 1891 to 1893 and the alleged abuses of power from 1896 to 1900. Instead, Brunet celebrated Mademba's initiatives with colonial cotton and his sons' roles in the war. "The war arrived, and he gave five of his sons to the Fatherland." Brunet ended by invoking the language Mademba had used during his 1906 Paris interviews. "This son of Senegal, brought up by Faidherbe, who by the natural attraction of his heart and by his sense of filial gratitude, he attached himself and expanded around him the cult of France . . . And this fierce devotion to France lives on in his sons."[87]

Brunet finished his eulogy and the dignitaries left. The intrigues, however, did not take long to begin. When Racine and Abd-el-Kader arrived in Sinsani a few days before the funeral, they convened a "family" gathering. I do not know exactly what transpired at this gathering, but it almost certainly included planning for the funeral, an assessment of Mademba's estate, and a discussion about the welfare and support of Mademba's widows and underage orphans. I also know that Mademba did not leave a will or any similar testament describing the distribution of his assets. Because Mademba's estate was not merely a family affair but one that touched on his role as king and as long-term colonial employee, Racine, as the eldest son and therefore the first in line to succeed his father as head of the household, invited Deputy Administrator Dionisi, now serving as Sinsani Resident, to attend these discussions. Racine wanted Dionisi to attend all family discussions because, in the absence of clear

---

[87] "Les obsèques du *Fama* Mademba, Discours du Lieutentant-Gouverneur," *JOHSN*, Sept. 1, 1918, 414.

indications of how Mademba wished to divide his estate, he wanted Dionisi to have the power of attorney in order to secure the official French validation for the distribution of the estate and to assure the "absolute authenticity" of the inventory of the estate. The first family gathering took place on August 15, 1918. Dionisi, accompanied by his interpreter, took part in all family discussions regarding Mademba's estate. Racine described the month-long collaboration with Dionisi as "extremely valuable." After having "resolved all the questions my presence required," Racine left Sinsani to return to his official position in Dakar. "Having conferred the further management of our affairs to my three brothers whose military service no longer required them to leave the family home, I left behind me a situation that was clean and clear." Racine here referred to his brothers Madiouma, Ben Daoud, and Abidine.[88] Racine did not mention his brother Abd-el-Kader.

By early September, a preliminary inventory of Mademba's estate revealed that he had left 63,325 francs in cash, some unspecified herds of livestock, four buildings in Saint Louis and in Kayes, and several unimproved lots in Segu and Kayes. In addition, the estate also controlled Mademba's palace and the *foraba* [Bambara: big field] in Sinsani. Lieutenant-governor Brunet estimated that this estate would be divided among Mademba's nineteen children, of whom five were still minors.[89] Brunet had earlier raised a concern that Mademba's fortune was actually far more "precarious" than previously assumed.[90] Mademba's declining health over the previous decade, the departure of his coercible labor, and the demands of a huge household had certainly taken a toll on his wealth. Brunet raised the issue of a pension to support Mademba's many wives and the minor children and pointed to the precedent of such a pension for Aguibu's widows and orphans. Brunet noted that the pension for Aguibu, who died in 1907, was set at 9,000 francs annually and was reduced gradually to 5,000 francs.[91] Governor-general Angoulvant wasted no time in approving Brunet's proposal, although he did not counter with any specific amount.[92] The status of the pension and the pool of Mademba's dependents eligible to participate remained part of what was becoming a contentious and "delicate" issue. But first back to the intrigues.

By September 15, when Racine left Sinsani, he was convinced that all of the big issues regarding Mademba's estate and its division had been clarified. By October 18, when he wrote his letter to Lieutenant-governor Brunet, the accord he had assumed was solid had already frayed. As soon as he left Sinsani, "certain persons did not remain inactive. Above all were griots from

[88] Racine Mademba, letter to lt.-gouv., Dakar, Oct. 18, 1918, ANM 2 D 87.
[89] Lt.-gouv., telegram to gouv.-gen., Kouluba, Sept. 6, 1918, ANS-AOF 15 G 176.
[90] Lt.-gouv., telegram to gouv.-gen., Kouluba, Aug. 12, 1918, ANS-AOF 15 G 176.
[91] Lt.-gouv., telegram to gouv.-gen., Kouluba, Sept. 6, 1918, ANS-AOF 15 G 176.
[92] Gouv.-gen., telegram to lt.-gouv., n.p., Sept. 18, 1918, ANS-AOF 15 G 176.

all parts of Haut-Sénégal-Niger, under the pretext of offering condolences at Sansanding, actually arrived with the intention of receiving presents. But they received nothing from me." Racine found the griots annoying. However, there was another group of malcontents who posed a more serious threat. This group, "holding grievances long contained, pursued political vengeance against our family. This is the case of the interpreter for M. Dionisi, whose father was considered a dangerous person and was expelled from Sansanding by our father. M. Dionisi, the Resident, must surely have known this since the reasons for the expulsion formed part of a report addressed to the Segu administrator." Racine did not specify what these intrigues were, but he noted that its purpose was to "reduce our situation in the land." By "reducing our situation," Racine almost certainly meant permitting others to claim parts of Mademba's accumulated wealth. Racine accused Dionisi of "being too complaisant to the authors" of these intrigues. Racine further accused Dionisi of meddling in the "private affairs of our family" and of holding up the delivery of the formal mandate of the estate, which "is absolutely indispensable in order to authorize repairs to our buildings, revise the leases, and pay and collect debts."[93] Racine's letter made its way up the administrative ladder to the governor-general, who ordered Brunet to issue "urgent instructions" for the inheritance to be regulated in a way that "respects the family of an excellent servant of France" while also moving "progressively to place the region of Sansanding under a normal administrative regime" and eliminating any possibility of "abuse on the part of those engaged in intrigues" against the family.[94] In a subsequent letter, Angoulvant elaborated his interpretation of those with "personal ambitions" who wished to put "in peril the resources of the family of a former chief." Angoulvant noted that disputes over Mademba's estate were "particularly delicate" were made more complex because of the size of this "very numerous family." Regulating these disputes required the "special attention of a competent court with the necessity of proceeding with extreme prudence by applying scrupulously the relevant customs that regulate succession and that will avoid any decision that might involve the consideration of interested persons." The most important part of Angoulvant's letter, however, had less to do with the distribution of Mademba's estate but with the status of Mademba's kingdom. "In renouncing a successor to the *Fama*, we have put to end a political situation that constituted an anachronism in French West Africa."[95] Angoulvant felt obliged to reiterate his position on ending the kingship of Sinsani because Abd-el-Kader had started his own political campaign to be appointed as Resident of Sinsani, an idea originally proposed by Lieutenant-governor Brunet.

---

[93] Racine Mademba, letter to lt.-gouv., Dakar, Oct. 18, 1918, ANM 2 D 87.
[94] Gouv.-gen., telegram to lt.-gouv., n.p., Oct. 23, 1918, ANS-AOF 15 G 176.
[95] Gouv.-gen., letter to lt.-gouv., [Dakar], Oct. 26, 1918, ANS-AOF 15 G 176.

Racine was clearly eager to leave Sinsani and return to Dakar. Abd-el-Kader, however, lingered in Sinsani and over the still unresolved issues of Mademba's estate, the pension for his father's household, and the succession to the *faama*-ship. Abd-el-Kader seems to have gotten a taste for prestige and celebrity not only because of his increased status as a high-ranking officer wounded in action in France but through his role in Blaise Diagne's recruitment entourage. Abd-el-Kader claimed that Lieutenant-governor Brunet had proposed the idea of becoming Resident directly to him, although when this occurred is not clear.[96] He clearly did not know or chose to ignore Angouvlant's firm rejection of this proposal. In October 1918, Abd-el-Kader drew on his own patronage network in France by sending telegrams to General Archinard and Blaise Diagne in which he urged his patrons to help him secure this position. Abd-el-Kader was sufficiently shrewd to frame his request not as a promotion for himself but out of a sense of duty to Sinsani and to the legacy of his father, which was being undermined by the current Resident.

> After agreement with my brothers, the Governor [Haut-Sénégal-] Niger knows my affection for Sansanding and proposes to second me from my military duties to become Resident until the end of hostilities. This proposal has strong approval from the Minister and corresponds to views expressed by Dakar. Since the death of the *Fama*, we are in a difficult and false situation [in Sinsani] due to the awkwardness of the current Resident.[97]

Abd-el-Kader's patrons most likely responded positively to his efforts since the minister of Colonies wrote to Governor-general Angouvlant asking whether "official information" that Abd-el-Kader was being considered as Resident of Sansanding "as compensation for the services rendered by his father" was true.[98] Angouvlant wrote back that rumor has absolutely no foundation and cited his telegram of August 12, 1918, in which he had already decided that in the interests of France, of the African subjects of Sinsani, and of Mademba's family, the kingdom of Sinsani would be "ended and placed under a regular administrative regime." Angouvlant also signaled to the minister that Racine Mademba "disavows all political intrigues," almost certainly referring to his brother. That same day, Angouvlant wrote to Lieutenant-governor Brunet, demanding to know the source of this "questionable information" regarding the proposal to promote Abd-el-Kader as Resident. Angouvlant reiterated to Brunet his opposition to this idea.[99]

---

[96] Abd-el-Kader Mademba, letter to gouv.-gen., Paris, May 2, 1919, ANS-AOF 15 G 176.

[97] Abd-el-Kader Mademba, telegram to General Archinard, Sinsani, Oct. 7, 1918, Abd-el-Kader Mademba, telegram to Deputy Diagne, Sinsani, Oct. 9, 1918, ANS-AOF 15 G 176.

[98] Min. Col., telegram to gouv.-gen., Paris, Dec. 4, 1918, ANS-AOF 15 G 176.

[99] Gouv.-gen., telegram to min. Col., Dakar, Dec. 8, 1918, gouv.-gen. telegram to lt.-gouv., Dakar, Dec. 8, 1918, ANS-AOF 15 G 176.

What message Abd-el-Kader received regarding his efforts to appeal directly to the minister of Colonies is not clear, but by early February 1919, he again sought the patronage of Blaise Diagne to return to France because his "current situation in Soudan has become unhappy."[100] Part of Abd-el-Kader's unhappiness may have stemmed from the still unresolved issues of the division of Mademba's estate and the status of the États de Sansanding. The problem with the division of the estate stemmed from the absence of Mademba's will or a clear set of instructions. On the other hand, as a Muslim, the division of Mademba's estate would have been governed by Islamic laws of inheritance in which shares of the estate were determined by lineage, gender, and marriage. One of the problems facing those trying to adjudicate the estate was to determine who was whom in Mademba's large household. In order to finally determine the order of inheritance, Abd-el-Kader brought the problem to the subdivision tribunal in Sinsani on February 26, 1919. Because of the absence of a qualified court secretary in Sinsani, the case was shifted to Segu, where the Sinsani judges presided over the case and Konila Diarra, serving as secretary, established a complete list of heirs. The judgment rendered "obeyed Muslim law." Crucial in this judgment was the fact that Abd-el-Kader sought to "admit only four wives as the heirs out of the 82 wives of his father." The court only recognized Garassy So, Bana Cisse, Nazika Tonko, and N'Tande Coulibaly as the legitimate wives.[101] According to Muslim law, a man can only have four wives at any one time, although the number of concubines in a household could be much larger.

The drama, however, continued. The lieutenant-governor responded to the Segu administrator's letter that the judgment of the Sinsani subdivision tribunal regarding Mademba's estate was "null and void" in part because Abd-el-Kader had no legal standing in the Sinsani subdivision tribunal because he was a French citizen and as such he could not bring disputes before a native court.[102] And second, already months before, Racine Mademba had received the official proxy of Mademba's estate drawn up by Resident Dionisi, which had resulted in "an amicable division of the cash found at the death of the *Fama*." Obviously, Abd-el-Kader was not pleased with this "amicable division" and thus pursued his legal options further. The lieutenant-governor was "surprised" that such an important case was not examined by a European

[100] Abd-el-Kader Mademba, telegram to Commissaire Général Diagne, Segu, Feb. 4, 1919, gouv.-gen., telegram to lt.-gouv., Feb. 4, 1919, Dakar, lt.-gouv., telegram to gouv.-gen., Kouluba, Feb. 15, 1919, min. Col., telegram, no addressee [but likely gouv.-gen.], Paris, Feb. 17, 1919, ANS-AOF 15 G 176.

[101] Admin. Segu, letter to lt.-gouv., Segu, Mar. 1, 1919, ANM 2 D 87.

[102] Abd-el-Kader Mademba became a naturalized French citizen on Aug. 14, 1916, which prevented him from bringing disputes before native courts. Min. Col., letter to min. War, Paris, Aug. 19, 1918, Dossiers personnels (Abd-el-Kader Mademba), SHD GRE 7 YE 882.

functionary who could have explained to the African judges the procedure to follow.[103] Abd-el-Kader, however, might not have been completely self-serving in this case regarding the further distribution of Mademba's estate. Abd-el-Kader may have been seeking to secure the welfare of at least some members of his father's extended household. He pursued this agenda through his persistent requests to increase the size of the pension promised by the French administration to Mademba's heirs.

Once back in Paris, Abd-el-Kader seemed to have yet another change of heart regarding his decision to leave Sinsani. Perhaps he longed for the respect and authority he imagined that his father commanded. In any case, in early May 1919, he wrote two simultaneous letters to the governor-general and to the minister of Colonies. Abd-el-Kader began

> France has put her confidence for 58 years in my deceased father, the *Fama* Mademba. She gave him the honor of having his own land – the États de Sansanding, which he administered for over 28 years following the policies of the government and following the principles that he was given. Today, now that he is no longer with us, I come, very respectfully to request in the name of the population of Sansanding my nomination as Resident of Sansanding in order to continue my father's tasks to deepen the ideas of civilization and to prove to the entire French West Africa that France retains always the confidence of the descendants of those, the first ones, who without restrictions, without ulterior motive, to give their body and soul to the triumph of France's cause.

Abd-el-Kader invoked the now standard narrative of Mademba's heroic participation in the conquest of the Soudan, his loyalty to the French military commanders, and their recognition and respect for Mademba's service. He detailed how Archinard had rewarded Mademba with the grant of the *faama*ship of Sinsani in 1891 and how in 1893 Archinard decided to "substract a portion of his domain" to Aguibu in order to facilitate Mademba's rule in Sinsani. This was, of course, a selective reading of Archinard's intentions, but it served Abd-el-Kader's narrative. "Always loyal and devoted to the French cause, my father understood the reasons that led to these decision and declared himself satisfied with the measures designed to help the wellbeing of the colony." Abd-el-Kader mentioned the numerous medals and honors Mademba received, but left out the troubles Mademba caused the French administration in 1891–1893 and from 1896 to 1900. "Since the day my father entered into his functions [as king] until the month of July 1918, the Government has always demonstrated its satisfaction with my father's manner of serving." Abd-el-Kader noted that just before his death, the Commissaire of the Republic Blaise Diagne, Governor-general Angoulvant, and Lieutenant-

---

[103] Lt.-gouv., telegram to Admin. Segu, [Kouluba], Mar. 24, 1919, ANM 2 D 87.

governor Brunet discussed nominating Mademba for the rank of commander in the Legion of Honor.

Having made the case for Mademba's long and loyal service to France, Abd-el-Kader then volunteered to continue the tasks his father began. Abd-el-Kader was careful to anticipate criticism of what appeared to be dynastic succession.

> It is in this manner that the formula for political succession corresponds to our time: the era of creating *Famas* is over. I thus request that you, M. the Governor-general, join this idea in order for us to safeguard a situation created by France that still to this day exerts an influence that ties this land to Greater France. In their rustic mentality, the Bambara of Sansanding should not doubt for a minute that the sons of the *Fama* have been abandoned by the Government. The old servants, the contemporaries of my deceased father should be assured by our example that the future will be happy for their families.

With that, Abd-el-Kader again respectfully reiterated his request that the governor-general nominate him, even provisionally, as Resident of the États de Sansanding. Abd-el-Kader stressed that his qualifications rested not merely on his lineage. Instead, he listed his classical education at the Lycée of Algiers, where he graduated in 1912 before returning to Sinsani to help with his aging father, only to join the *Tirailleurs Sénégalais* right when the war broke out. He noted that he served with "frozen feet" in Champagne during the winter of 1914, was severely wounded at Dardenelles in 1915, and served with distinction in the Somme and at Verdun. He listed the citations he received from his military superiors and how he was recruited by Deputy Diagne to serve on his 1918 recruitment mission, during which he alone recruited more than 300 sons of chiefs from among the Mossi.

Abd-el-Kader also used this letter to press the governor-general on the still unresolved pension issue. Abd-el-Kader appreciated the pension of 9,000 francs that the colony of Haut-Senegal-Niger had already approved, but he pushed for an increase.

> My father left 20 old women and 18 children of whom only two (Racine as an agricultural engineer and myself as a lieutenant in the Colonial Infantry) are capable of supporting ourselves in the condition respecting our status and education. In addition, we have in our charge 10 old *sofa* or my father's companions-in-arms who have also participated in the last campaigns of conquest and most recently in 1915–1916 in police actions in the Volta region. All of these men have been wounded in action and have received citations and medals of honor. Since 1893, they have also served as the police in the États de Sansanding.[104]

---

[104] Abd-el-Kader Mademba, letter to gouv.-gen., Paris, May 2, 1919, ANS-AOF 15 G 176. He sent the exact same letter to Blaise Diagne.

Abd-el-Kader also attached three lists in his letter: a list of Mademba's eighteen children, a list of his twenty-one wives (despite his statement earlier in the letter that there were only twenty wives), and a list of the ten old *sofa*. All of this was designed to bolster his request for an increased pension for Mademba's household. Abd-el-Kader sent the exact same letter to Blaise Diagne, the deputy of Senegal, with the request that he forward the letter the minister of Colonies. In his covering note to the minister, Diagne argued that Abd-el-Kader's request for an increased pension was "incontestably justified." Diagne did not, however, comment on Abd-el-Kader's request to become the Resident of Sinsani.[105]

Abd-el-Kader's persistence in pushing the administration to increase the annual pension for Mademba's surviving household paid off. After some back and forth between Paris, Dakar, and Kouluba, Governor-general Angoulvant agreed to increase the pension from 9,000 to 15,000 francs, payable out of the general budget of the Haut-Sénégal-Niger colony. This increased pension was designed to "support primarily [Mademba's] wives and *sofa*."[106] The new lieutenant-governor of Haut-Sénégal-Niger agreed to this charge, but asked in response if this pension would at some point expire. The new governor-general replied that the current decision did not envision a date at which the pension would be reduced or eliminated, choosing instead to kick this decision down the road. On October 11, 1919, the governor-general and the lieutenant-governor enacted a formal decree authorizing this pension to the heirs of *Faama* Mademba.[107] As part of his campaign for increased support for Mademba's household, Abd-el-Kader also sought to secure better administrative positions for his younger brothers: Ben Daoud, Abidine, and Madiouma. All three had been trained at the Lycée of Algiers. Abd-el-Kader wanted Ben Daoud to be admitted into the general administrative service of French West Africa and that Abidine and Madiouma be advanced to clerks in the Treasury Department given their competence in French. The director of Personnel Services for French West Africa examined these requests. In Ben Daoud's case, he already possessed a "superior metropolitan diploma and a certificate in pedagogy" and was already employed in the Education Department of the Haut-Sénégal-Niger colony. The director declined the petition to employ Abidine and Midouma in the Treasury Department

---

[105] Commissaire Général des Effectifs Coloniaux, letter to min. col., Paris, May 2, 1919, ANS-AOF 15 G 176.

[106] Gouv.-gen., telegram to min. Col., [Dakar], June 19, 1919, ANS-AOF 15 G 176.

[107] Lt.-gouv., telegram to gouv.-gen., Kouluba, Sept. 18, 1919, gouv.-gen., telegram to lt.-gouv., Dakar, Sept. 30, 1919, decree 1311, Haut-Sénégal-Niger, Oct. 11, 1919, ANS-AOF 15 G 176.

because both needed to have the requisite diplomas as identified in a recently updated decree.[108] It was clear that patronage worked only so far, particularly in a world increasingly organized by a semblance of regularity and bureaucratic order.

The archival record is silent on any further efforts by Abd-el-Kader to seek dynastic succession. Abd-el-Kader obviously relished the pomp and ceremony that accompanied royalty. While in Paris in 1919, Abd-el-Kader did not hesitate to present himself as an African prince and did not seek to dissuade others of his royalty. In an article on General Mangin in 1919, Paul Adam referred to Abd-el-Kader, the son of *Faama* Mademba, as a "young prince of the Niger," who was recruited as a simple *tirailleur*, but who rose to become lieutenant in the Colonial Infantry and a knight in the Legion of Honor.[109] In a retrospective article on African troops during World War I, Alfred Guignard described how Blaise Diagne surrounded himself with "brothers of his race" during his recruitment mission.

> These were young men belonging to the first families of our West Africa, former students of our lycées, recruited as simple tirailleurs during their mobilization, but today they are officers of the sword, experienced, honored, legionnaires [of Honor], such as the prince Abd-el-Kader Mademba, a delicate poet of his times, and his brothers, the sons of the old king of Sansanding, our loyal friend of six decades.[110]

Abd-el-Kader basked in this recognition. To help celebrate Bastille Day in 1922, the government of French West Africa recruited twenty-seven "grand chiefs of French West Africa. Officers or knights of the Legion of Honor, holders of numerous other honors, these small sovereigns, several of whom are the most formidable and are today the most loyal collaborators of our colonial government have enjoyed the admiration of the Parisian population." Greeting them was a delegate from the French West African government, a deputy from the National Assembly, a delegate from the Ministry of Colonies, a military officer, and Captain Abd-el-Kader Mademba.[111]

---

[108] Chef du Service du Personnel, note to Chef du Service des Affaires Civiles, Dakar, Oct. 15, 1919, ANS-AOF 15 G 176.

[109] Paul Adam, "Un Grand Chef: Le Général Mangin," *La Revue Hebdomadaire*, Oct. 18, 1919, 297. Already in 1915, when Abd-el-Kader was a mere corporal, Paul Adam referred to him as a "young prince," "La Reverie du caporal," *Le Galois*, Feb. 19, 1915.

[110] Alfred Guignard, "Les troupes noires pendant la guerre," *Revue des Deux Mondes*, 89, May 1, 1919, 877.

[111] "Grands Chefs d'Afrique occidentale à Paris," *Le Petit Journal*, July 10, 1922. In 1919, Abd-el-Kader had a falling out with Diagne and with the military. Abd-el-Kader published two critical articles on Diagne, which resulted in a military reprimand, although he recovered and went on to have an important military career. For more detail, see Dossiers personnels (Abd-el-Kader Mademba), SHD GRE 7 YE 882.

The Final (Almost) Revision of Mademba

Of all of Mademba's surviving sons, Abd-el-Kader took on the task of writing Mademba's life. All of his sons who had obtained the educational requirements for admission had been trained at least partially at the Lycée of Algiers. Several had studied with the White Fathers in Segu and some had been sent to the College de Saint Louis du Sénégal prior to attending Lycée of Algiers. Three (Gustave, Souleymane, and Abdoulaye) apparently could not tolerate the "climate" in Algiers and returned to Saint Louis.[112] At the Lycée of Algiers, students were offered a classic French education. Abd-el-Kader pursued this coursework up to the second level of the Bac, before he returned to Sinsani in 1912. With the outbreak of the war, Abd-el-Kader, together with his brothers Racine, Cheikh, Abdoul Karim, and Lamine, enlisted.[113] Ben Daoud, Abidine, and Madiouma were rejected probably for medical reasons. Of these three, only Ben Daoud graduated the Lycée of Algiers with a certificate in pedagogy. Ben Daoud went on to have a long career in the Soudanese Education Department. Racine, the eldest son, went on from Algiers to France for further training as an agricultural engineer. In January 1918, Racine was appointed to serve as military attaché to the French West African government in Dakar in the section devoted to the supply of subsistence and provisions for the African troops serving in the metropole.[114] Racine continued in colonial governmental service as an agricultural engineer, based in Bamako, until around 1926, when he entered the commercial sector full-time.[115] Both Ben Daoud and Racine published articles on their respective areas of expertise.[116] Given their education and scholarly inclinations, why did Abd-el-Kader emerge as the author of Mademba's biography? And would a biography of Mademba written by an agricultural engineer or a school teacher have been different than one authored by a career military officer?

The aftermath of the devastation and sacrifice of the war ushered in a period of memorialization. Monuments were erected and speeches given honoring the sacrifice of individuals as well as collectivities.[117] Shortly after the armistice, General Archinard and Deptuy Blaise Diagne established a committee – Les Amis des Troupes Noires – to raise funds to commission a monument to

---

[112] Mademba, *Au Sénégal*, 109.

[113] Abd-el-Kader Mademba, letter to gouv.-gen., Paris, May 2, 1919, ANS-AOF 15 G 176.

[114] *JOAOF*, Jan. 31, 1918.

[115] *JOAOF*, Aug. 9, 1926.

[116] See, for example, Ben Daoud Mademba, "La dernière étape d'un conquérant: Odyssée des dernières anées du Sultan Ahmadou de Ségou, racontée par son cousin et compagnon d'infortune Mohammadou Hassmiou Tall," *Bulletin du Comité des études historiques et scientifiques de l'AOF* 1921 (3) July–Sept.: 473–480; Racine Mademba, "Les céréales d'été en Égypte," *L'Agronomie coloniale* I (12) June 1914: 166–174.

[117] For more context, see Pierre Nora, ed. *Lieux de mémoire* (Paris: Gallimard, 1984–1992).

the "heroes of the Black Army" that fought for France. Of the 200,000 African soldiers recruited, 130,000 fought on the European front; nearly 30,000 died. By 1922, Archinard and Diagne's committee had raised sufficient funds to commission two copies of a statue designed by Paul Moreau-Vauthier celebrating the African soldiers of Mangin's Force Noire in their defense of France. In 1924, ceremonies were held in the French city of Reims, where African soldiers helped defend the city, and in Bamako, the capital of the French Soudan, from which the majority of African soldiers in the Force Noire had been recruited.[118] The end of the war also brought forth nostalgia for the heroes of French conquest of empire. As Archinard was busy raising funds for the "heroes of the Black Army," he also began raising fund to memorialize Gallieni.[119]

Abd-el-Kader was obviously caught up in the excitement of the nostalgia for this era. In 1922, Abd-el-Kader was promoted to captain, thus helping to break the glass ceiling for African officers. Writing to Archinard in April 1924, in response to a pamphlet Archinard had sent him in which Archinard praised the "disappeared founders" of French West Africa and the *Tirailleurs Sénéglais*, Abd-el-Kader wrote that he was pleased that their memories would be perpetuated in Bamako. "It was to the Niger that you decided, my General, on the heels of Borgnis-Desbordes, that our land should be forever French. It was there, that you said to our fathers: to serve France, that is to serve humanity." Such service to France, he continued, "became the most precious part of our patrimony." "The times may have changed," he continued, "but the sons [of this glorious period] have the same faith as their fathers."[120] It could be that this postwar nostalgia contributed to Abd-el-Kader's inclination to memorialize his father as part of this wider enthusiasm for commemoration. Not insignificantly, Abd-el-Kader penned this letter to Archinard from stationary emblazoned with "Bibliothèque des Officiers, Place de Frejus." This library for officers at the major French military base at Frejus was certain to have a rich collection of reports and memoires written by the heroes of the French conquest of the Soudan. Given the pervasive sense of nostalgia and the new-found celebration of empire, could Abd-el-Kader have resisted the draw of these memoires that celebrated his father's role in conquest and colonization?

[118] Wikipedia, "Monument aux héros de l'Armée Noire," https://fr.wikipedia.org/wiki/Monument_aux_h%C3%A9ros_de_l%27Arm%C3%A9e_noire. See also Cuttier, *Portrait du colonialism triomphant*, 535. The base of the two statues differed, however. The one in Reims stood atop a base designed to look like a Western Sudanese *tata*, while the one in Bamako stood atop the French military heroes, including Archinard. In 1940, the Germans destroyed the monument in Reims.

[119] Cuttier, *Portrait du colonialism triomphant*, 536.

[120] Abd-el-Kader Mademba, letter to Archinard, Frejus, Apr. 4, 1924, SHD Papiers Réquin (Mademba letters to Archinard) 1 K 108.

Abd-el-Kader wrote again to Archinard in March 1925 while he was en route to Madagascar for his new posting, thanking him for exchanging photographs.

> I thank you from all my heart, my General, for myself and for my son, who I wish to raise in the spirit, not only of France – he is French – but of the Fatherland ... [I wish to raise him] in the spirit of the great chiefs who, after having conquered the land through force of arms, but also through their hearts, have given us the flag and confided us with representing them as the leader of the Blacks.

It is not completely clear what Abd-el-Kader was driving at in this passage, but it suggests that France was increasingly delegating military and political authority to black African officers and administrators. Abd-el-Kader would shortly be promoted to brigade commander and the leader of black troops. For the first time in this letter, Abd-el-Kader refers to himself not only as the son of the *faama* of Sansanding, which he had already invoked in numerous letters, but as the grandchild of Amadu Shehu, thus the great-grandson of Al Hajj Umar. In the biography of his father, which he published in 1930, Abd-el-Kader noted that after the conquest of Segu in 1890 and Nioro in 1891 in which the harem of the rulers was divided, Mademba married Jenuba Oumou Tall, the daughter of Amadu and that he was born of that union.[121] Abd-el-Kader certainly liked being referred to as a "prince," as he was in the press during the early 1920s. Perhaps his invocation of his heritage from the rulers of the Umarians may have bolstered this part of his self-image, although it remained paradoxical since the Umarians were only three decades before the inveterate enemies of the French.

Following his posting to Madagascar late in 1926, Abd-el-Kader sought and received permission to spend part of his vacation in the Soudan, where he would shortly begin another posting at the military base in Kati. Writing from Segu, Abd-el-Kader informed Archinard about his visit to Sinsani and to his father's tomb. Abd-el-Kader found all those in his family who remained in Sinsani well and that his father's succession, which had been "a source of conflicts," was amicably resolved. He noted that all of his father's real property has been sold for 500,000 francs, most of which his brother Racine had invested in a commercial house in Bamako. After noting that his own financial situation was somewhat challenged, Abd-el-Kader wrote that "Racine has succeeded very well in the Soudan. At the moment, he sits on a small fortune that will continue to grow because of the economic development of the land."[122] Abd-el-Kader only slightly begrudged his brother. Brothers of different

---

[121] Abd-el-Kader Mademba, letter to Archinard, Tananarive, Mar. 24, 1912, SHD Papiers Réquin (Mademba letters to Archinard) 1 K 109; Mademba, *Au Sénégal*, 40–41.

[122] Abd-el-Kader Mademba, letter to Archinard, Segu, Oct. 17, 1926, SHD Papiers Réquin (Mademba letters to Archinard) 1 K 108.

mothers in polygynous households often had rivalries. "Despite our different ancestors," Abd-el-Kader wrote of his brother, whom people described as a "millionaire," Racine offered "only kindness to my wife and myself. Every Sunday, he puts his motorcar at our disposal." He also told Archinard that "From time to time, I receive visits of other members of my family, which is now totally dispersed. No one remains in Sansanding."[123] Abd-el-Kader spent the next two years in Kati together with his wife and their son, where he served as commander of a brigade. Whether in Kati or nearby in Bamako, Abd-el-Kader likely consulted with visiting family members and Mademba's old servants as he prepared to write his biography.

The late 1920s and early 1930s were an especially fecund time to reimagine and reassess French empire and the men who created it. Empire had proven itself crucial to the metropole in terms of men to fight on its battlefields, commodities crucial to supply the war effort, and in less tangible things like glory of military successes. More statues were built and speeches given. Archinard benefitted from this resurgence of interest in empire and in conquest. His long career had been marred by periodic political censures that often left him in a political and administrative wilderness. Archinard's prominence in the resurgence of interest in empire helped resurrect his image as the hero of African conquest. In the late 1920s, plans were underway to celebrate the centenary of French conquest of Algeria in 1930 and to celebrate the military's role in colonization at the International Colonial Exposition in Paris to be held in 1931. The year 1929 marked the cinquantenaire of Borgnis-Desbordes's start of military conquest in the Soudan. As one of the architects of conquest, Archinard played an important role in the committees and spectacles celebrating the French conquest of West Africa.

Several books were in production to celebrate the French empire, including the multivolume *Histoire des colonies françaises et l'expansion de France dans le monde,* edited by Gabriel Hanotaux and Alfred Martineau.[124] This series, which was published in 1929, consisted of six fat volumes, including one dedicated to Africa. In 1931, Jacques Méniaud, published a massive two-volume history of the first fifteen years of conquest of the French Soudan entitled *Les Pionniers du Soudan: Avant, Avec, et Après Archinard, 1879–1894.*[125] Méniaud's book was a celebration of Archinard and the military's role in French colonial expansion. Former Governor-general Ernest Roume's preface to Méniaud's book lauds the author's meticulous research in original documents. Roume argued that Méniaud was especially well positioned for this task since he spent most of his career in the regions that he

---

[123] Abd-el-Kader Mademba, letter to Archinard, Kati, Dec. 31, 1926, SHD Papiers Réquin (Mademba letters to Archinard) 1 K 108.

[124] Gabriel Hanotaux and Alfred Martineau, eds., *Histoire des colonies françaises et l'expansion de France dans le monde* (Paris: Société de l'histoire nationale and Plon, 1929).

[125] Méniaud, *Pionniers.*

wrote about and that he knew many of the principle actors personally. Most importantly, Roume argued, "every one of his assertions is based on authentic and indisputable documents."[126] Standards of citation and references to "indisputable documents" were rather looser in the hands of amateur historians of the 1930s than what we are now used to, but at least Méniaud often gives the reader a general reference if not a note that we could trace back directly to the source in question.[127]

Archinard died in 1932, but he was still alive when Méniaud's book appeared. The very next year, designed to celebrate the cinquantenaire of Bosgnis-Desbordes's arrival in Bamako in 1883, a formal National Committee under the titular leadership of Presidents of the Republic Paul Doumer and Albert Lebrun was established. The actual work of the committee fell to Secretary-general Jacques Méniaud and to Assistant Secretary-general Commandant Abd-el-Kader Mademba, "the great grandson of El Hadj Oumar." Abd-el-Kader's role on the committee carried significant symbolic weight. "Unique in history, the sons of the emperors and kings whose peoples were conquered by the French, these indigenous notables of French West Africa have spontaneously associated themselves with this tribute to the two great workers of its colonial expansion."[128] The National Committee's task was to fund two statues, one of Borgnis-Desbordes and the other of Archinard, to be erected in Bamako and Segu, respectively. It could be that this was the first time that Méniaud and Abd-el-Kader had served together or that they even knew each other, but the worlds of a high-ranking Soudanese soldier and a former high-ranking Soudanese administrator, who were both in Paris, must have overlapped. Abd-el-Kader must have known about Méniaud's historical project on Archinard. But even if they did not overlap, Abd-el-Kader's interest in writing his biography of Mademba was certainly piqued by the waves of commemoration and nostalgia for the heroic time of the conquest and the establishment of French colonialism in the Soudan.

In late 1930, Abd-el-Kader Mademba published a long article entitled "Au Sénégal et au Soudan Français" in the *Bulletin du Comité d'Études historiques et scientifiques de l'Afrique occidentale francaise* in 1930.[129] Several months later in 1931, *Au Sénégal et au Soudan Français* was published as a slender

---

[126] E. Roume, "Préface," in Méniaud, *Pionniers*, vol. 1, vii–viii.

[127] For context on the peculiar history of footnotes, see Anthony Grafton, *The Footnote: A Curious History* (Cambridge, MA: Harvard University Press, 1997).

[128] "Pourquoi ce Cinquantinaire," *Le Monde Colonial Illustré*, 124, Dec. 1933, 180.

[129] *Bulletin du Comité d'Etudes historiques et scientifiques de l'Afrique occidentale française* XIII (2) Apr.–June 1930: 100–216. Included in this article is a letter from Archinard to Abd-el-Kader dated Oct. 16, 1930, which suggests that the publication date of this issue – Apr.–June – was nominal.

book in exactly the same format as it had appeared in the previous year.[130] Abd-el-Kader dedicated his book to General Archinard, "who gave to France: an empire, the Soudan; an army, the *Tirailleurs Sénégalais*," and to Battalion Commander Goetzmann of the Colonial Infantry, "who always commanded the Blacks as they wished to be commanded: with a spirit of justice, of humanity, and of disinterest that placed the well-being of the people above the personal satisfactions of those who govern." Archinard, in turn, sent Abd-el-Kader a letter that served as a preface. "My Captain, I have read with much interest and passion your work, 'Au Sénégal et au Soudan – le *Fama* Mademba'. In writing this, you have brought to the memory of your father a monument worthy of him to all those who, like me, have known him, appreciate him, and loved him, we are grateful to you." Archinard went on to restrain himself from making even the mildest of criticism of Abd-el-Kader's work "because it would make [*Faama* Mademba] lose something of his peculiar flavor," which Archinard did not elaborate. Archinard noted that "in occupying the Soudan, France not only enlarged itself territorially, but she enlarged herself morally by augmenting the number of her sons and capturing their hearts. Your pages of history will certainly be appreciated and it is with all my heart that I congratulate you for having written them."[131]

Abd-el-Kader dedicated his book to the memory of his father "Le *Fama* Mademba-Sy," his brother "the Under-Lieutenant Cheikh Mademba-Sy," his uncle "the Captain Mahmadou Racine-Sy," interpreter first-class "Amadi Coumba-Sy," and to his sons Cheikh-Claude Mademba-Sy and Racine-Charles-Mangin Mademba-Sy, and to his daughter Myriem-Josette Mademba-Sy. What is striking in these dedications was the reference to the patronym Mademba-Sy. In the formal, colonial legal documents, including those dealing with his death, Mademba is referred to simply as Mademba or using his patronym Sèye. During the course of his reign as *faama*, Mademba was sometimes referred to as Mademba Sy or Mademba Si. The shift in spelling of his patronym is not insignificant. Near the beginning of his biography, Abd-el-Kader notes

> it was 1847 that marks the beginning of the loyalty of the Mademba-Sy family towards France ... M'Baye-Sy, father of Mademba, was of the Torodo tribe, who did not admit that there was any other prophet other than Mohammad. Entering in a struggle with al hajj Umar, he preferred to seek refuge in Saint Louis, near Faidherbe, who had proclaimed, in the name of France, the respect of all religions.[132]

---

[130] Mademba, *Au Sénégal*. In the following discussion, I will refer to the book version rather than the article version, even though they are exactly the same.

[131] Archinard, letter to Abd-el-Kader, Villiers-le-Bel, Oct. 16, 1930, reprinted as a front piece in *Au Sénégal*.

[132] Mademba, *Au Sénégal*, 8–9.

Abd-el-Kader's *Au Sénégal et au Soudan Français* is a work of hagiography shaped by the context in which he produced it. This was a time of heightened nostalgia and fevered memorialization of a heroic past in the quest of empire and the grandeur of France. It was also written by a loyal son, who was a decorated career military officer, whose own sense of self was shaped both by his own military exploits and by his thwarted ambition to succeed his father. But it also bears the stamp of filial loyalty that has deep roots in West Africa cultures, where "no child shall speak ill of his parents."[133] Unsurprisingly, *Au Sénégal et au Soudan Français* reflected the now standard event-driven narrative of Mademba's rise from a telegraph clerk to a leader of men to the inner circle of trusted advisors to the French military leaders, during conquest in which he earned their loyalty and respect and was rewarded by Archinard by being named *faama* or king of Sinsani. I do not know anything about when and how Abd-el-Kader wrote his history, but he clearly relied on published accounts, letters written to Mademba that likely were found in Mademba's palace, and oral histories. Nearly a quarter of this slender book appears in direct quotes. Sometimes the source is identified, but most often it is not. Footnotes occasionally appear, but they are merely explanations of terms used in the text. There are no citations of the kind we would now expect from a work of history. Abd-el-Kader included in his book photographs of several letters written to Mademba. Abd-el-Kader also notes that some of the events and stories he used came from Mademba's own memories, probably mostly stories that Mademba had told his sons. Abd-el-Kader also cites oral narratives recited by the interpreter Amadi Coumba-Sy.[134] In terms of historical substance, this book is very much as Archinard described it: a monument to the heroic work of an African deeply committed to French conquest and colonization. Missing from this book, as we would expect for a work of hagiography, is any sustained discussion of Mademba's alleged misdeeds and abuses of power. Abd-el-Kader refers in passing to the "intrigues . . . by malevolent people" that led to Mademba's house arrest in Kayes from November 1899 to October 1900. Instead, he quotes at length Lieutenant-governor Ponty's letters to Mademba exonerating him of his alleged abuses of power and then jumps quickly to Mademba's award of an agricultural medal for his promotion of Soudanese cotton.[135] Abd-el-Kader concluded his story of Mademba with long quotes from Lieutenant-governor Brunet's eulogy at Mademba's funeral in August 1918.

---

[133] I heard this refrain numerous times as I conducted oral history on household tensions and divorce in particular. I was not successful in getting my elderly informants to corroborate the evidence I had from court cases.

[134] See for example, Mademba, *Au Sénégal*, 13, 24, 42.

[135] Mademba, *Au Sénégal*, 104–111.

History is never settled. We are constantly engaged with reassessing the past as we probe ever more deeply into historical sources. We know that few historical sources are ever purely "authentic and indisputable" as Governor-general Roume suggested. We also know that we understand history and probe its meaning through the prism of the present. Mademba's story will be rewritten many times to come, at least I hope so.

Conclusion

On April 8, 2014, Claude Mademba Sy died at the age of ninety. As his father, Abd-el-Kader Mademba Sy, and his grandfather, Mademba Sèye, before him, Claude served loyally his two fatherlands, France and Senegal. Born in Versailles in 1923, Claude was heir to a rich tradition of family service to the state.[1] While studying law in Tunis, where his mother had resettled and remarried following the death of Abd-el-Kader in 1932, Claude joined the Allied military forces when Germany invaded. Rising through the ranks of *Tirailleurs Sénégalais*, just as his father had done, Claude served admirably in the battles to liberate France. Because of his service to France and because of his abilities to lead, Claude was rewarded by being sent to Saint-Cyr for advanced military training. He continued to serve France in Indochina and Algeria and, like his father, became captain and battalion commander. Upon Senegal's independence in 1960, Léopold Senghor invited Claude to return to Senegal to help remake the colonial troops into the new nation's army. Claude was next promoted into the diplomatic corps of the new nation and served as Senegal's ambassador to Zaire (Congo), Yugoslavia, Italy, and Austria. Claude eventually joined the UN's diplomatic cadre and served the UN's atomic agency in Austria and in South Africa before his retirement. Even in retirement, Claude took up the campaign to pressure France to increase the paltry pensions that African veterans received from their service to France during World War II. In recognition of his services to France, in 2012, Claude Mademba Sy was awarded the Legion of Honor's Grand Officer medal.[2]

---

[1] Service to the state has long been a vehicle for Africans to promote themselves and their families. In precolonial Asante, for example, bureaucratic skills were often inherited from fathers to sons. See Ivor Wilks, "Aspects of Bureaucratization in Ashanti in the Nineteenth Century," *JAH* 7 (2) 1966: 215–232 and T. C. MacCaskie, *State and Society in Precolonial Asante* (Cambridge: Cambridge University Press, 1995). Claude Mademba Sy is the same person as Cheikh-Claude Mademba-Sy. Sometime in the course of his life, he slightly modified his name to be Claude Mademba Sy.

[2] "Claude Mademba Sy, tirailleur exemplaire," http://africamix.blog.lemonde.fr/2007/10/25/claude-mademba-sy-tirailleur-exemplaire/; see also "La mort de Claude Mademba Sy, grande figure des tirailleurs sénégalais," *L'Opinion*, Apr. 9, 2014, and "Claude Mademba Sy, doyen des tirailleurs sénégalais, est mort," *Jeune Afrique*, Apr. 9, 2014. Several of these

There is no question that Claude Mademba Sy was a national hero and a war hero. There is no question that Claude's father, Abd-el-Kader Mademba Sy, was a hero of World War I and served France loyally, rising as major in the *Tirailleurs Sénégalais*. And there is no question that Claude's grandfather, Mademba Sèye, served France loyally and occasionally heroically during the early phase of colonial conquest and colonial rule in the French Soudan. But to serve the state loyally and to become a hero does not absolve us of the need to probe more deeply into the complexities of human behavior. And to identify flaws in human behavior does not simply demand that we reassess the individual's reputation; instead, it is part of the historical craft to situate individuals and their actions within larger contexts. That has been the task of this study.

As I have argued in this study, I approached this study of Mademba with considerable trepidation. I had long encountered Mademba as part of my research into the social history of the French Soudan and Mademba has appeared in several of my previous studies. Part of my wariness of focusing too much on an individual was my strong belief that history is made by ordinary people struggling to achieve justice and equity as they themselves defined it. Ordinary people, like heroes, make history out of the structures of power and the opportunities that cracks in those structures afford them. Given the nature of our historical records, we know more about heroes than ordinary people. Thus, I turned to this detailed study of Mademba not as a study of a hero but as a historian more concerned with what Mademba can tell us about the nature of colonialism, about power, and about the struggles against power during the early phase of French colonialism in the Soudan.

Mademba tells us a great deal about these structures of power, about the challenges to them, and about the strategies men and women used to navigate these changes. Mademba became a "hero" in no small measure due to the bargains of collaboration through which those in subaltern positions demonstrated their loyalty to superior powers and are rewarded for their actions. The rewards for such bargains were manifold and include power, prestige, and wealth. Not all loyal subalterns became kings, as Mademba did, but all benefitted from these bargains. Such bargains, however, persisted only as long as the structures of power remained intact. When they shifted, the bargains made must be reassessed and reasserted or they crumbled. Mademba faced these shifting bargains as colonialism in the French Soudan changed from

obituaries actually confused Claude's grandfather with Mamadou Racine Sy. See also Echenberg, *Colonial Conscripts*, 182–183 fn. 89.

Archinard's model of indirect rule to French efforts to impose a more robust system of the rule of law and administrative regularity.

Changes in colonialism thus formed a central argument in this study. The three nested investigations into Mademba's alleged abuses of power and crimes from 1899 to 1900 refracted the uneven process of attempting colonial reform and efforts to implement a civilian rule of law. That Mademba was ultimately cleared of these charges testified to the power of those bargains of collaboration that brought him to power in the first place; these investigations also revealed that these bargains were fraying. Structures of power only occasionally change precipitously. Recognizing that these structures of power were actually changing, even if not radically, provided Mademba with the opportunities to remake himself, which he did by promoting himself as an indigenous modernizer. Promoting cotton for export to France became the vehicle for Mademba's abilities to ride the waves of metropolitan interest in colonial sources of raw material and to mitigate the potential challenges to his anomalous position within the colonial state. Mademba made excellent use of his visit to France in 1906, where he was celebrated as the model of an enlightened indigenous leader and as a close collaborator of France's mission to develop her colonies. Mademba took the opportunity of his celebrity to promote a new image of himself by recasting his own history for local newspapers. Upon the return to his kingdom, however, Mademba's promotion of a bright cotton future flamed out as his army of coerced labor that worked his cotton fields revolted and sought their independence.

Mademba's 1906 efforts to remold himself after his critical encounter with the rule of law investigations of 1899–1900 are a reminder of Mademba's long history of refashioning himself. Mademba's revising of himself reflects the theme of bricoleur discussed in this study. Drawing creatively on seemingly disparate aspects of changing cultures in the "middle ground" of recently created colonial spaces, Mademba's bricolage was himself. Emerging from both Qur'anic schools and Faidherbe's *école des otages*, Mademba then joined the colonial state as an entry-level post and telegraph clerk. After languishing for nearly a decade in a small telegraph outpost south of Rufisque, a fortuitous promotion sent him to the newly created military command in the French Soudan, where he became the head of a telegraph building team. As head of this team, Mademba wanted a uniform to reflect his new status, but such uniforms were normally not available to African civilian employees. With the support of his French military patrons, Mademba succeeded in getting his uniform. As Mademba built the telegraph that helped the colonial armies in their conquest, Mademba also deepened his loyalty to the French military command and tested his capacity for leadership in mounting the first of many military missions. In 1891, Colonel Archinard, the French military commander to whom Mademba had proven his loyalty and his service rewarded

Mademba by making him king (*faama*) in a newly conquered region of the French Soudan that had never had kings before. From a telegraph clerk and occasionally leader of African auxiliary forces, Mademba remade himself as king in a tradition of kingship that he had himself invented. Because Mademba had no legitimate claim on kingship and because Mademba's actions as king were inconsistent with regional practices, these actions contributed to a widespread revolt in 1891–1892 that necessitated French military action to rescue Mademba from his besieged fortress in his newly created kingdom. The bargains of collaboration were tested, but they held. Instead of removing Mademba as *faama* as Archinard had done to another king he had established at Segu, he admonished Mademba, diminished the size of his kingdom, but left him enthroned.

In the intervening years from 1892 to 1899, Mademba remade himself periodically, but Janus-faced: one side faced the French in which he promoted himself as a benevolent and enlightened African ruler intent on promoting his sons through French schools and in experimenting with new crops; and the other side faced his subjects in which he deepened his autocratic nature, amassed a huge hareem of girls and women whom he fancied regardless of their age, marital status, or consent, and coerced his subjects to grow cotton. Mademba's African subjects began to voice their complaints to the French colonial administration, which led to initial investigations into his alleged abuses of power in 1896–1897. The evidence of Mademba's abuses of power were compelling, but French colonial commitments to the rule of law remained elastic. Mademba had survived yet another challenge to this authority.

Mademba's abilities to remake himself with an eye toward specific audiences caught the attention of Félix Dubois in 1894–1895, who described Mademba's attributes and attire as a strange bricolage of French metropolitan and invented African traits. "I admit," Dubois wrote, "that he has, just a small resemblance, to a king of the theater who appears to have just left the storeroom of the accessories. At the very least, however, he avoids looking ridiculous in vest and jacket."[3] Mademba's ability and willingness to remake himself periodically demonstrates his skills as a bricoleur. Mademba's skills to play both to different audiences and to changed audiences were part of his success in withstanding challenges to his power and authority. In the end, Mademba was undone not by the rule of law or the promotion of bureaucratic regularity but by old age. Mademba died just before the end of World War I in 1918. But even in death, Mademba has been made over again. In his eulogy, the lieutenant-governor of the Soudan drew on many of the stories that

---

[3] Dubois, *Tombouctou la mystérieuse,* 91.

Mademba himself had presented to the French press in 1906.[4] His son, Abd-el-Kader Mademba, continued this tradition of remaking Mademba in his 1931 book on his father's heroic life. My version of Mademba presented here is and should be only another phase in our understanding of how Africans lived the great transformations of colonialism.

---

[4] "Les obsèques du *Fama* Mademba, Discours du Lieutenant-Gouverneur," *JOAOF*, Sept. 1, 1918, 414.

BIBLIOGRAPHY

Archival Sources

(List of Archival Series cited. For more detail on documents, see footnotes)

Archives Nationales de France d'Outre-Mer (ANOM)

AOF: I-1, I-4, I-6, VII-2
Comité Française pour l'Outre-Mer: 183
Direction du Contrôle: 894, 903
Dossiers personnels (Mademba): 2862, (Danel) 3540
Sénégal et dépendances: IV-8, IV-9, IV-73 bis, IV-77, IV-79 bis, IV-84, IV-90, IV-93, IV-95, XII-117
Soudan: I-1, I a, I-2, I-2 bis, I-6, I-7, I-11, III-4, VII-1, VIII-2, XIII-1, XIII-13, XIX-1

Archives Nationales du Mali (ANM)

Series B: Correspondances politiques: 70, 77, 83, 150, 165
Series 1 B: Correspondances politiques: 150, 172
Series 1 D: Rapports et études: 15, 55, 102, 127, 206
Series 2 D: Rapports et études: 87, 94, 102, 105
Series 5 D: Recensement: 43
Series 1 E: Rapports politiques, cercles: 71, 72, 74, 113, 177, 219, 220
Series 1 G: Éducation: 177
Series J: Poste et télégraphe: 1, 43
Series 2 M: Justice: 1, 4, 9, 34, 54, 59, 73, 89, 92, 94, 459
Series 1 R: Rapports économiques: 79, 118

Archives Nationales du Sénégal section l'Afrique Occidentale Française (ANS-AOF)

Series 1 D: Affaires militaires: 56, 59, 90, 92, 93, 95, 105, 117, 137
Series 1 G: Études générales: 32, 83, 115, 138, 158, 209, 229, 248
Series 15 G: Soudan, affaires politiques, administratives et musulmanes: 29, 33, 57, 58, 60, 72, 92, 95, 98, 172, 174, 175, 176

Series 17 G: AOF, affaires politiques, généralités: 18
Series 18 G: AOF, affaires administratives, généralités: 2, 4
Series M: Justice: 90, 115

Service Historique de la Défense (SHD; Vincennes)

Dossiers personnels (Abd-el-Kader Mademba): GRE 7 YE 882, (Gustave Emmanuel Lambert) GR 7 YF 72626
Papiers Meynier: 1 KT 1001
Papiers Réquin (Mademba letters to Archinard): 1 K 108, 1 K 109

Oral Interviews Cited

Alamake Togora, July 12, 1992, Sinsani
Alassane Togora, July 12, 1992, Sinsani
Al Hajj Ismaila Fane, Mar. 15, 1977, Tesserela
Al Hajj Soumaila Fane, Jan. 24, 1984, Tesserela
Al Hajj Soumaila Fane, July 15, 1992, Tesserela
Binke Baba Kuma, Dec. 19, 1976, Sinsani
Binke Baba Kuma, Mar. 21, 1977, Sinsani
Binke Baba Kuma, July 7, 1992, Sinsani
Binke Baba Kuma, July 9, 1992, Sinsani
Binke Sadiki Traoré, BaKoroba Kuma, and Binke Baba Kume, July 17, 1992, Sinsani
Ce-Baba Kuma, Dec. 28, 1976, Sinsani
Cekoro Kulubali, Feb. 26, 1977, Segu
Dahou Traoré, July 19, 1992, Sibila
Gausu Cisse, July 12, 1992, Sinsani

Unpublished Dissertations and Papers

Bouche, Denise. "L'enseignement dans les Territoires français de l'Afrique Occidentale de 1817 à 1920: Mission civilisatrice ou formation d'une élite?" Université Paris I, unpublished PhD dissertation, June 8, 1974 (Lille: Atelier Reproduction des Thèses, 1975).

Hammond, Jr., Charles Hubert. "Neither Lenient nor Draconian: The Evolution of French Military Justice during the Early Third Republic," University of California, Davis, unpublished dissertation, 2005.

Pérignon, Aristide Auguste François. "Album de 100 photographies du Sénégal, du Soudan français, du Dahomey," Bibliothèque nationale de France, département Société de Géographie, SGE SG WE-513, 1897–1900.

Sy, Mamoudou. "Capitaine Mamadou Racine Sy (1838–1902)," unpublished paper, Dakar, 2010.

Ward, Jennifer. "The French–Bambara Relationship, 1880–1915," University of California, Los Angeles, unpublished PhD dissertation, 1976.

Published Journals, Bulletins, and Newspapers

Bulletin de l'Association cotonnière coloniale
Dépêche Coloniale
Le Figaro
Le Gallois
Jeune Afrique
Journal officiel de l'Afrique Occidentale française
Journal officiel du Haut-Sénégal-Niger
La Lanterne
Le Monde Colonial Illustré
Moniteur du Sénégal
L'Opinion
Le Petit Journal
Questions Diplomatiques et coloniales
La Revue hebdomadaire
Revue des Deux Mondes
Les Temps
Textile World Record

Published Books and Articles

Afigbo, Adiele Eberechukwu. *The Warrant Chiefs: Indirect Rule in Southeastern Nigeria, 1891–1929* (London: Longman, 1972).

Allain, Jean-Claude. "L'Indépendance câblière de la France au début du XXè siècle," *Guerres mondiales et conflits contemporains* 166 (April) 1992: pp. 115–131.

Amselle Jean-Loup. *Vers un multiculturalisme français: L'empire de la coutume* (Paris: Aubier, 1996).

Andrew, Christopher Maurice, Peter Grupp, and Alexander Sydney Kanya-Forstner. "Le mouvement colonial français et ses principales personnalités, 1890–1914," *Revue française d'histoire d'Outre-Mer* 42 (4) 1975: pp. 640–673.

Andrew, Christopher Maurice, and Alexander Sydney Kanya-Forstner. "The French 'Colonial Party': Its Composition, Aims and Influence, 1885–1914," *Historical Journal* 14 (1) 1971: pp. 99–128.

"Gabriel Hanotaux, the Colonial Party and the Fashoda Strategy," *The Journal of Imperial and Commonwealth History* 3 (1) 1974: pp. 55–104.

Anonymous. "*Fama* de Sansanding, Distinctions honorifiques," *Bulletin Administratif du Gouvernement général de l'Afrique occidentale française* Sept. 1904: p. 645.

Archinard, Colonel. *Le Soudan en 1893* (Le Havre: Imprimerie de la Société des Anciens Courtiers, 1895).

Archinard, Lieutenant-colonel. *Le Soudan Français en 1889–1890: Rapport militaire du Commandant Supérieur* (Paris: Imprimerie Nationale, 1891).

Archinard, Louis. *Soudan français: Croquis pour suivre les opérations de la campagne 1890-1891* (Paris: Sous-secrétariat d'État des colonies, ca. 1891).

Aubry, André (ed.). *Lettres et carnets de route du Commandant Briquelot de 1871 à 1896: Correspondances* (Paris: Manuscrit.com, 2003).

Bâ, Amadou Hampaté. *The Fortunes of Wangrin*, translated by Aina Pagolini Taylor (Bloomington: Indiana University Press, 1999).

"The Living Tradition," in Jacqueline Ki-Zerbo (ed.), *General History of Africa: Methodology and Prehistory* (London: Heinemann, 1981): pp. 166-203.

Babou, Cheikh Anta. *Fighting the Greater Jihad: Amadou Bamba and the Founding of the Muridiyya of Senegal, 1853-1913* (Athens: Ohio University Press, 2007).

Baillaud, Émile. *Sur les routes du Soudan* (Toulouse: Imprimerie Édouard Privat, 1902).

Barjot, Dominique, Éric Anceau, Isabelle Lescent-Giles, and Bruno Marnot (eds.). *Les entrepreneurs du Second Empire* (Paris: Presses Université Paris-Sorbonne, 2003).

Barrows, Leland. "Louis Léon César Faidherbe (1818-1889)," in Lewis Henry Gann and Peter Duignan (eds.), *African Proconsuls: European Governors in Africa* (New York: Free Press, 1978): pp. 51-79.

Barry, Boubacar. *Senegambia and the Atlantic Slave Trade*, translated by Ayi Kwei Armah (Cambridge: Cambridge University Press, 1998).

Bathily, Abdoulaye, "Mamadou Lamine Dramé et la Résistance antiimpérialiste dans le Haut-Sénégal (1885-1887)," *Notes Africaines* 125 1970: pp. 20-32.

Bayly, Christopher Alan. *Empire and Information: Intelligence Gathering and Social Communication in India, 1780-1870* (Cambridge: Cambridge University Press, 1996).

Beckert, Sven. *Empire of Cotton: A New History of Global Capitalism* (New York: Alfred A. Knopf, 2014).

Benton, Lauren. *A Search for Sovereignty: Law and Geography in European Empires, 1400-1900* (New York: Cambridge University Press, 2010).

Benton, Lauren, and Lisa Ford. *Rage for Order: The British Empire and the Origins of International Law, 1800-1850* (Cambridge, MA: Harvard University Press, 2016).

Berman, Bruce, and John Lonsdale. *Unhappy Valley: Conflict in Kenya and Africa* (Athens: Ohio University Press, 1992).

Bermann, George A., and Étienne Picard. "Administrative Law," in George A. Bermann and Étienne Picard (eds.), *Introduction to French Law* (Alphen aan den Rijn: Kluwer Law International, 2012): pp. 57-102.

Bernault, Florence (ed.). *Enfermement, prison et châtiments en Afrique: Du 19e siècle à nos jours* (Paris: Karthala, 1999).

Berry, Sara. *No Condition Is Permanent: The Social Dynamics of Agrarian Change in Sub-Saharan Africa* (Madison: University of Wisconsin Press, 1993).

Bingham, Tom. *The Rule of Law* (London: Penguin Books, 2010).

Bonnardel, Régine. *Saint-Louis du Sénégal: Mort ou naissance?* (Paris: L'Harmattan, 1992).

Bonnier, Chef d'Escadron. *Mission au Pays de Ségou: Campagne dans le Gueniekalary et le Sansanding en 1892* (Paris: Imprimerie Nationale, 1897).

Bouche, Denise. *Les Villages de liberté en Afrique noire française, 1887–1910* (Paris: Mouton, 1968).

"L'école française et les musulmans au Sénégal de 1850 à 1920," *Revue française d'histoire d'outre-mer* 61 (223) 1974: pp. 218–235.

Bredin, Jean-Denis. *L'Affaire* (Paris: Fayard, 1993).

Brunschwig, Henri. *Noirs et Blancs dans l'Afrique noire française: Comment le colonisé devient colonisateur, 1870–1914* (Paris: Flammarion, 1983).

Buell, Raymond Leslie. *The Native Problem in Africa* (original New York: Macmillan, 1928; reprinted London: Frank Cass, 1965).

Burbank, Jane, and Frederick Cooper. *Empires in World History: Power and the Politics of Difference* (Princeton, NJ: Princeton University Press, 2010).

Burrill, Emily, and Richard Roberts. "Domestic Violence, Colonial Courts, and the End of Slavery in the French Soudan, 1905–1912," in Emily Burrill, Richard Roberts, and Elizabeth Thornberry (eds.), *Domestic Violence and the Law in Africa: Historical and Contemporary Perspectives* (Athens: University of Ohio Press, 2010): pp. 33–53.

Butel, Paul (ed.). *Un officier et la conquête coloniale: Emmanuel Ruault (1878–1896)* (Bordeaux: Presses Universitaires de Bordeaux, 2007).

Cahm, Eric. *The Dreyfus Affair in French Society and Politics* (London: Longman, 1996).

Caron, Lieutenant de Vaisseau E. *De Saint-Louis au Port de Tombouctou: Voyage d'une canonnière française* (Paris: Augustin Challamel, 1891).

Cerullo, John. *Minotaur: French Military Justice and the Aernoult-Rousset Affair* (Dekalb: Northern Illinois University Press, 2011).

Chafer, Tony, and Amanda Sackur. *Promoting the Colonial Idea: Propaganda and Visions of Empire in France* (New York: Palgrave, 2002).

Chanock, Martin. *Law, Custom, and Social Order: The Colonial Experience in Malawi and Zambia* (Cambridge: Cambridge University Press, 1985).

Cohen, Thomas V. "The Macrohistory of Microhistory," *Journal of Medieval and Early Modern Studies* 47 (1) 2017: pp. 55–73.

Combes, André. *Histoire de la Franc-Maçonnerie au XIXè siècle* (Monaco: Éditions du Rocher, 1999).

Conklin, Alice L. *A Mission to Civilize: The Republican Idea of Empire in France and West Africa, 1895–1930* (Stanford, CA: Stanford University Press, 1997).

Conklin, Alice L., Sarah Fishman, and Robert Zaretsky. *France and Its Empire since 1870* (New York: Oxford University Press, second edition, 2015).

Conrad, David (ed.). *A State of Intrigue: The Epic of Bamana Segu according to Tayiru Banbera* (Oxford: Oxford University Press for the British Academy, 1990).

Conrad, David, and Barbara Hoffman (eds.). *Status and Identity in West Africa: Nyamakalaw of Mande* (Bloomington: Indiana University Press, 1995).

Cooper, Frederick. *Citizenship between Empire and Nation: Remaking France and French Africa, 1945–1960* (Princeton, NJ: Princeton University Press, 2014).

Coquery-Vidrovitch, Catherine. "Nationalité et citoyenneté en Afrique occidentale française: Originaires et citoyens dans le Sénégal colonial," *JAH* 42 (2) 2001: pp. 285–305.

Cordell, Dennis D. *Dar al-Kuti and the Last Years of the Trans-Saharan Slave Trade* (Madison: University of Wisconsin Press, 1985).

Crowder, Michael. "Indirect Rule: French and British Style," *Africa* 34 (3) 1964: pp. 197–205.

Curtin, Philip. *Economic Change in Precolonial Africa: Senegambia in the Era of the Slave Trade* (Madison: University of Wisconsin Press, 1975).

"The Impact of Europe," in Philip Curtin, Steven Feierman, Leonard Thompson and Jan Vansina, *African History: From Earliest Times to Independence* (New York; London: Longman, second edition, 1995): pp. 423–445.

Cuttier, Martine. *Portrait du colonialisme triomphant: Louis Archinard (1850–1932)* (Panazol: Lavauzelle, 2006).

Daniel, Jean. *La Légion d'Honneur: Histoire et organisation de l'Ordre National* (Paris: Éditions André Bonne, 1948).

Daughton, James P. "A Colonial Affair?: Dreyfus and the French Empire," *Historical Reflections/Réflexions historiques* 31 (3) 2005: pp. 469–483.

David, Philippe. *Inventaire général des cartes postales Fortier* (St. Julien au Sault: self-published, 1986).

Debré, Jean-Louis. *La justice au XIXè siècle: Les magistrats* (Paris: Librairie Académique Perrin, 1981).

Delafosse, Maurice. *Haut-Sénégal-Niger*, three vols. (original Paris: Champion, 1912; republished Paris: Larose, 1972).

Delavignette, Robert, *Les vrais chefs de l'empire* (Paris: Gaillmard, 1939).

Delavignette, Robert L. *Freedom and Authority in French West Africa* (London: F. Cass, 1968).

Deschamps, Hubert. "Et maintenant, Lord Lugard," *Africa* 33 (4) 1963: pp. 293–306.

Despagnet, Frantz. "Les protectorats," in Maxime Petit (ed.), *Les colonies françaises: Petite encyclopédie coloniale publiée sous la direction de M. Maxime Petit* (Paris: Larousse, 1902), vol. 1: pp. 53–54.

Diamond, Larry. *Ill Winds: Saving Democracy from Russian Rage, Chinese Ambition, and American Complacency* (New York: Penguin, 2019).

Dion, Isabelle. *Vers le Lac Tchad: Expéditions françaises et résistances africaines, 1890–1900* (Milan: Collections Histoires d'outre-mer, 2014).

Diouf, Mamadou. *Le Kajoor au XIXe siècle: Pouvoir ceddo et conquête coloniale* (Paris: Karthala, 1990).

"The French Colonial Policy of Assimilation and the Civility of the Originaires of the Four Communes (Senegal): A Nineteenth Century Globalization Project," *Development and Change* 29 1998: pp. 671–696.

Dirks, Nicholas. "'From Little King to Landlord': Colonial Discourse and Colonial Rule," in Nicolas Dirks (ed.), *Colonialism and Culture* (Ann Arbor: University of Michigan Press, 1992): pp. 1–25.

Dislère, Paul. *Traité de législation coloniale* (Paris: P. Dupont, 1914).

Djata, Sundiata A. *The Bamana Empire by the Niger: Kingdom, Jihad and Colonization, 1712–1920* (Princeton, NJ: Markus Weiner Publisher, 1997).

Dubois, Félix. *Tombouctou la mystérieuse* (Paris: Flammarion, 1897).

Duguit, Léon. "The Rule of Law," in Alfred Jules Émile Fouillée, Joseph Charmont, René Demogue, and Léon Duguit (eds.), *Modern French Legal Philosophy*, translated by Franklin Scott and Joseph P. Chamberlain (Boston: The Boston Book Co., 1916): pp. 285–338.

"The State and Law, as Concrete Facts Rather Than Abstract Conceptions," in Alfred Jules Émile Fouillée, Joseph Charmont, René Demogue, and Léon Duguit (eds.), *Modern French Legal Philosophy*, translated by Franklin Scott and Joseph P. Chamberlain (Boston: The Boston Book Co., 1916): pp. 339–346.

Duke Bryant, Kelly M. *Education as Politics: Colonial Schooling and Political Debate in Senegal, 1850s–1914* (Madison: University of Wisconsin Press, 2015).

"Changing Childhood: 'Liberated Minors', Guardianship, and the Colonial State in Senegal, 1895–1911," *JAH* 60 (2) 2019: pp. 209–228.

Echenberg, Myron. *Colonial Conscripts: The Tirailleurs Sénégalais in French West Africa, 1857–1960* (Portsmouth, NH: Heinemann, 1991).

Africa in the Time of Cholera: A History of Pandemics from 1817 to the Present (New York: Cambridge University Press, 2012).

Eckert, Andreas. "Cultural Commuters: African Employees in Late Colonial Tanzania," in Benjamin Lawrance, Emily Osborn, and Richard Roberts (eds.), *Intermediaries, Interpreters, and Clerks: African Employees in the Making of Colonial Africa* (Madison: University of Wisconsin Press, 2006): pp. 248–269.

Enders, Armelle. "L'École Nationale de la France d'Outre-Mer et la formation des administrateurs coloniaux," *Revue d'histoire moderne et contemporaine* 40 (2), 1993: pp. 272–288.

Evans, Martin (ed.). *Empire and Culture: The French Experience, 1830–1940* (London: Palgrave, 2004).

(ed.). *The French Colonial Mind*, two vols. (Lincoln: University of Nebraska Press, 2011).

Faidherbe, Général. *Le Sénégal: La France dans l'Afrique occidentale* (Paris: Hachette, 1889).

Fairgrieve, Duncan, and Françoise Lichère. "The Liability of Public Authorities in France," in Ken Oliphant (ed.), *The Liability of Public Authorities in Comparative Perspective* (Cambridge: Intersentia, 2016): pp. 156–175.

Feierman, Steven. "African Histories and the Dissolving of World History," in Robert H. Bates, Valentin-Yves Mudimbe, and Jean O'Barr (eds.), *Africa and the Disciplines: The Contributions of Research in Africa to the Social Sciences and Humanities* (Chicago: University of Chicago Press, 1993): pp. 167–211.

Fieldhouse, David Kenneth. *Colonialism, 1870–1945: An Introduction* (London, Weidenfeld and Nicolson, 1981).

Freeman, Daniel, and Jason Freeman. *Paranoia: A Twenty-first Century Fear* (Oxford: Oxford University Press, 2008).

Gallieni, Joseph Simon. *Voyage au Soudan Français (Haut-Sénégal et pays de Ségou), 1879–1881* (Paris: Hachette, 1885).

Gallieni, Lieutenant-colonel. *Deux campagnes au Soudan Français, 1886–88* (Paris: Hachette, 1891).

Garrigues, Jean. *Le Général Boulanger* (Paris: O. Orban, 1991).

Gaucher, Joseph. *Les débuts de l'enseignement en Afrique francophone: Jean Dard et l'École Mutuelle de Saint-Louis du Sénégal* (Paris: Le Livre Africain, 1968).

Gerkrath, Jorg. "Military Law in France," in Georg Nolte (ed.), *European Military Law Systems* (Berlin: De Gruyter Recht, 2003): pp. 277–336.

Getz, Trevor. *Slavery and Reform in West Africa: Toward Emancipation in Nineteenth Century Senegal and the Gold Coast* (Athens: Ohio University Press, 2004).

Getz, Trevor R., and Liz Clarke. *Abina and the Import Men: A Graphic History* (New York: Oxford University Press, second edition, 2016).

Girault, Arthur. *Principes de colonisation et de législation coloniale* (Paris: L. Tenin, fourth edition, 1921–1923).

Glasman, Joël. *Les corps habillés au Togo: Genèse coloniale des métiers de police* (Paris: Karthala, 2014).

Glineur, Cédric. *Histoire des Institutions administratives, Xè–XIXè siècle* (Paris: Économica, 2017).

Gomez, Michael A. *Pragmatism in the Age of Jihad: The Precolonial State of Bundu* (Cambridge: Cambridge University Press, 1992).

Goody, Jack. *The Domestication of the Savage Mind* (Cambridge: Cambridge University Press, 1977).

Gouvernement Général de l'AOF. *Les Postes et Télégraphes en Afrique Occidentale* (Corbeil: Éditions Crété, 1907).

Grafton, Anthony. *The Footnote: A Curious History* (Cambridge, MA: Harvard University Press, 1997).

Grant, John P., and J. Craig Barker (eds.). *Parry and Grant Encyclopedic Dictionary of International Law* (Dobbs Ferry, NY: Oceana Publications, second edition, 2004).

Green, Toby. *The Rise of the Trans-Atlantic Slave Trade in Western Africa, 1300–1589* (Cambridge: Cambridge University Press, 2012).

Guyver, Christopher. *The Second French Republic, 1848–1852: A Political Reinterpretation* (London: Palgrave Macmillan, 2016).

Hale, Thomas. *Griots and Griottes: Masters of Words and Music* (Bloomington, Indiana University Press, 1998).

Hanotaux, Gabriel, and Alfred Martineau (eds.). *Histoire des colonies françaises et l'expansion de France dans le monde* (Paris: Société de l'histoire nationale and Plon, 1929).

Hanretta, Sean. *Islam and Social Change in French West Africa: History of an Emancipatory Community* (New York: Cambridge University Press, 2009).

Harding, James. *The Astonishing Adventure of General Boulanger* (New York: Scribner, 1971).

Harms, Robert. *The Diligent: A Voyage through the Worlds of the Slave Trade* (New York: Basic Books, 2002).

Harrison, Christopher. *France and Islam in West Africa 1860–1960* (Cambridge: Cambridge University Press, 1988).

Hazareesingh, Sudhir, and Vincent Wright. *Francs-Maçons sous le Second Empire: Les loges provinciales du Grand-Orient à la veille de la Troisième République* (Rennes: Presses Universitaires de Rennes, 2001).

Headrick, Daniel R. *The Tools of Empire: Technology and European Imperialism in the Nineteenth Century* (New York: Oxford University Press, 1981).

The Invisible Weapon: Telecommunications and International Politics, 1851–1945 (New York: Oxford University Press, 1991).

Henry, Yves. *Le coton dans l'Afrique occidentale française* (Paris: Augustin Challamel, 1906).

Herbst, Jeffrey. *States and Power in Africa: Comparative Lessons in Authority and Control* (Princeton, NJ: Princeton University Press, 2000).

Hoffmann, Stefan-Ludwig. *The Politics of Sociability: Freemasonry and German Civil Society, 1840–1918* (Ann Arbor: University of Michigan Press, 2007).

Homberg, Octave. *L'École des colonies* (Paris: Plon, 1929).

Hopkins, Antony Gerald. "Lessons of 'Civilizing Missions' Are Mostly Unlearned," *New York Times*, Mar. 23, 2003, sec. 4, p. 5.

Hourst, Lieutenant de Vaisseau. *Sur le Niger et au Pays des Touaregs: La Mission Hourst* (Paris: Plon, 1898).

Humphrys, Stephen. *Theater of the Rule of Law: Transnational Legal Intervention in Theory and Practice* (Cambridge: Cambridge University Press, 2010).

Irvine, William D. *The Boulanger Affair Reconsidered: Royalism, Boulangism, and the Origins of the Radical Rights in France* (New York: Oxford University Press, 1989).

Jaime, Lieutenant de Vaisseau. *De Koulikoro à Tombouctou à bord du "Mage," 1889–1890* (Paris: E. Dentu, 1892).

Jankowski, Paul. "The Republic and Justice," in Edward Berenson, Vincent Duclert, and Christophe Prochassan (eds.), *The French Republic: History, Values, Debates* (Ithaca, NY: Cornell University Press, 2011): pp. 154–162.

Jennings, Robert, and Arthur Watts (eds.). *Oppenheim's International Law* (Harlow: Longman, ninth edition, 1992).

Jézéquel, Jean-Hervé. "'Collecting Customary Law': Educated Africans, Ethnographic Writing, and Colonial Justice in French West Africa," in Benjamin N. Lawrence, Emily L. Osborn, and Richard Roberts (eds.), *Intermediaries, Interpreters, and Clerks: African Employees in the Making of Colonial Africa* (Madison: University of Wisconsin Press, 2006): pp. 139–158.

Joalland, General. *Le drame de Dankori: Mission Voulet–Chanoine: Mission Joalland–Meynier* (Paris: Argo, 1931).

Johnson, Douglas. *France and the Dreyfus Affair* (London: Blandford, 1966).

Johnson, G. Wesley. *The Emergence of Black Politics in Senegal: The Struggle for Power in the Four Communes, 1900–1920* (Stanford, CA: Stanford University Press, 1971).

"William Ponty and Republican Paternalism in French West Africa (1866–1915)," in Lewis Henry Gann and Peter Duignan (eds.), *African Proconsuls: European Governors in Africa* (New York: Free Press, 1978): pp. 127–156.

Jones, Hilary. *The Métis of Senegal: Urban Life and Politics in French West Africa* (Bloomington: Indiana University Press, 2013).

Kamanda, Alfred M. *A Study of the Legal Status of Protectorates in Public International Law* (Ambilly: The Graduate Institute, Geneva, 1961).

Kanya-Forstner, Alexander Sydney. *The Conquest of the Western Sudan: A Study in French Military Imperialism* (Cambridge: Cambridge University Press, 1969).

Kessler-Harris, Alice. "AHR Roundtable: Why Biography?" *American Historical Review* 114 (3), 2009: pp. 625–630

Kirk-Greene, Anthony H. M. "Thin White Line: The Size of the British Colonial Service in Africa," *African Affairs* 79, 1980: pp. 26–44.

Klein, Martin A. *Islam and Imperialism in Senegal: Sin-Saloum, 1847–1914* (Stanford, CA: Stanford University Press, 1968).

"Social and Economic Factors in the Muslin Revolution in Senegambia," *JAH* 13 (4), 1972: pp. 419–441.

Slavery and Colonial Rule in French West Africa (New York: Cambridge University Press, 1998).

Klobb, Jean François Arsène, Colonel, and Lieutenant Octave Meynier. *À la recherche de Voulet: Sur les traces sanglantes de la mission Afrique centrale, 1898–1899*, Chantal Ahounou (ed.) (Paris: Cosmopole, 2001).

Kopytoff, Larissa. "French Citizens and Muslim Law: The Tensions of Citizenship in Early Twentieth-Century Senegal," in Richard Marback and Marc W. Kruman (eds.), *The Meaning of Citizenship* (Detroit: Wayne State University Press, 2011): pp. 320–337.

Krygier, Martin. "Four Puzzles about the Rule of Law: Why, What, Where? And Who Cares?" in James E. Fleming (ed.), *Getting to the Rule of Law* (New York: New York University Press, 2011): pp. 64–104.

"The Rule of Law (and Rechtstaat)," *International Encyclopedia of the Social and Behavioral Sciences* 20 (2015): pp. 780–787, second edition.

Larkin, Maurice. "Fraternité, solidarité et sociabilité: Les racines herbeuses du Grand Orient de France (1900–1920)," in Sudhir Hazareesingh (ed.), *L'héritage jacobin dans la France d'aujourd'hui: Essais en l'honneur de Vincent Wright* (Oxford: Oxford University Press, 2002).

Lautour, Gaston, Lieutenant. *Journal d'un Spahi au Soudan, 1897–1899* (Paris: Perin et Cie., 1909).

Lawrance, Benjamin, Emily Osborn, and Richard Roberts. "Introduction: African Intermediaries and the 'Bargain' of Collaboration," in Benjamin Lawrance, Emily Osborn, and Richard Roberts (eds.), *Intermediaries, Interpreters, and*

Clerks: African Employees in the Making of Colonial Africa (Madison: University of Wisconsin Press, 2006): pp. 3–34.

Lawrance, Benjamin, and Richard Roberts (eds.). *Trafficking in Slavery's Wake: Law and the Experience of Women and Children* (Athens: Ohio University Press, 2012).

Lecomte, Henri. *Le coton: Monographie, culture et histoire économique* (Paris: Carré et Naud, 1900).

Lee, Brandy X. (ed.). *The Dangerous Case of Donald Trump: 27 Psychiatrists and Mental Health Experts Assess a President* (New York: St. Martin's Press, 2017).

Lévi-Strauss, Claude. *Savage Mind* (Chicago: University of Chicago Press, 1966).

Levitsky, Steven, and Daniel Ziblatt. *How Democracies Die* (New York: Crown, 2018).

Lewis, David Levering. *Race to Fashoda: European Colonialism and African Resistance in the Scramble for Africa* (New York: Weidenfeld and Nicolson, 1987).

Lewis, Mary Dewhurst. *Divided Rule: Sovereignty and Empire in French Tunisia, 1881–1938* (Berkeley: University of California Press, 2014).

Lugard, Frederick John Dealtry, Baron. *The Dual Mandate in Tropical Africa* (Edinburgh; London: W. Blackwood and Sons, 1922).

Political Memoranda, Revision of Instructions to Political Officers on Subjects Chiefly, Political and Administrative 1913–1918 (original London: F. Cass, 1906; republished 1970).

Lydon, Ghislaine. "Obtaining Freedom at the Muslims' Tribunal: Colonial Kadijustiz and Women's Divorce Litigation in Ndar (Senegal)," in Shamil Jeppie, Ebrahim Moosa, and Richard Roberts (eds.), *Muslim Family Law in Sub-Saharan Africa: Colonial Legacies and Post-colonial Challenges* (Amsterdam: Amsterdam University Press, 2010): pp. 135–164.

Mademba, Abd-el-Kader. "Au Sénégal et au Soudan Français," *Bulletin du Comité d'études historiques et scientifiques de l'Afrique occidentale français* 13 (2) April–June 1930: pp. 100–216.

Au Sénégal et au Soudan Français (Paris: Larose, 1931).

Mademba, Ben Daoud. "La dernière étape d'un conquérant: Odyssée des dernières années du Sultan Ahmadou de Ségou, racontée par son cousin et compagnon d'infortune Mouhamadou Hassimiou Tall," *Bulletin du Comité des études historiques et scientifiques de l'AOF* 3 1921: pp. 473–480.

Mademba, Racine. "Les céréales d'été en Égypte," *L'Agronomie coloniale* 1 (12) 1914: pp. 166–174.

Mage, Eugène. *Voyage dans le Soudan occidental* (Paris: Hachette, 1868).

Mann, Gregory. *Native Sons: West African Veterans and France in the Twentieth Century* (Durham, NC: Duke University Press, 2006).

Marion, Marcel. *Dictionnaire des Institutions de la France aux XVIIè et XVIIIè siècles* (Paris: Auguste Picard, 1923).

Mark, Peter, and José da Silva Horta. *The Forgotten Diaspora: Jewish Communities in West Africa and the Making of the Atlantic World* (Cambridge: Cambridge University Press, 2011).

M'Baye, Saliou. *Histoire des institutions coloniales françaises en Afrique de l'Ouest: 1816–1960* (Dakar: Imprimerie St. Paul, 1991).

Mbayo, Tamba. *Muslim Interpreters in Colonial Senegal, 1850–1920: Mediations of Knowledge and Power in the Lower and Middle Senegal River Valley* (Lanham, MD: Lexington Books, 2016).

McAuliffe, Mary. *Dawn of the Belle Époque: The Paris of Monet, Zola, Bernhardt, Eiffel, Debussy, Clemenceau, and Their Friends* (Lanham, MD: Rowman and Littlefield, 2011).

McIlwraith, Malcolm. "The Declaration of a Protectorate over Egypt and Its Legal Effects," *Journal of the Society of Comparative Legislation* 17 (1–2) 1917: pp. 238–259.

Meillassoux, Claude. "Esclavage à Gumbu," in Claude Meillassoux (ed.), *Esclavage en Afrique précoloniale* (Paris: Maspero, 1975): pp. 221–251.

Méniaud, Jacques (ed.). *Les pionniers du Soudan: Avant, avec, et après Archinard, 1879–1894* (Paris: Société des Publications Modernes, 1931).

Merriman, John M. *The Agony of the Republic: The Repression of the Left in Revolutionary France, 1848–1851* (New Haven, CT: Yale University Press, 1978).

Meynier, Octave. *La Mission Jolland–Meynier* (Paris: Éditions de l'Empire français, 1947).

Michel, Marc. *Gallieni* (Paris: Fayard, 1989).

    Les Africains et la Grande Guerre: L'appel à l'Afrique (1914–1918) (Paris: Karthala, 2003).

Miers, Suzanne. *Britain and the Ending of the Slave Trade* (New York: Africana Publishing Co., 1975).

Moitt, Bernard. "Slavery and Emancipation in Senegal's Peanut Basin: The Nineteenth and Twentieth Centuries," *International Journal of African Historical Studies* 22 (1) 1989: pp. 27–50.

Monson, Jamie. "Claims to History and the Politics of Memory in Southern Tanzania, 1940–1960," *International Journal of African Historical Studies* 33 (3) 2000: pp. 543–565.

Moyd, Michelle. *Violent Intermediaries: African Soldiers, Conquest, and Everyday Colonialism in German East Africa* (Athens: Ohio University Press, 2014).

Newbury, Colin. "The Formation of the Government General of French West Africa," *JAH* 1 (1) 1960: pp. 111–128.

    Patrons, Clients, and Empire: Chieftaincy and Over-rule in Asia, Africa, and the Pacific (Oxford: Oxford University Press, 2003).

Ngalamulume, Kalala. *Colonial Pathologies, Environment, and Western Medicine in Saint-Louis-du-Sénégal, 1867–1920* (New York: Peter Lang, 2012).

Nora, Pierre (ed.). *Lieux de mémoire*, seven vols. (Paris: Gallimard, 1984–1992).

Nord, Philip. *The Republican Moment: Struggles for Democracy in Nineteenth-Century France* (Cambridge, MA: Harvard University Press, 1995).

Ochonu, Moses E. *Colonialism by Proxy: Hausa Imperial Agents and Middle Belt Consciousness in Nigeria* (Bloomington: Indiana University Press, 2014).

Odo, Georges. *La Franc-Maçonnerie dans les colonies, 1738–1960* (Paris: Éditions Maçonniques de France, 2001).

Osborn, Emily. "'Circle of Iron': African Colonial Employees and the Interpretation of Colonial Rule in French West Africa," *JAH* 44 (1) 2003: pp. 29–50.

Our New Husbands Are Here: Households, Gender, and Politics in a West African State from the Slave Trade to Colonial Rule (Athens: Ohio University Press, 2011).

Pacteau, Bernard. *Contentieux administratif* (Paris: Presses Universitaires de France, 1985).

Parsons, Timothy. *The African Rank-and-File: Social Implications of Colonial Military Service in the King's African Rifles, 1902–1964* (Portsmouth, NH: Heinemann, 1999).

Peabody, Sue. "Microhistory, Biography, and Fiction: The Politics of Narrating the Lives of People under Slavery," *Transatlantica: Revue d'études américaines, American Studies Journal* 2 (2012): pp. 1–19.

Peabody, Sue, and Keila Grinberg (eds.). *Free Soil in the Atlantic World* (London: Routledge, 2015).

Pérignon, Aristide Auguste François. *Haut-Sénégal et Moyen-Niger: Kita et Ségou* (Paris: J. André, 1901).

Perinbam, B. Marie. *Family Identity and the State in the Bamako Kafu, c. 1800–c. 1900* (Boulder, CO: Westview Press, 1997).

Person, Yves. *Samori: Une Révolution Dyula*, three vols. (Dakar: IFAN, 1968–1974).

Pietri, Capitaine. *Les Français au Niger: Voyages et combats* (Paris: Hachette, 1885).

Press, Steven. "Sovereignty at Guantánamo: New Evidence and a Comparative Historical Interpretation," *Journal of Modern History* 85 (3) 2013: pp. 592–631.

Rogue Empires: Contracts and Conmen in Europe's Scramble for Africa (Cambridge, MA: Harvard University Press, 2017).

Price, Roger. *A Concise History of France* (Cambridge: Cambridge University Press, third edition, 2014).

Ranger, Terence. "The Invention of Tradition in Colonial Africa," in Eric Hobsbawm and Terence O. Ranger (eds.), *The Invention of Tradition* (Cambridge: Cambridge University Press, 1983): pp. 211–262.

Rebérioux, Madeleine. *La République radicale? 1898–1914* (Paris: Éditions du Seuil, 1975).

Ridely, Frederick F., and Jean Blondel. *Public Administration in France* (London: Routledge and Kegan Paul, 1969).

Roberts, Richard. "The Emergence of a Grain Market in Bamako, 1883–1908," *Canadian Journal of African Studies* 14 (1) 1980: pp. 37–54.

Warriors, Merchants and Slaves: The State and the Economy in the Middle Niger Valley, 1700–1914 (Stanford, CA: Stanford University Press, 1987).

"The End of Slavery in the French Soudan, 1905–1914," in Suzanne Miers and Richard Roberts (eds.), *The End of Slavery in Africa* (Madison: University of Wisconsin Press, 1988): pp. 282–307.

"*Guinée* Cloth: Linked Transformations within France's Empire in the Nineteenth Century," *Cahiers d'études africaines* 32 (128) 1992: pp. 597–627.

Two Worlds of Cotton: Colonial and the Regional Economy in the French Soudan, 1800–1949 (Stanford, CA: Stanford University Press, 1996).

Litigants and Households: African Disputes and Colonial Courts in the French Soudan, 1895–1912 (Portsmouth, NH: Heinemann, 2005).

"Custom and Muslim Family Law in Native Courts of the French Soudan, 1905–1912," in Shamil Jeppie, Ebrahim Moosa, and Richard Roberts (eds.), *Muslim Family Law in Sub-Saharan Africa: Colonial Legacies and Post-colonial Challenges* (Amsterdam: Amsterdam University Press, 2010): pp. 85–108.

"Slavery, the End of Slavery, and the Intensification of Work in the French Soudan, 1883–1912," *African Economic History* 49 (1) 2021: pp. 47–72.

Roberts, Richard, and Martin A. Klein. "The Banamba Slave Exodus of 1905 and the Decline of Slavery in the Western Sudan," *JAH* 21 (3) 1980: pp. 375–394.

Roberts, Sophie B. *Citizenship and Antisemitism in Colonial Algeria, 1870–1962* (Cambridge: Cambridge University Press, 2018).

Roberts, Stephen H. *History of French Colonial Policy (1870–1925)* (London: P. S. King and Son, 1929).

Robinson, David. *Chiefs and Clerics: Abdul Bokar Kane and Futa Toro, 1853–1891* (Oxford: Clarendon Press, 1975).

The Holy War of Umar Tall: The Western Sudan in the Mid-Nineteenth Century (Oxford: Clarendon Press, 1985).

Paths of Accommodation: Muslim Societies and French Colonial Authorities in Senegal and Mauritania, 1880–1920 (Athens: Ohio University Press, 2000).

Robinson, Ronald. "Non-European Foundations of European Imperialism: Sketch for a Theory of Collaboration," in Roger Owen and Bob Sutcliffe (eds.), *Studies in the Theory of Imperialism* (London: Longman, 1972): pp. 117–142.

Rolland, Jacques-François. *Le Grand Capitaine* (Paris: Bernard Grasset, 1976).

Roume, Ernest. "Préface," in Jacques Méniaud (ed.), *Les pionniers du Soudan: Avant, avec, et après Archinard, 1879–1894* (Paris: Société des Publications Modernes, 1931): vol. 1, pp. vii–viii.

Royer, Jean-Pierre, Nicolas Derasse, Jean-Pierre Allinne, Bernard Durand, and Jean-Paul Jean. *Histoire de la justice en France du XVIIIè siècle à nos jours* (Paris: Presses Universitaires de France, 1995).

Royer, Jean-Pierre, Renée Martinage, and Pierre Lecocq. *Juges et notables au XIXè siècle* (Paris: Presses Universitaires de France, 1982).

Rudorff, Raymond. *Belle Époque: Paris in the Nineties* (London: Hamish Hamilton, 1972).

Saada, Emmanuelle. "The Republic and the *Indigènes*," in Edward Berenson, Vincent Duclert, and Christophe Prochasson (eds.), *The French Republic: History, Values, Debates* (Ithaca, NY: Cornell University Press, 2011): pp. 224–225.

Empire's Children: Race, Filiation, and Citizenship in the French Colonies, translated by Arthur Goldhammer (Chicago: University of Chicago Press, 2012).

Sabatié, Alexandre Camille. *Le Sénégal: Sa conquête et son organisation (1364–1925)* (Saint Louis: Imprimerie du Gouvernement, 1925).

Saint-Martin, Yves-Jean. "Un fils d'El Hadj Omar: Aguibou, roi du Dinguiray et du Macina (1843?–1907)," *Cahiers d'études africaines* 8 (29) 1968: pp. 144–178.

Le Sénégal sous le Second Empire: Naissance d'un empire colonial (1850–1871) (Paris: Karthala, 1989).

Félix Dubois, 1862–1945: Grand reporter et explorateur de Panama à Tamanrasset (Paris: L'Harmattan, 1999).

Sanoko, Soumaïla. *Le royaume du Kénédougou, 1825–1898* (Bamako: Nouvelle Imprimerie Bamakoise, 2010).

Sarr, Dominique, and Richard Roberts. "The Jurisdiction of Muslim Tribunals in Colonial Senegal, 1857–1932," in Kristin Mann and Richard Roberts (eds.), *Law in Colonial Africa* (Portsmouth, NH: Heinemann, 1991): pp. 131–145.

Saul, Mahir, and Patrick Royer. *West African Challenge to Empire: Culture and History in the Volta-Bani Anticolonial War* (Athens: Ohio University Press, 2001).

Schneider, William. *An Empire for the Masses: The French Popular Image of Africa, 1870–1900* (Westport, CN: Greenwood Press, 1982).

Schwartz, Bernard. *French Administrative Law and the Common-Law World* (New York: New York University Press, 1954).

Searing, James F. *"God Alone Is King": Islam and Emancipation in Senegal: The Wolof Kingdoms of Kajoor and Bawol, 1859–1914* (Portsmouth, NH: Heinemann, 2002).

Sharkey, Heather. *Living with Colonialism: Nationalism and Culture in the Anglo-Egyptian Sudan* (Berkeley: University of California Press, 2003).

Shereikis, Rebecca. "From Law to Custom: The Shifting Legal Status of Muslim *Originaires* in Kayes and Médine, 1903–13," *JAH* 42 (2) 2001: pp. 261–283.

Shiers, George (ed.). *The Electric Telegraph: An Historical Anthology* (New York: Arno Press, 1977).

Sibeud, Emmanuelle. *Une science impériale pour l'Afrique? La construction des savoirs Africanistes en France, 1878–1930* (Paris: Ecole des hautes études en sciences sociales, 2002).

Simoën, Jean-Claude. *Le Fils de rois: Le crépuscle sanglangt de l'aventure afriaine* (Paris: J.-C. Lattès, 1996).

Soares, Benjamin F. *Islam and the Prayer Economy: History and Authority in Malian Town* (Ann Arbor: University of Michigan Press, 2005).

Soleillet, Paul. *Voyage à Ségou, 1878–1879, rédigé d'aprés les notes et journaux de Soleillet par Gabriel Gravier* (Paris: Challamel, 1887).

Spear, Thomas. "Neo-traditionalism and the Limits of Invention in British Colonial Africa," *JAH* 44 (1) 2003: pp. 3–27.

Steiner, Eva. *French Law: A Comparative Approach* (Oxford: Oxford University Press, 2018).

Stockreiter, Elke E. "Islamic and Colonial Discourses on Gender Relations and Female Status in Zanzibar, 1900–1950s," in Emily Burrill, Richard Roberts, and Elizabeth Thornberry (eds.), *Domestic Violence and the Law in Africa: Historical and Contemporary Perspectives* (Athens: Ohio University Press, 2010): pp. 118–132.

Sy, Seydou Madani. *Le capitaine Mamadou Racine Sy (1838–1902): Une figure sénégalaise au temps des Tirailleurs* (Paris: Karthala, 2014).

Taithe, Bertrand. *The Killer Trail: A Colonial Scandal in the Heart of Africa* (New York: Oxford University Press, 2009).

Tamari, Tal. *Les castes de l'Afrique occidentale: Artisans et musiciens endogames* (Nanterre: Société d'ethnologie, 1997).

Thiriet, Emile. *Au Soudan Français: Souvenirs 1892–1893, Macina–Tombouctou* (Paris: Imprimerie André Lisot, 1932).

Thobie, Jacques. "La France coloniale de 1870 à 1914," in Jean Meyer, Jean Tarrade, Annie Rey-Goldzeiguer, and Jacques Thobie (eds.), *Histoire de la France coloniale: Des origines à 1914* (Paris: Armand Colin, 1991): pp. 555–746.

Tilly, Charles. "Retrieving European Lives," in Olivier Zunz (ed.), *Reliving the Past: The Worlds of Social History* (Chapel Hill: University of North Carolina Press, 1985): pp. 11–52.

Todd, David. "A French Imperial Meridian, 1814–1870," *Past and Present* 210 (Feb. 2011): pp. 155–186.

Traoré, Samba Lamine. *La saga de la ville historique de Ségou* (Paris: L'Harmattan, 2011).

Tulard, Jean, François Monnier, and Olivier Echappé (eds.). *La Légion d'honneur: Deux siècles d'histoire* (Paris: Perrin, 2004).

Tupper, Lewis. "Customary and Other Law in the East Africa Protectorate," *Journal of the Society of Comparative Legislation* 8 (2) 1907: pp. 172–184.

Tymowski, Michal. "Les esclaves du Commandant Quinquandon," *Cahiers d'études africaines* 158 2000: pp. 351–361.

United Nations Department of Peacekeeping Operations and Office of the High Commissioner of Human Rights. *The United Nations Rule of Law Indicators: Implementation Guide and Project Tools* (New York: United Nations Publications, 2011).

Urban, Yerri. *L'indigène dans le droit colonial français, 1865–1955* (Clermont-Ferrand: Fondation Verenne, 2010).

"La citoyenneté dans l'Empire colonial français est-elle spécifique," *Jus Politicum: Review de droit politique* 14 2017: pp. 151–187.

Ware III, Rudolph T. *The Walking Qur'an: Islamic Education, Embodied Knowledge, and History in West Africa* (Chapel Hill: University of North Carolina Press, 2014).

Wattel, Michel, and Béatrice Wattel. *Les Grand-Croix de la Légion d'Honneur de 1805 à nos jours: Titulaires français et étrangers* (Paris: Archives et culture, 2009).

Webb, James L. A., Jr. *Desert Frontier: Ecological and Economic Change along the Western Sahel, 1600–1850* (Madison: University of Wisconsin Press, 1995).

Weingast, Barry R. "The Political Foundations of Democracy and the Rule of Law," *American Political Science Review* 91 (2) 1997: pp. 245–263.

White, Luise. *Speaking with Vampires: Rumor and History in Colonial Africa* (Berkeley: University of California Press, 2000).

White, Luise, and Douglas Howland (eds.). *State of Sovereignty: State, Laws, Populations* (Bloomington: Indiana University Press, 2009).

White, Owen. "Networking: Freemasons and the Colonial State in French West Africa, 1895–1914," *French History* 19 (1) 2005: pp. 94–95.

White, Richard. *The Middle Ground: Indians, Empires, and Republics in the Great Lakes Region, 1650–1815*, twentieth anniversary edition (New York: Cambridge University Press, 2011).

Wikipedia. "Monument aux héros de l'Armée Noire," https://fr.wikipedia.org/wiki/Monument_aux_h%C3%A9ros_de_l%27Arm%C3%A9e_noire.

"Paranoia," https://en.wikipedia.org/wiki/Paranoia.

Wilks, Ivor. "Aspects of Bureaucratization in Ashanti in the Nineteenth Century," *JAH* 7 (2) 1966: pp. 215–232.

Willms, Johannes. *Paris, Capital of Europe: From the Revolution to the Belle Époque* (New York: Homes and Meier, 1997).

Worger, William. "Parsing God: Conversations about the Meaning of Words and Metaphors in Nineteenth Century Southern Africa," *JAH* 42 (3) 2001: pp. 417–447.

Wright, Marcia. *Strategies of Slaves and Women: Life-stories from East/Central Africa* (New York: L. Barber Press, 1993).

Zeldin, Theodore. *France 1848–1945* (Oxford: Clarendon Press, 1973), vol. 1.

INDEX

African Studies Series

CPSIA information can be obtained
at www.ICGtesting.com
Printed in the USA
LVHW081132290322
714682LV00005B/311